Zodiac P.I.

ALSO AVAILABLE FROM TOKYOPOP®

MANGA

.HACK//LEGEND OF THE TWILIGHT (September 2003)
@LARGE (COMING SOON)
ANGELIC LAYER*
BABY BIRTH* (September 2003)
BATTLE ROYALE*
BRAIN POWERED*
BRIGADOON* (August 2003)
CARDCAPTOR SAKURA
CARDCAPTOR SAKURA: MASTER OF THE CLOW*
CHOBITS*
CHRONICLES OF THE CURSED SWORD
CLAMP SCHOOL DETECTIVES*
CLOVER
CONFIDENTIAL CONFESSIONS*
CORRECTOR YUI
COWBOY BEBOP*
COWBOY BEBOP: SHOOTING STAR*
DEMON DIARY
DIGIMON*
DRAGON HUNTER
DRAGON KNIGHTS*
DUKLYON: CLAMP SCHOOL DEFENDERS*
ERICA SAKURAZAWA*
FAKE* (September 2003)
FORBIDDEN DANCE* (August 2003)
GATE KEEPERS*
G GUNDAM*
GRAVITATION*
GTO*
GUNDAM WING
GUNDAM WING: BATTLEFIELD OF PACIFISTS
GUNDAM WING: ENDLESS WALTZ*
GUNDAM WING: THE LAST OUTPOST*
HAPPY MANIA*
HARLEM BEAT
I.N.V.U.
INITIAL D*
ISLAND
JING: KING OF BANDITS*
JULINE
KARE KANO*
KINDAICHI CASE FILES, THE*
KING OF HELL
KODOCHA: SANA'S STAGE*
LOVE HINA*
LUPIN III*
MAGIC KNIGHT RAYEARTH* (August 2003)
MAGIC KNIGHT RAYEARTH II* (COMING SOON)

MAN OF MANY FACES*
MARMALADE BOY*
MARS*
MIRACLE GIRLS
MIYUKI-CHAN IN WONDERLAND* (October 2003)
MONSTERS, INC.
PARADISE KISS*
PARASYTE
PEACH GIRL
PEACH GIRL: CHANGE OF HEART*
PET SHOP OF HORRORS*
PLANET LADDER*
PLANETES* (October 2003)
PRIEST
RAGNAROK
RAVE MASTER*
REALITY CHECK
REBIRTH
REBOUND*
RISING STARS OF MANGA
SABER MARIONETTE J*
SAILOR MOON
SAINT TAIL
SAMURAI DEEPER KYO*
SAMURAI GIRL: REAL BOUT HIGH SCHOOL*
SCRYED*
SHAOLIN SISTERS*
SHIRAHIME-SYO: SNOW GODDESS TALES* (Dec. 2003)
SHUTTERBOX (November 2003)
SORCERER HUNTERS
THE SKULL MAN*
THE VISION OF ESCAFLOWNE
TOKYO MEW MEW*
UNDER THE GLASS MOON
VAMPIRE GAME*
WILD ACT*
WISH*
WORLD OF HARTZ (COMING SOON)
X-DAY* (August 2003)
ZODIAC P.I. *

For more information visit www.TOKYOPOP.com

*INDICATES 100% AUTHENTIC MANGA (RIGHT-TO-LEFT FORMAT)

CINE-MANGA™

CARDCAPTORS
JACKIE CHAN ADVENTURES (COMING SOON)
JIMMY NEUTRON (September 2003)
KIM POSSIBLE
LIZZIE MCGUIRE
POWER RANGERS: NINJA STORM (August 2003)
SPONGEBOB SQUAREPANTS (September 2003)
SPY KIDS 2

NOVELS

KARMA CLUB (April 2004)
SAILOR MOON

TOKYOPOP KIDS

STRAY SHEEP (September 2003)

ART BOOKS

CARDCAPTOR SAKURA*
MAGIC KNIGHT RAYEARTH*

ANIME GUIDES

COWBOY BEBOP ANIME GUIDES
GUNDAM TECHNICAL MANUALS
SAILOR MOON SCOUT GUIDES

6-5-03

Zodiac P.I.

Vol.2
Natsumi Ando

Los Angeles • Tokyo • London

Translator - Takae Brewer
English Adaptation - Chris Poole
Copy Editor - Amy Court Kaemon
Retouch and Lettering - James Lee
Cover Layout - Raymond Makowski

Senior Editor - Julie Taylor
Managing Editor - Jill Freshney
Production Coordinator - Antonio DePietro
Production Manager - Jennifer Miller
Art Director - Matthew Alford
Director of Editorial - Jeremy Ross
VP of Production - Ron Klamert
President & C.O.O. - John Parker
Publisher & C.E.O. - Stuart Levy

Email: editor@TOKYOPOP.com
Come visit us online at www.TOKYOPOP.com

A TOKYOPOP® Manga

TOKYOPOP® is an imprint of Mixx Entertainment, Inc.
5900 Wilshire Blvd. Suite 2000, Los Angeles, CA 90036

©2001 Natsumi Ando. All rights reserved. First published in Japan in 2001
by Kodansha Ltd., Tokyo. English publication rights arranged through Kodansha Ltd.

English text © 2003 by Mixx Entertainment, Inc.
TOKYOPOP is a registered trademark of Mixx Entertainment, Inc.

All rights reserved. No portion of this book may be reproduced or
transmitted in any form or by any means without written permission
from the copyright holders. This manga is a work of fiction.
Any resemblance to actual events or locales or persons,
living or dead, is entirely coincidental.

ISBN: 1-59182-384-6

First TOKYOPOP® printing: September 2003

10 9 8 7 6 5 4 3 2 1

Printed in the USA

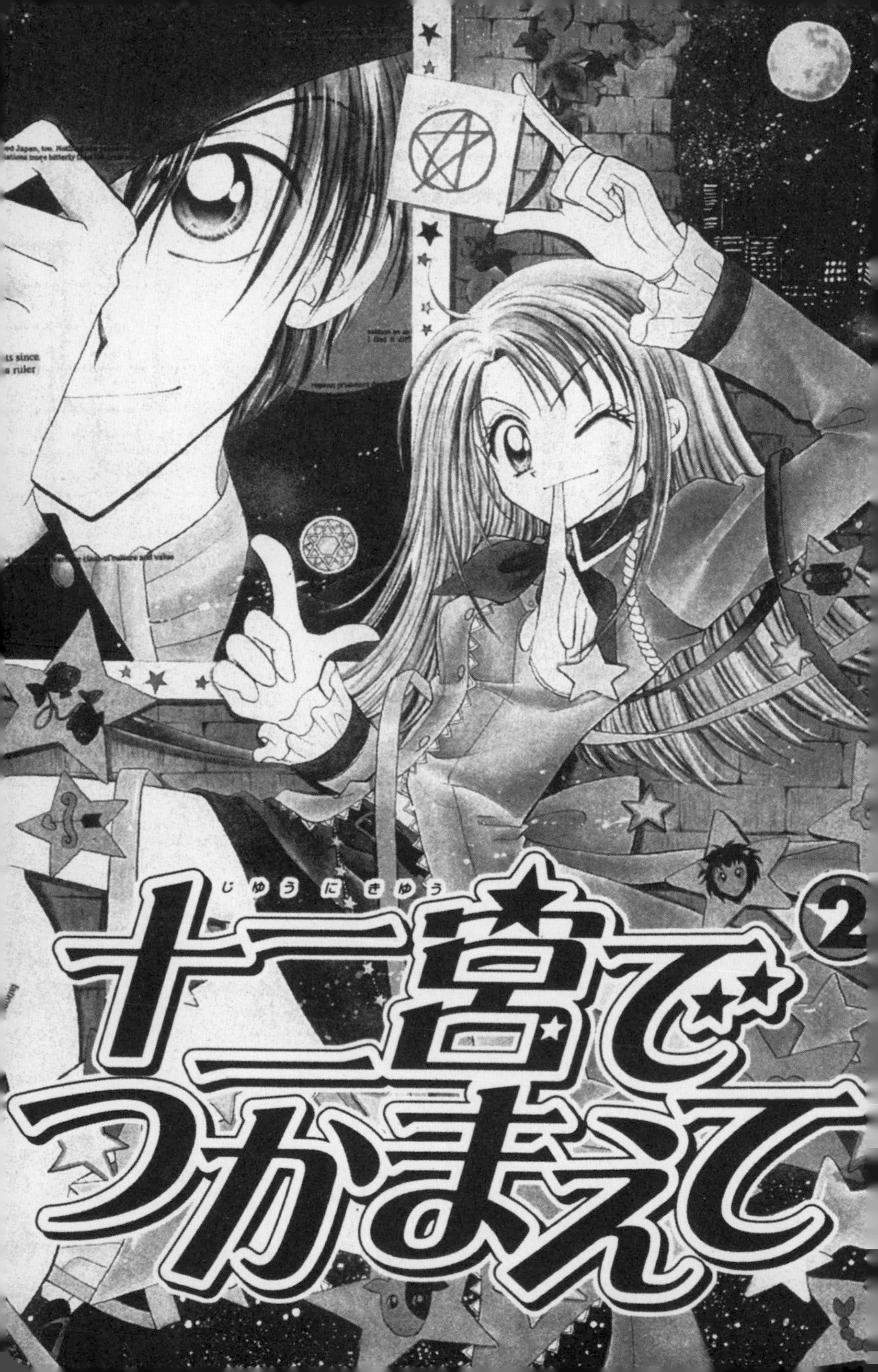
じゅうにきゅう
十二宮でつかまえて
2

十二宮でつかまえて

★ WHO'S WHO ★

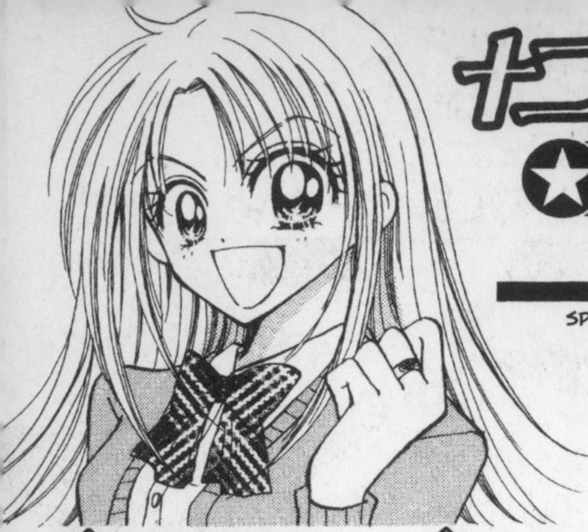

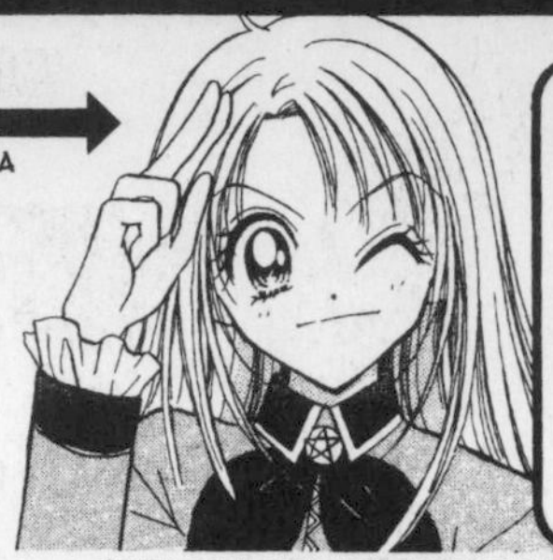

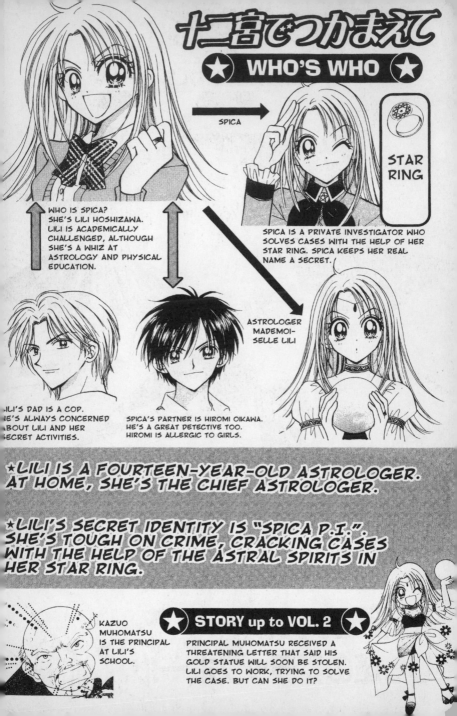

SPICA

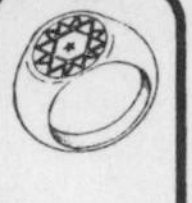

STAR RING

WHO IS SPICA?
SHE'S LILI HOSHIZAWA.
LILI IS ACADEMICALLY CHALLENGED, ALTHOUGH SHE'S A WHIZ AT ASTROLOGY AND PHYSICAL EDUCATION.

SPICA IS A PRIVATE INVESTIGATOR WHO SOLVES CASES WITH THE HELP OF HER STAR RING. SPICA KEEPS HER REAL NAME A SECRET.

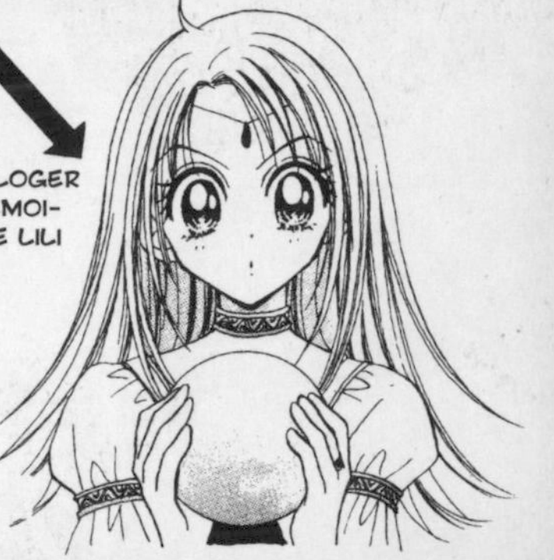

ASTROLOGER MADEMOISELLE LILI

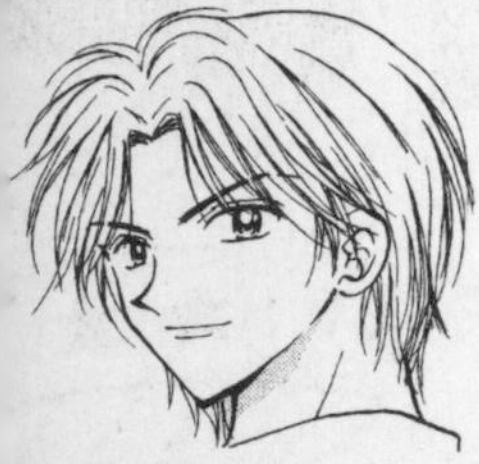

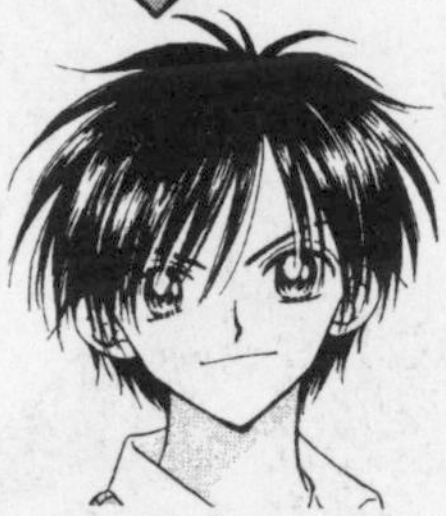

LILI'S DAD IS A COP.
HE'S ALWAYS CONCERNED ABOUT LILI AND HER SECRET ACTIVITIES.

SPICA'S PARTNER IS HIROMI OIKAWA.
HE'S A GREAT DETECTIVE TOO.
HIROMI IS ALLERGIC TO GIRLS.

★LILI IS A FOURTEEN-YEAR-OLD ASTROLOGER. AT HOME, SHE'S THE CHIEF ASTROLOGER.

★LILI'S SECRET IDENTITY IS "SPICA P.I.". SHE'S TOUGH ON CRIME, CRACKING CASES WITH THE HELP OF THE ASTRAL SPIRITS IN HER STAR RING.

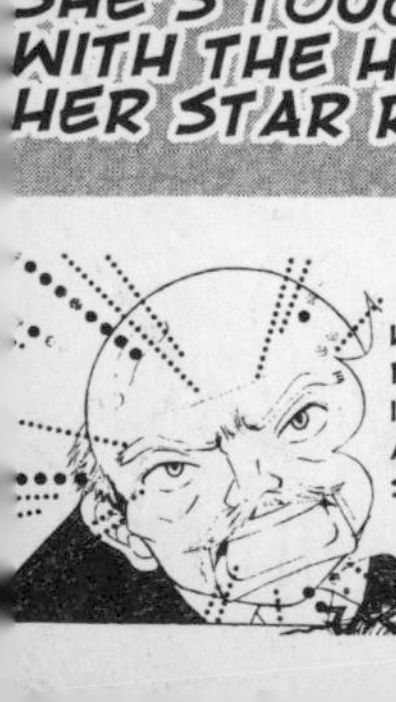

KAZUO MUHOMATSU IS THE PRINCIPAL AT LILI'S SCHOOL.

★ STORY up to VOL. 2 ★

PRINCIPAL MUHOMATSU RECEIVED A THREATENING LETTER THAT SAID HIS GOLD STATUE WILL SOON BE STOLEN. LILI GOES TO WORK, TRYING TO SOLVE THE CASE. BUT CAN SHE DO IT?

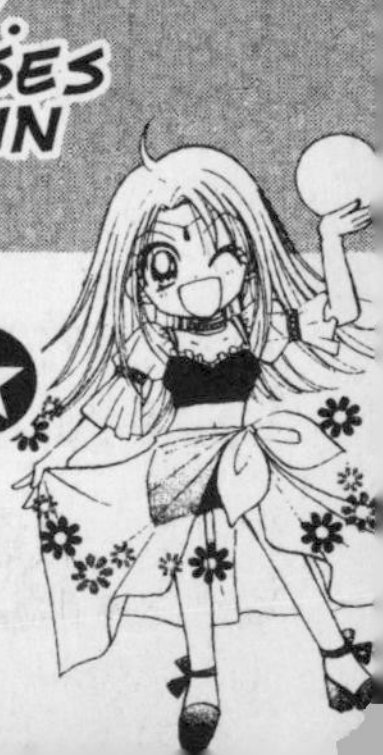

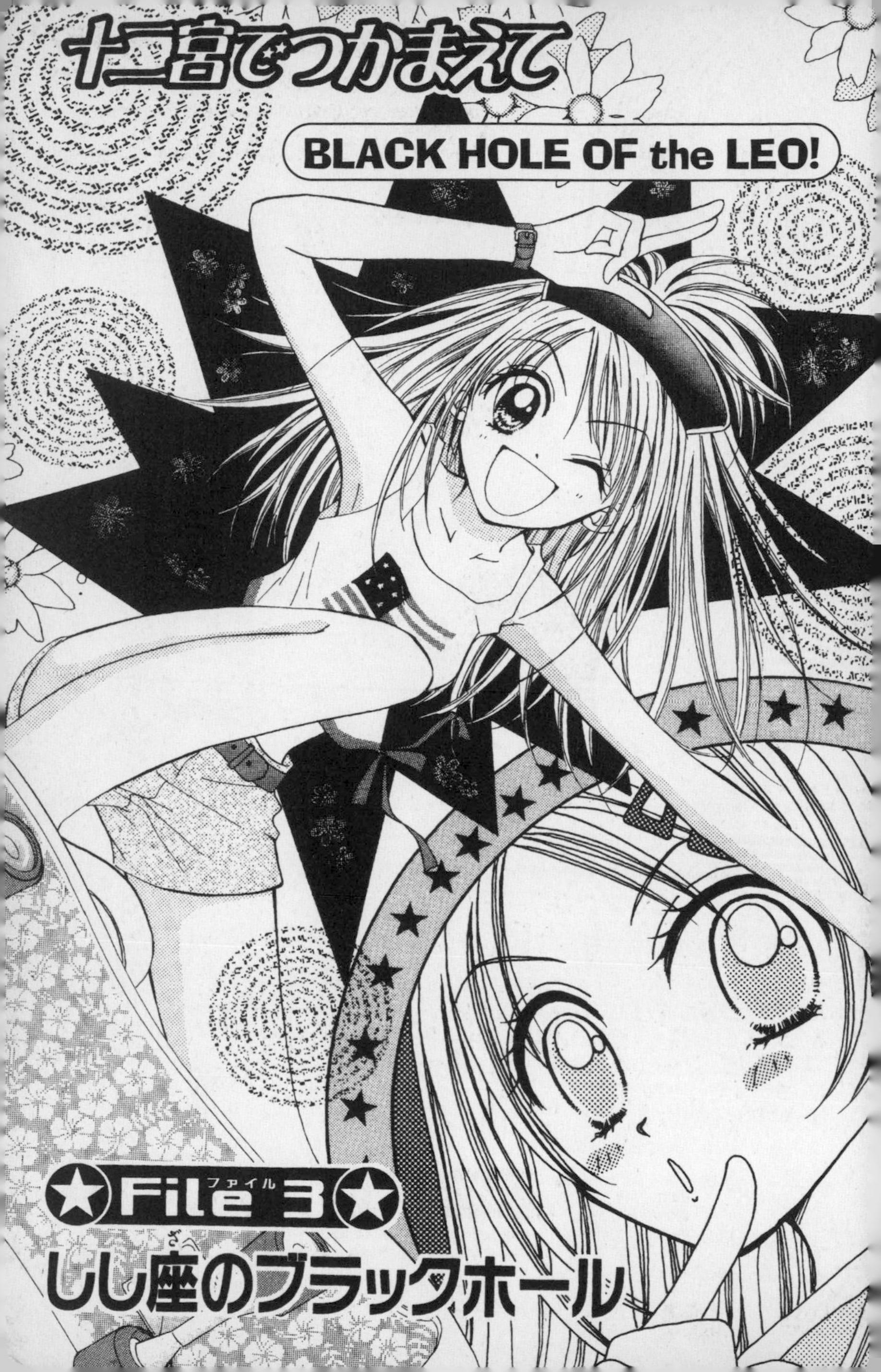
十二宮でつかまえて
BLACK HOLE OF the LEO!
★File 3★
しし座のブラックホール

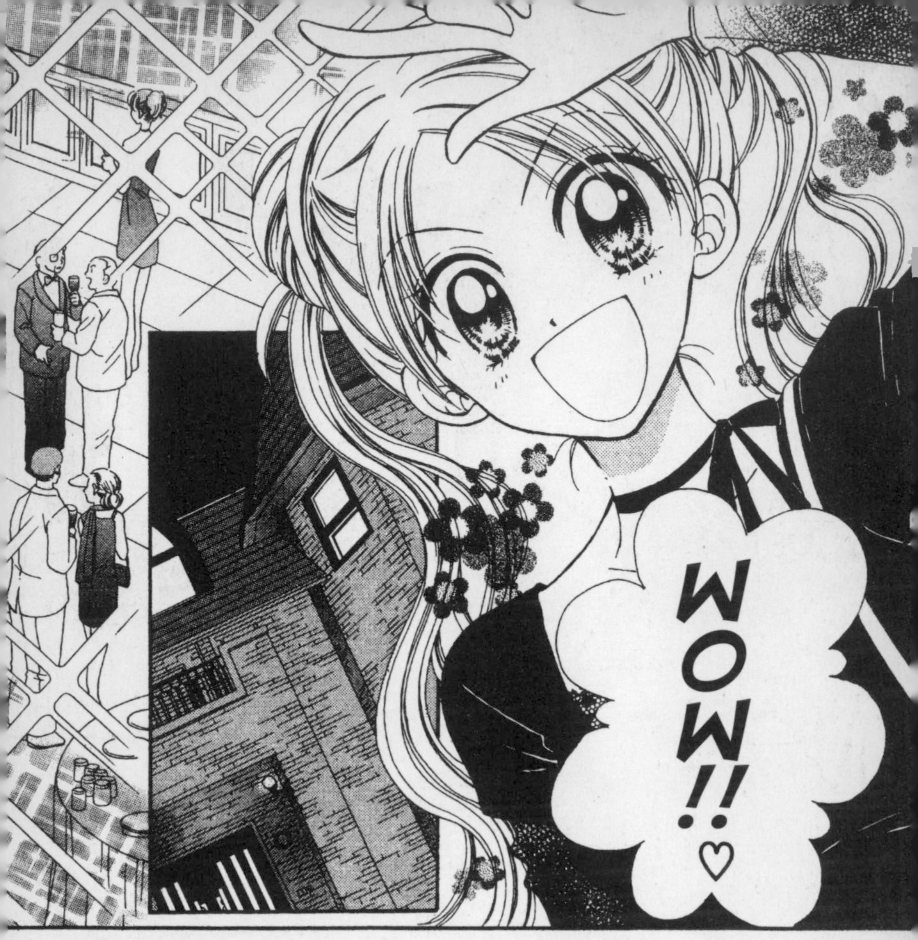
WOW!! ♡

Mademoiselle Lili's Astrology (5)

What brings you luck?
That depends on your lucky day and lucky color of your zodiac sign.

- ♈ Aries – Tuesday, red
- ♉ Taurus – Friday, navy blue
- ♊ Gemini – Wednesday, yellow
- ♋ Cancer – Monday, white
- ♌ Leo – Sunday, orange
- ♍ Virgo – Wednesday, beige
- ♎ Libra – Friday, pink and light blue
- ♏ Scorpio – Tuesday, dark red
- ♐ Sagittarius – Thursday, purple
- ♑ Capricorn – Saturday, brown and black
- ♒ Aquarius – Saturday, blue
- ♓ Pisces – Thursday, marine blue

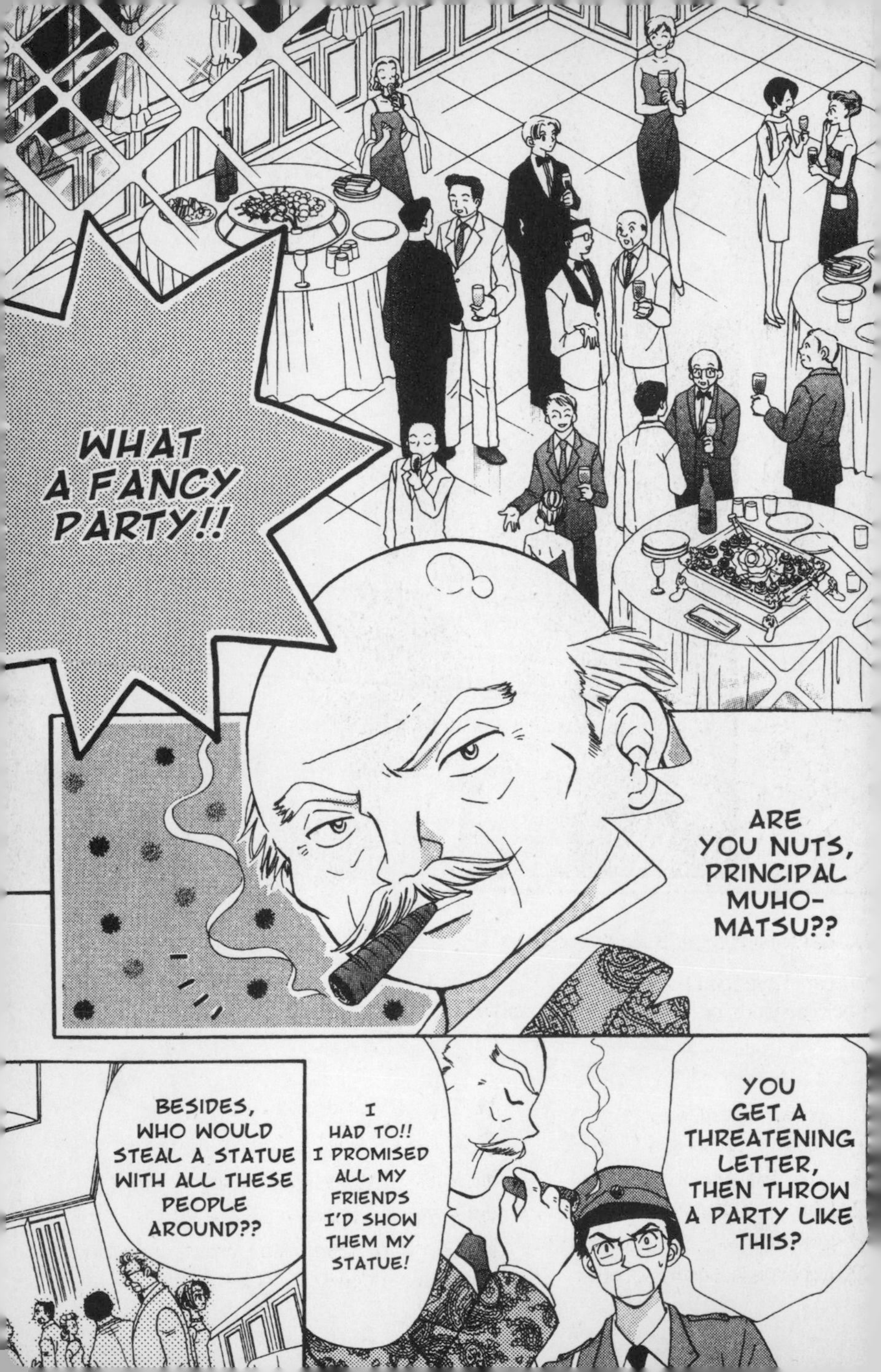
WHAT A FANCY PARTY!!
ARE YOU NUTS, PRINCIPAL MUHO-MATSU??
YOU GET A THREATENING LETTER, THEN THROW A PARTY LIKE THIS?
I HAD TO!! I PROMISED ALL MY FRIENDS I'D SHOW THEM MY STATUE!
BESIDES, WHO WOULD STEAL A STATUE WITH ALL THESE PEOPLE AROUND??

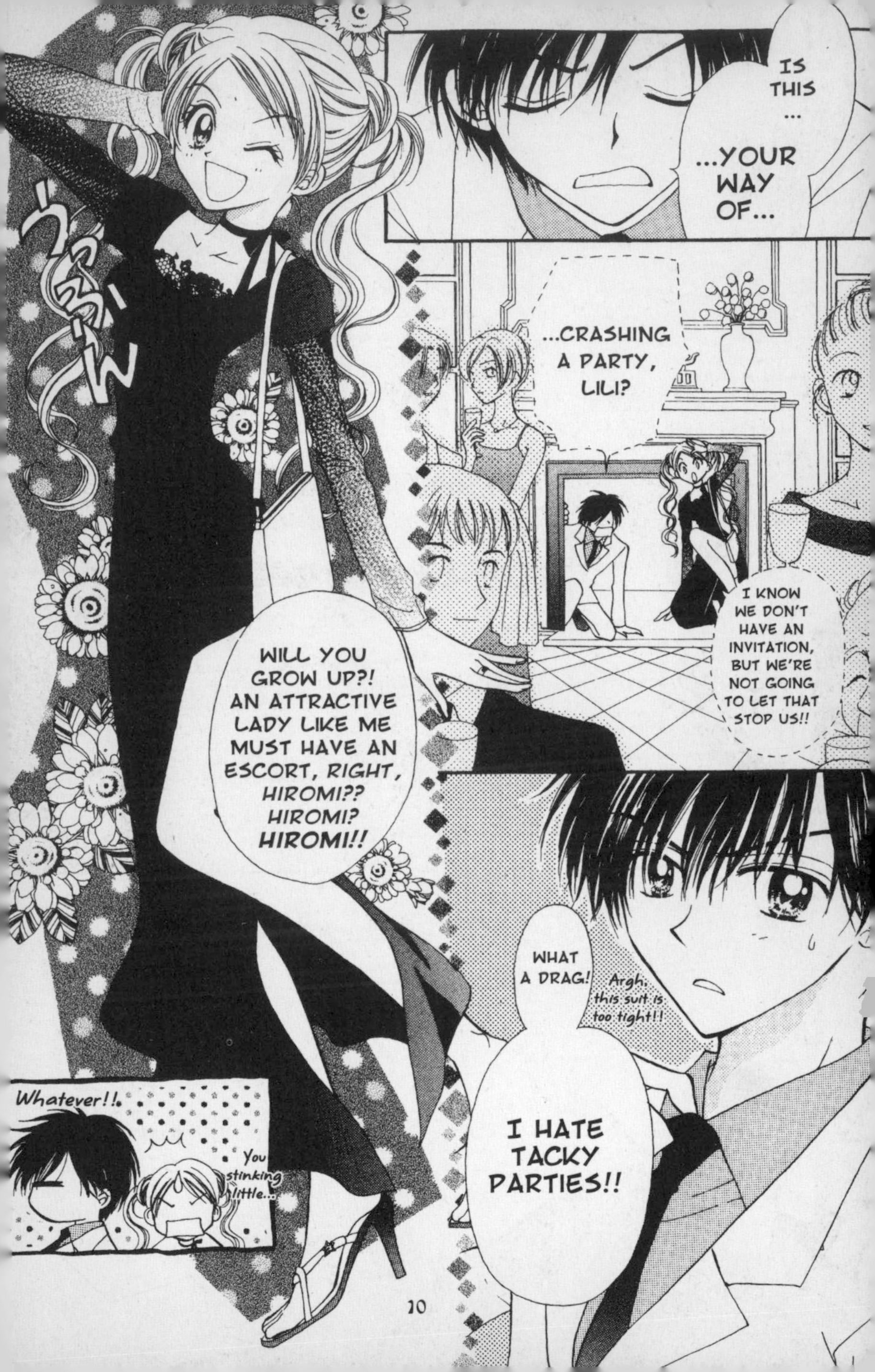
IS THIS ...
...YOUR WAY OF...
...CRASHING A PARTY, LILI?
I KNOW WE DON'T HAVE AN INVITATION, BUT WE'RE NOT GOING TO LET THAT STOP US!!
WHAT A DRAG!
Argh, this suit is too tight!!
I HATE TACKY PARTIES!!
WILL YOU GROW UP?! AN ATTRACTIVE LADY LIKE ME MUST HAVE AN ESCORT, RIGHT, HIROMI?? HIROMI? HIROMI!!
Whatever!!
You stinking little...

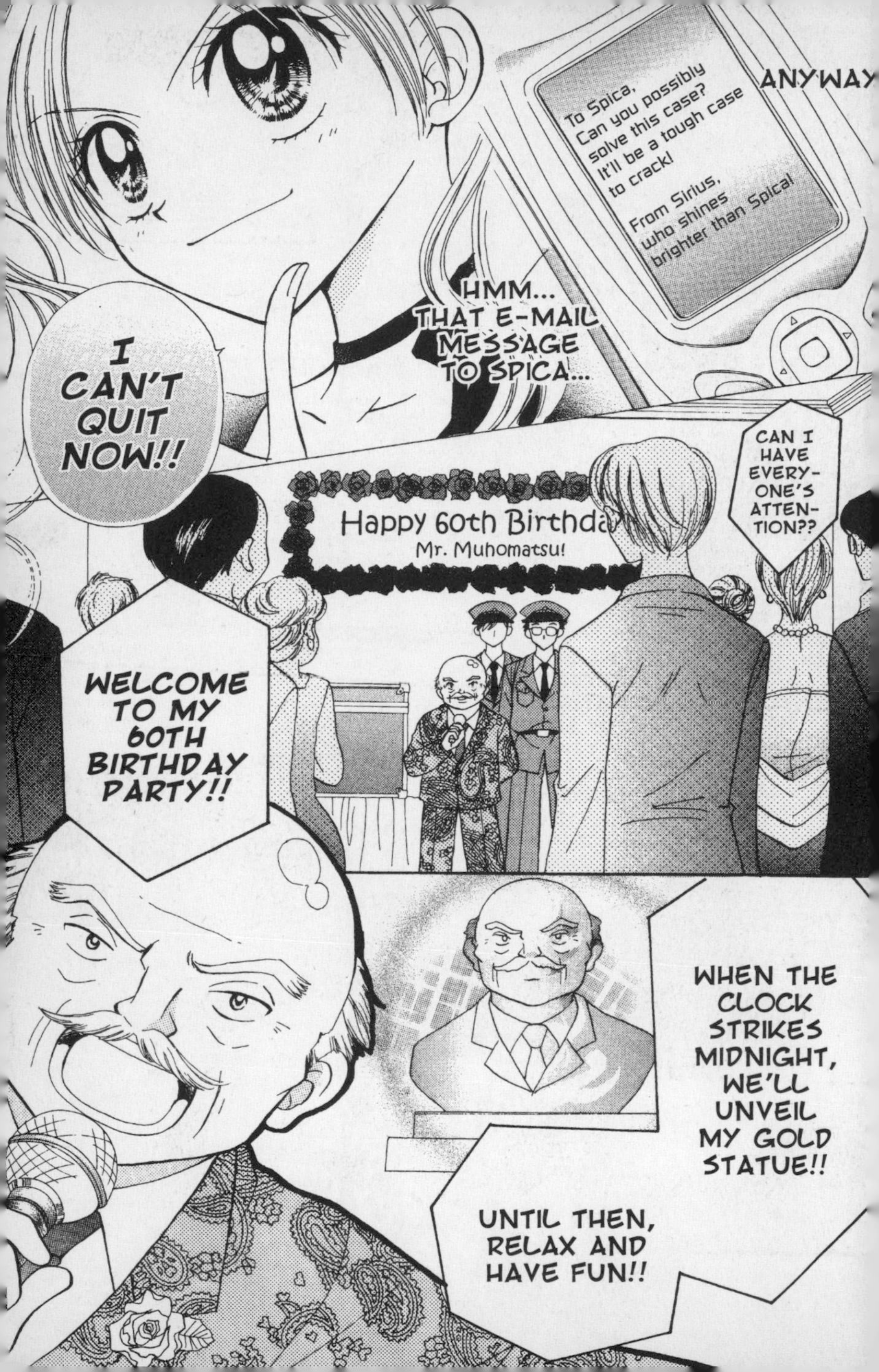
ANYWAY
To Spica,
Can you possibly solve this case? It'll be a tough case to crack!
From Sirius, who shines brighter than Spica!
HMM... THAT E-MAIL MESSAGE TO SPICA...
I CAN'T QUIT NOW!!
CAN I HAVE EVERY-ONE'S ATTEN-TION??
Happy 60th Birthda
Mr. Muhomatsu!
WELCOME TO MY 60TH BIRTHDAY PARTY!!
WHEN THE CLOCK STRIKES MIDNIGHT, WE'LL UNVEIL MY GOLD STATUE!!
UNTIL THEN, RELAX AND HAVE FUN!!

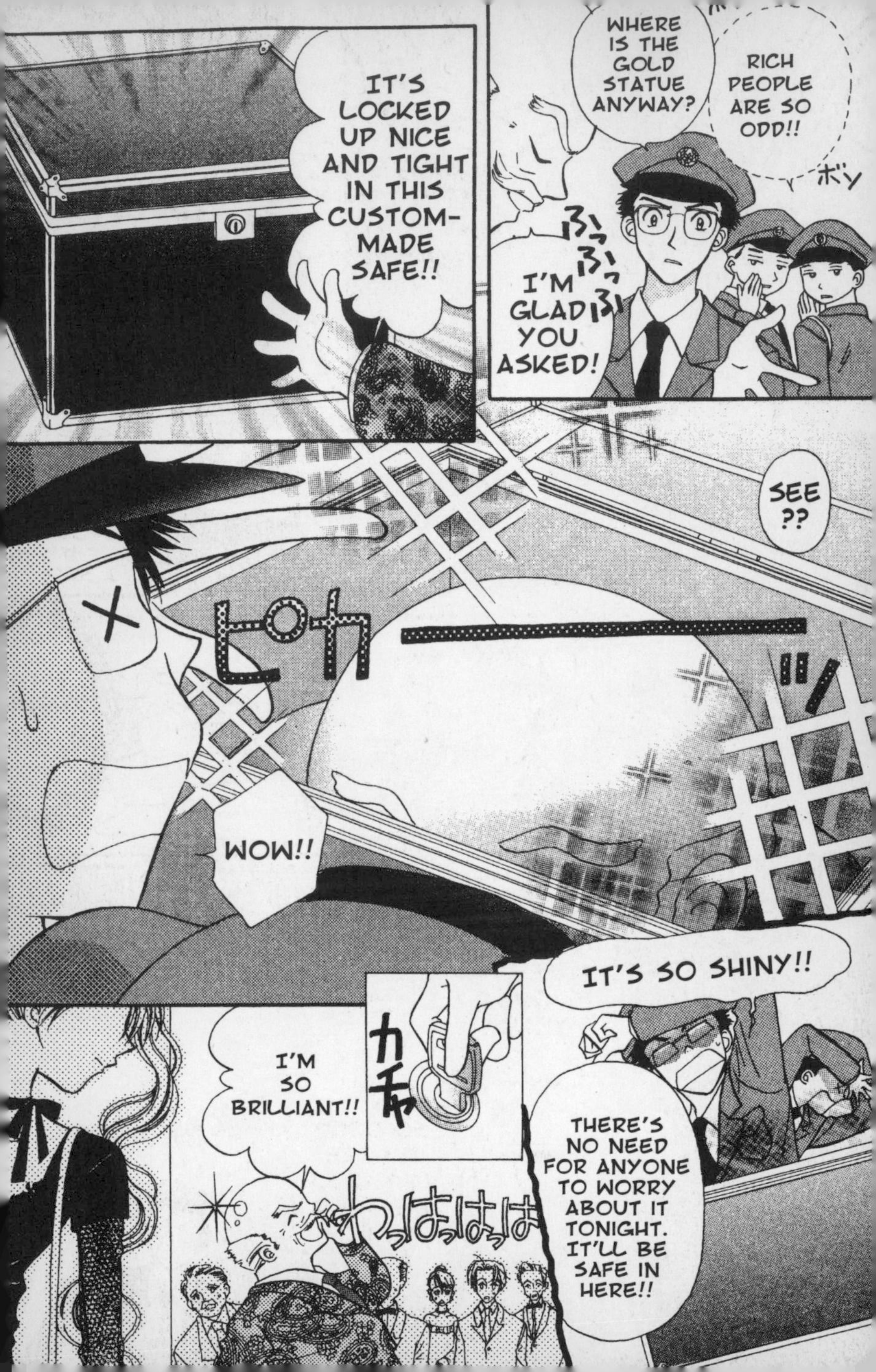

WHERE IS THE GOLD STATUE ANYWAY?
RICH PEOPLE ARE SO ODD!!
ボソ
ふっふっふ
I'M GLAD YOU ASKED!
IT'S LOCKED UP NICE AND TIGHT IN THIS CUSTOM-MADE SAFE!!
SEE??
ピカー
WOW!!
IT'S SO SHINY!!
THERE'S NO NEED FOR ANYONE TO WORRY ABOUT IT TONIGHT. IT'LL BE SAFE IN HERE!!
わっはっはっは
カチャ
I'M SO BRILLIANT!!

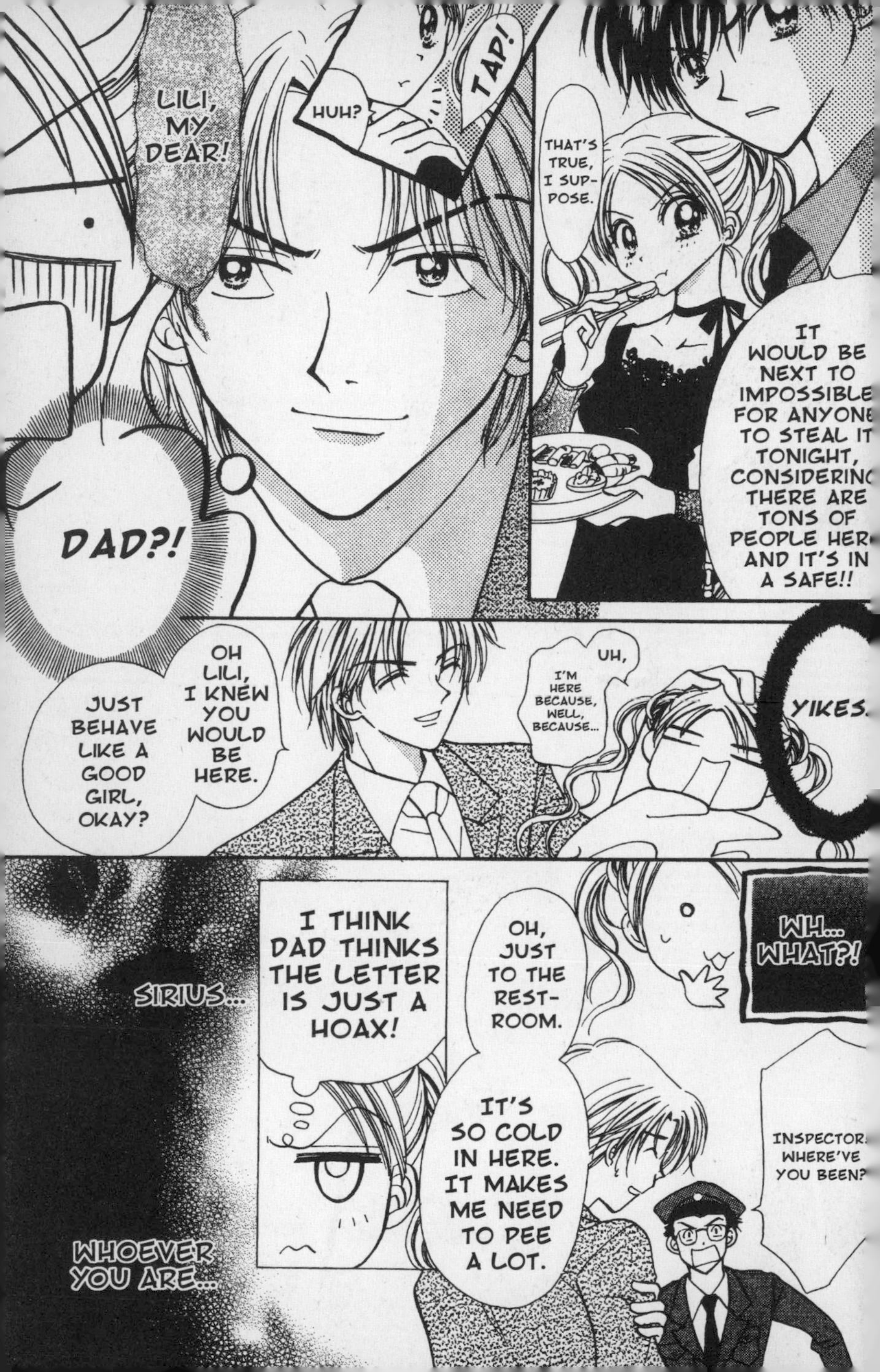
IT WOULD BE NEXT TO IMPOSSIBLE FOR ANYONE TO STEAL IT TONIGHT, CONSIDERING THERE ARE TONS OF PEOPLE HERE AND IT'S IN A SAFE!!
THAT'S TRUE, I SUP-POSE.
TAP!
HUH?
LILI, MY DEAR!
DAD?!
YIKES.
UH,
I'M HERE BECAUSE, WELL, BECAUSE...
OH LILI, I KNEW YOU WOULD BE HERE.
JUST BEHAVE LIKE A GOOD GIRL, OKAY?
WH... WHAT?!
INSPECTOR! WHERE'VE YOU BEEN?
OH, JUST TO THE REST-ROOM.
IT'S SO COLD IN HERE. IT MAKES ME NEED TO PEE A LOT.
I THINK DAD THINKS THE LETTER IS JUST A HOAX!
SIRIUS...
WHOEVER YOU ARE...

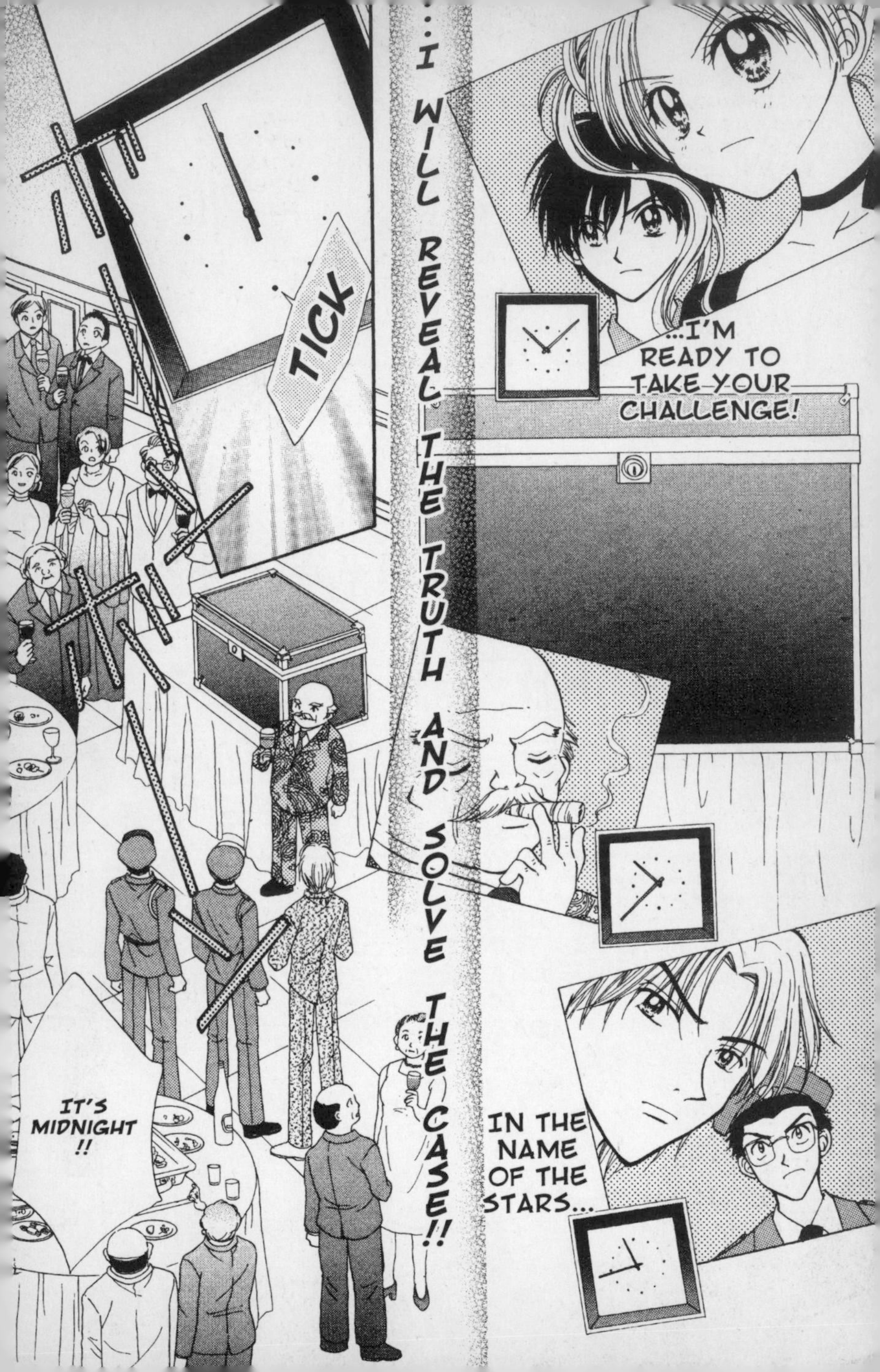
...I'M READY TO TAKE YOUR CHALLENGE!
IN THE NAME OF THE STARS...
...I WILL REVEAL THE TRUTH AND SOLVE THE CASE!!
TICK
IT'S MIDNIGHT!!

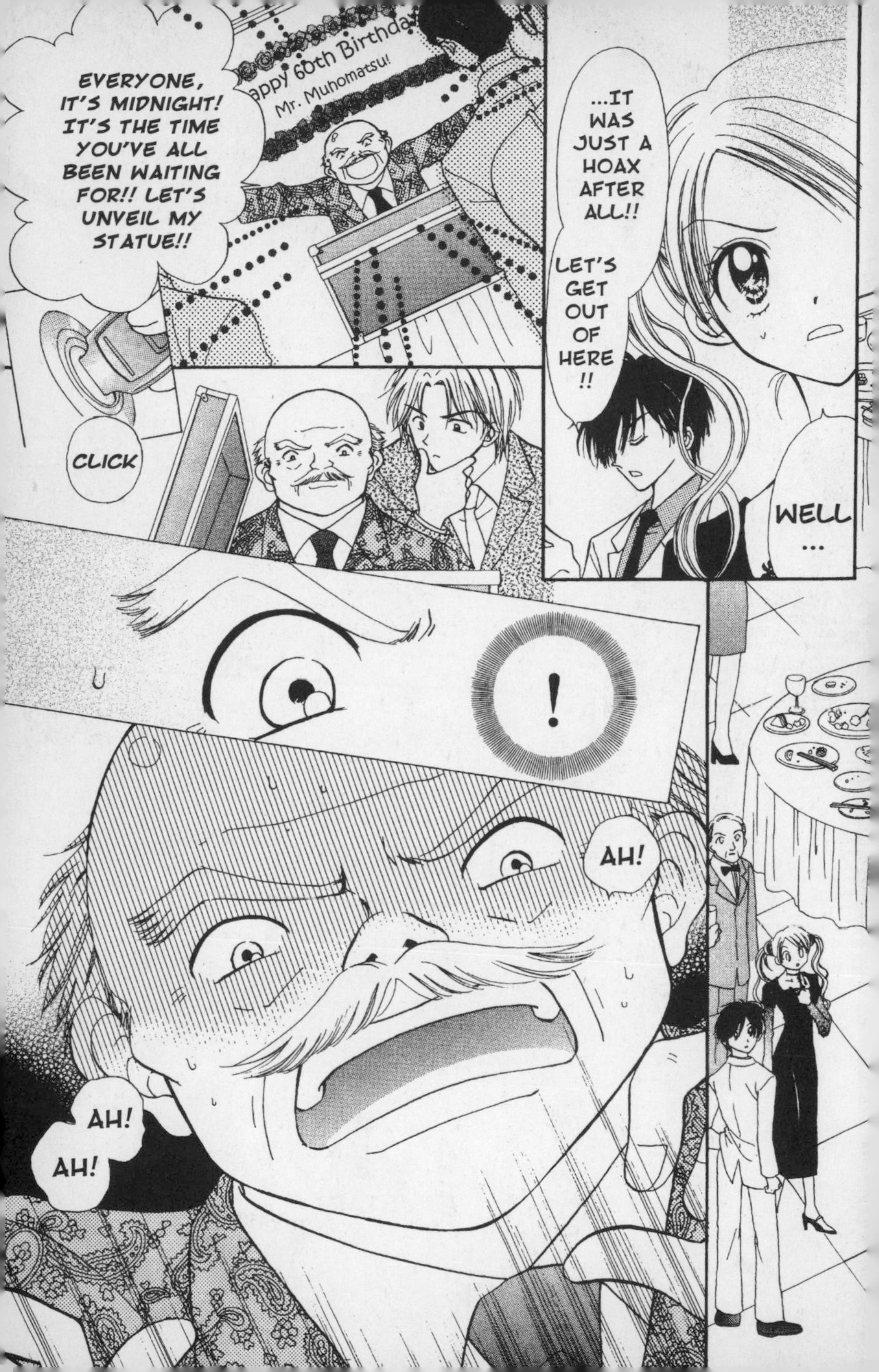
...IT WAS JUST A HOAX AFTER ALL!!
LET'S GET OUT OF HERE!!
WELL...
appy 60th Birthday
Mr. Muhomatsu!
EVERYONE, IT'S MIDNIGHT! IT'S THE TIME YOU'VE ALL BEEN WAITING FOR!! LET'S UNVEIL MY STATUE!!
CLICK
!
AH!
AH!
AH!

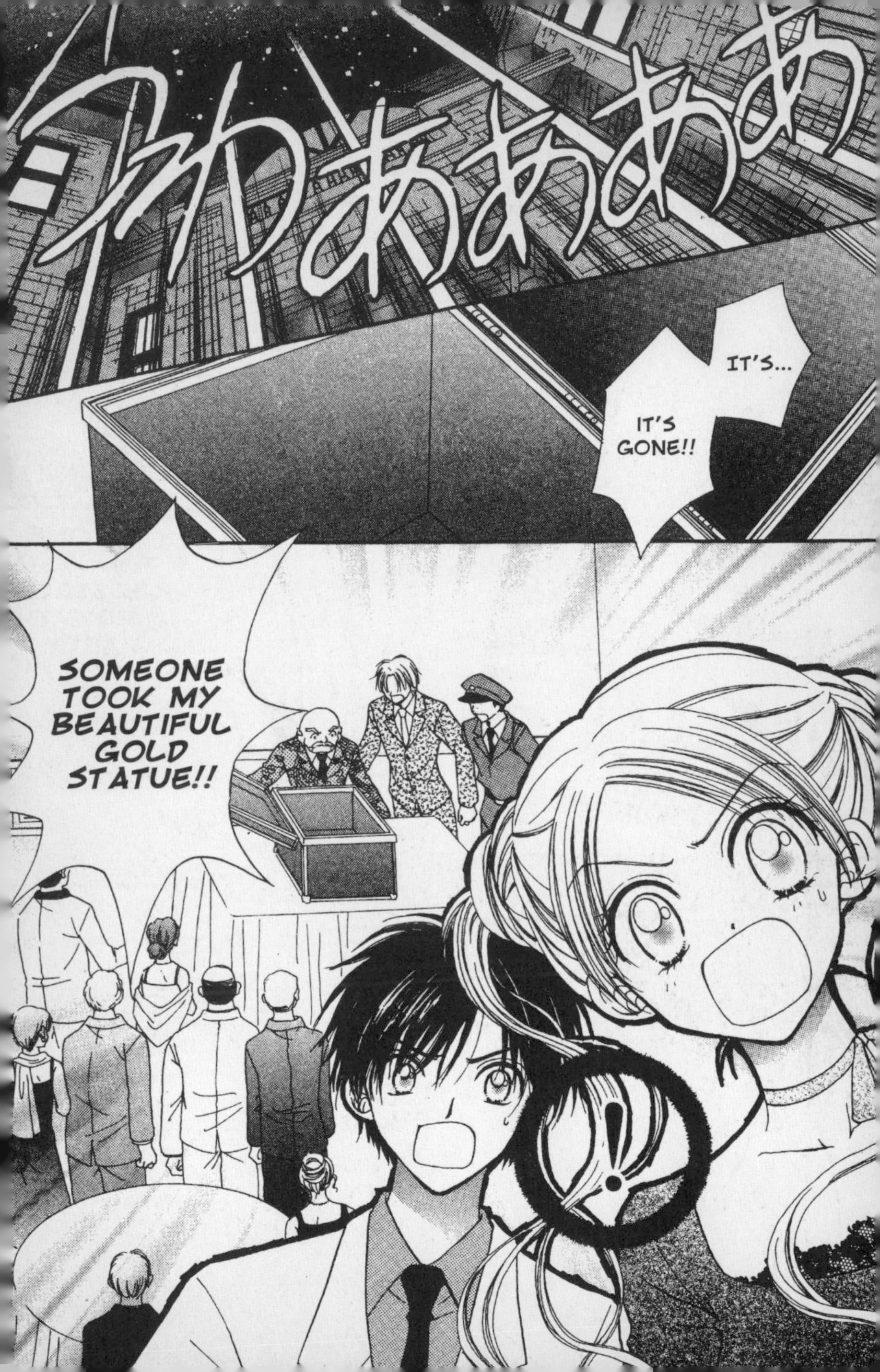
うわああああ
IT'S...
IT'S GONE!!
SOMEONE TOOK MY BEAUTIFUL GOLD STATUE!!
!

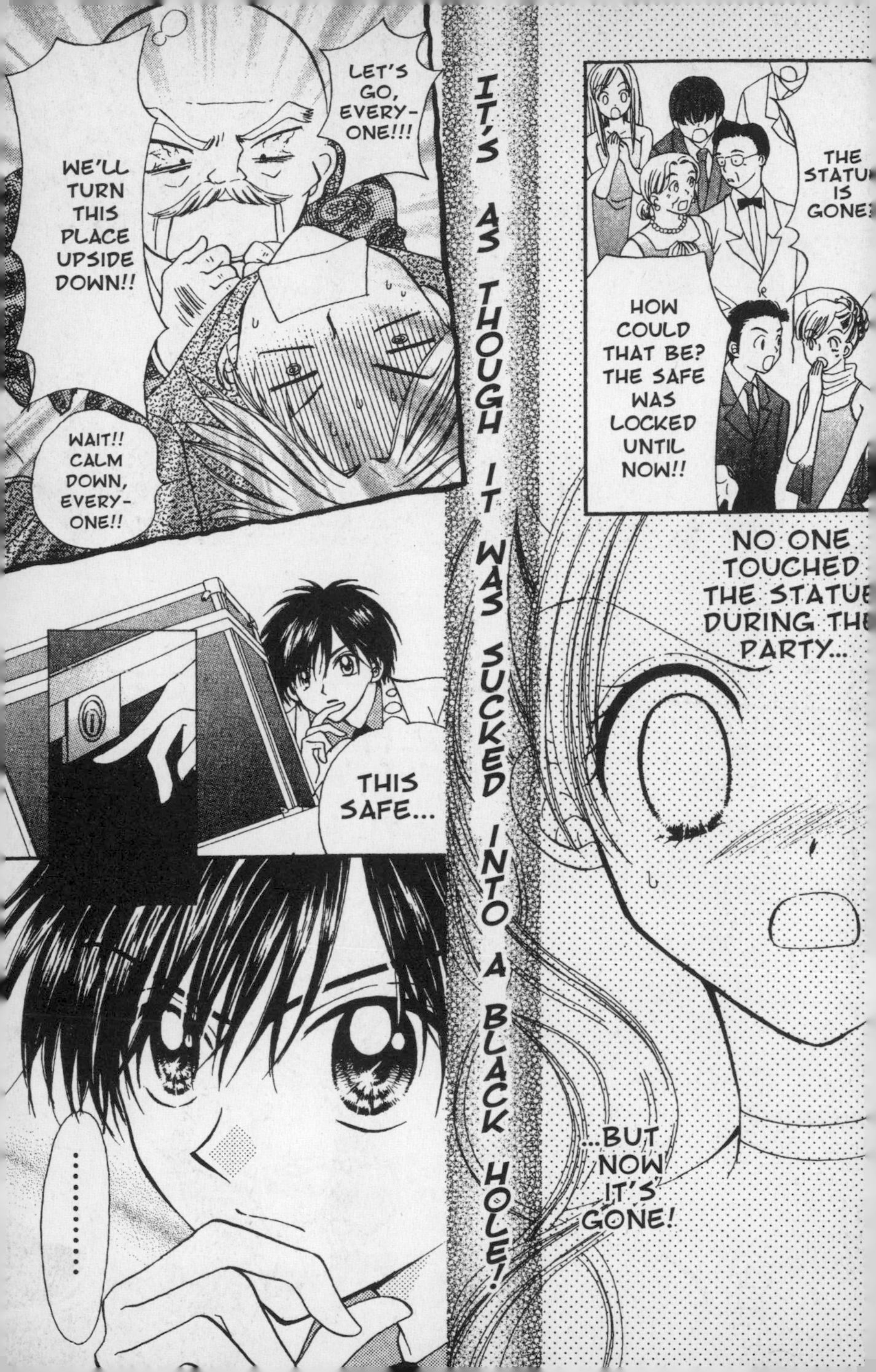
THE STATUE IS GONE!
HOW COULD THAT BE? THE SAFE WAS LOCKED UNTIL NOW!!
NO ONE TOUCHED THE STATUE DURING THE PARTY...
...BUT NOW IT'S GONE!
IT'S AS THOUGH IT WAS SUCKED INTO A BLACK HOLE!
LET'S GO, EVERY-ONE!!!
WE'LL TURN THIS PLACE UPSIDE DOWN!!
WAIT!! CALM DOWN, EVERY-ONE!!
THIS SAFE...
......

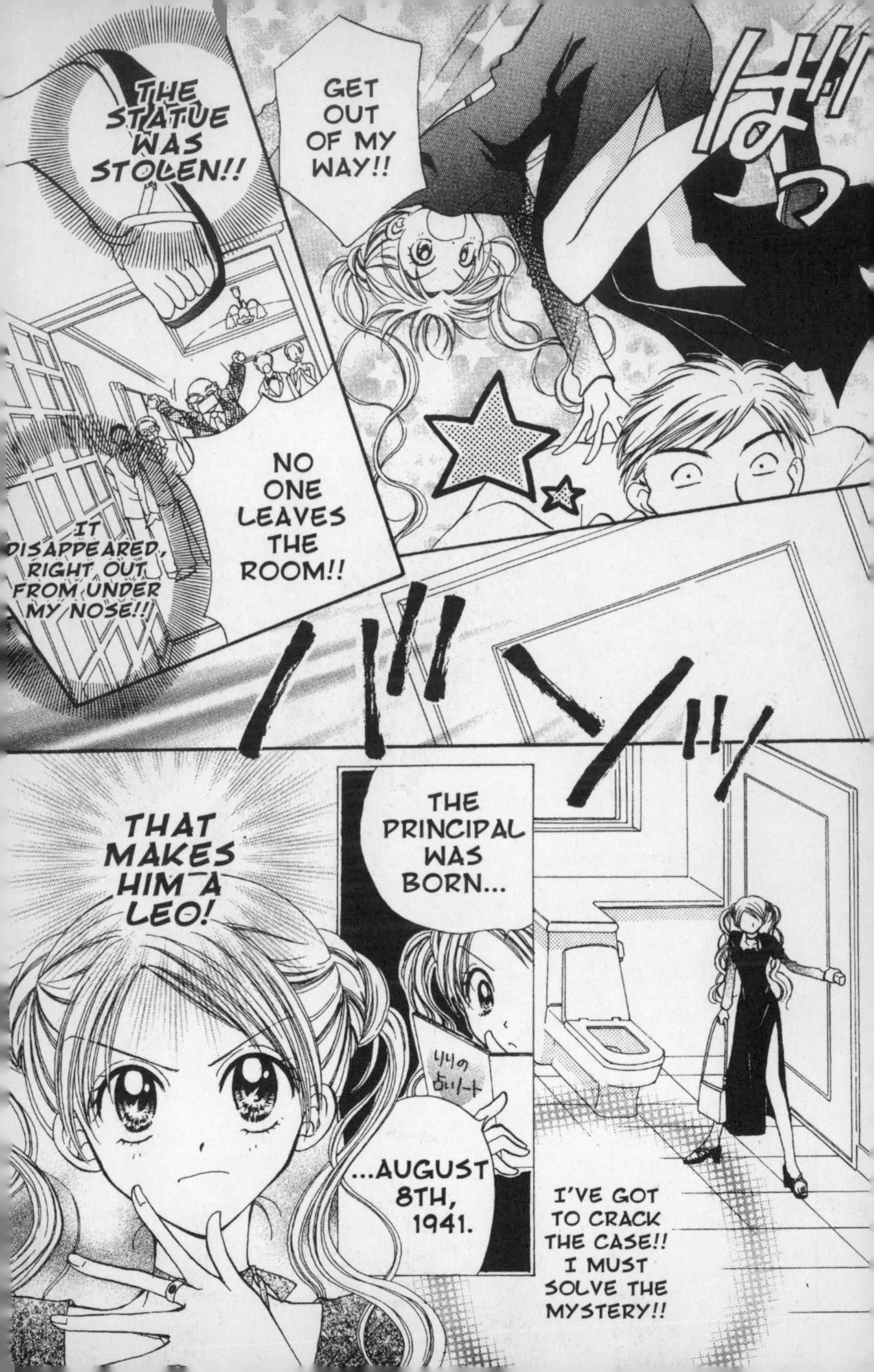
ぱっ
GET OUT OF MY WAY!!
THE STATUE WAS STOLEN!!
NO ONE LEAVES THE ROOM!!
IT DISAPPEARED, RIGHT OUT FROM UNDER MY NOSE!!
I'VE GOT TO CRACK THE CASE!! I MUST SOLVE THE MYSTERY!!
THE PRINCIPAL WAS BORN...
...AUGUST 8TH, 1941.
THAT MAKES HIM A LEO!

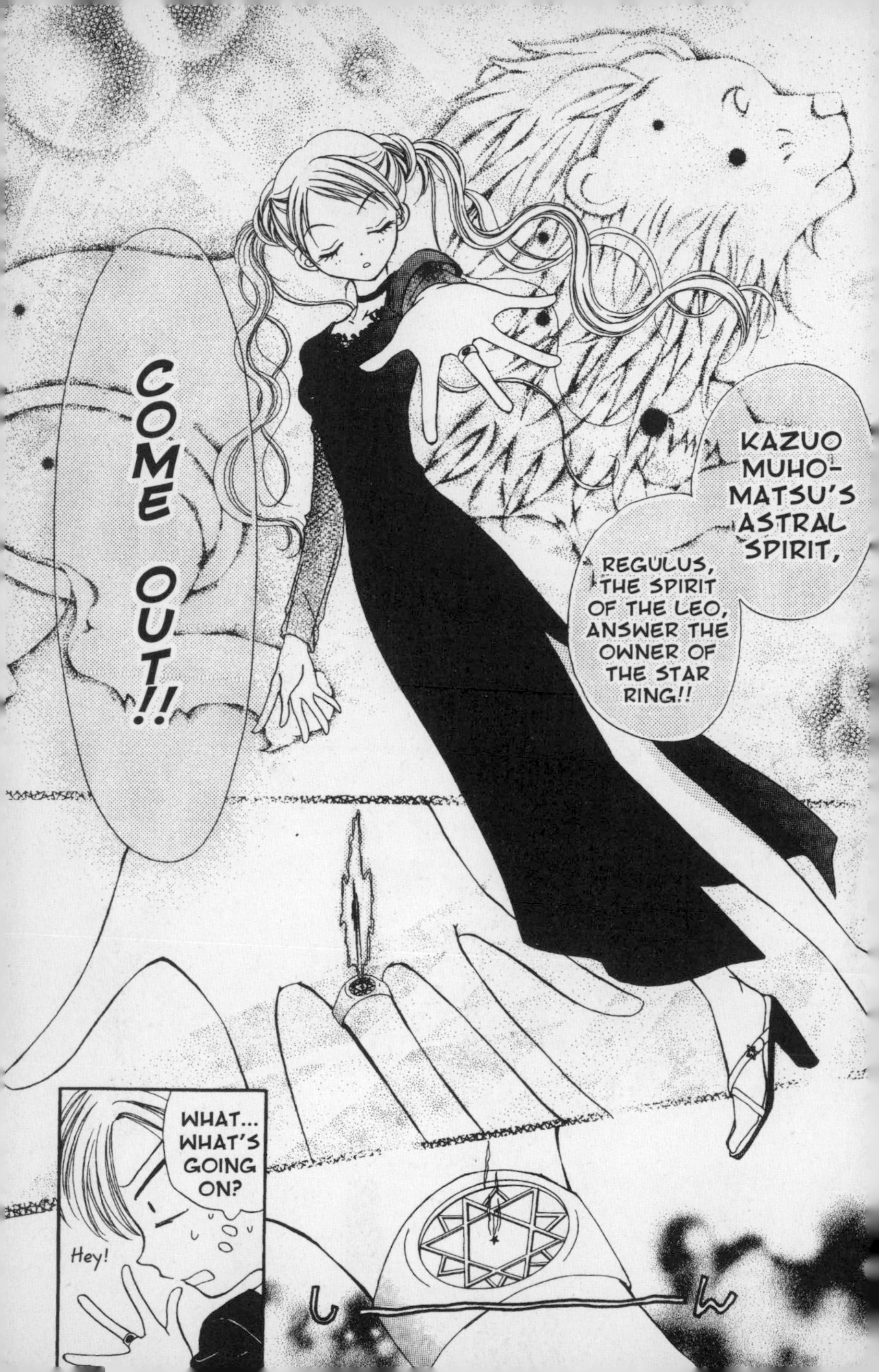
KAZUO MUHO-MATSU'S ASTRAL SPIRIT,
REGULUS, THE SPIRIT OF THE LEO, ANSWER THE OWNER OF THE STAR RING!!
COME OUT!!
WHAT... WHAT'S GOING ON?
Hey!

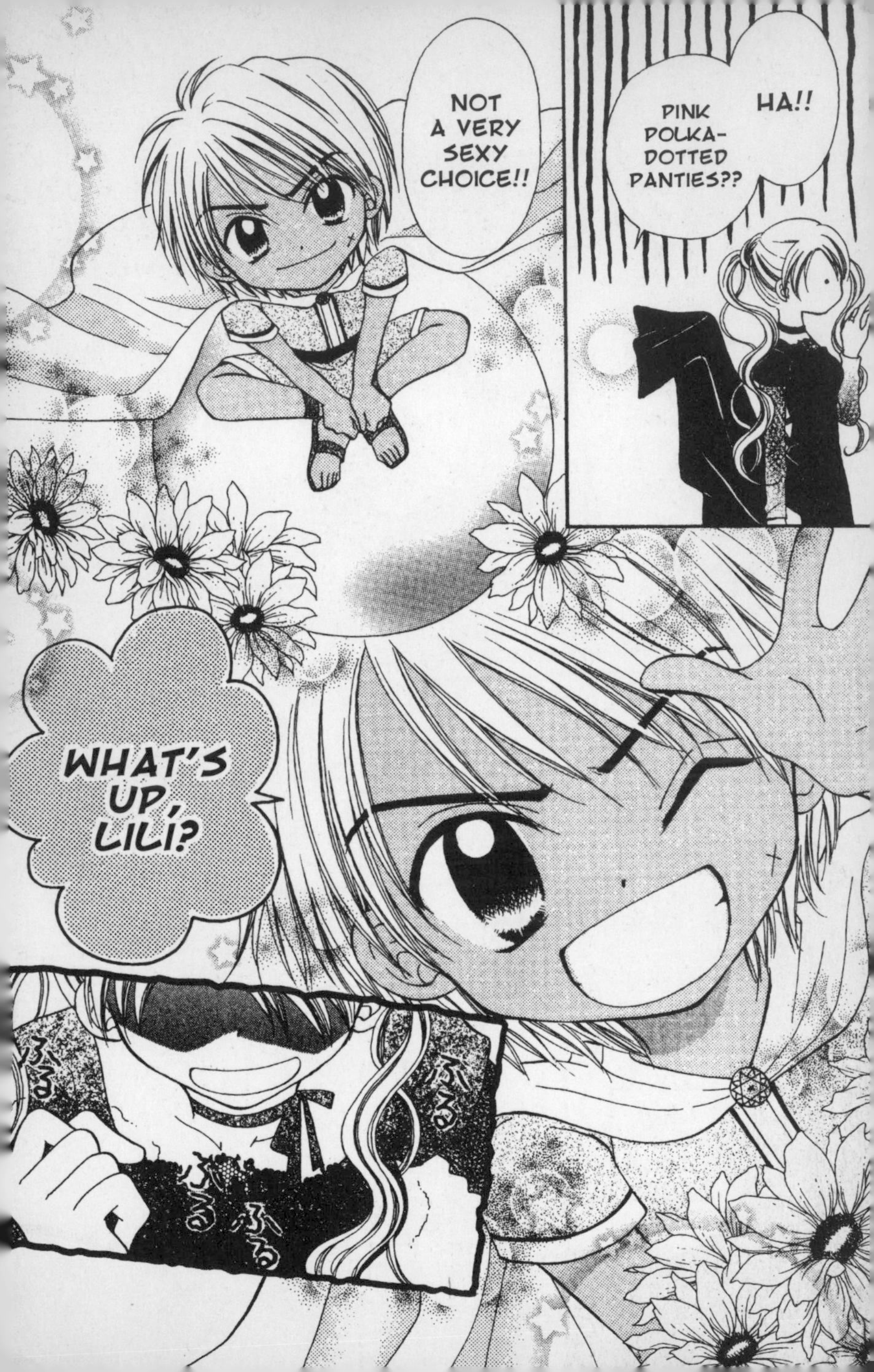
HA!! PINK POLKA-DOTTED PANTIES??
NOT A VERY SEXY CHOICE!!
WHAT'S UP, LILI?
ふる ふる
ふる ふる ふる

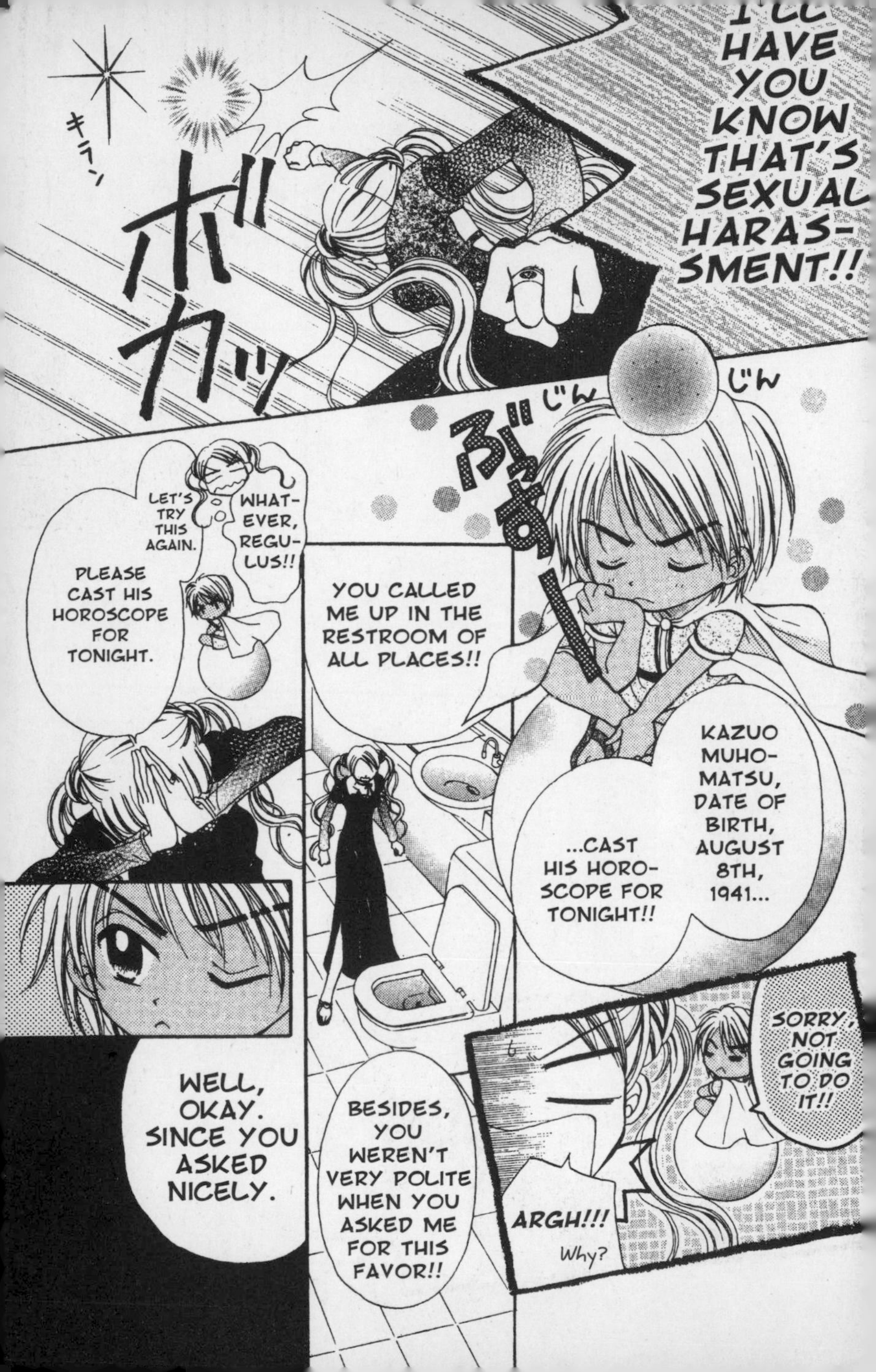
I'LL HAVE YOU KNOW THAT'S SEXUAL HARAS-SMENT!!
キラン
ボカッ
じんじん
ぶすー
YOU CALLED ME UP IN THE RESTROOM OF ALL PLACES!!
LET'S TRY THIS AGAIN.
WHAT-EVER, REGU-LUS!!
PLEASE CAST HIS HOROSCOPE FOR TONIGHT.
KAZUO MUHO-MATSU, DATE OF BIRTH, AUGUST 8TH, 1941...
...CAST HIS HORO-SCOPE FOR TONIGHT!!
SORRY, NOT GOING TO DO IT!!
ARGH!!!
Why?
BESIDES, YOU WEREN'T VERY POLITE WHEN YOU ASKED ME FOR THIS FAVOR!!
WELL, OKAY. SINCE YOU ASKED NICELY.

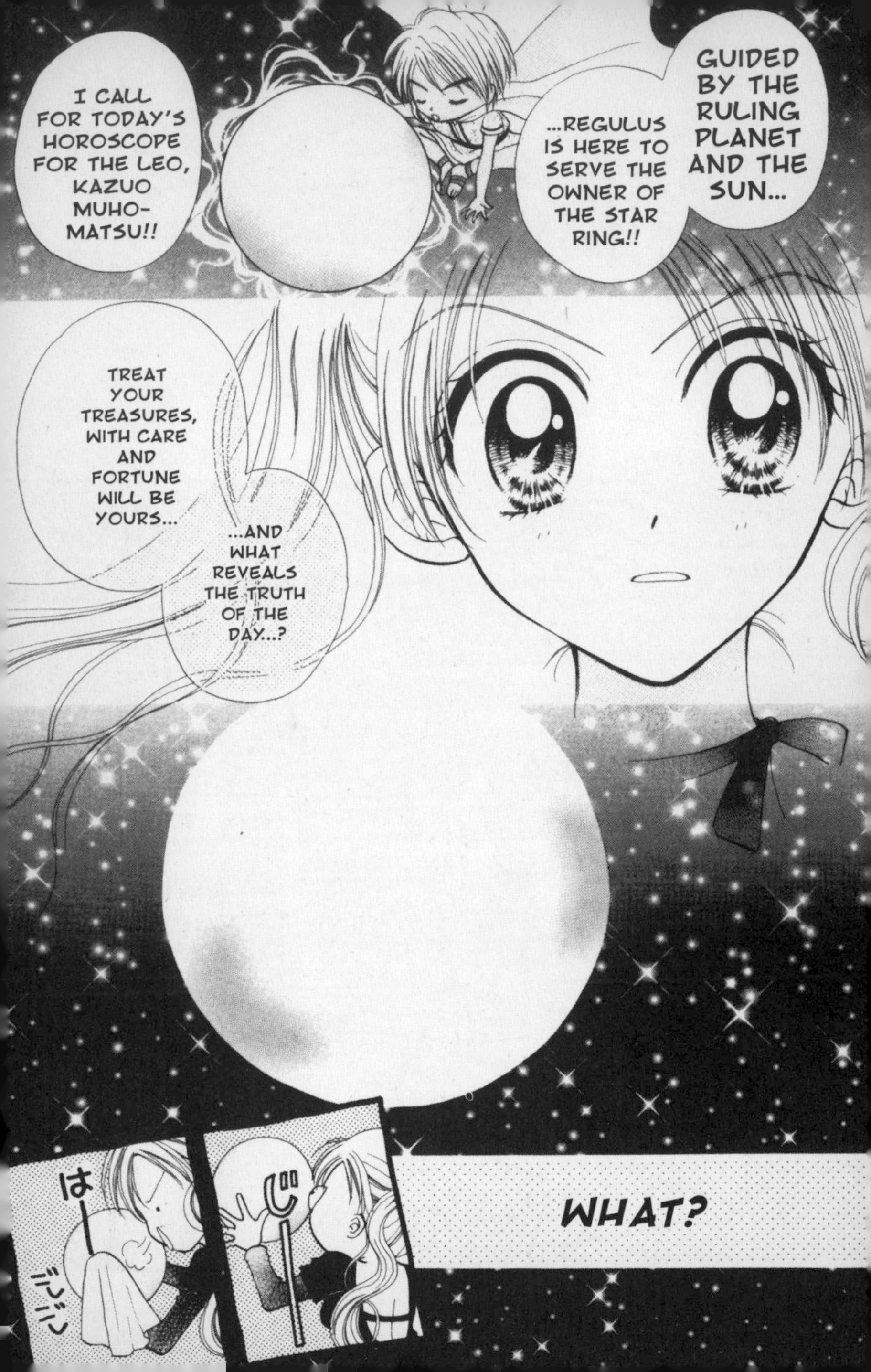
GUIDED BY THE RULING PLANET AND THE SUN...
...REGULUS IS HERE TO SERVE THE OWNER OF THE STAR RING!!
I CALL FOR TODAY'S HOROSCOPE FOR THE LEO, KAZUO MUHO-MATSU!!
TREAT YOUR TREASURES, WITH CARE AND FORTUNE WILL BE YOURS...
...AND WHAT REVEALS THE TRUTH OF THE DAY...?
WHAT?
じ
は

Greetings

Hello, everyone. Long time no see! This is the second volume of Zodiac P.I. Since I started this series, I've been watching detective shows on TV. My favorites are:

Mitsuhiko Asami's Detective Stories:
I like the hero. He's a sharp detective who cracks all the toughest cases. However, he does have trouble standing up to his mother and brother. Overall, he's a likable guy.

Judge Ayako Takabayashi:
You get to see some great crime-solving tricks. Azuma Mano, the actress who plays the heroine, is very pretty. I try to emulate her!

Attorney Yuko Kasumi:
I like the attorney's husband, who reminds me of Masuo in Sazae-san.

In short, I like detective stories with strong women characters-!

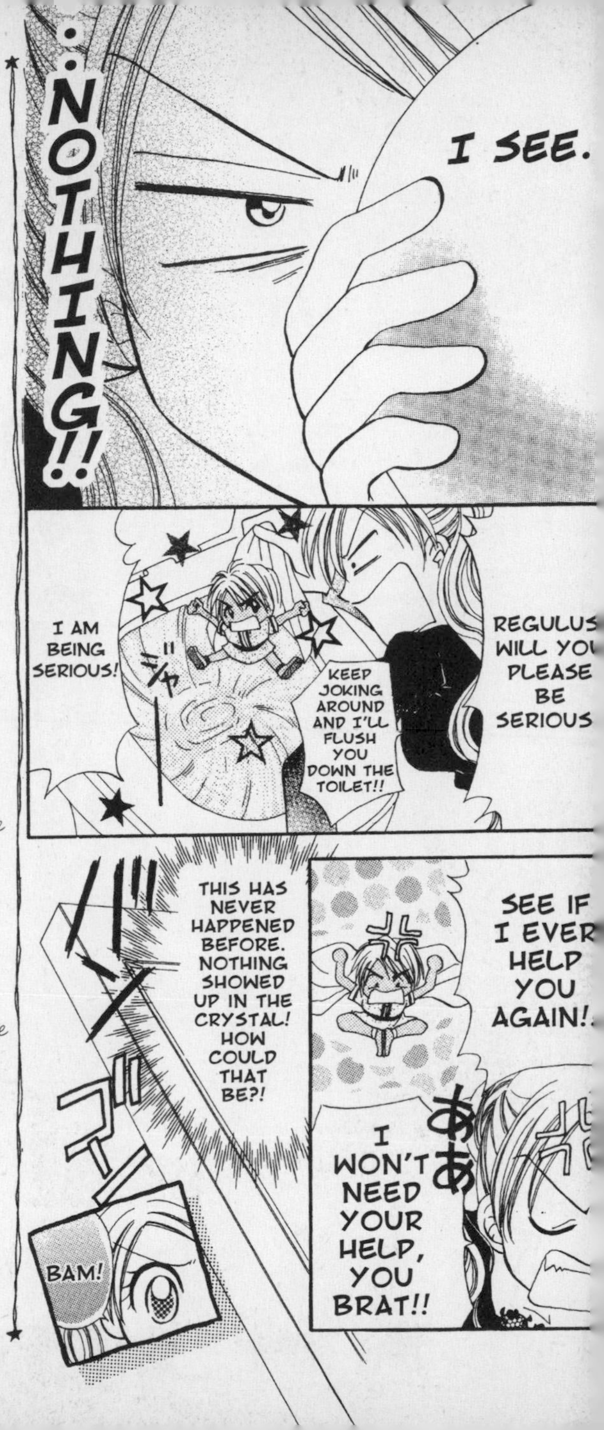
I SEE.
...NOTHING!!
REGULUS WILL YOU PLEASE BE SERIOUS
KEEP JOKING AROUND AND I'LL FLUSH YOU DOWN THE TOILET!!
I AM BEING SERIOUS!
SEE IF I EVER HELP YOU AGAIN!!
I WON'T NEED YOUR HELP, YOU BRAT!!
THIS HAS NEVER HAPPENED BEFORE. NOTHING SHOWED UP IN THE CRYSTAL! HOW COULD THAT BE?!
BAM!

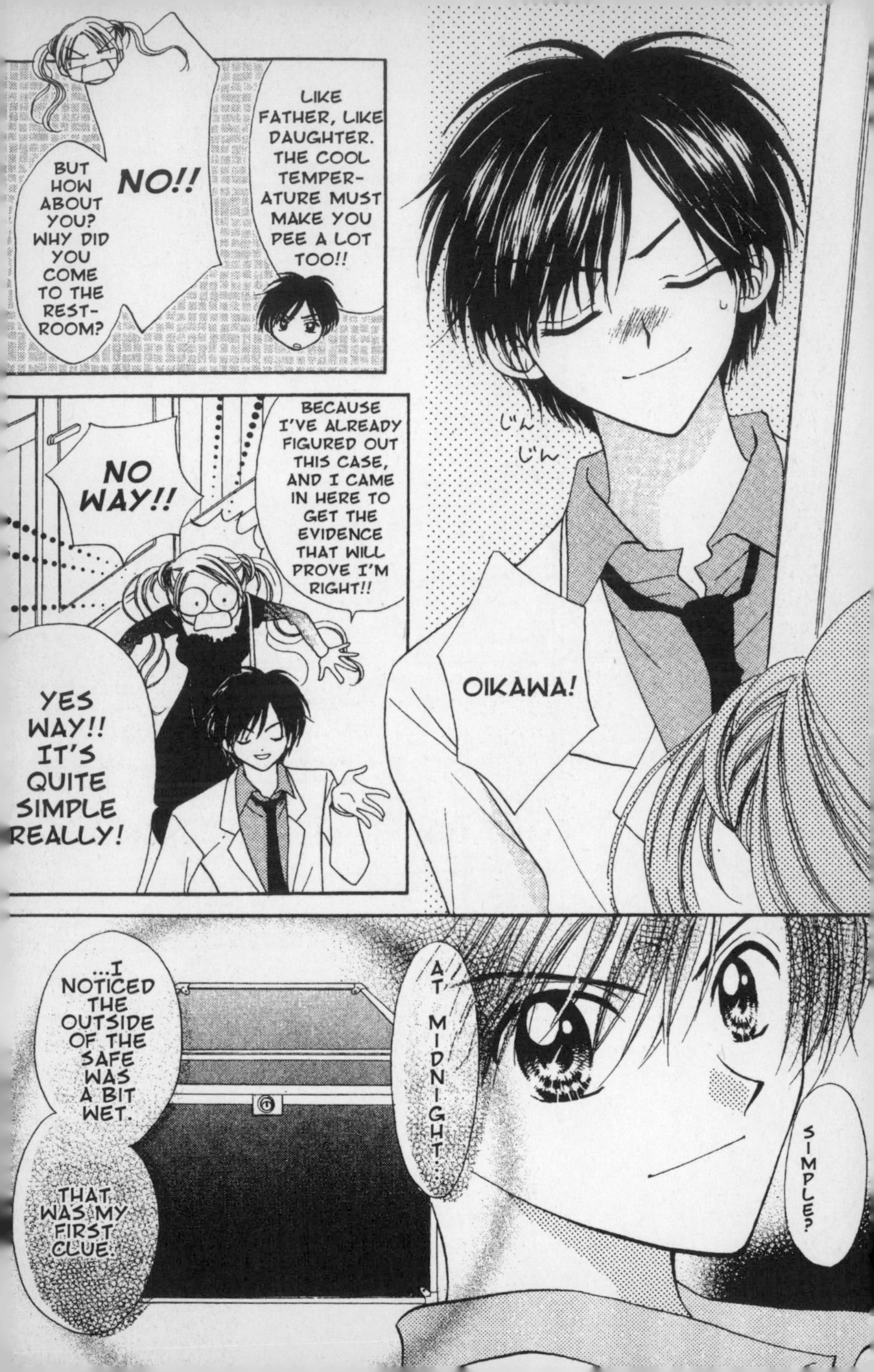
じん じん
OIKAWA!
LIKE FATHER, LIKE DAUGHTER. THE COOL TEMPER-ATURE MUST MAKE YOU PEE A LOT TOO!!
NO!!
BUT HOW ABOUT YOU? WHY DID YOU COME TO THE REST-ROOM?
BECAUSE I'VE ALREADY FIGURED OUT THIS CASE, AND I CAME IN HERE TO GET THE EVIDENCE THAT WILL PROVE I'M RIGHT!!
NO WAY!!
YES WAY!! IT'S QUITE SIMPLE REALLY!
SIMPLE?
AT MIDNIGHT...
...I NOTICED THE OUTSIDE OF THE SAFE WAS A BIT WET.
THAT WAS MY FIRST CLUE.

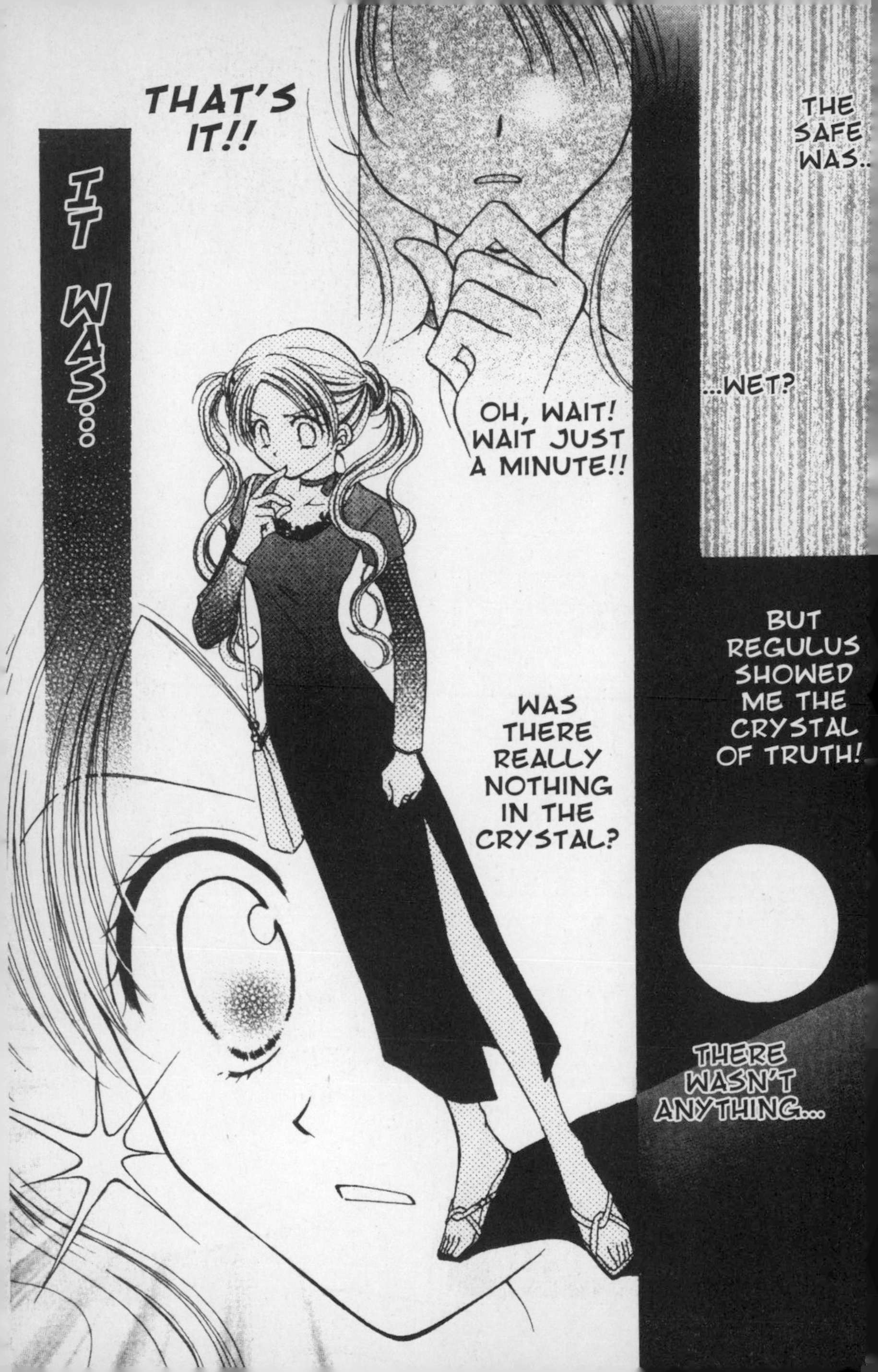
THE SAFE WAS..
...WET?
BUT REGULUS SHOWED ME THE CRYSTAL OF TRUTH!
THERE WASN'T ANYTHING...
OH, WAIT! WAIT JUST A MINUTE!!
WAS THERE REALLY NOTHING IN THE CRYSTAL?
THAT'S IT!!
IT WAS...

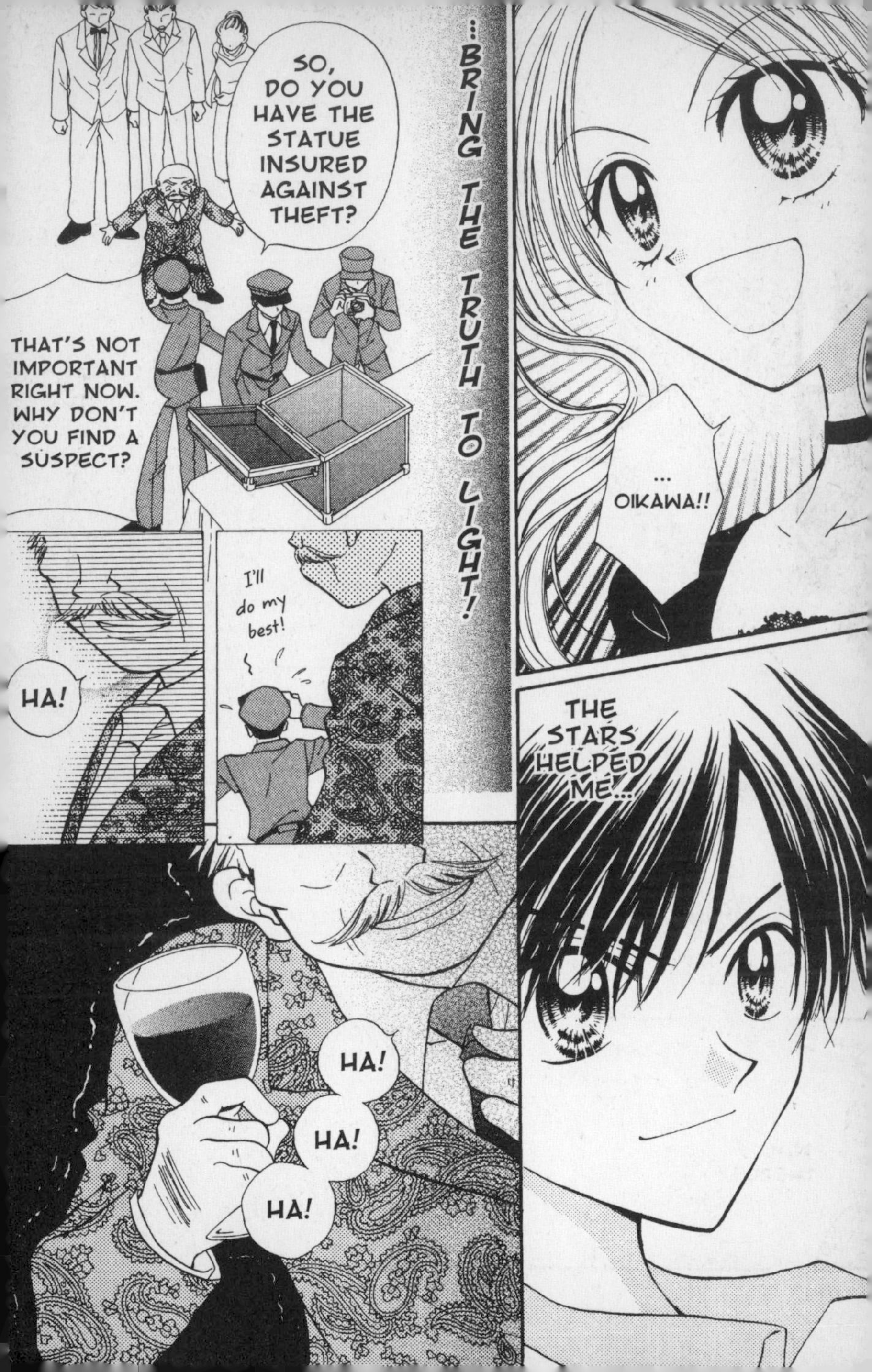
...OIKAWA!!
THE STARS HELPED ME...
...BRING THE TRUTH TO LIGHT!
SO, DO YOU HAVE THE STATUE INSURED AGAINST THEFT?
THAT'S NOT IMPORTANT RIGHT NOW. WHY DON'T YOU FIND A SUSPECT?
I'll do my best!
HA!
HA!
HA!
HA!

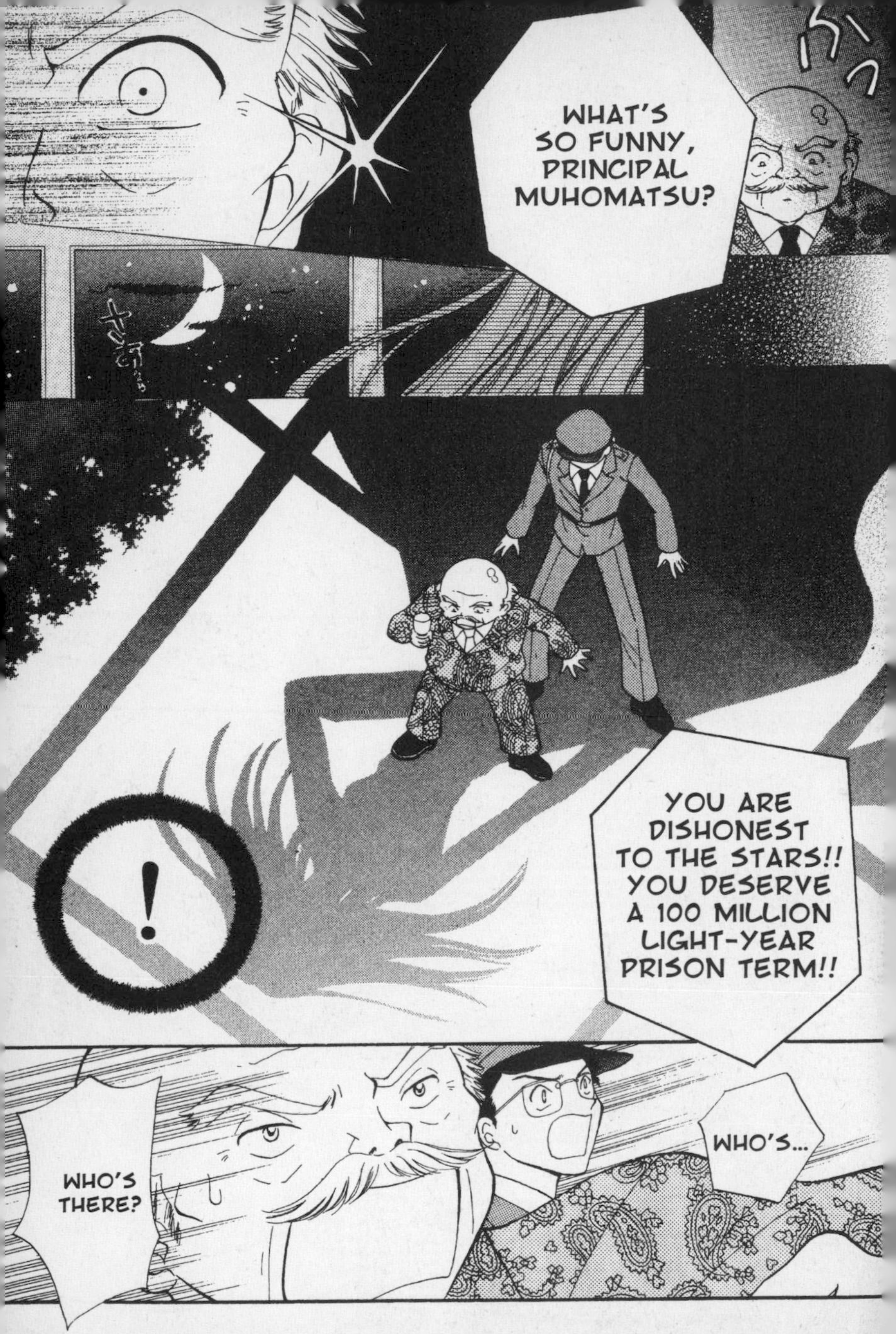
WHAT'S SO FUNNY, PRINCIPAL MUHOMATSU?
YOU ARE DISHONEST TO THE STARS!! YOU DESERVE A 100 MILLION LIGHT-YEAR PRISON TERM!!
!
WHO'S...
WHO'S THERE?

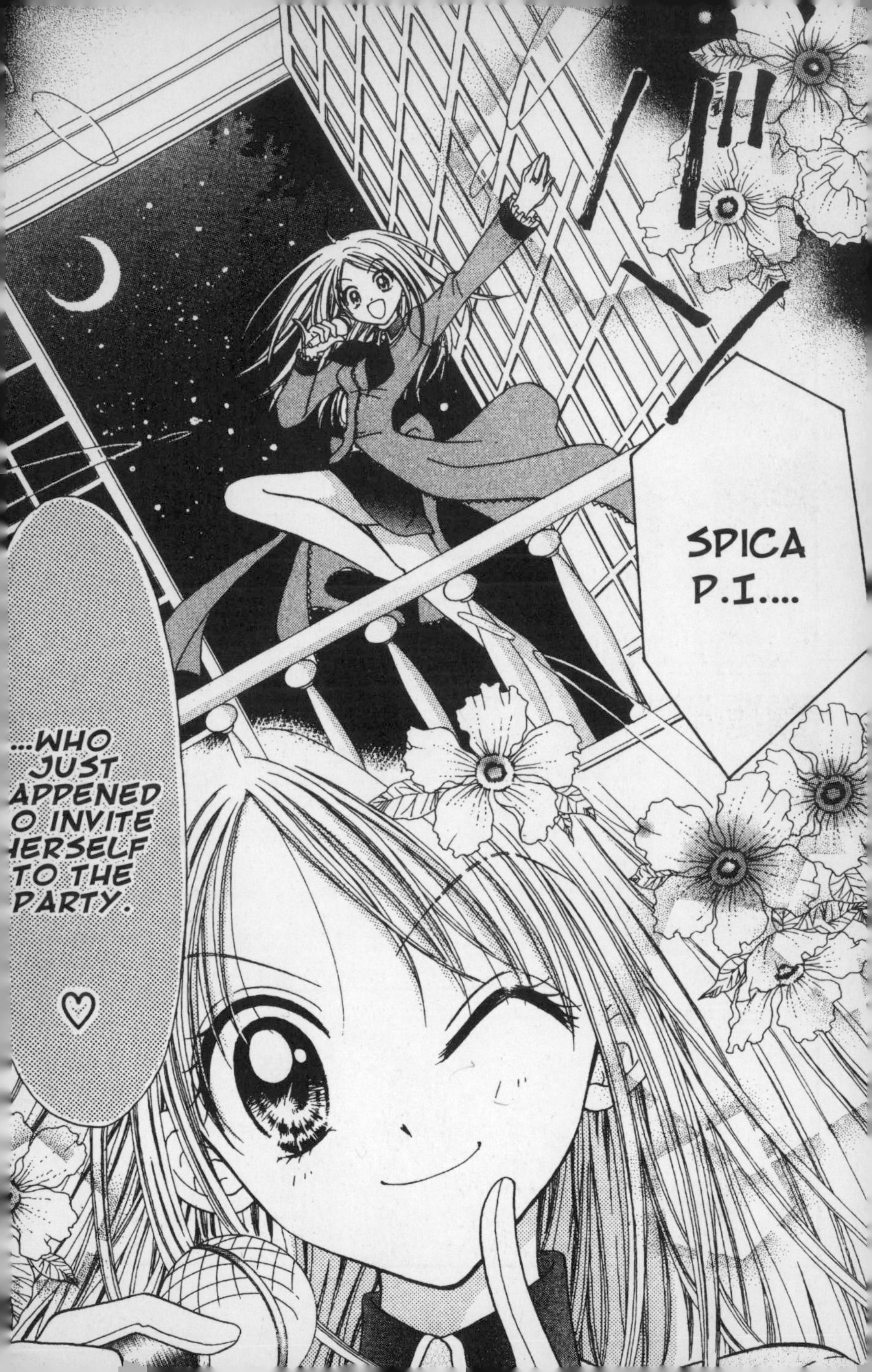
SPICA P.I....
...WHO JUST APPENED O INVITE HERSELF TO THE PARTY. ♡

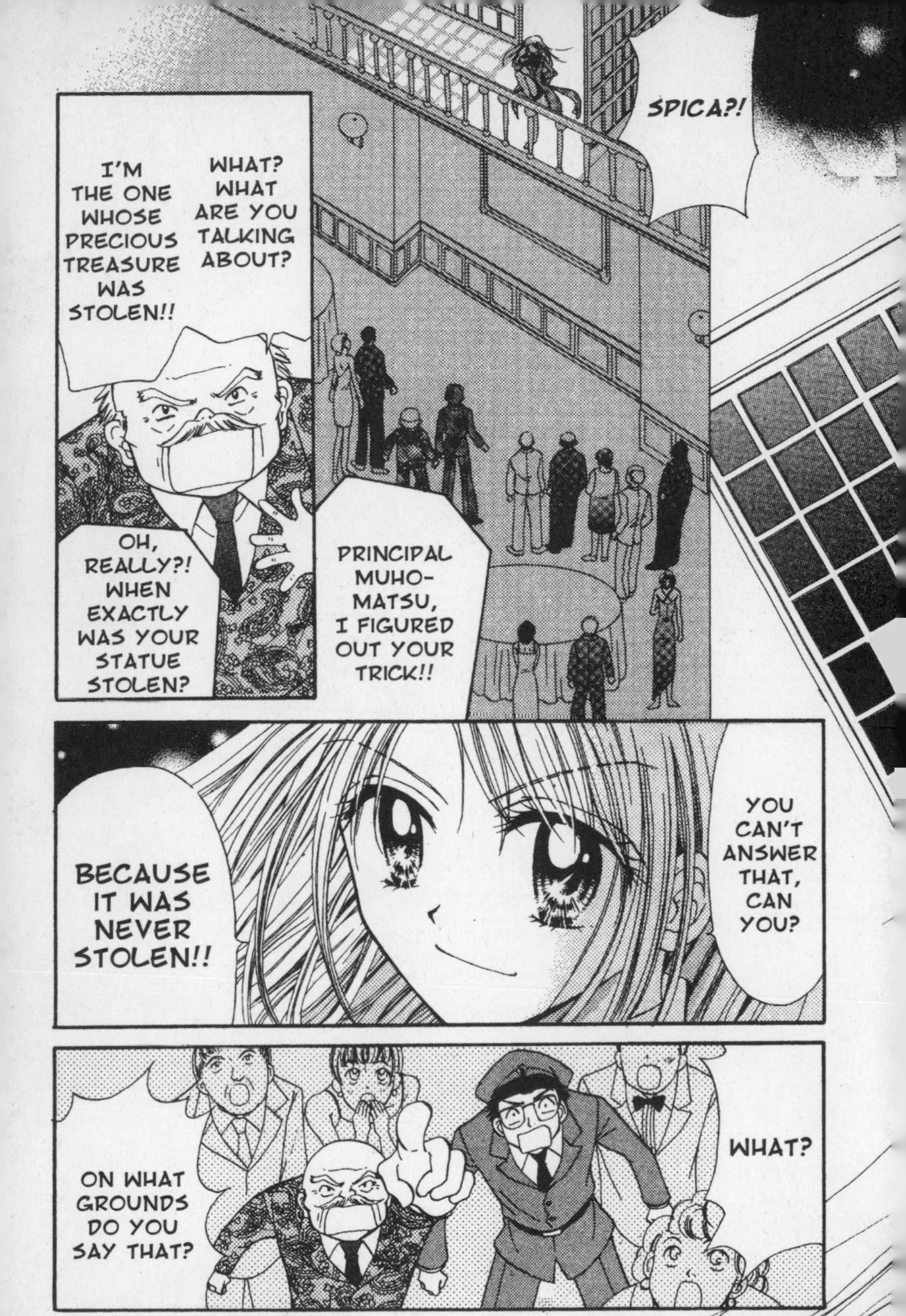
SPICA?!
PRINCIPAL MUHO-MATSU, I FIGURED OUT YOUR TRICK!!
WHAT? WHAT ARE YOU TALKING ABOUT?
I'M THE ONE WHOSE PRECIOUS TREASURE WAS STOLEN!!
OH, REALLY?! WHEN EXACTLY WAS YOUR STATUE STOLEN?
YOU CAN'T ANSWER THAT, CAN YOU?
BECAUSE IT WAS NEVER STOLEN!!
WHAT?
ON WHAT GROUNDS DO YOU SAY THAT?

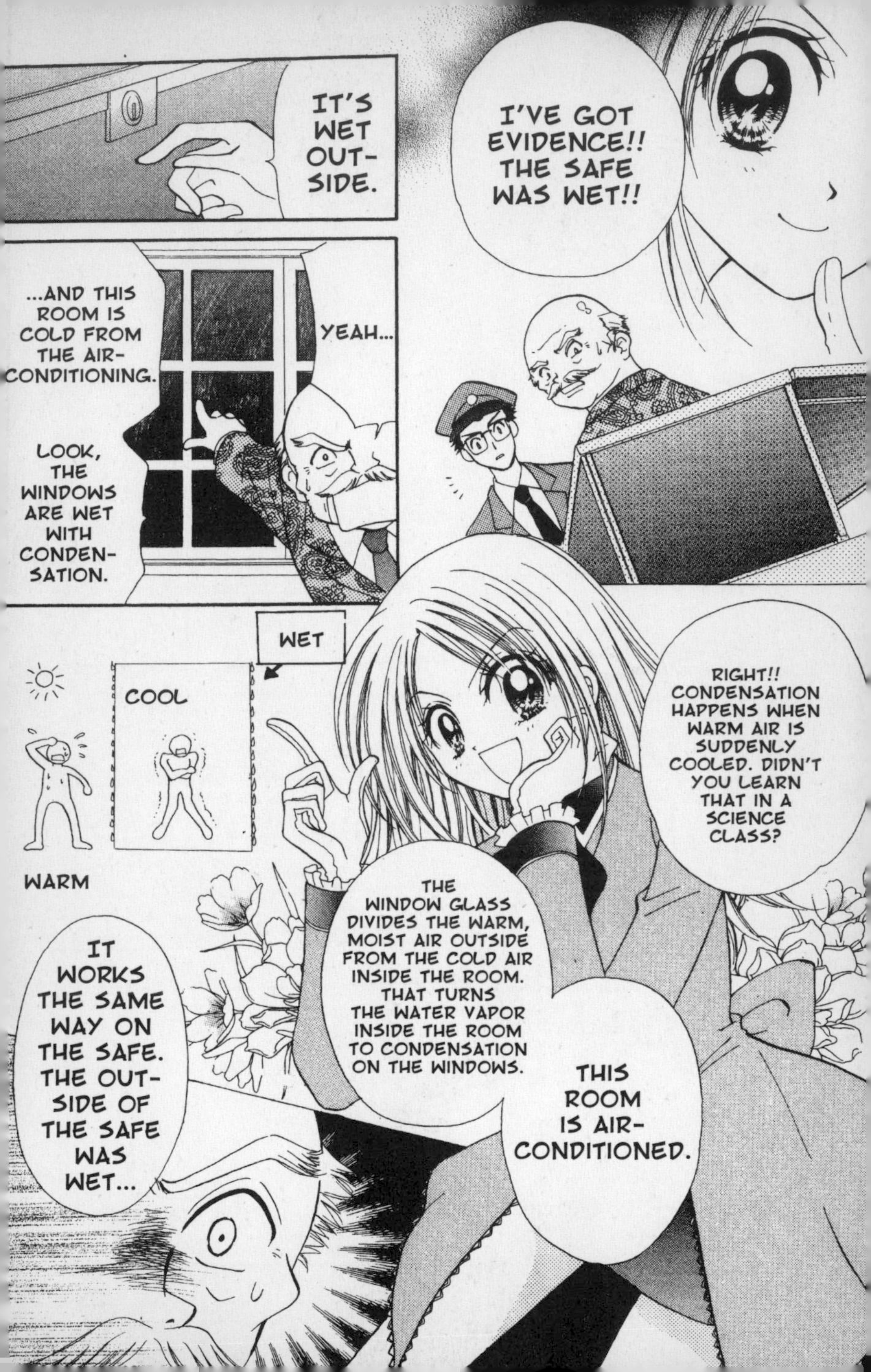
I'VE GOT EVIDENCE!! THE SAFE WAS WET!!
IT'S WET OUT-SIDE.
YEAH...
...AND THIS ROOM IS COLD FROM THE AIR-CONDITIONING.
LOOK, THE WINDOWS ARE WET WITH CONDEN-SATION.
RIGHT!! CONDENSATION HAPPENS WHEN WARM AIR IS SUDDENLY COOLED. DIDN'T YOU LEARN THAT IN A SCIENCE CLASS?
WET
COOL
WARM
THIS ROOM IS AIR-CONDITIONED.
THE WINDOW GLASS DIVIDES THE WARM, MOIST AIR OUTSIDE FROM THE COLD AIR INSIDE THE ROOM. THAT TURNS THE WATER VAPOR INSIDE THE ROOM TO CONDENSATION ON THE WINDOWS.
IT WORKS THE SAME WAY ON THE SAFE. THE OUT-SIDE OF THE SAFE WAS WET...

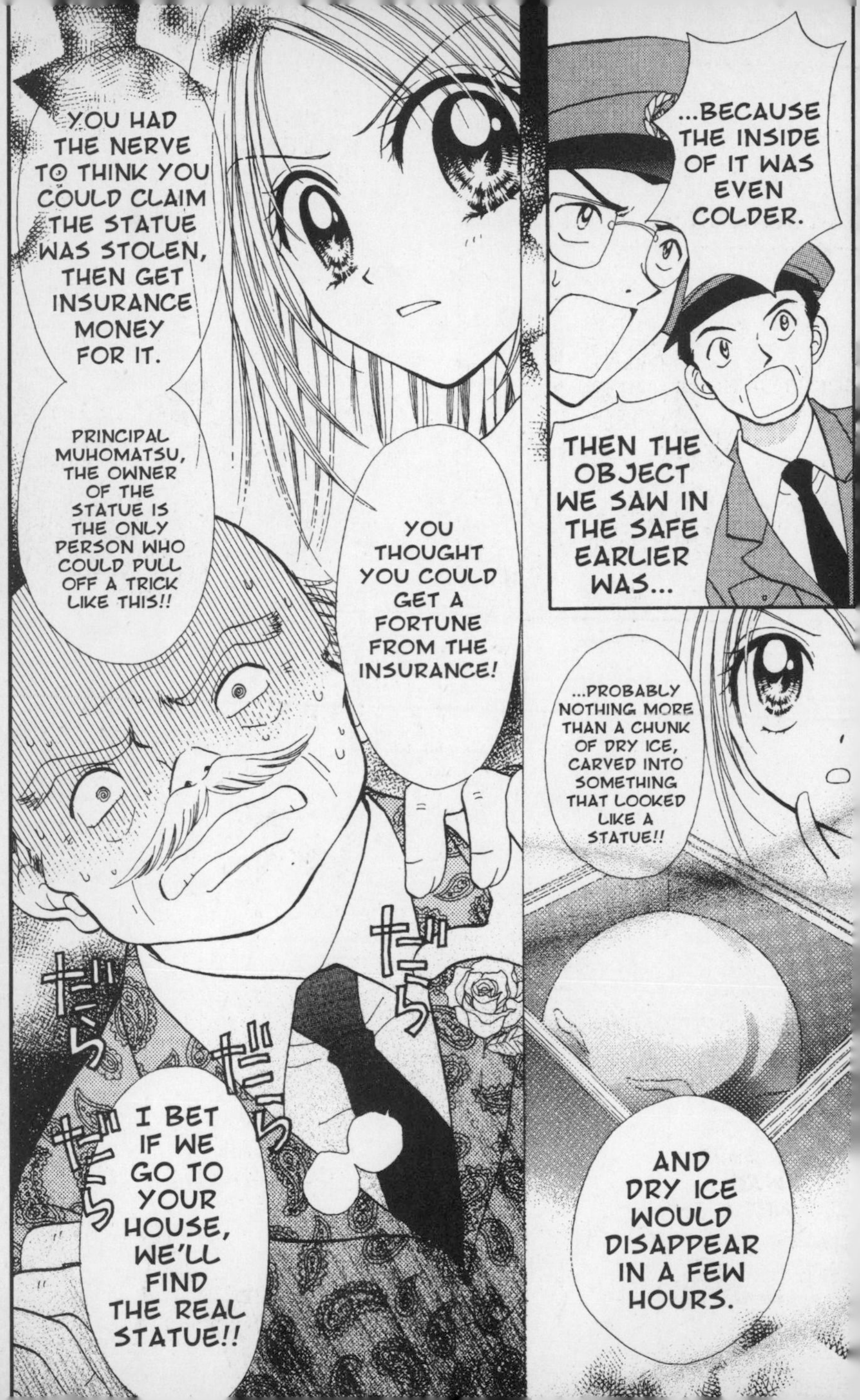
...BECAUSE THE INSIDE OF IT WAS EVEN COLDER.
THEN THE OBJECT WE SAW IN THE SAFE EARLIER WAS...
...PROBABLY NOTHING MORE THAN A CHUNK OF DRY ICE, CARVED INTO SOMETHING THAT LOOKED LIKE A STATUE!!
AND DRY ICE WOULD DISAPPEAR IN A FEW HOURS.
YOU HAD THE NERVE TO THINK YOU COULD CLAIM THE STATUE WAS STOLEN, THEN GET INSURANCE MONEY FOR IT.
PRINCIPAL MUHOMATSU, THE OWNER OF THE STATUE IS THE ONLY PERSON WHO COULD PULL OFF A TRICK LIKE THIS!!
YOU THOUGHT YOU COULD GET A FORTUNE FROM THE INSURANCE!
だら
だら
だら
だら
I BET IF WE GO TO YOUR HOUSE, WE'LL FIND THE REAL STATUE!!

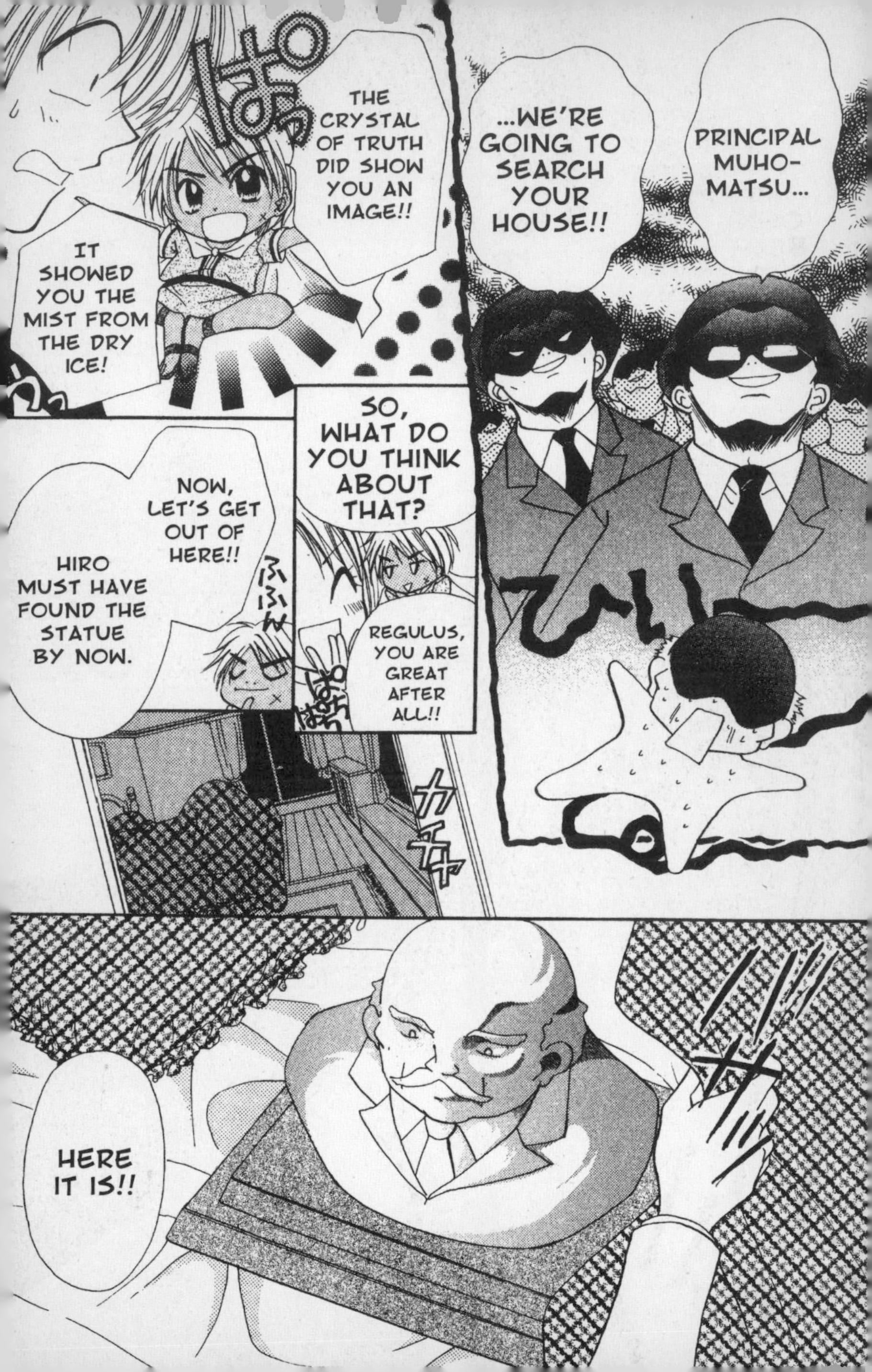
PRINCIPAL MUHO-MATSU...
...WE'RE GOING TO SEARCH YOUR HOUSE!!
ぱっ
THE CRYSTAL OF TRUTH DID SHOW YOU AN IMAGE!!
IT SHOWED YOU THE MIST FROM THE DRY ICE!
SO, WHAT DO YOU THINK ABOUT THAT?
REGULUS, YOU ARE GREAT AFTER ALL!!
ぱちぱち
NOW, LET'S GET OUT OF HERE!!
ふふん
HIRO MUST HAVE FOUND THE STATUE BY NOW.
カチャ
HERE IT IS!!

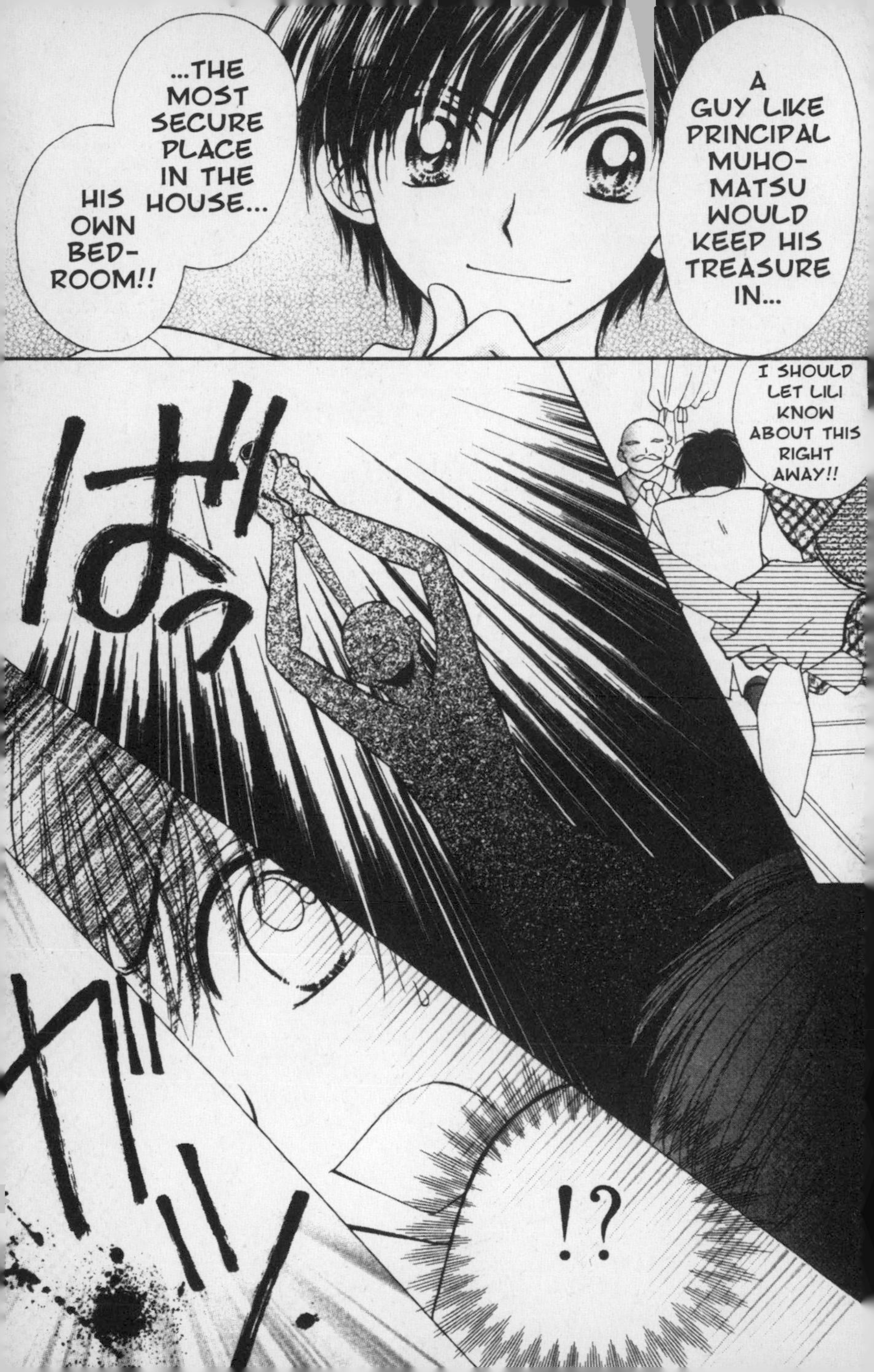
A GUY LIKE PRINCIPAL MUHO-MATSU WOULD KEEP HIS TREASURE IN...
...THE MOST SECURE PLACE IN THE HOUSE...
HIS OWN BED-ROOM!!
I SHOULD LET LILI KNOW ABOUT THIS RIGHT AWAY!!
はっ
ガバッ
!?

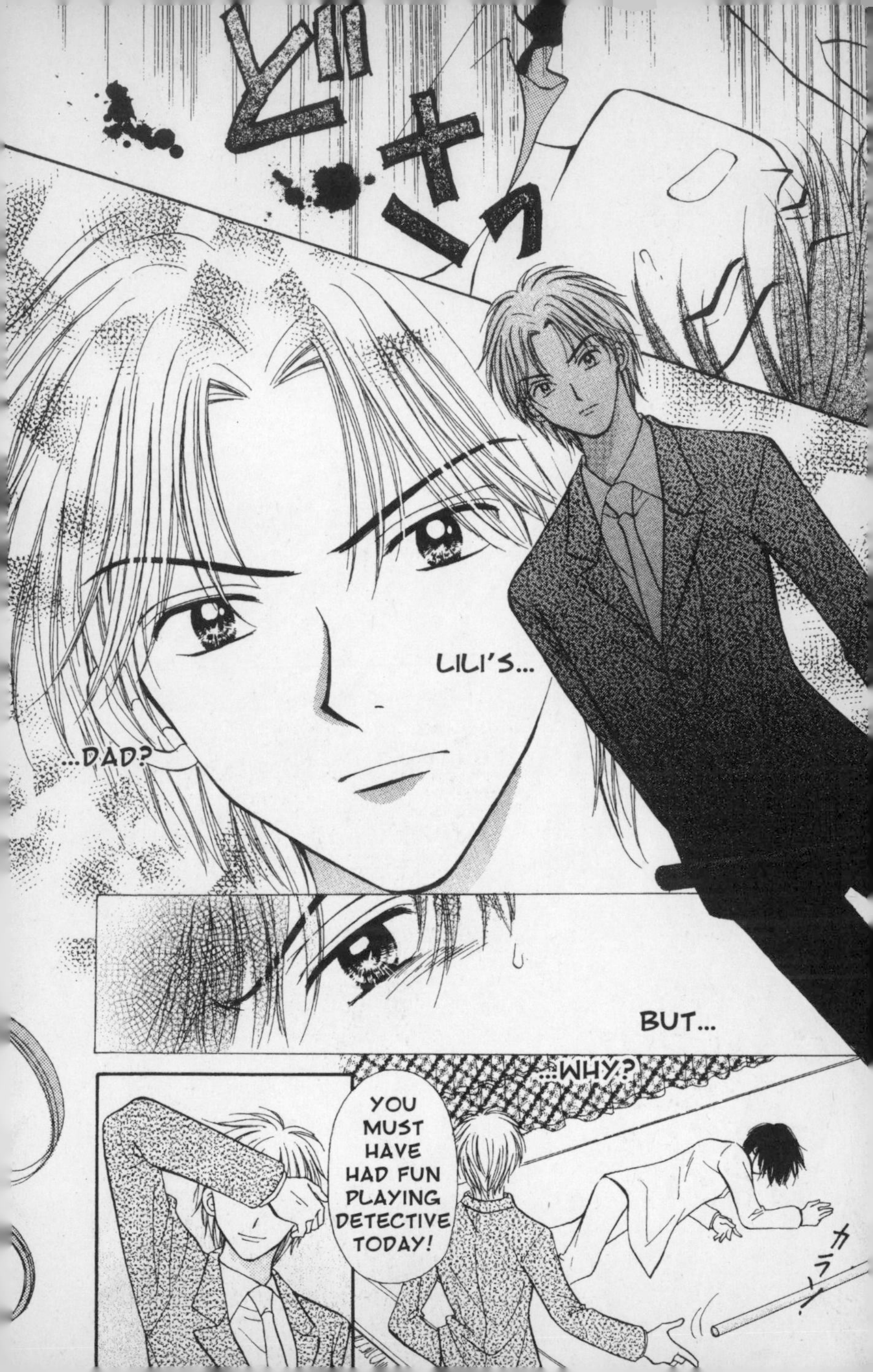
ビキッ
LILI'S...
...DAD?
BUT...
...WHY?
カラ
YOU MUST HAVE HAD FUN PLAYING DETECTIVE TODAY!

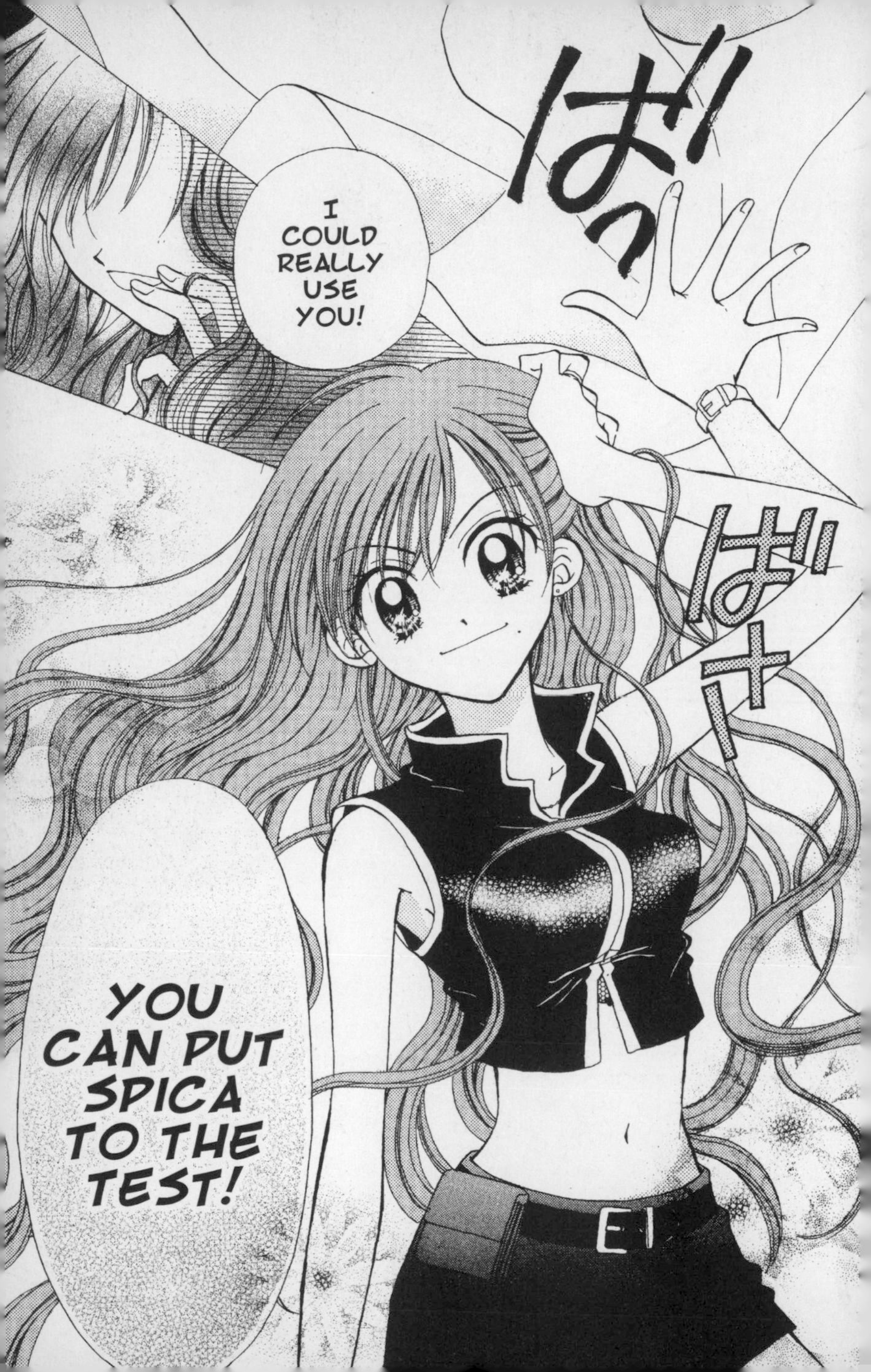
ぱっ
I COULD REALLY USE YOU!
YOU CAN PUT SPICA TO THE TEST!

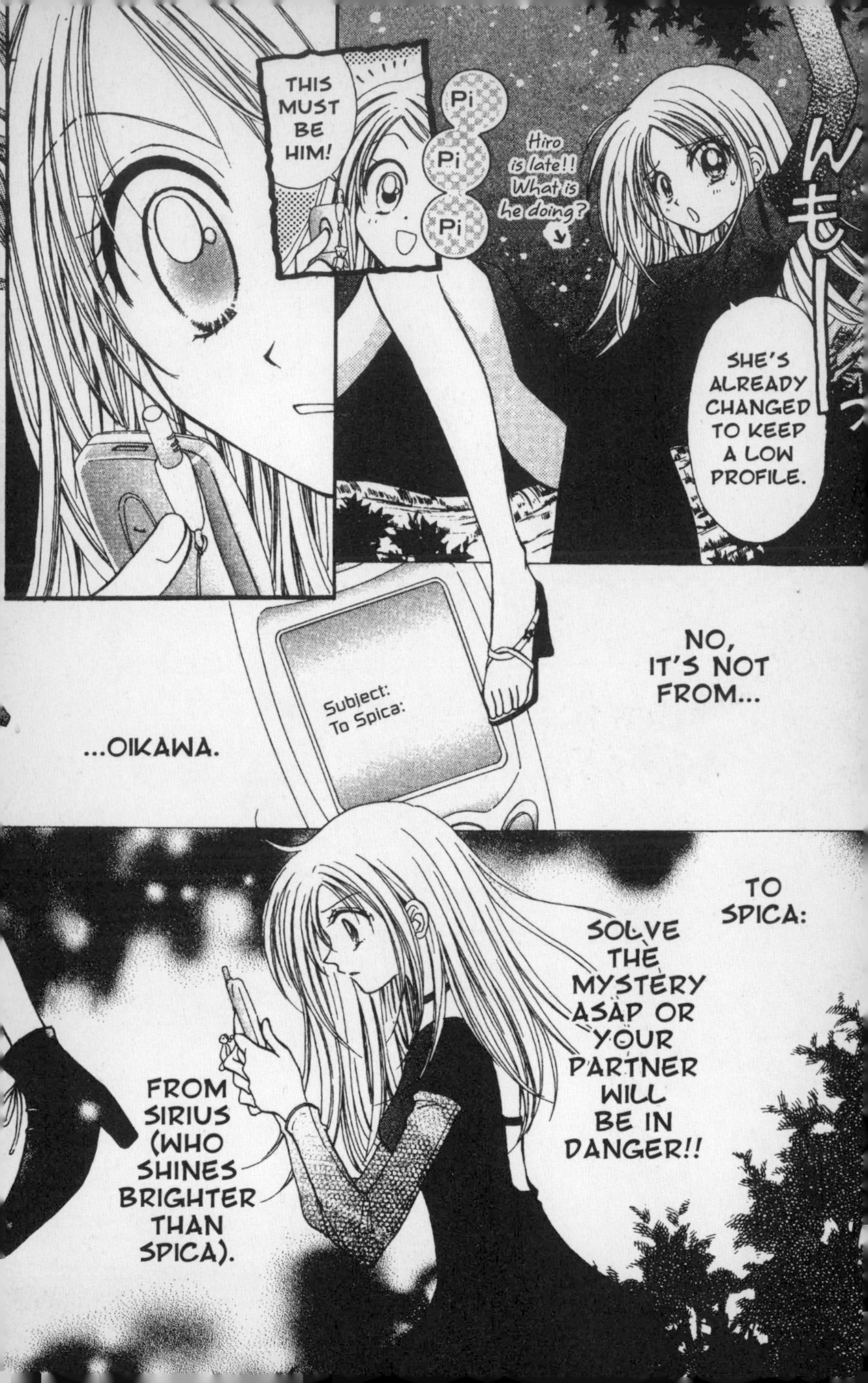
んもーっ
Hiro is late!! What is he doing?
SHE'S ALREADY CHANGED TO KEEP A LOW PROFILE.
Pi Pi Pi
THIS MUST BE HIM!
NO, IT'S NOT FROM...
Subject: To Spica:
...OIKAWA.
TO SPICA:
SOLVE THE MYSTERY ASAP OR YOUR PARTNER WILL BE IN DANGER!!
FROM SIRIUS (WHO SHINES BRIGHTER THAN SPICA).

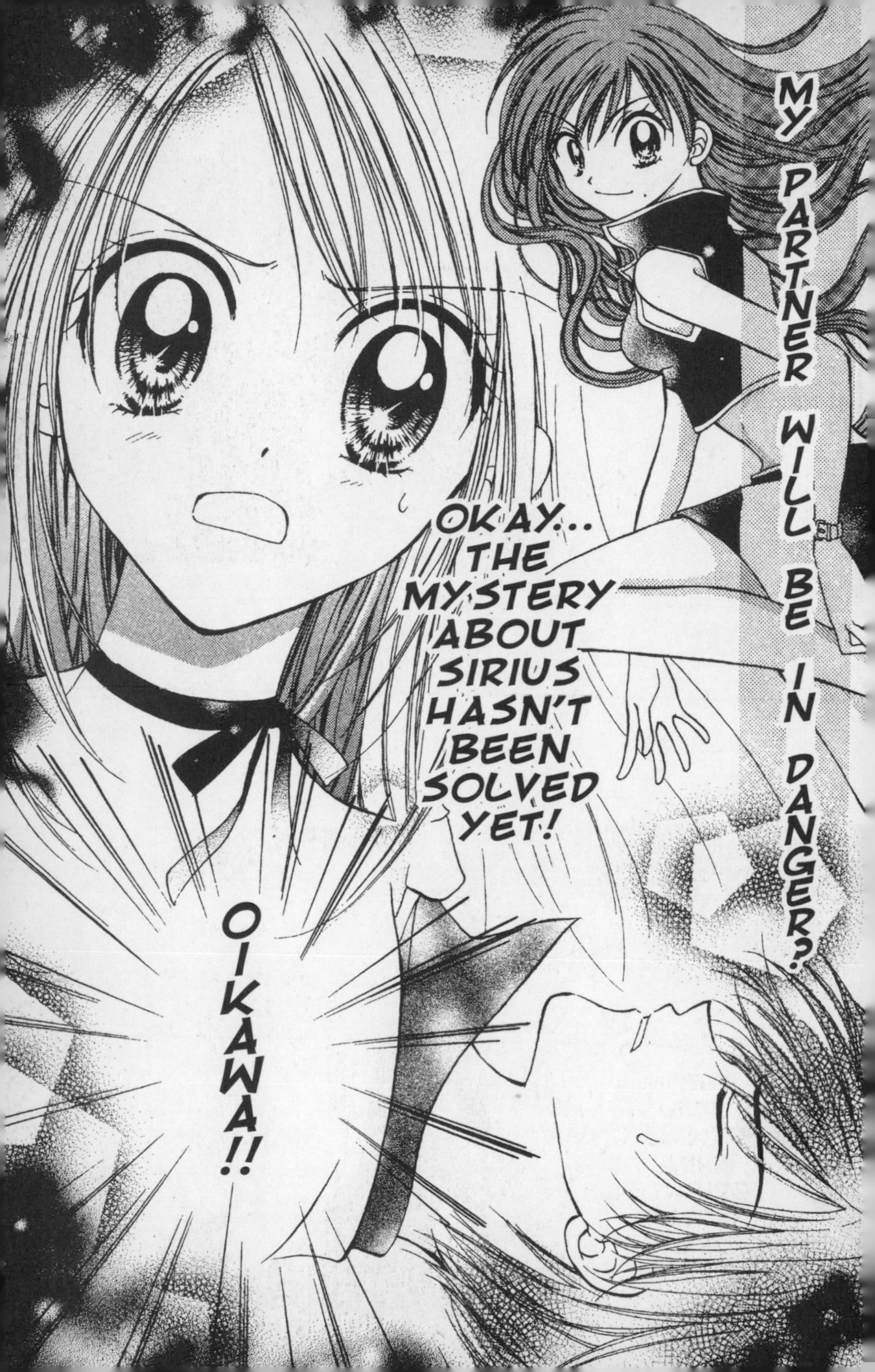
MY PARTNER WILL BE IN DANGER?
OKAY... THE MYSTERY ABOUT SIRIUS HASN'T BEEN SOLVED YET!
OIKAWA!!

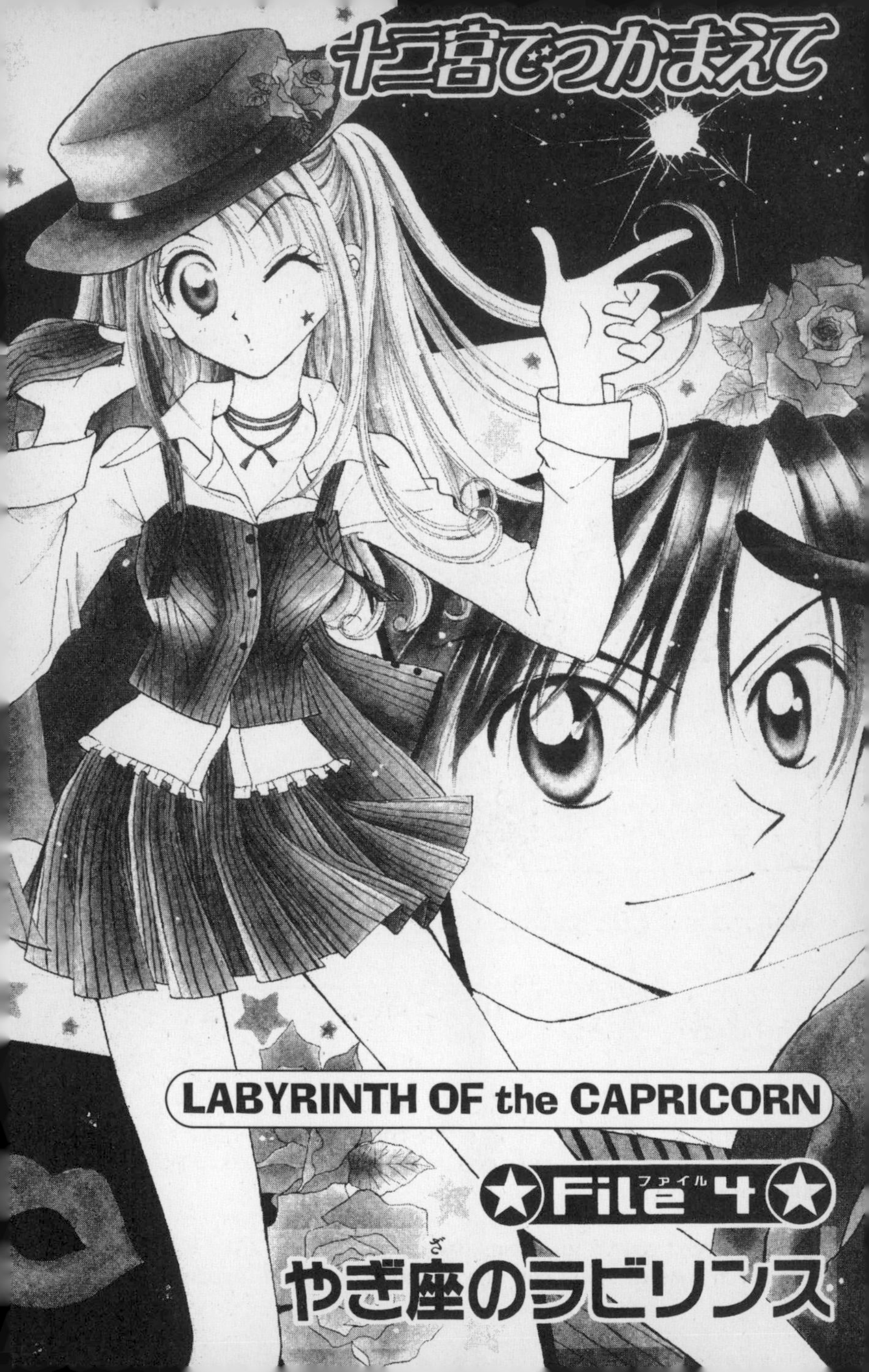
十二宮でつかまえて
LABYRINTH OF the CAPRICORN
File 4
やぎ座のラビリンス

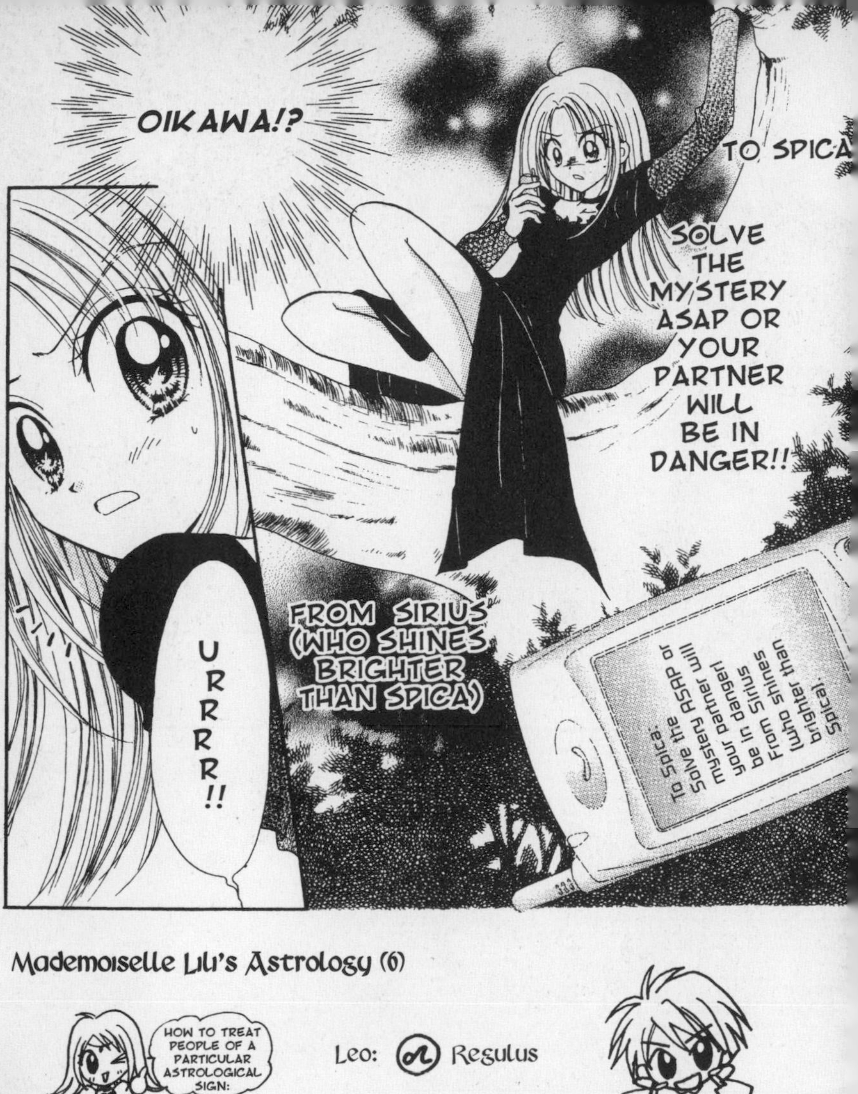
TO SPICA
SOLVE THE MYSTERY ASAP OR YOUR PARTNER WILL BE IN DANGER!!
OIKAWA!?
FROM SIRIUS (WHO SHINES BRIGHTER THAN SPICA)
URRRR!!

Mademoiselle Lili's Astrology (6)

HOW TO TREAT PEOPLE OF A PARTICULAR ASTROLOGICAL SIGN:

Leo: ♌ Regulus

Regulus is the name of a star in the constellation Leo. Regulus is very competitive and a natural leader. He tries to fulfill people's expectations. He has a cheerful personality and lives life to the fullest. He is very stubborn, though!

Leo boys tend to like easy going, sweet girls. When a Leo is in love, it's often easy to figure out who the object of his affection is!

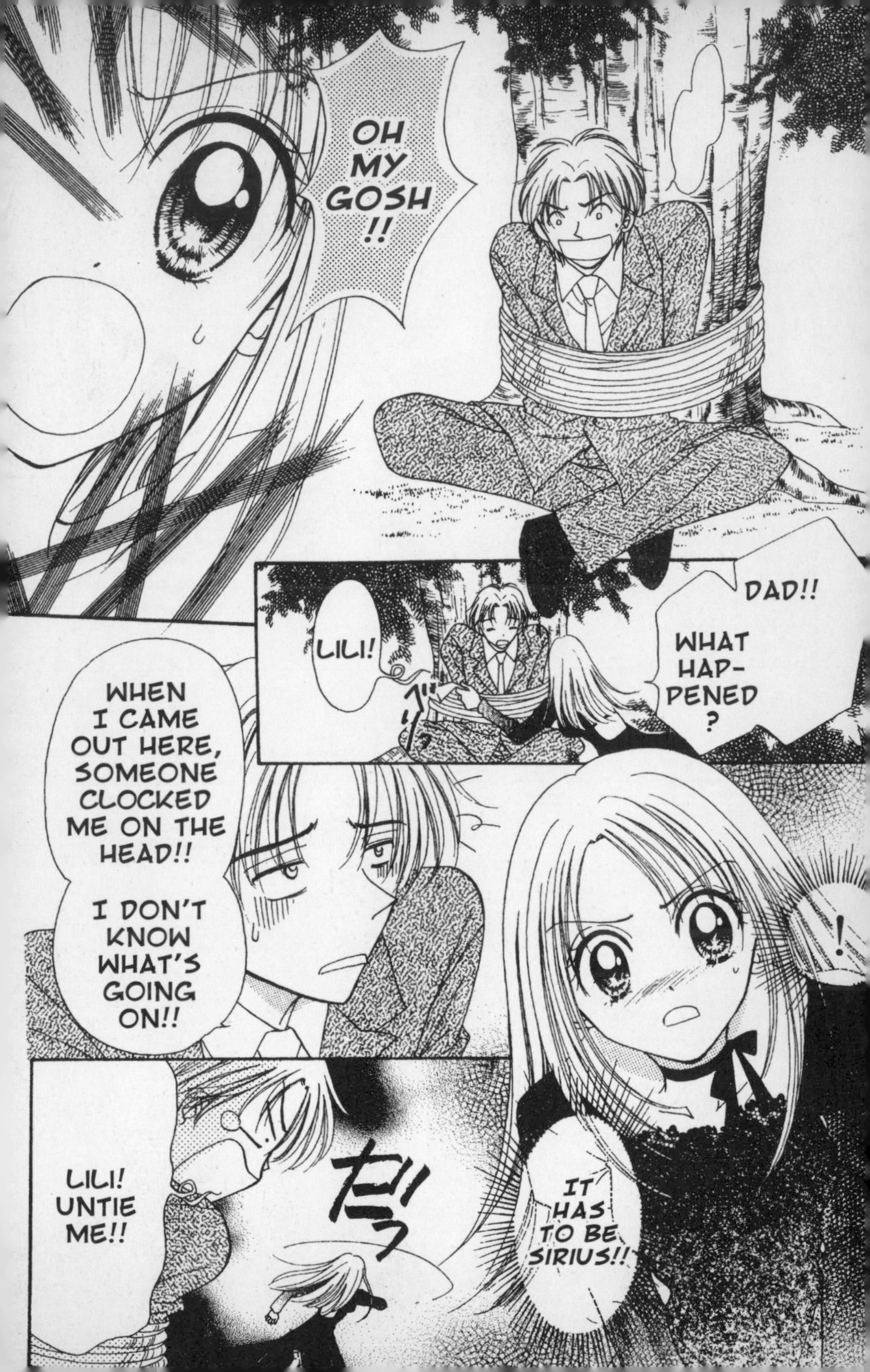
OH MY GOSH!!
DAD!!
WHAT HAP-PENED?
LILI!
WHEN I CAME OUT HERE, SOMEONE CLOCKED ME ON THE HEAD!!
I DON'T KNOW WHAT'S GOING ON!!
!
IT HAS TO BE SIRIUS!!
LILI! UNTIE ME!!

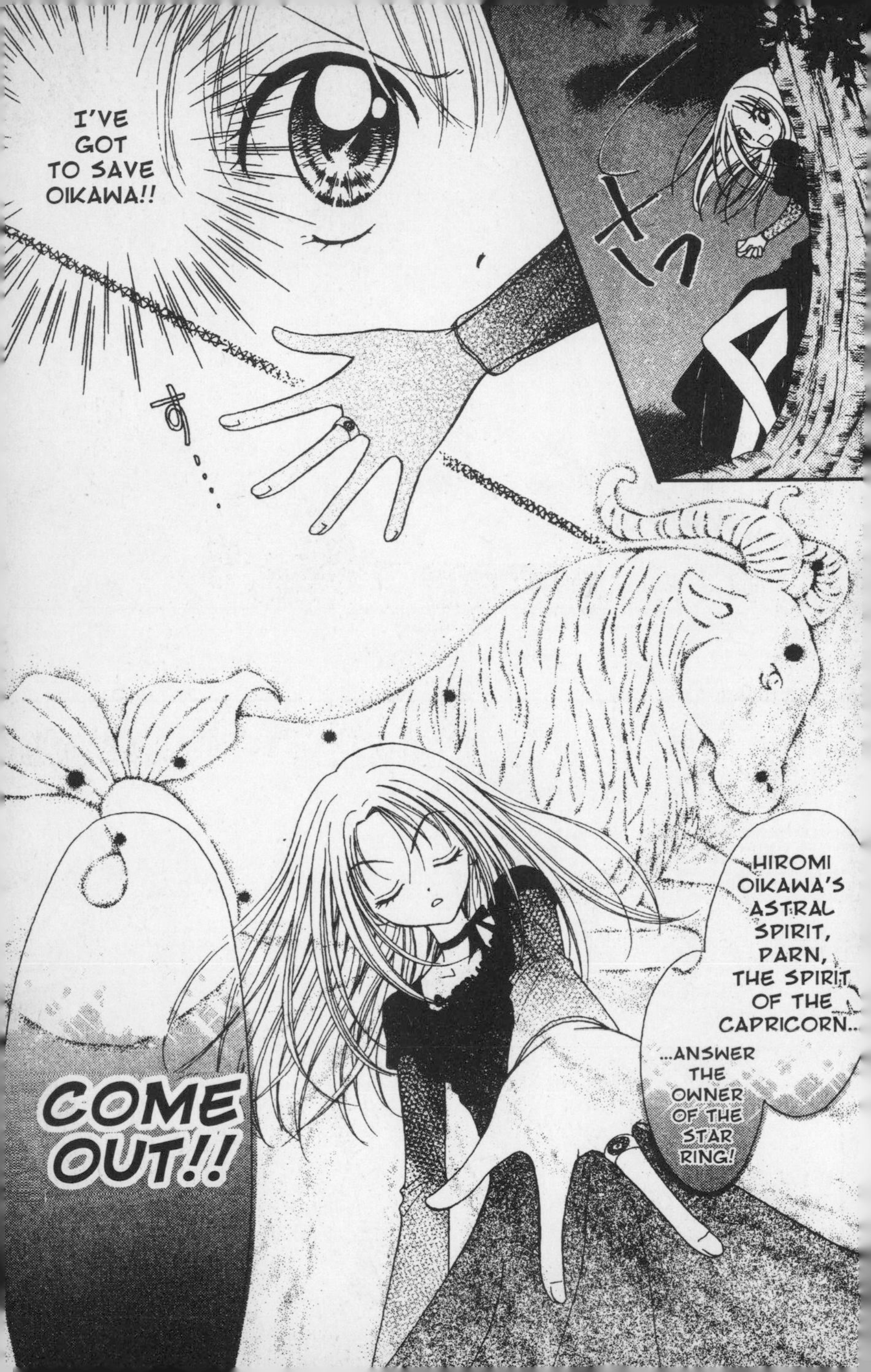
I'VE GOT TO SAVE OIKAWA!!
HIROMI OIKAWA'S ASTRAL SPIRIT, PARN, THE SPIRIT OF THE CAPRICORN..
...ANSWER THE OWNER OF THE STAR RING!
COME OUT!!

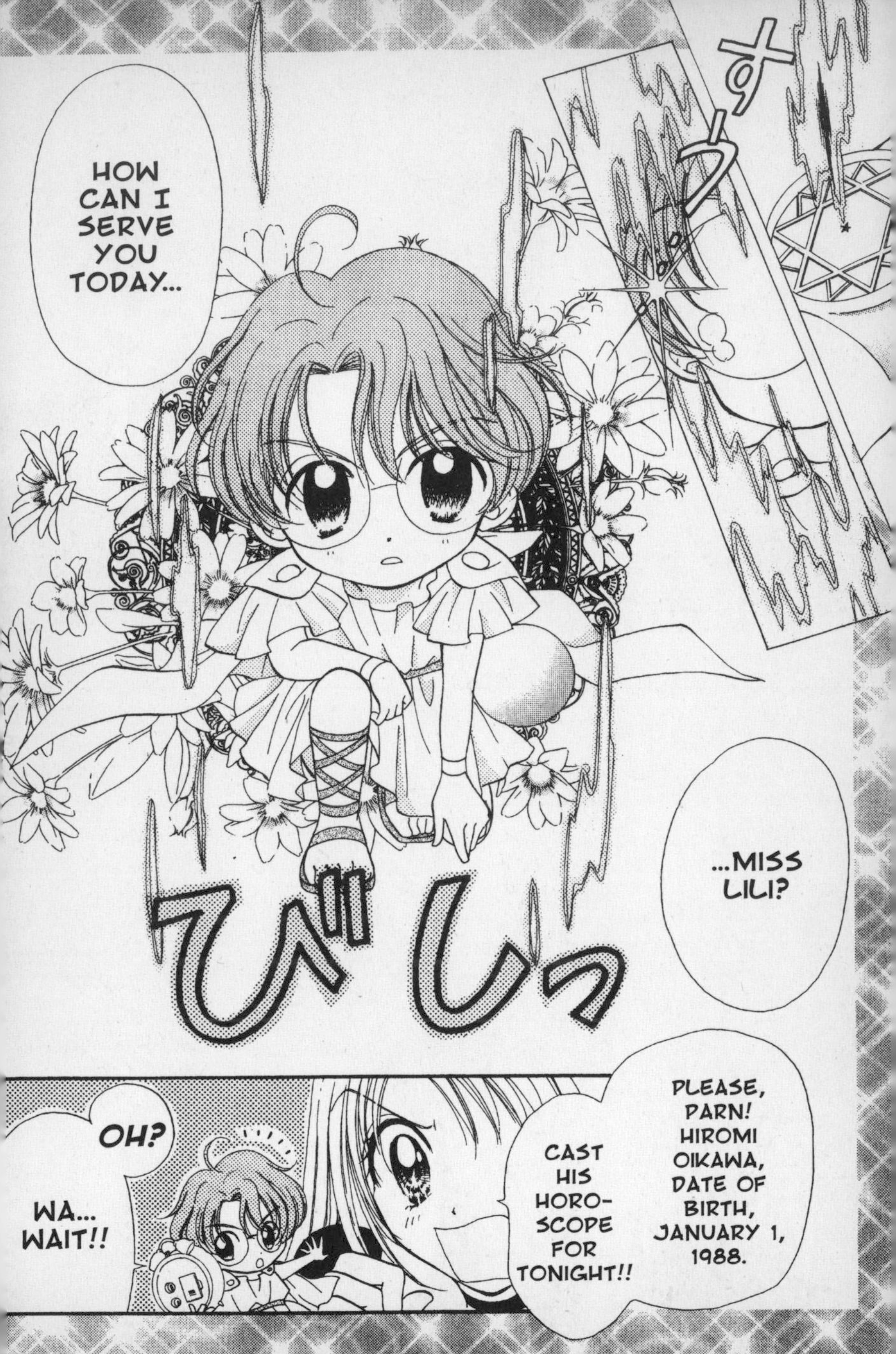

すうっ
HOW CAN I SERVE YOU TODAY...
...MISS LILI?
びしっ
PLEASE, PARN! HIROMI OIKAWA, DATE OF BIRTH, JANUARY 1, 1988.
CAST HIS HOROSCOPE FOR TONIGHT!!
OH?
WA... WAIT!!

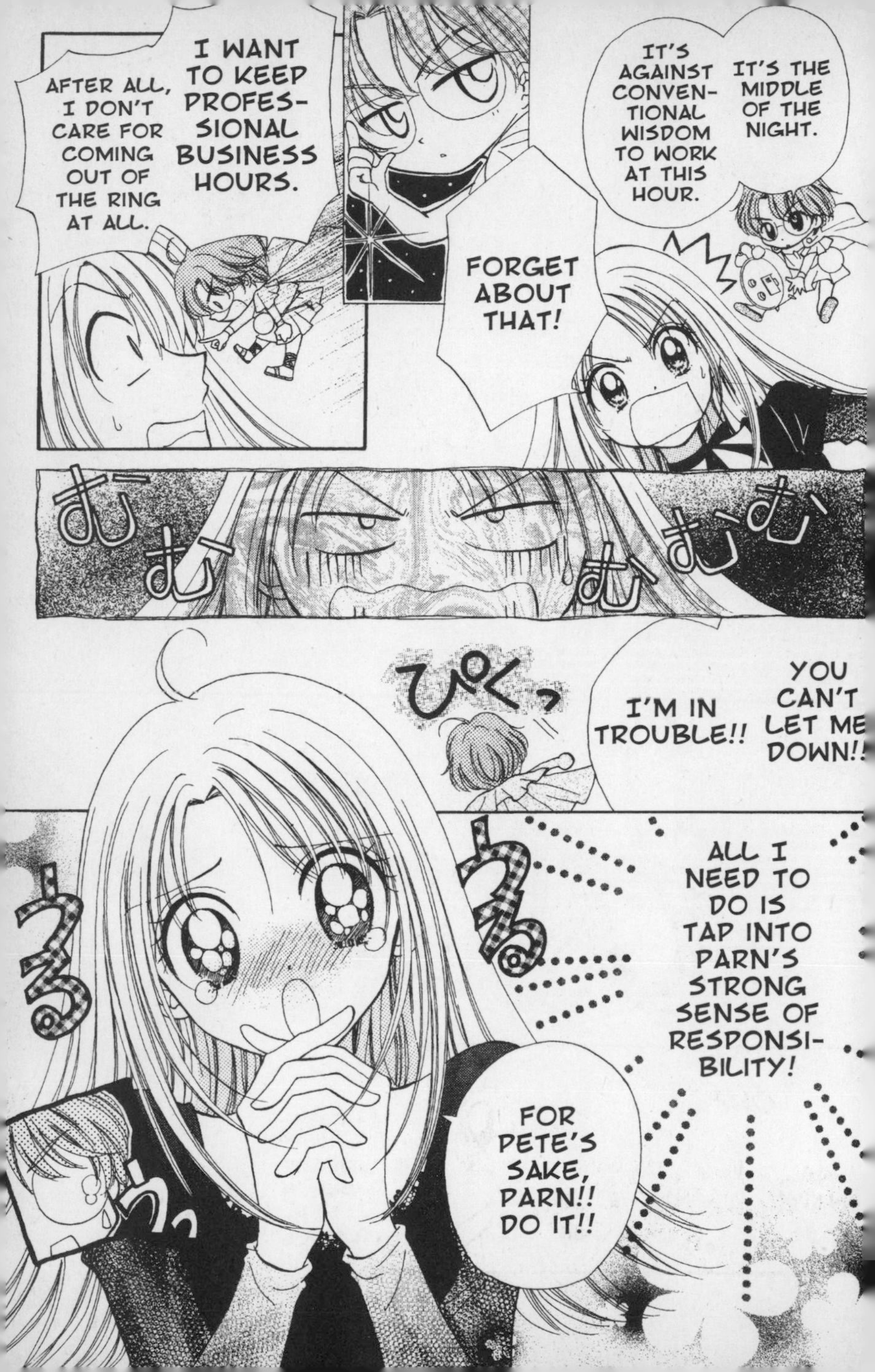
IT'S THE MIDDLE OF THE NIGHT.
IT'S AGAINST CONVENTIONAL WISDOM TO WORK AT THIS HOUR.
FORGET ABOUT THAT!
I WANT TO KEEP PROFESSIONAL BUSINESS HOURS.
AFTER ALL, I DON'T CARE FOR COMING OUT OF THE RING AT ALL.
YOU CAN'T LET ME DOWN!!
I'M IN TROUBLE!!
ぴくっ
ALL I NEED TO DO IS TAP INTO PARN'S STRONG SENSE OF RESPONSIBILITY!
うる
うる
FOR PETE'S SAKE, PARN!! DO IT!!
うっ

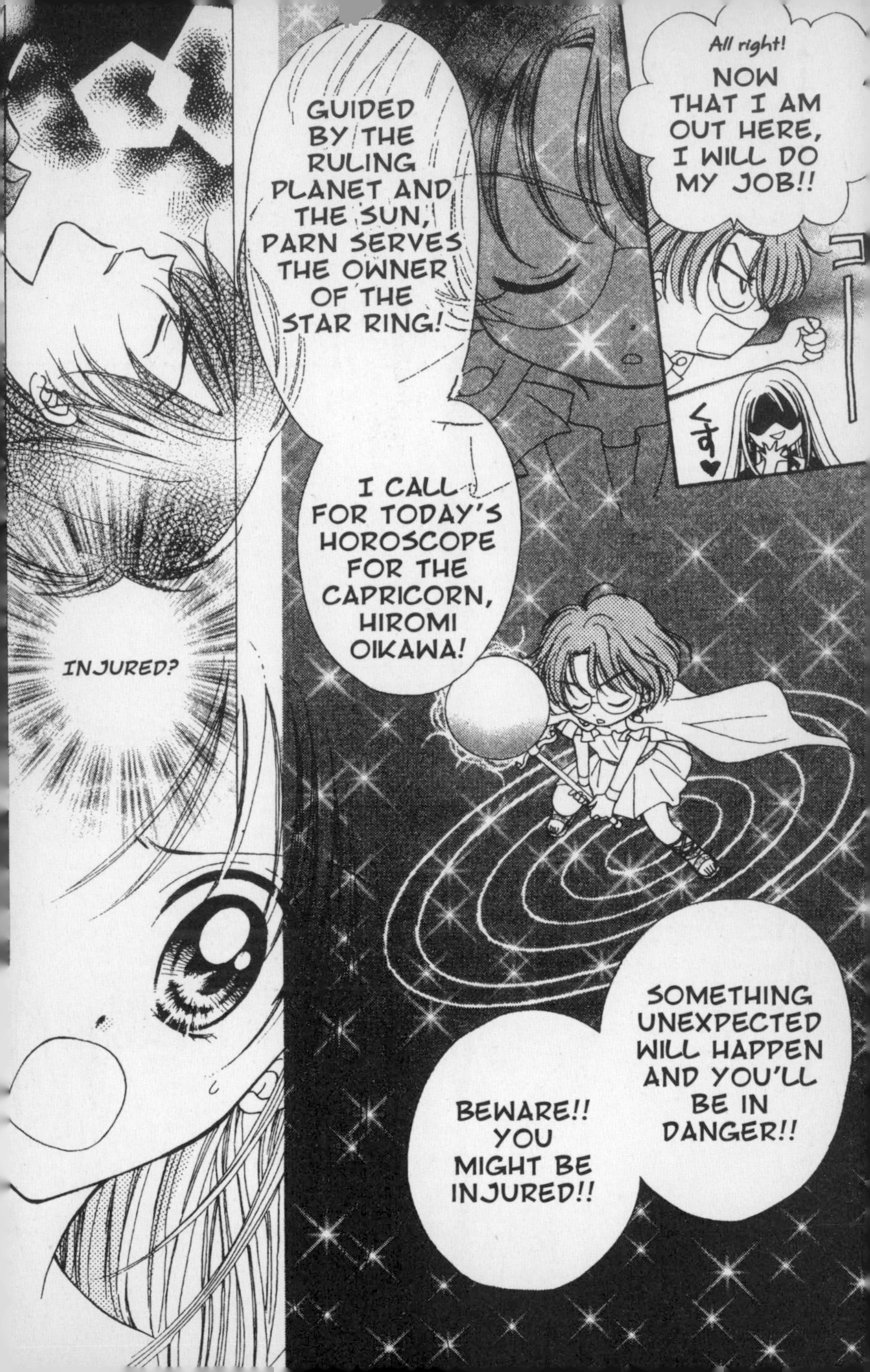
All right!
NOW THAT I AM OUT HERE, I WILL DO MY JOB!!
くす♥
GUIDED BY THE RULING PLANET AND THE SUN, PARN SERVES THE OWNER OF THE STAR RING!
I CALL FOR TODAY'S HOROSCOPE FOR THE CAPRICORN, HIROMI OIKAWA!
SOMETHING UNEXPECTED WILL HAPPEN AND YOU'LL BE IN DANGER!!
BEWARE!! YOU MIGHT BE INJURED!!
INJURED?

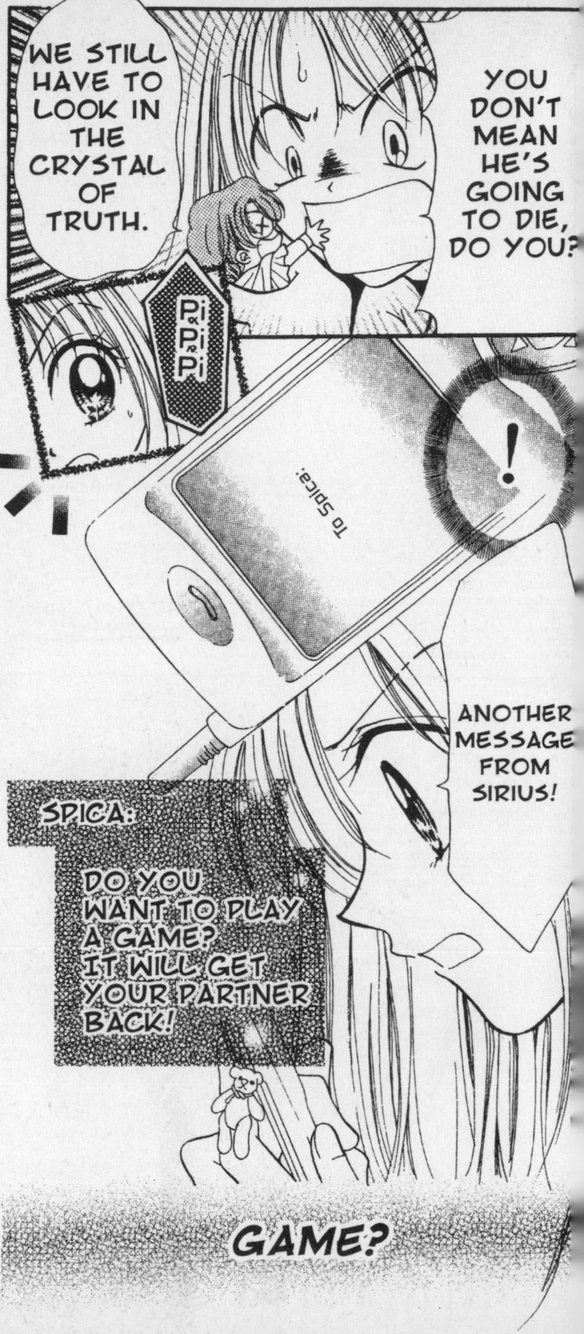
YOU DON'T MEAN HE'S GOING TO DIE, DO YOU?
WE STILL HAVE TO LOOK IN THE CRYSTAL OF TRUTH.
Pi Pi Pi
!
To Spica:
ANOTHER MESSAGE FROM SIRIUS!
SPICA:
DO YOU WANT TO PLAY A GAME? IT WILL GET YOUR PARTNER BACK!
GAME?

Pampering Myself

My first experience with massage therapy was with a technique called reflexology. It's popular in Japan so I decided to give it a try. At first it was painful., but after awhile I started to get used to it. The therapist massaged my feet. It made me feel like a rich woman!

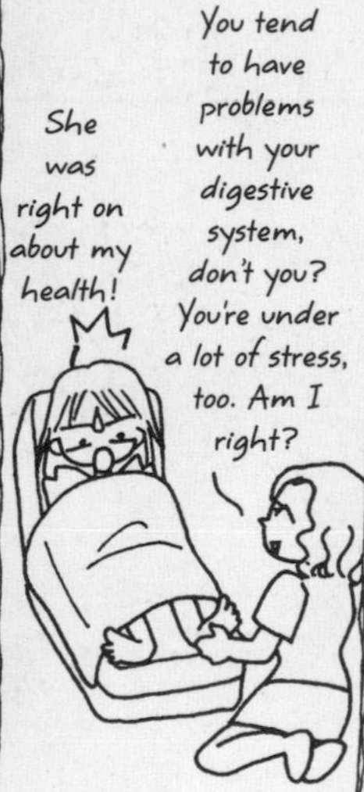
You tend to have problems with your digestive system, don't you? You're under a lot of stress, too. Am I right?
She was right on about my health!

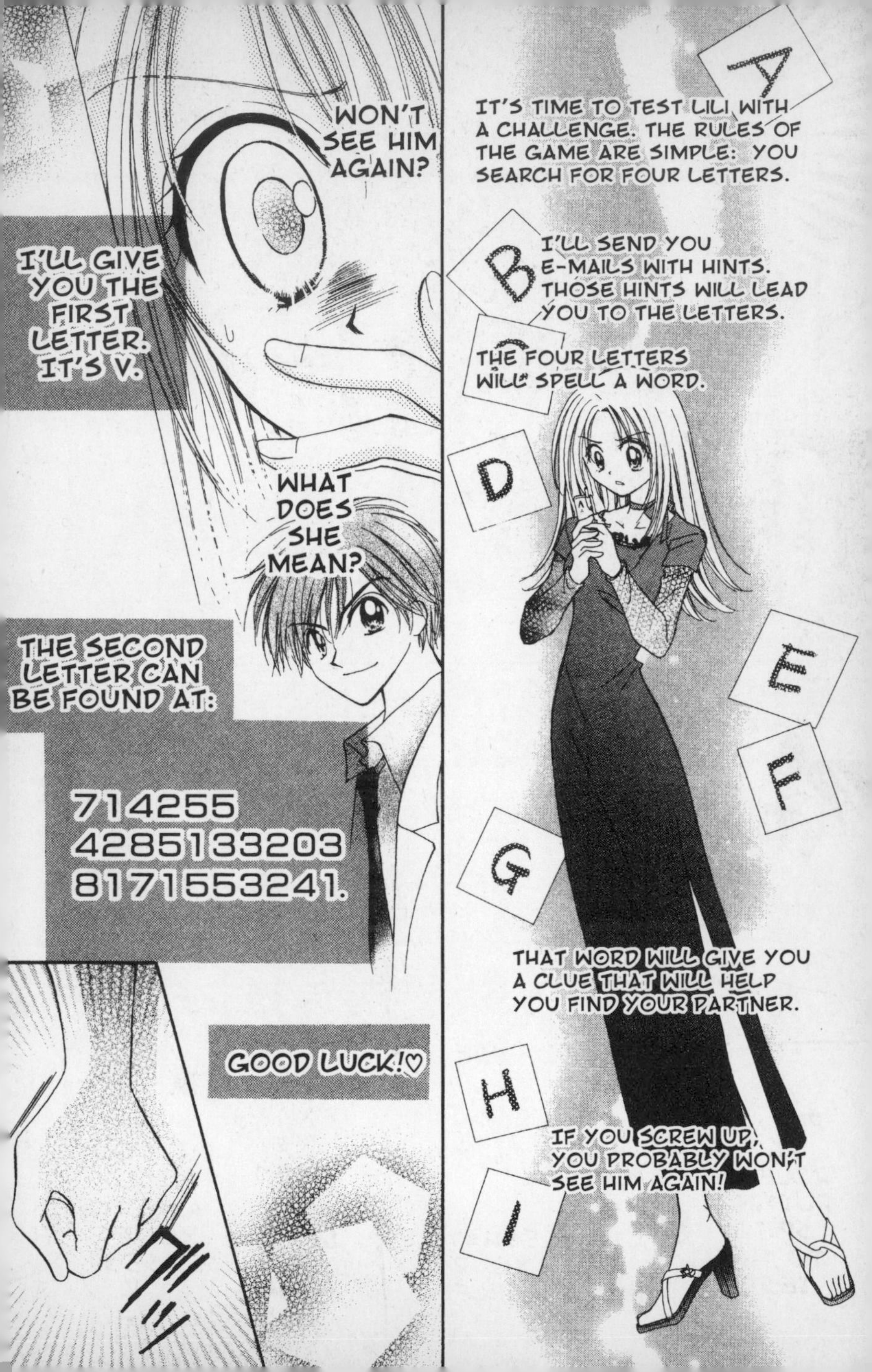
A
IT'S TIME TO TEST LILI WITH A CHALLENGE. THE RULES OF THE GAME ARE SIMPLE: YOU SEARCH FOR FOUR LETTERS.
B
I'LL SEND YOU E-MAILS WITH HINTS. THOSE HINTS WILL LEAD YOU TO THE LETTERS.
THE FOUR LETTERS WILL SPELL A WORD.
D
E
F
G
THAT WORD WILL GIVE YOU A CLUE THAT WILL HELP YOU FIND YOUR PARTNER.
H
IF YOU SCREW UP, YOU PROBABLY WON'T SEE HIM AGAIN!
I
WON'T SEE HIM AGAIN?
I'LL GIVE YOU THE FIRST LETTER. IT'S V.
WHAT DOES SHE MEAN?
THE SECOND LETTER CAN BE FOUND AT:
714255
4285133203
8171553241.
GOOD LUCK!♡

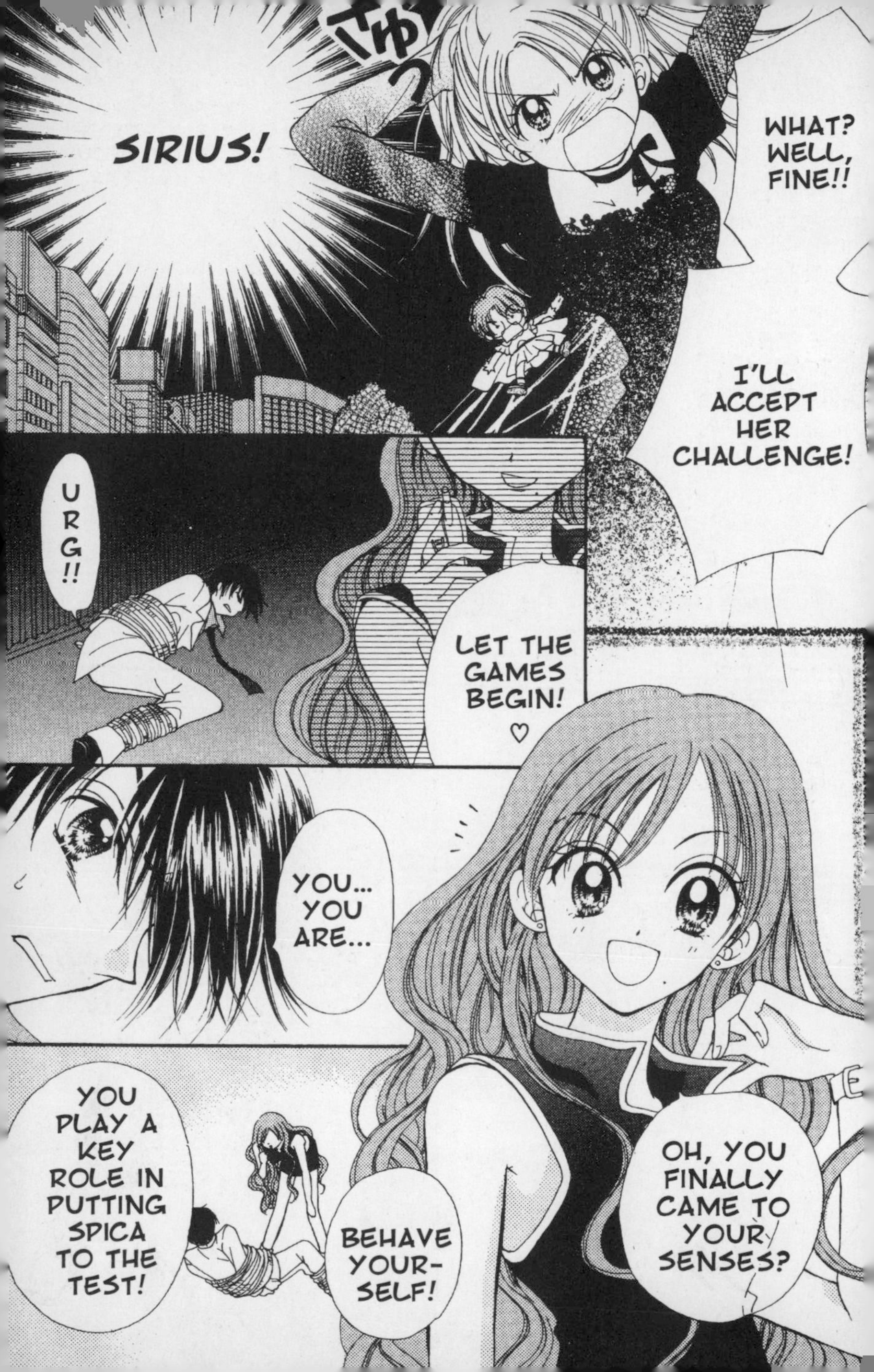
WHAT? WELL, FINE!!
SIRIUS!
I'LL ACCEPT HER CHALLENGE!
LET THE GAMES BEGIN! ♡
URG!!
OH, YOU FINALLY CAME TO YOUR SENSES?
YOU... YOU ARE...
BEHAVE YOURSELF!
YOU PLAY A KEY ROLE IN PUTTING SPICA TO THE TEST!

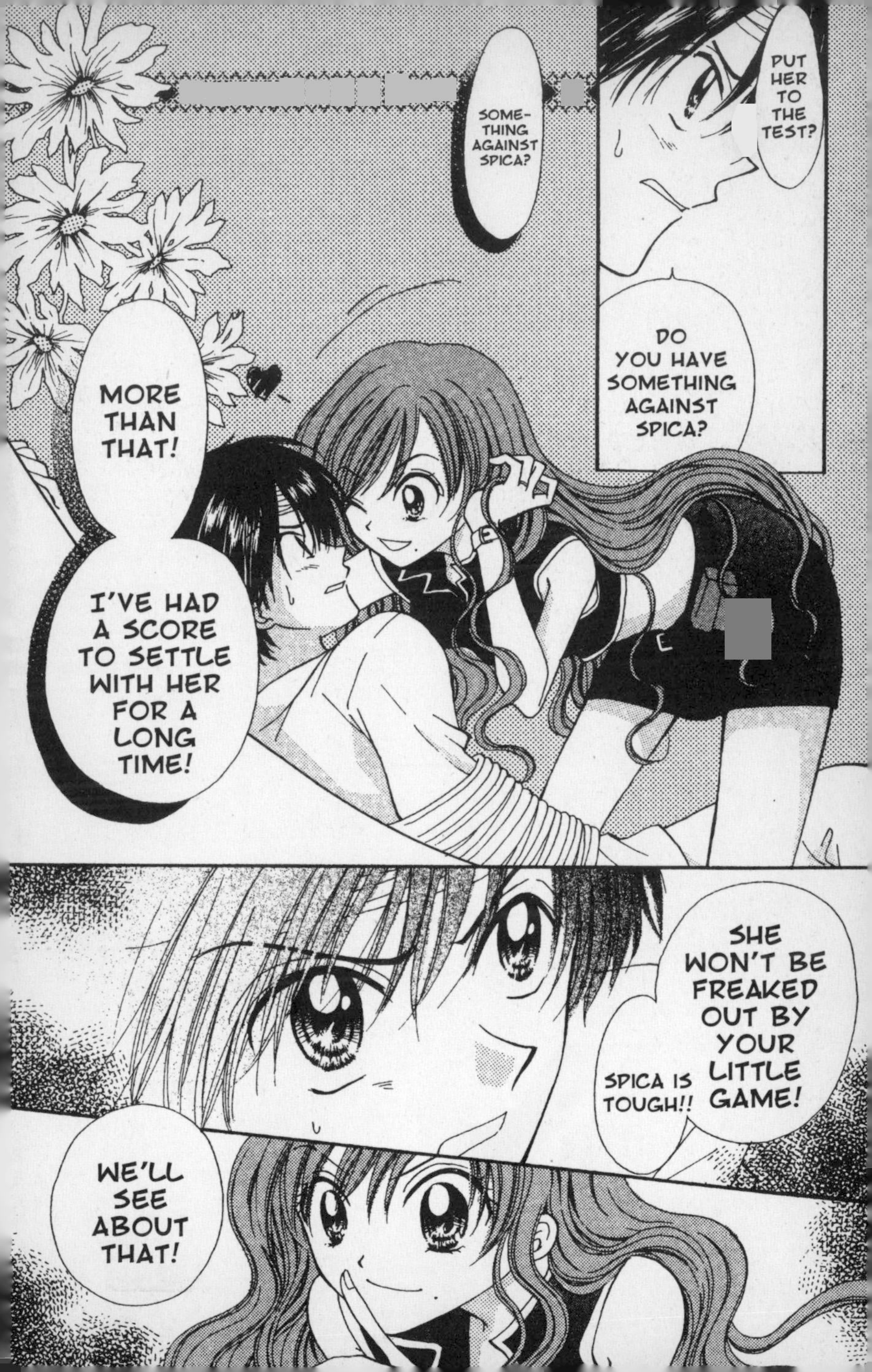
PUT HER TO THE TEST?
DO YOU HAVE SOMETHING AGAINST SPICA?
SOME-THING AGAINST SPICA?
MORE THAN THAT!
I'VE HAD A SCORE TO SETTLE WITH HER FOR A LONG TIME!
SHE WON'T BE FREAKED OUT BY YOUR LITTLE GAME!
SPICA IS TOUGH!!
WE'LL SEE ABOUT THAT!

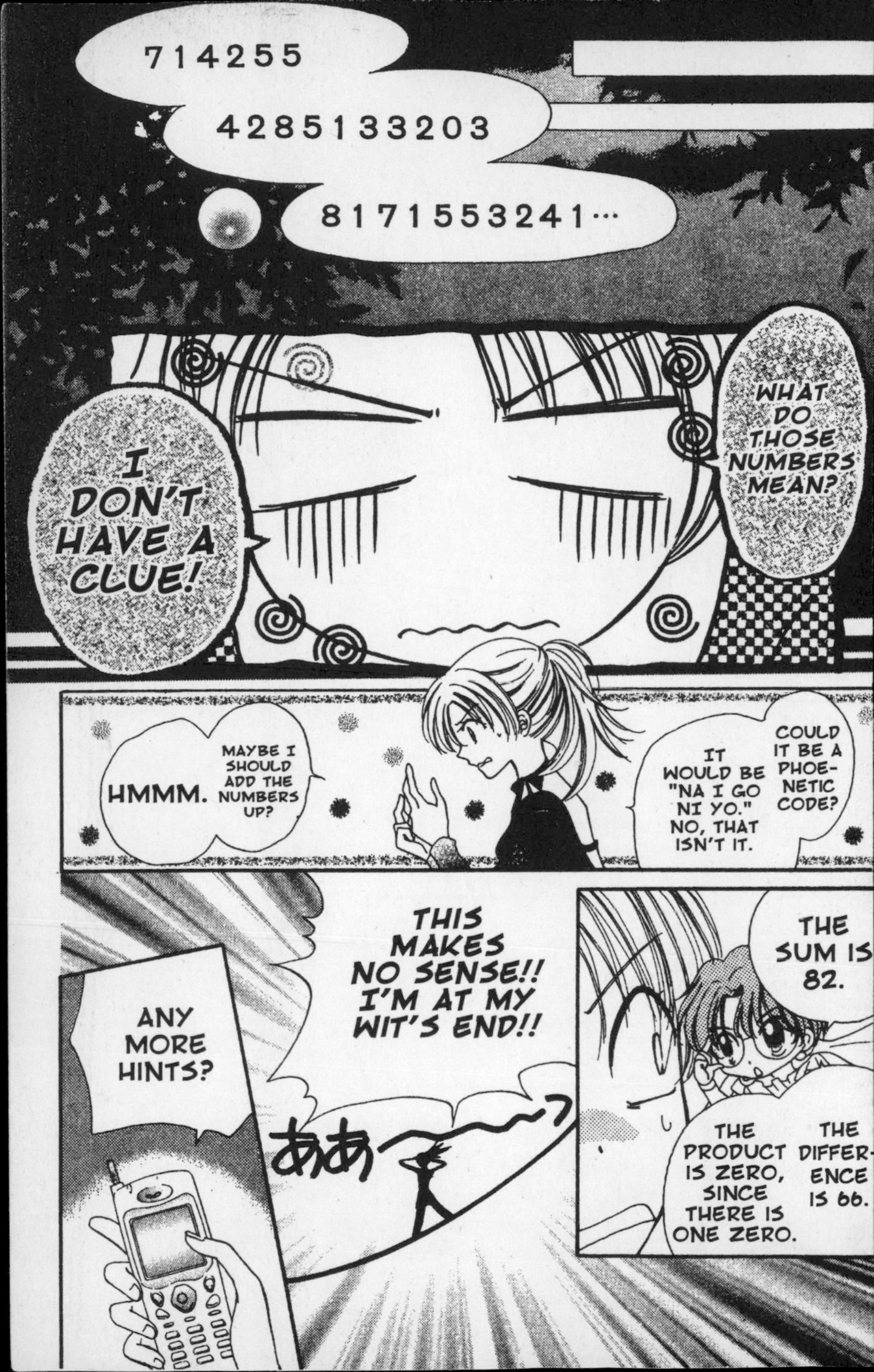
714255
4285133203
8171553241…
WHAT DO THOSE NUMBERS MEAN?
I DON'T HAVE A CLUE!
COULD IT BE A PHOENETIC CODE?
IT WOULD BE "NA I GO NI YO." NO, THAT ISN'T IT.
MAYBE I SHOULD ADD THE NUMBERS UP?
HMMM.
THE SUM IS 82.
THE DIFFERENCE IS 66.
THE PRODUCT IS ZERO, SINCE THERE IS ONE ZERO.
THIS MAKES NO SENSE!! I'M AT MY WIT'S END!!
ああ〜〜〜っ
ANY MORE HINTS?

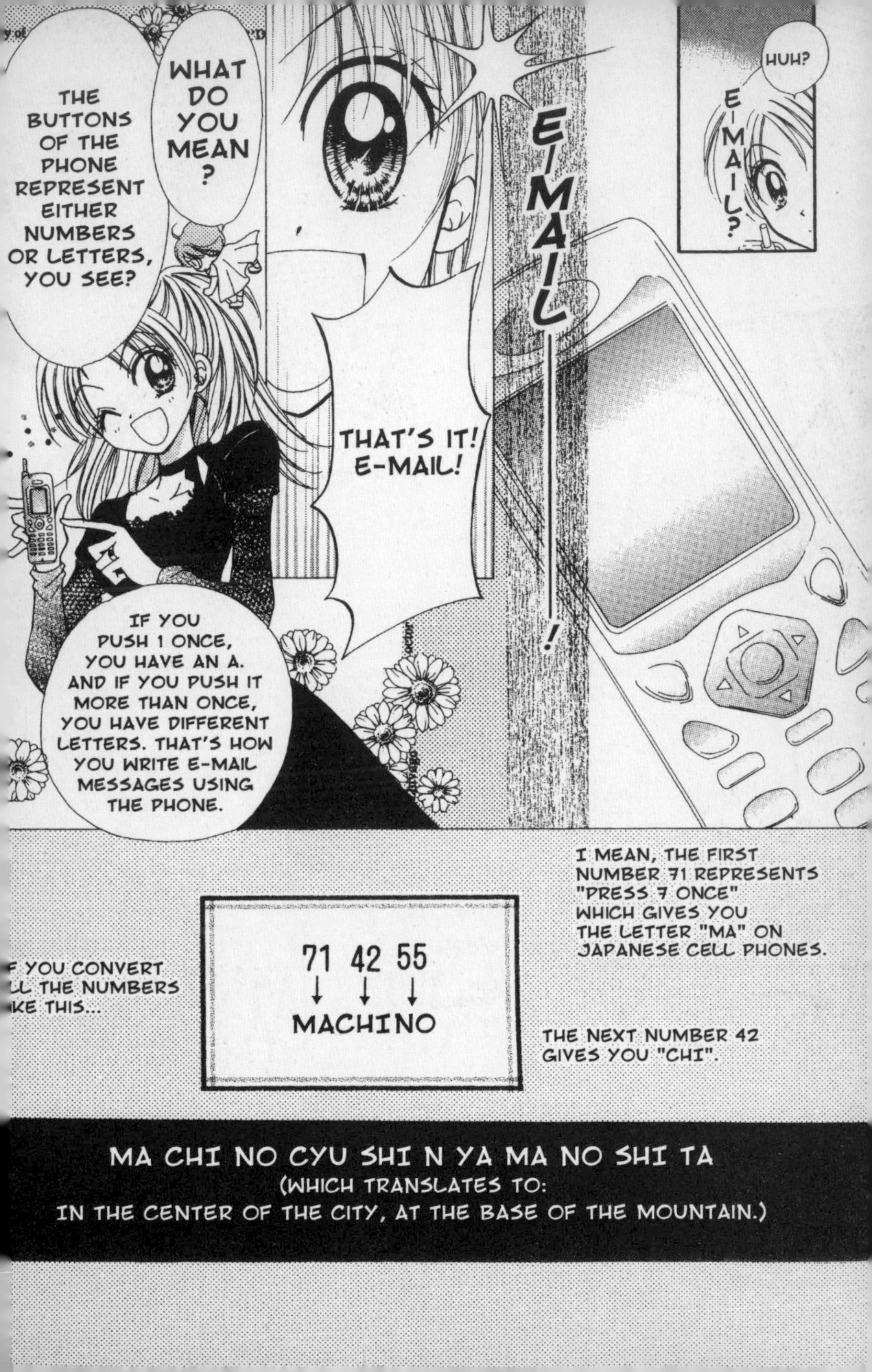
HUH?
E-MAIL?
E-MAIL—!
THAT'S IT! E-MAIL!
WHAT DO YOU MEAN?
THE BUTTONS OF THE PHONE REPRESENT EITHER NUMBERS OR LETTERS, YOU SEE?
IF YOU PUSH 1 ONCE, YOU HAVE AN A. AND IF YOU PUSH IT MORE THAN ONCE, YOU HAVE DIFFERENT LETTERS. THAT'S HOW YOU WRITE E-MAIL MESSAGES USING THE PHONE.

F YOU CONVERT
LL THE NUMBERS
KE THIS...

71 42 55
↓ ↓ ↓
MACHINO

I MEAN, THE FIRST NUMBER 71 REPRESENTS "PRESS 7 ONCE" WHICH GIVES YOU THE LETTER "MA" ON JAPANESE CELL PHONES.

THE NEXT NUMBER 42 GIVES YOU "CHI".

MA CHI NO CYU SHI N YA MA NO SHI TA

(WHICH TRANSLATES TO:
IN THE CENTER OF THE CITY, AT THE BASE OF THE MOUNTAIN.)

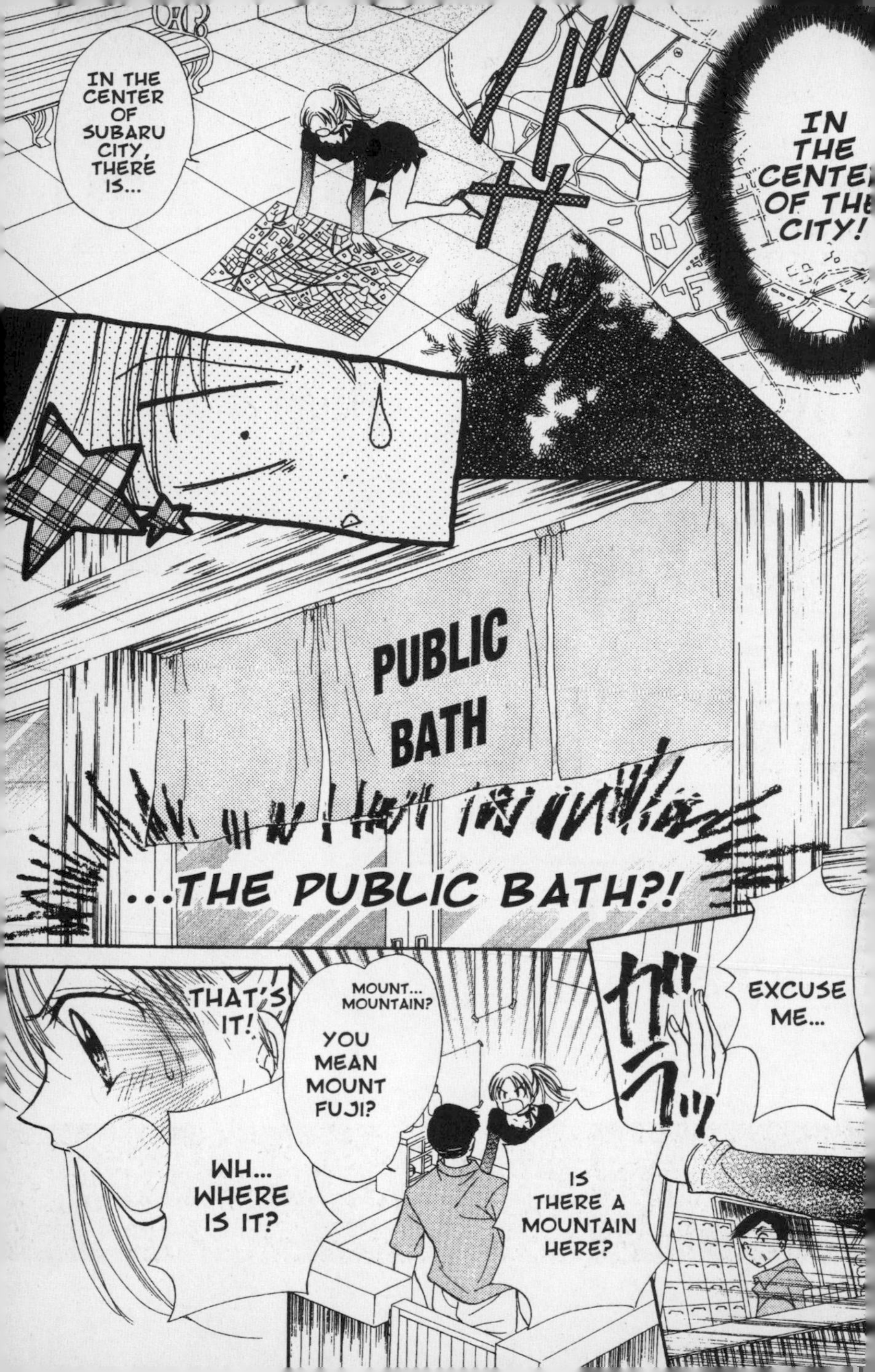
IN THE CENTE OF THE CITY!
IN THE CENTER OF SUBARU CITY, THERE IS...
PUBLIC BATH
...THE PUBLIC BATH?!
EXCUSE ME...
IS THERE A MOUNTAIN HERE?
MOUNT... MOUNTAIN?
YOU MEAN MOUNT FUJI?
THAT'S IT!
WH... WHERE IS IT?

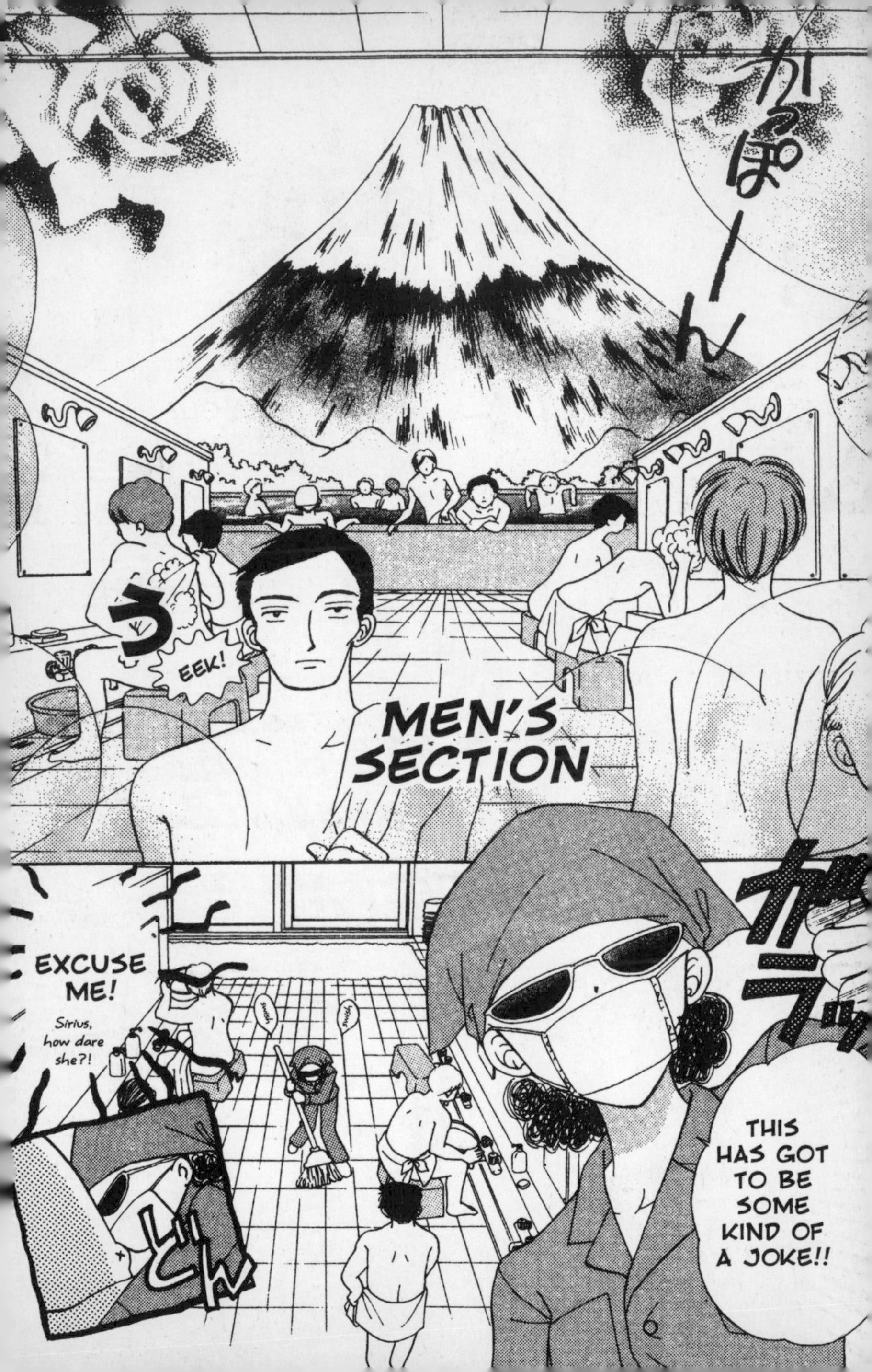
かっぽーーん
つ
EEK!
MEN'S SECTION
カラッ
THIS HAS GOT TO BE SOME KIND OF A JOKE!!
swish
swish
EXCUSE ME!
Sirius, how dare she?!
じーん

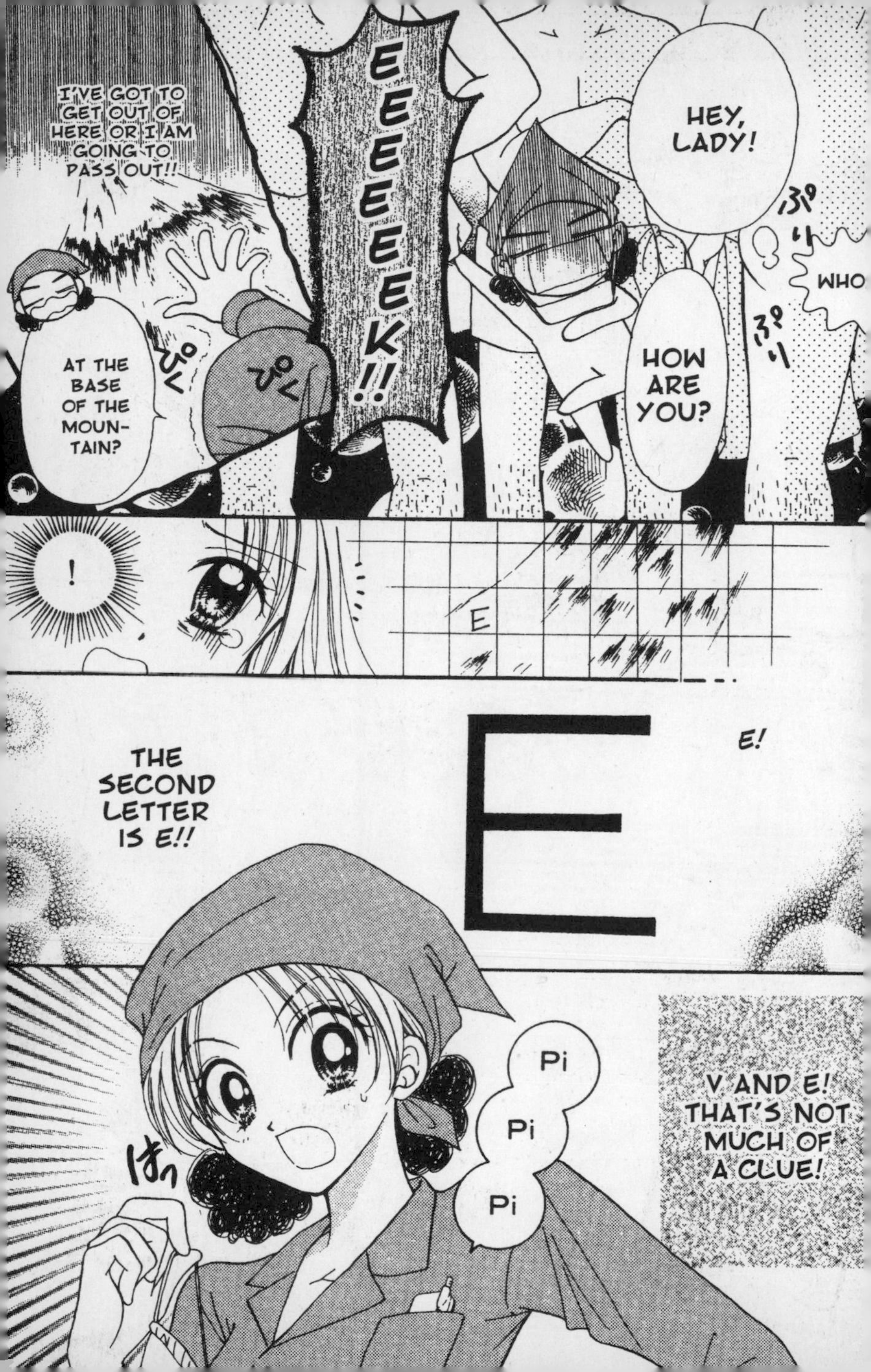
WHO
ぷり
ぷり
HEY, LADY!
HOW ARE YOU?
EEEEEEK!!
ぴく
ぴく
I'VE GOT TO GET OUT OF HERE OR I AM GOING TO PASS OUT!!
AT THE BASE OF THE MOUN-TAIN?
!
E
E!
E
THE SECOND LETTER IS E!!
V AND E! THAT'S NOT MUCH OF A CLUE!
Pi
Pi
Pi
はっ

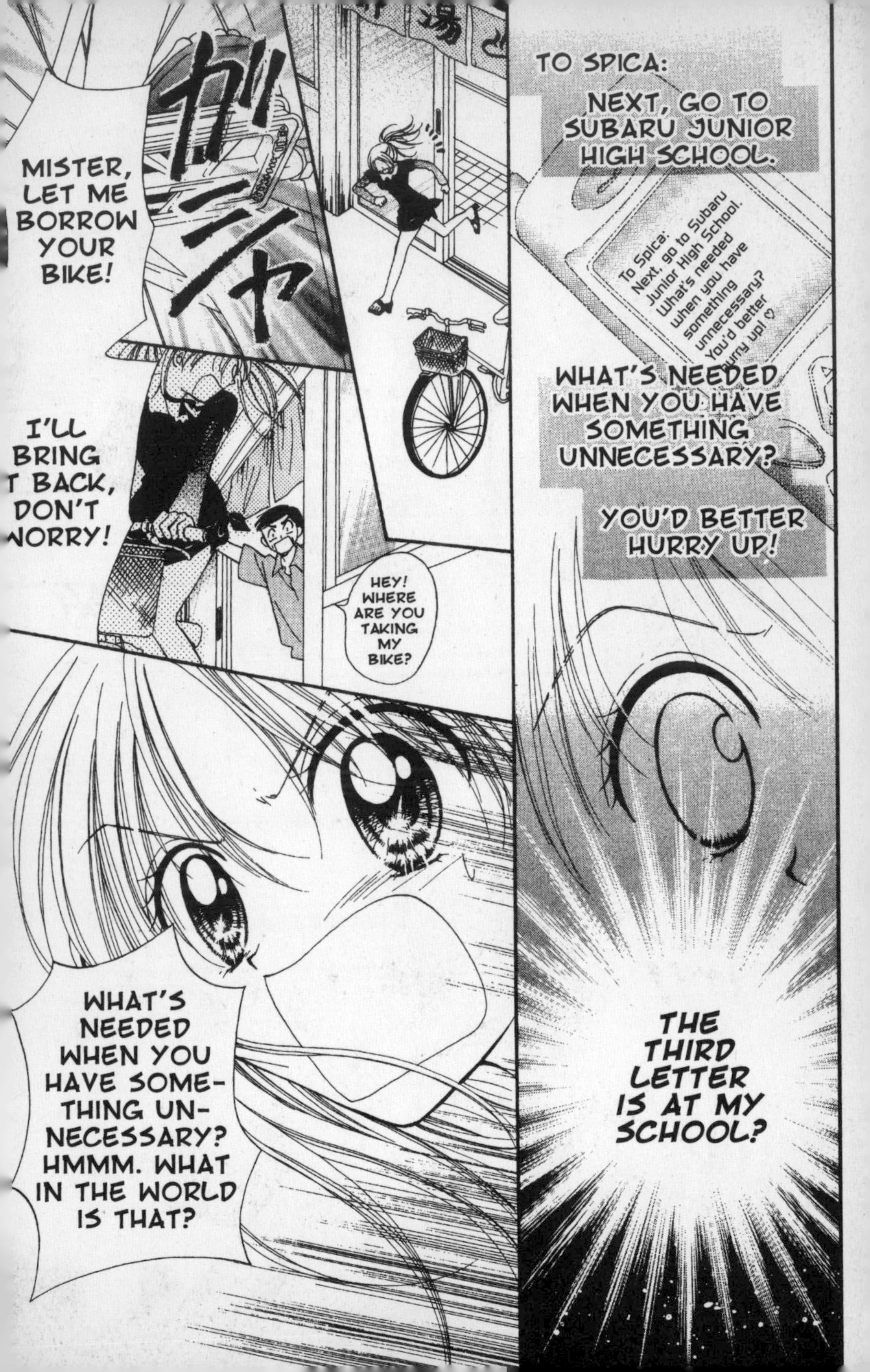
TO SPICA:
NEXT, GO TO SUBARU JUNIOR HIGH SCHOOL.
To Spica: Next, go to Subaru Junior High School. What's needed when you have something unnecessary? You'd better hurry up! ♡
WHAT'S NEEDED WHEN YOU HAVE SOMETHING UNNECESSARY?
YOU'D BETTER HURRY UP!
THE THIRD LETTER IS AT MY SCHOOL?
ガシャ
MISTER, LET ME BORROW YOUR BIKE!
I'LL BRING T BACK, DON'T ORRY!
HEY! WHERE ARE YOU TAKING MY BIKE?
WHAT'S NEEDED WHEN YOU HAVE SOME- THING UN- NECESSARY? HMMM. WHAT IN THE WORLD IS THAT?

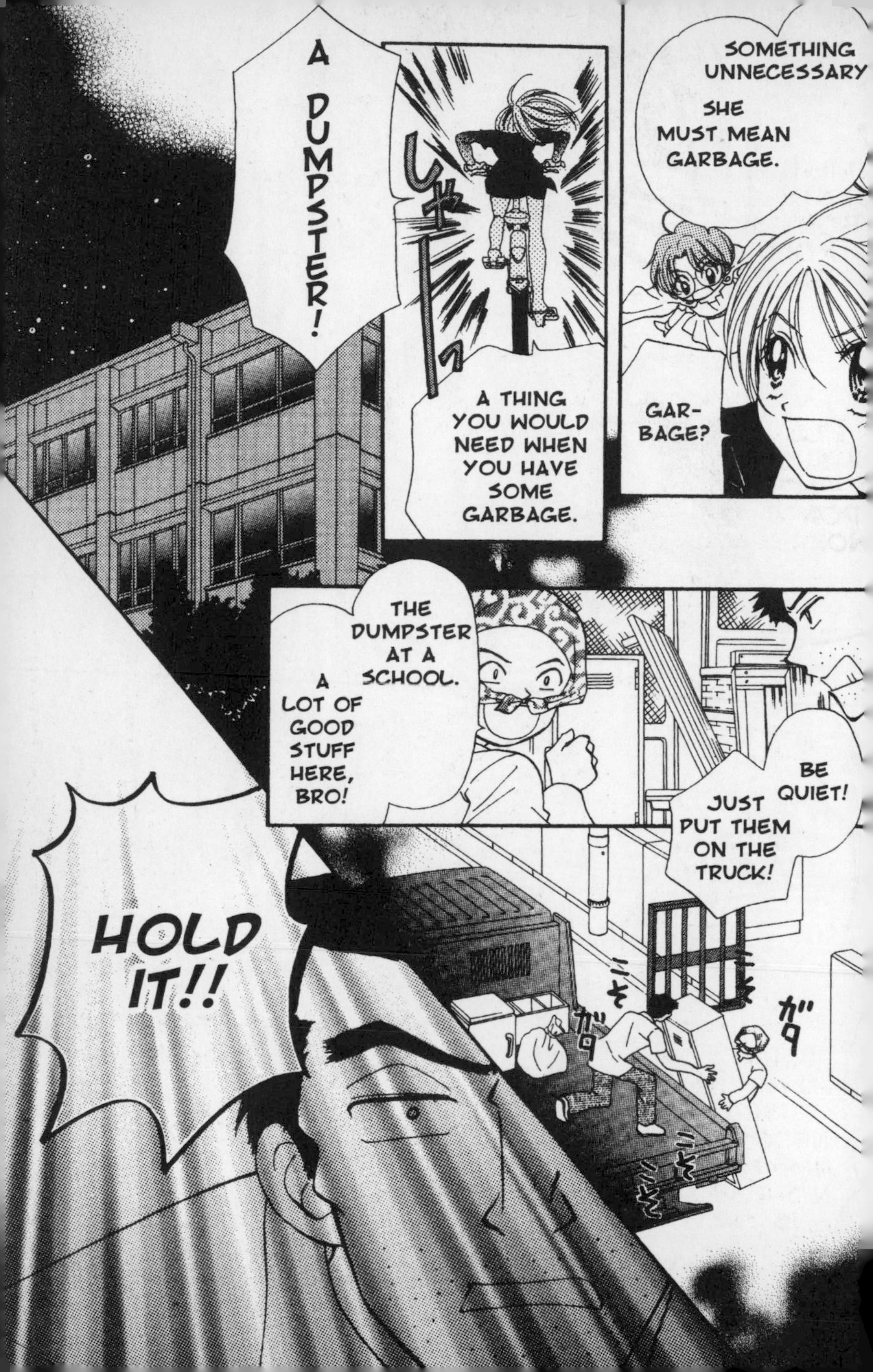
SOMETHING UNNECESSARY
SHE MUST MEAN GARBAGE.
GAR-BAGE?
A THING YOU WOULD NEED WHEN YOU HAVE SOME GARBAGE.
A DUMPSTER!
THE DUMPSTER AT A SCHOOL.
A LOT OF GOOD STUFF HERE, BRO!
BE QUIET!
JUST PUT THEM ON THE TRUCK!
HOLD IT!!

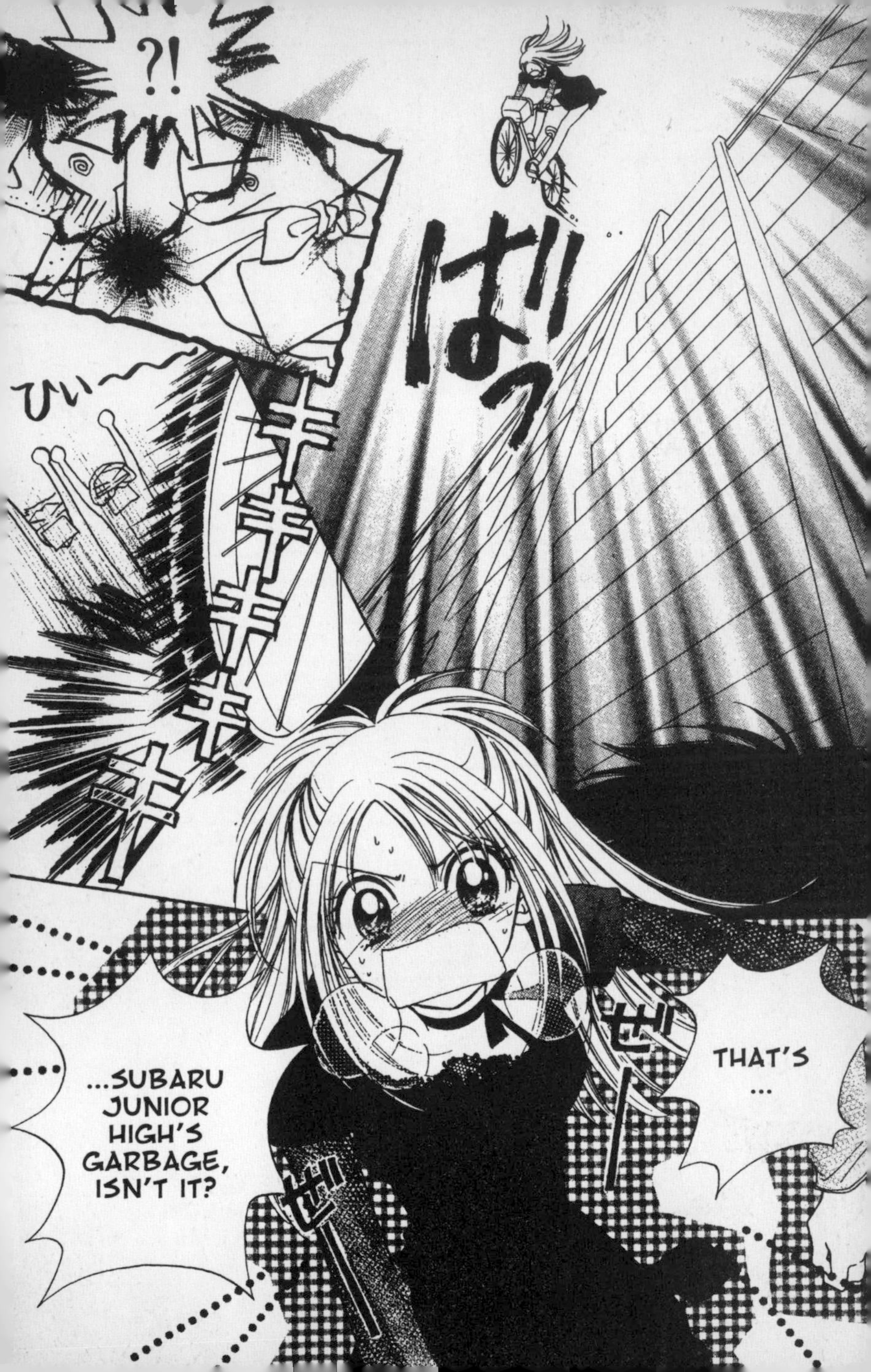
ぱっ
?!
ひぃ〜
キキキキキ
ぜー
ぜー
THAT'S ...
...SUBARU JUNIOR HIGH'S GARBAGE, ISN'T IT?

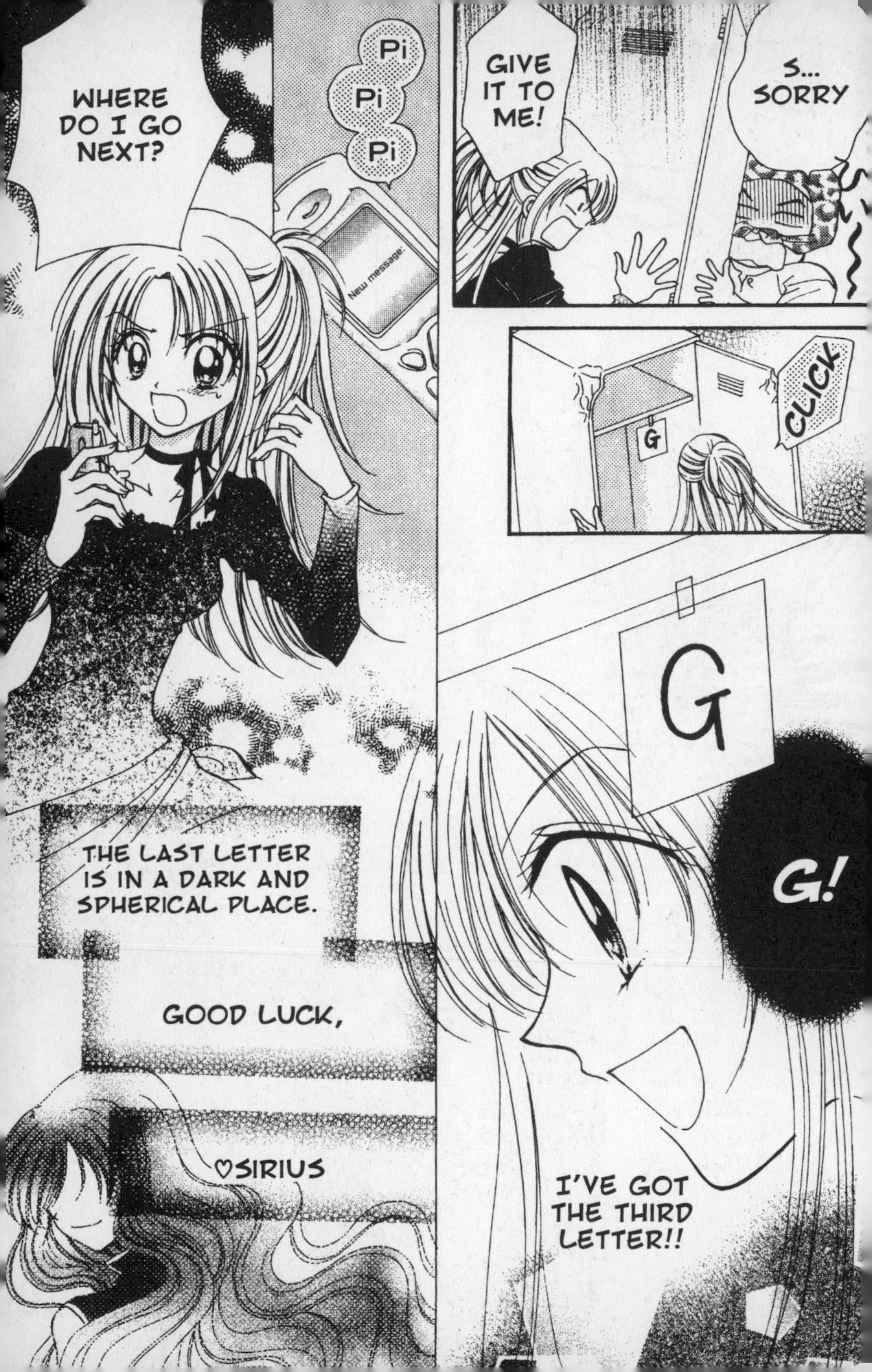
GIVE IT TO ME!
S... SORRY
CLICK
G
G
G!
I'VE GOT THE THIRD LETTER!!
Pi
Pi
Pi
New message:
WHERE DO I GO NEXT?
THE LAST LETTER IS IN A DARK AND SPHERICAL PLACE.
GOOD LUCK,
♡SIRIUS

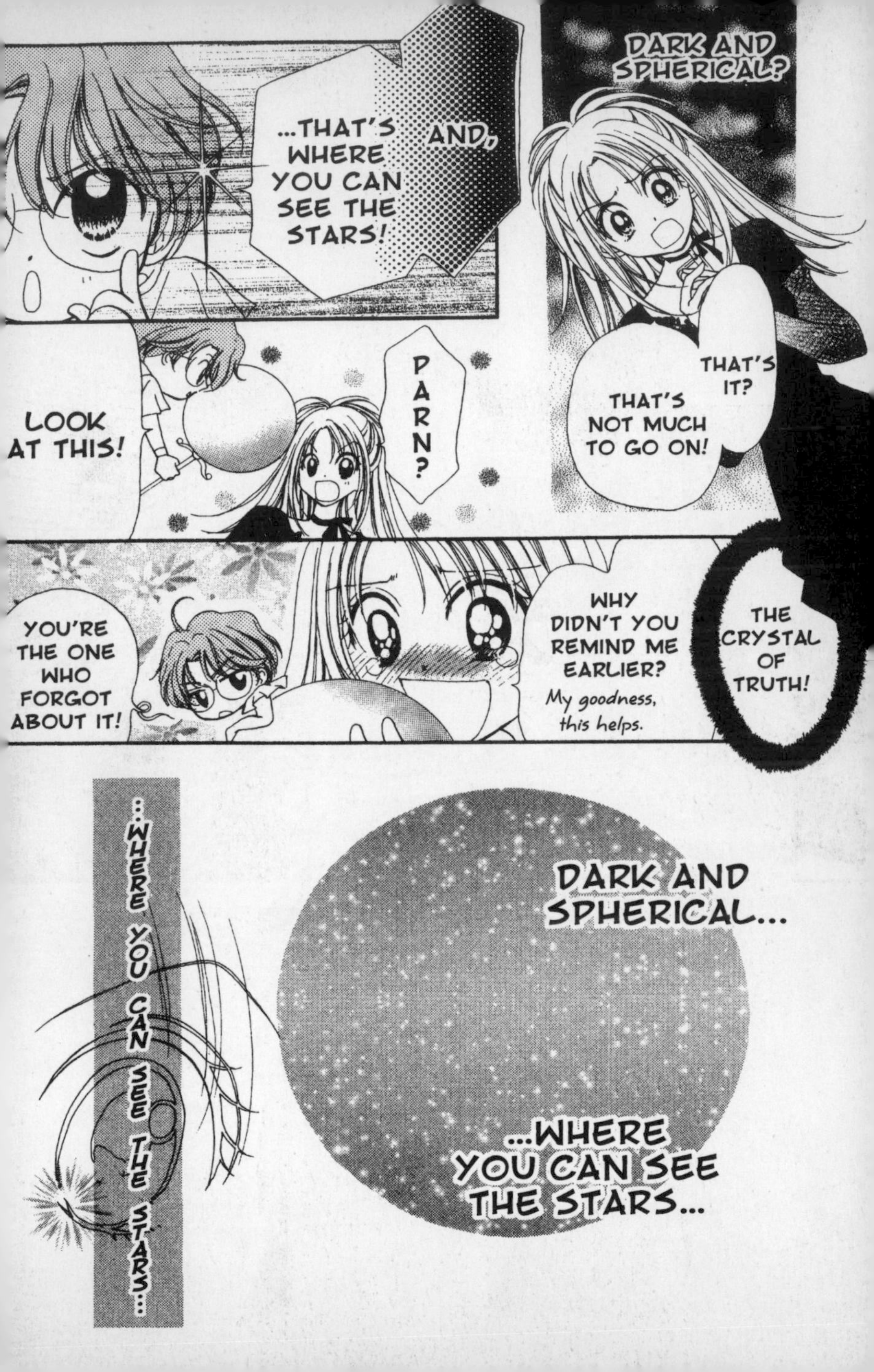
DARK AND SPHERICAL?
THAT'S IT?
THAT'S NOT MUCH TO GO ON!
AND,
...THAT'S WHERE YOU CAN SEE THE STARS!
PARN?
LOOK AT THIS!
THE CRYSTAL OF TRUTH!
WHY DIDN'T YOU REMIND ME EARLIER?
My goodness, this helps.
YOU'RE THE ONE WHO FORGOT ABOUT IT!
DARK AND SPHERICAL...
...WHERE YOU CAN SEE THE STARS...
...WHERE YOU CAN SEE THE STARS...

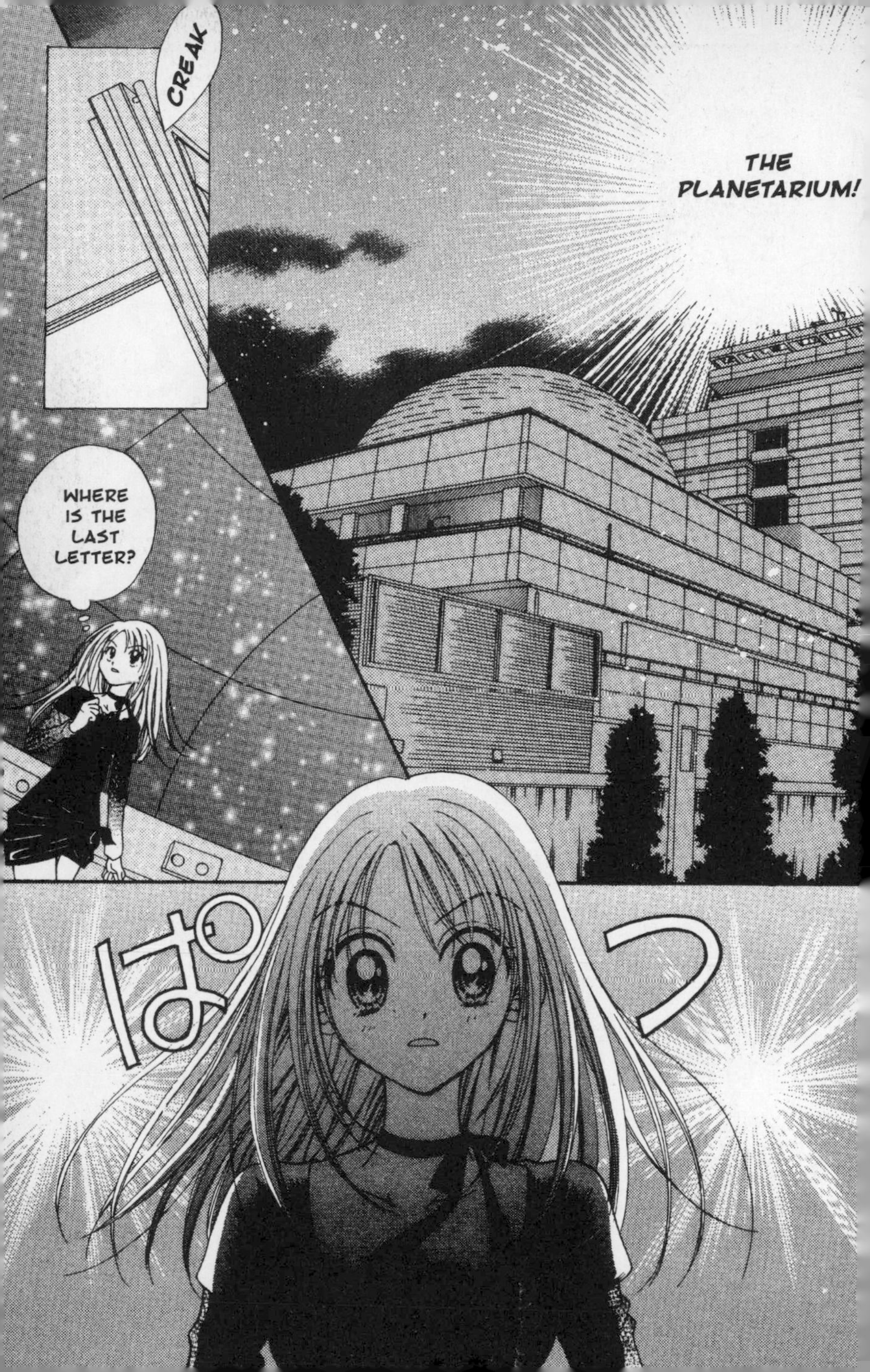
THE PLANETARIUM!
CREAK
WHERE IS THE LAST LETTER?
ぱっ

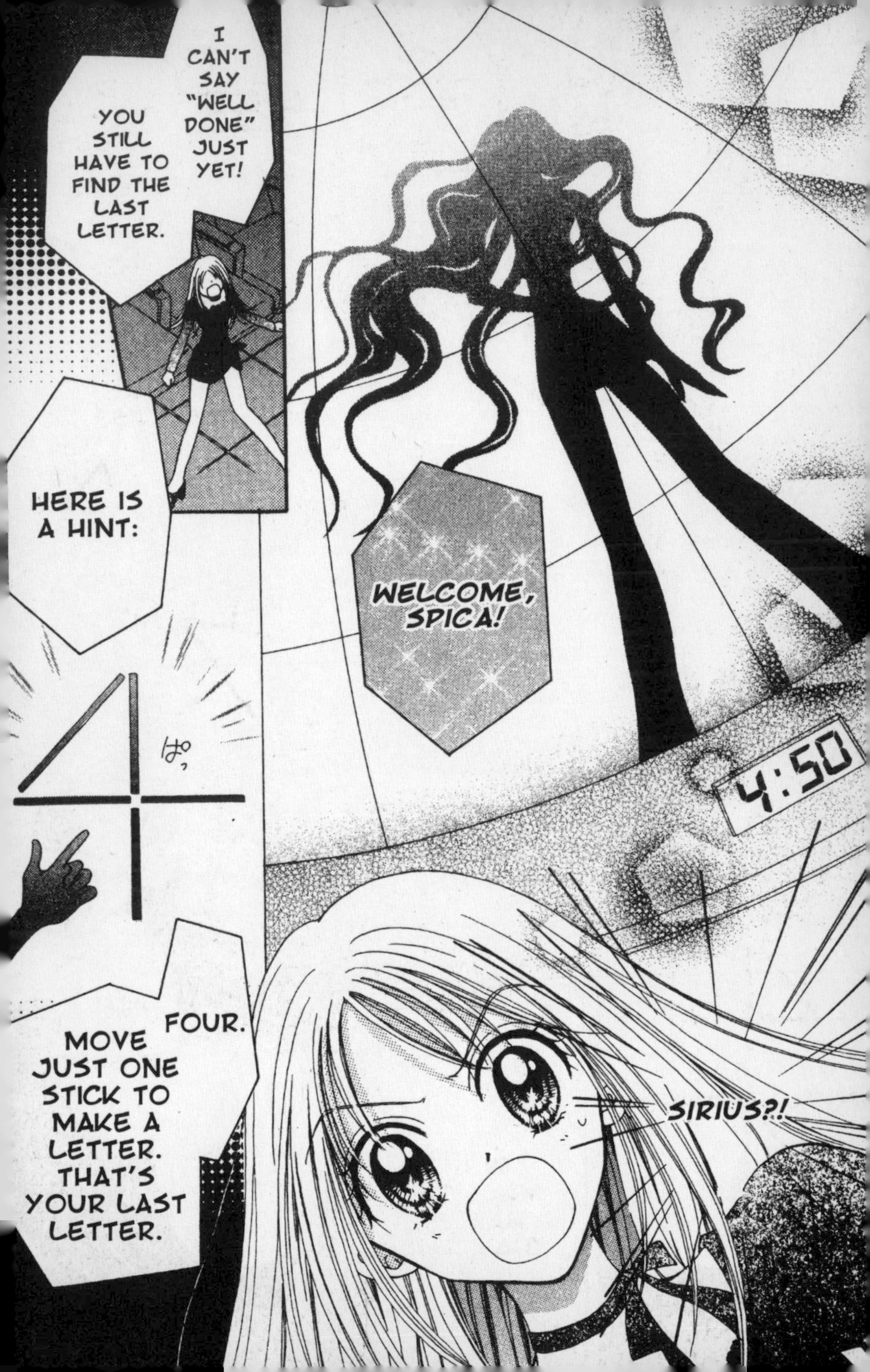
WELCOME, SPICA!
4:50
SIRIUS?!
I CAN'T SAY "WELL DONE" JUST YET!
YOU STILL HAVE TO FIND THE LAST LETTER.
HERE IS A HINT:
ぱっ
FOUR. MOVE JUST ONE STICK TO MAKE A LETTER. THAT'S YOUR LAST LETTER.

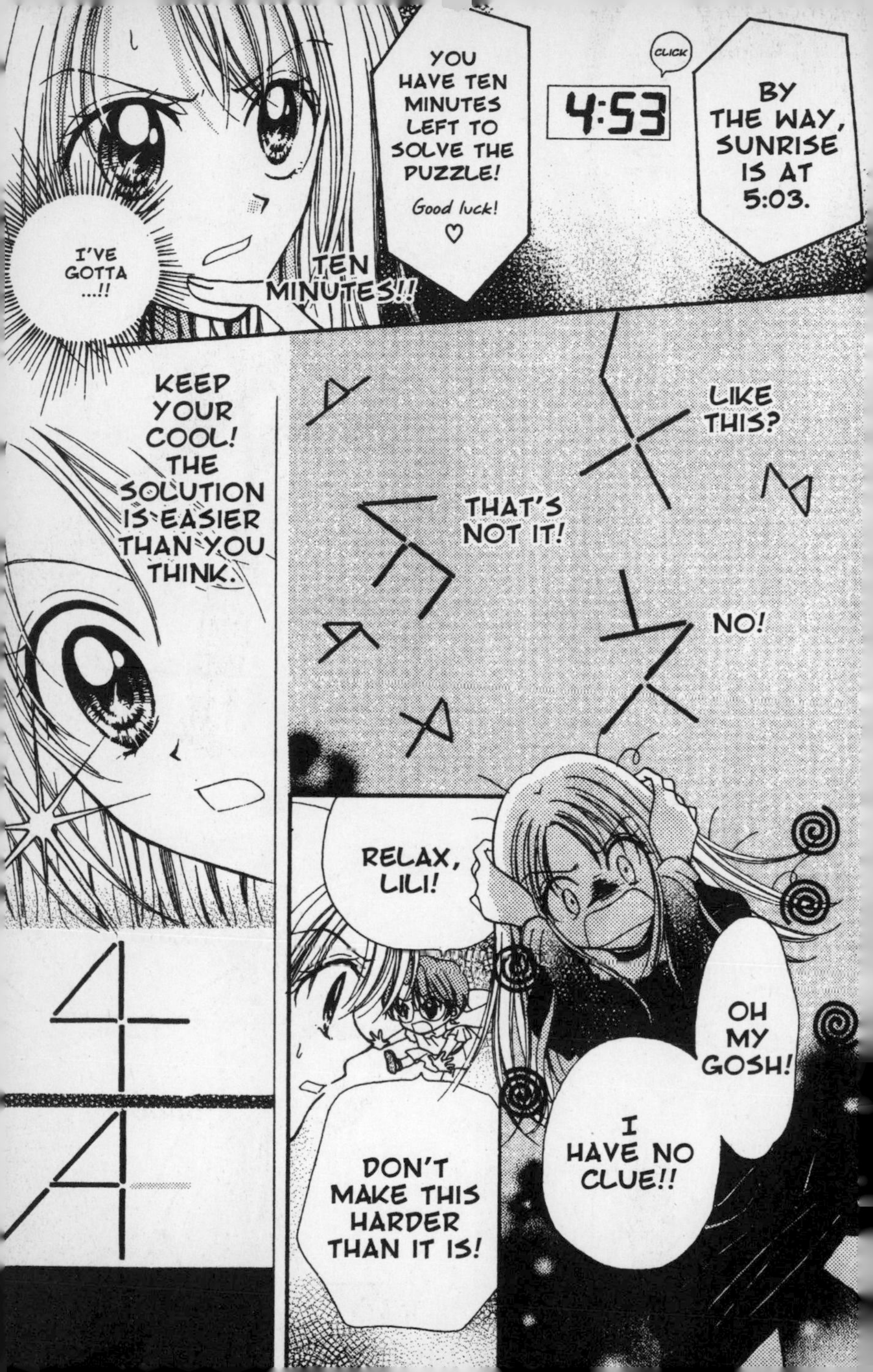
CLICK
4:53
BY THE WAY, SUNRISE IS AT 5:03.
YOU HAVE TEN MINUTES LEFT TO SOLVE THE PUZZLE!
Good luck! ♡
TEN MINUTES!!
I'VE GOTTA ...!!
LIKE THIS?
THAT'S NOT IT!
NO!
OH MY GOSH!
I HAVE NO CLUE!!
RELAX, LILI!
DON'T MAKE THIS HARDER THAN IT IS!
KEEP YOUR COOL! THE SOLUTION IS EASIER THAN YOU THINK.

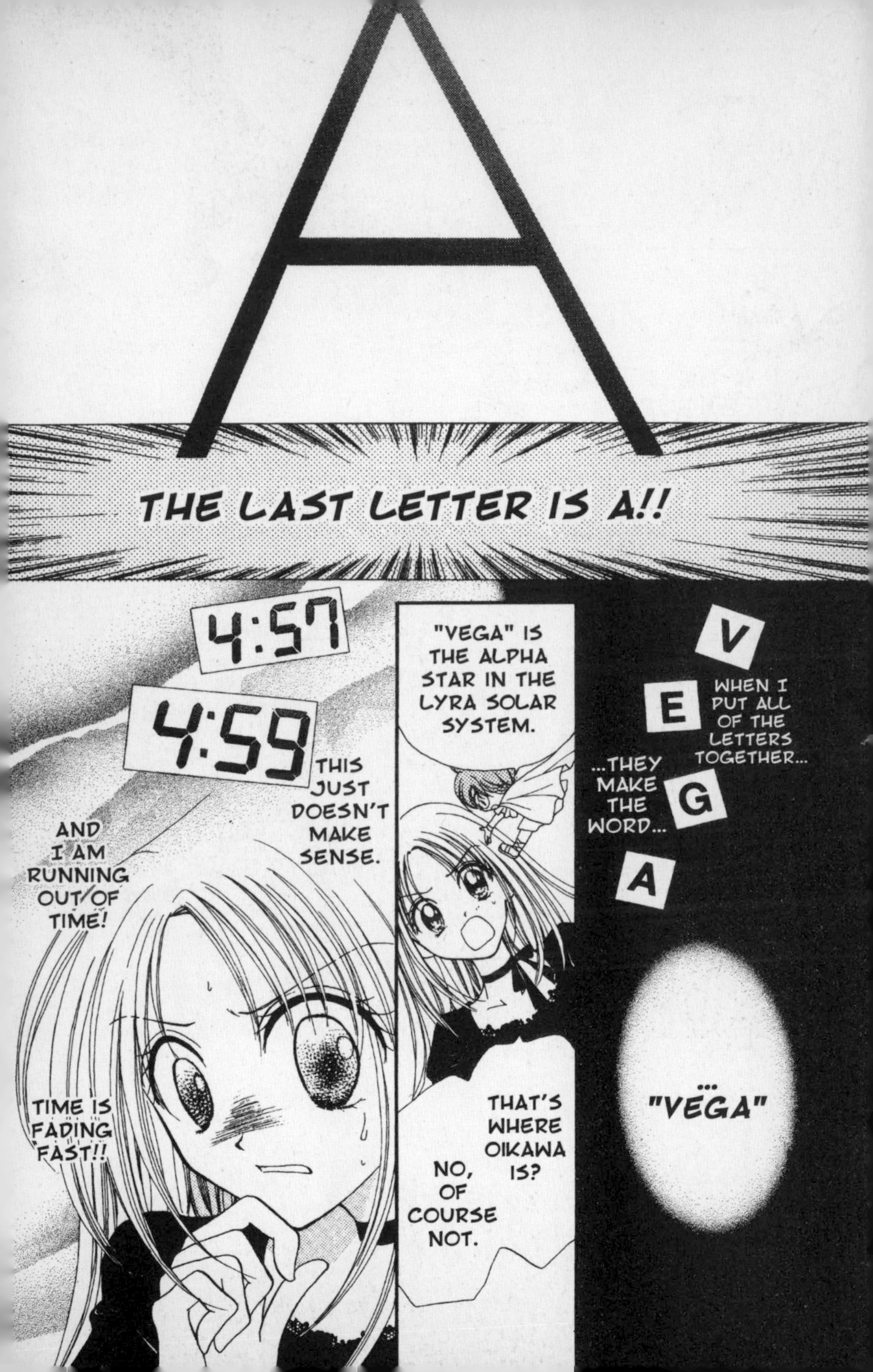
A
THE LAST LETTER IS A!!
V
E
G
A
WHEN I PUT ALL OF THE LETTERS TOGETHER...
...THEY MAKE THE WORD...
..."VEGA"
"VEGA" IS THE ALPHA STAR IN THE LYRA SOLAR SYSTEM.
THAT'S WHERE OIKAWA IS?
NO, OF COURSE NOT.
4:57
4:59
THIS JUST DOESN'T MAKE SENSE.
AND I AM RUNNING OUT OF TIME!
TIME IS FADING FAST!!

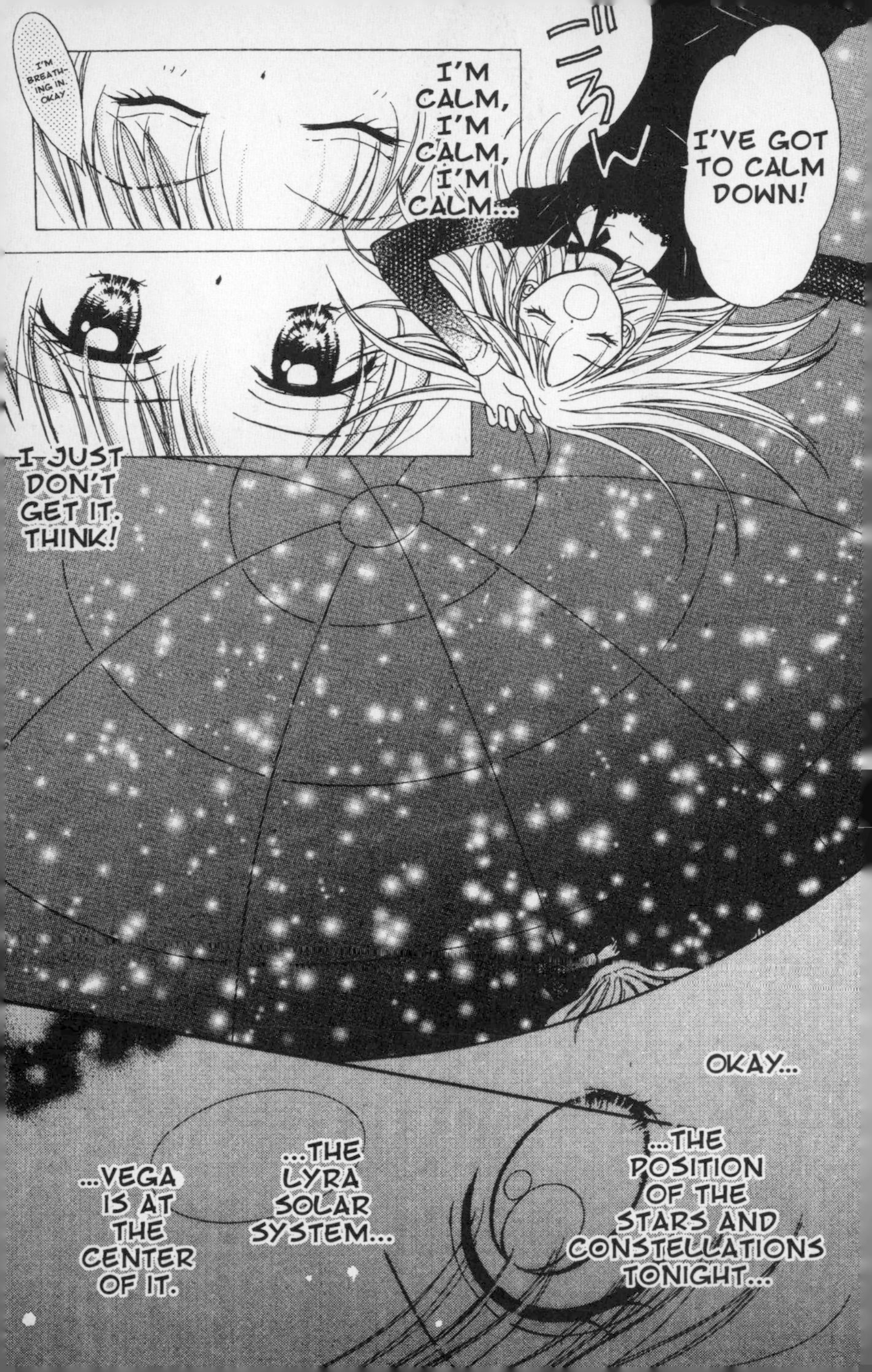
I'VE GOT TO CALM DOWN!
I'M CALM, I'M CALM, I'M CALM...
I'M BREATHING IN. OKAY
I JUST DON'T GET IT. THINK!
OKAY...
...THE POSITION OF THE STARS AND CONSTELLATIONS TONIGHT...
...THE LYRA SOLAR SYSTEM...
...VEGA IS AT THE CENTER OF IT.

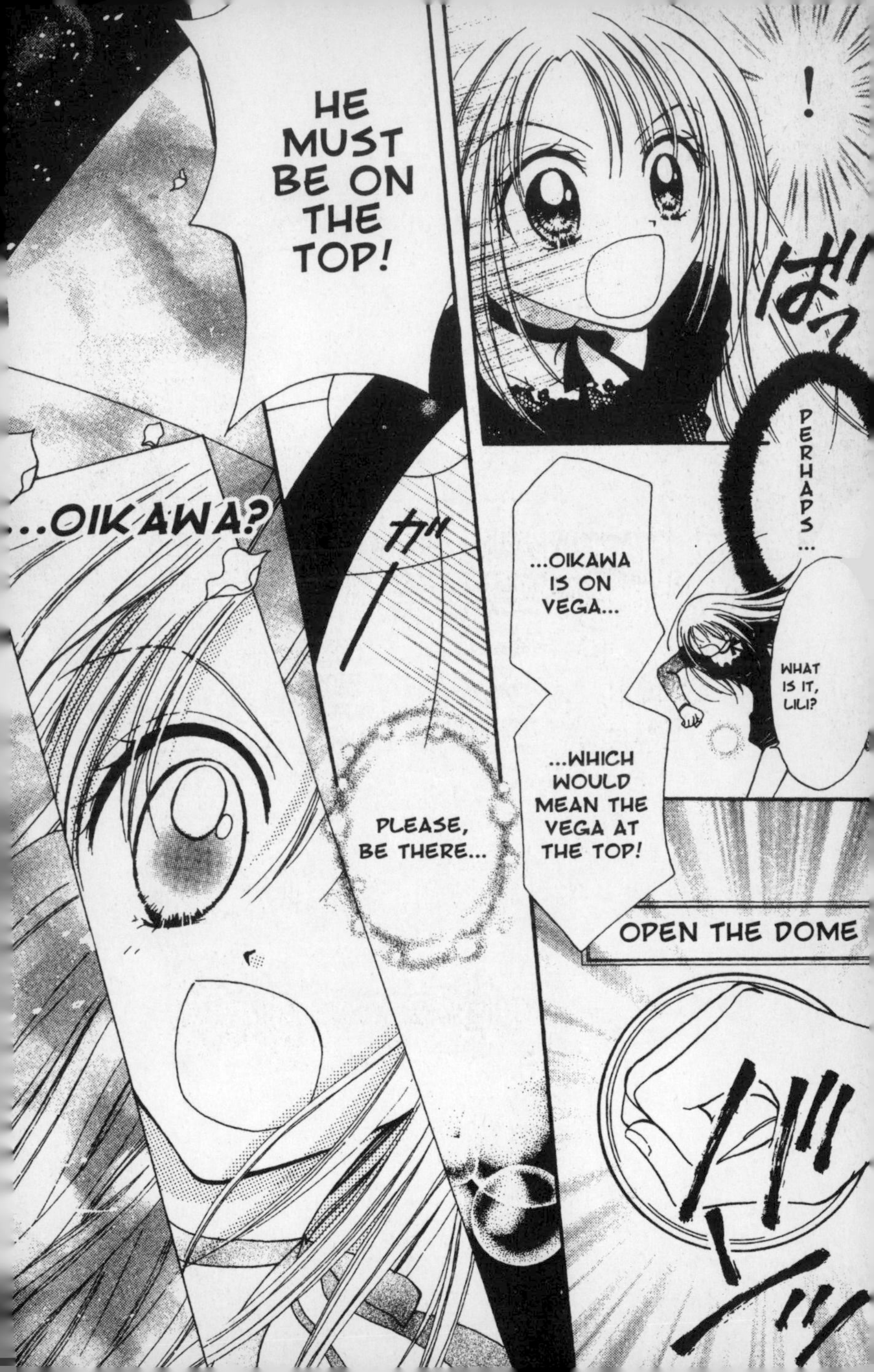
!
ぱっ
HE MUST BE ON THE TOP!
PERHAPS...
WHAT IS IT, LILI?
...OIKAWA IS ON VEGA...
...WHICH WOULD MEAN THE VEGA AT THE TOP!
OPEN THE DOME
...OIKAWA?
PLEASE, BE THERE...

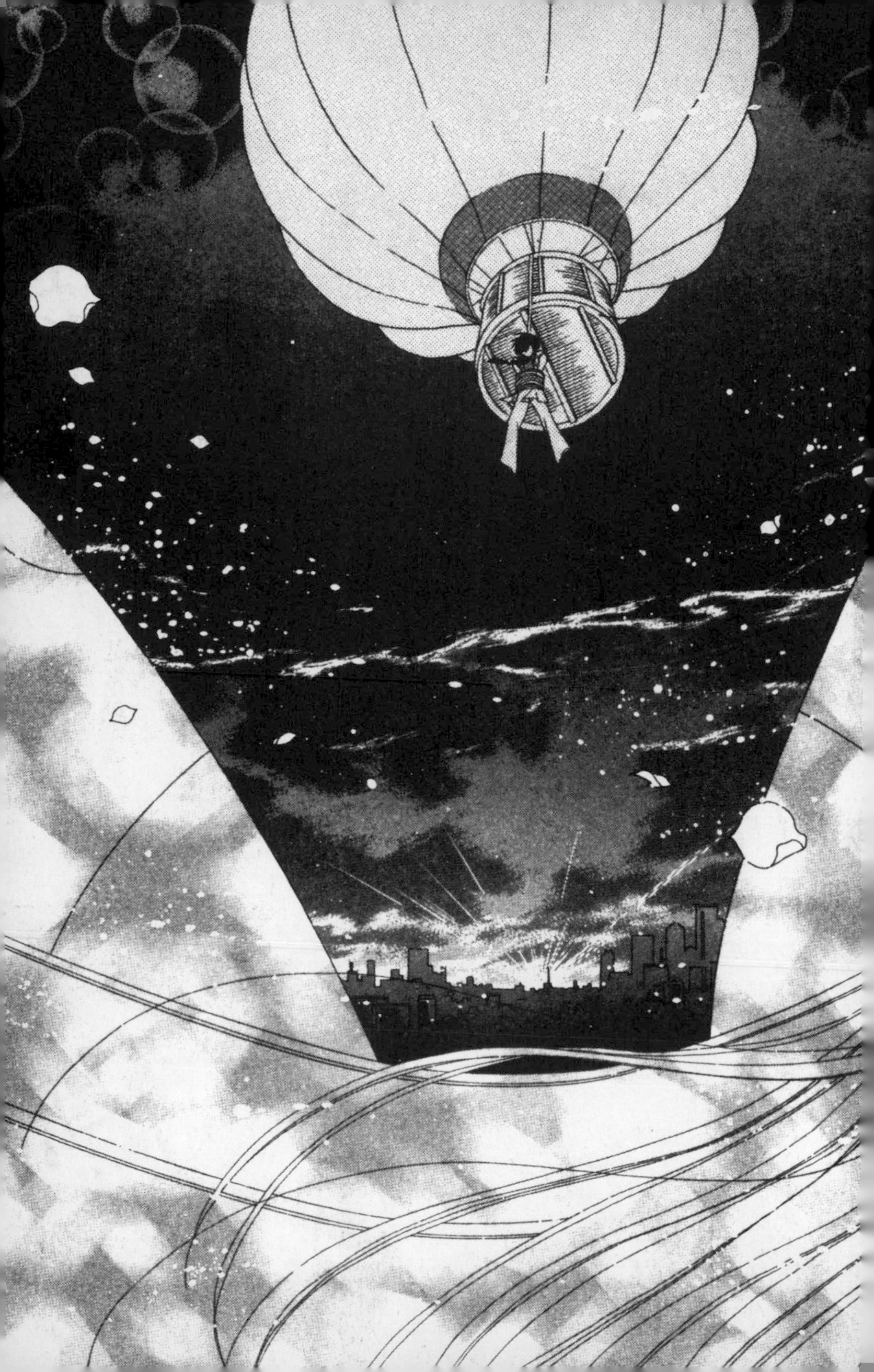

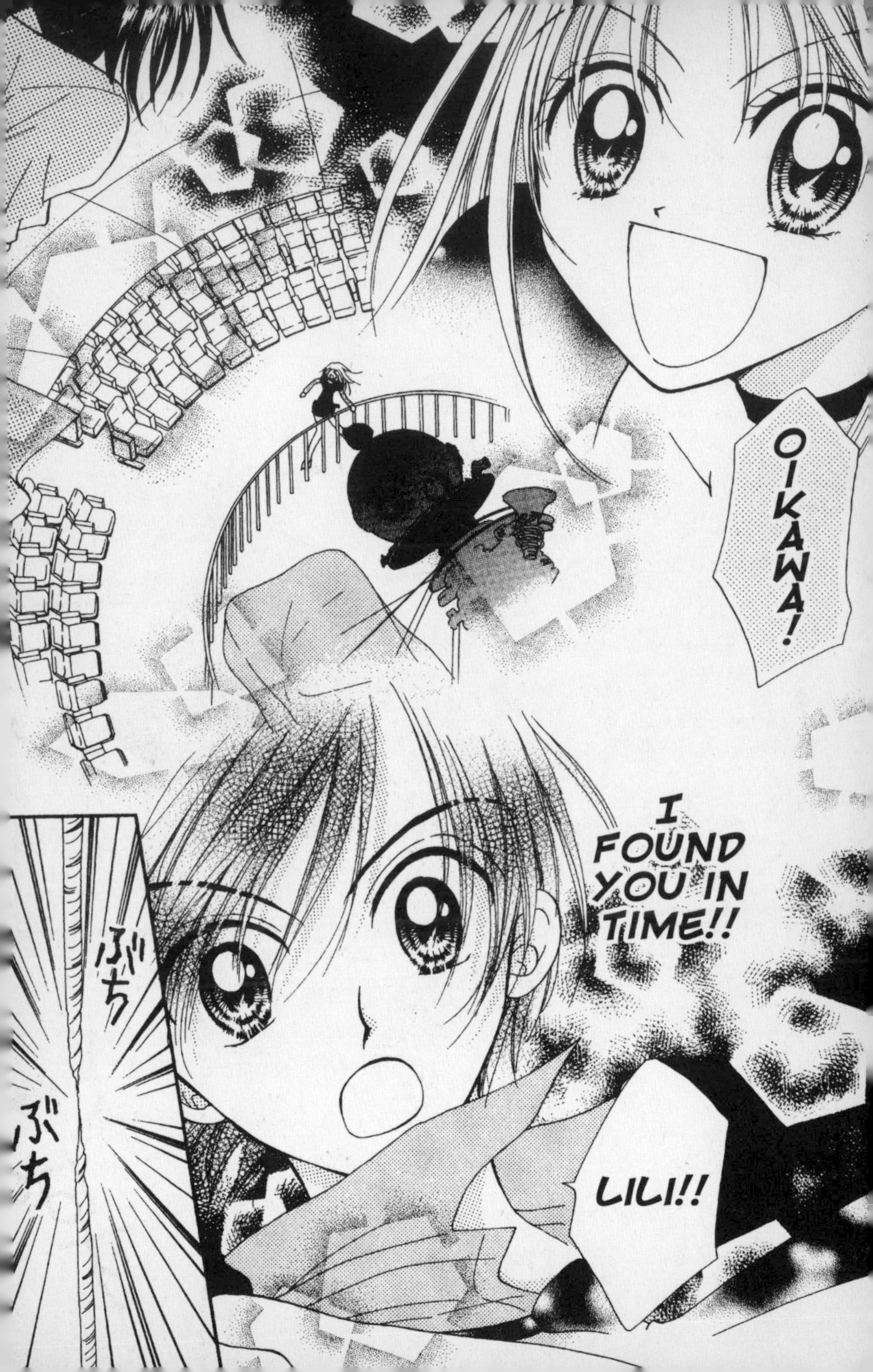
OIKAWA!
I FOUND YOU IN TIME!!
ぶちぶち
LILI!!

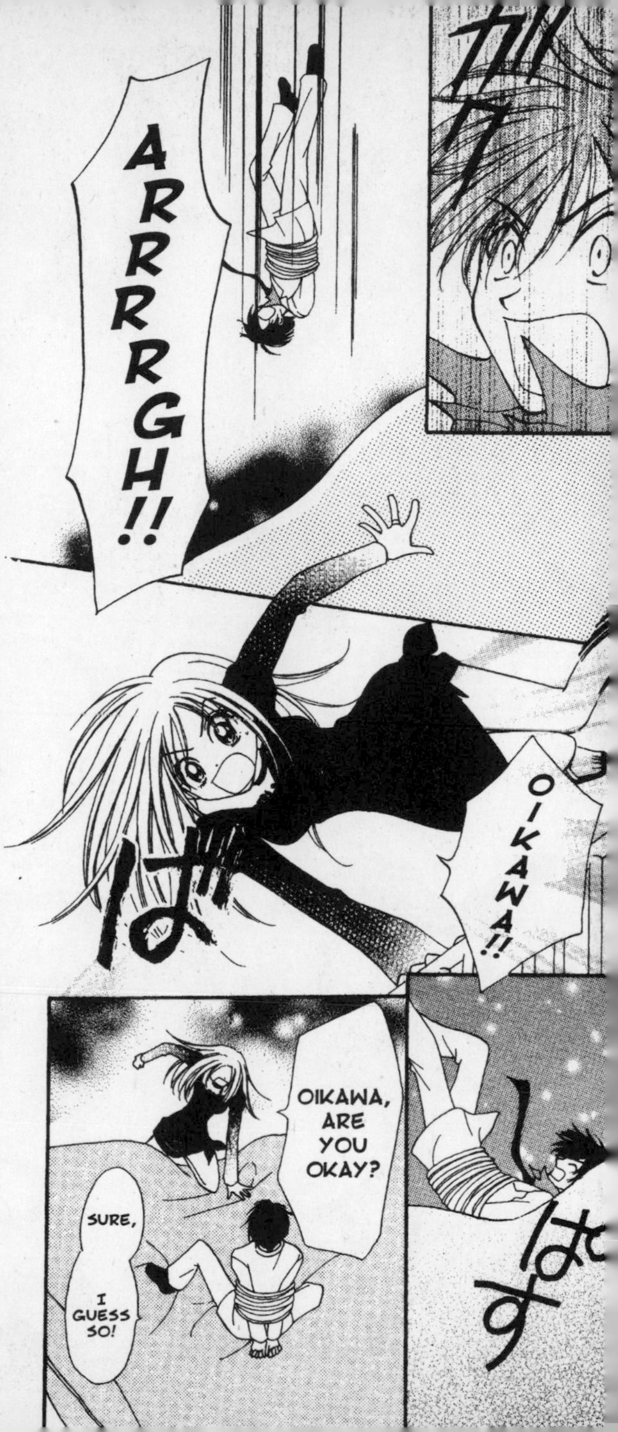
ARRRRGH!!
OIKAWA!!
OIKAWA, ARE YOU OKAY?
SURE, I GUESS SO!

My Trip -

One day I had the urge to take a trip, so I headed to Hiroshima. I decided on Hiroshima because it's warm and there are lots of sights to see. (I wanted to visit sites with lots of heritage.) Hiroshima is close enough that I didn't have to fly. I've always wanted to go to the Itsukushima Shrine in Miyajima. It must be great to see the shrine on the water. But what amazes me in Hiroshima are the trolley cars. They are one of the most popular ways to get around. They are every bit as popular as the subway. Hiroshima is amazing. I've never seen another place like it. The A-Bomb Dome and the Peace Memorial are breathtaking.

Yeah, quite a trip!

It was amazing!

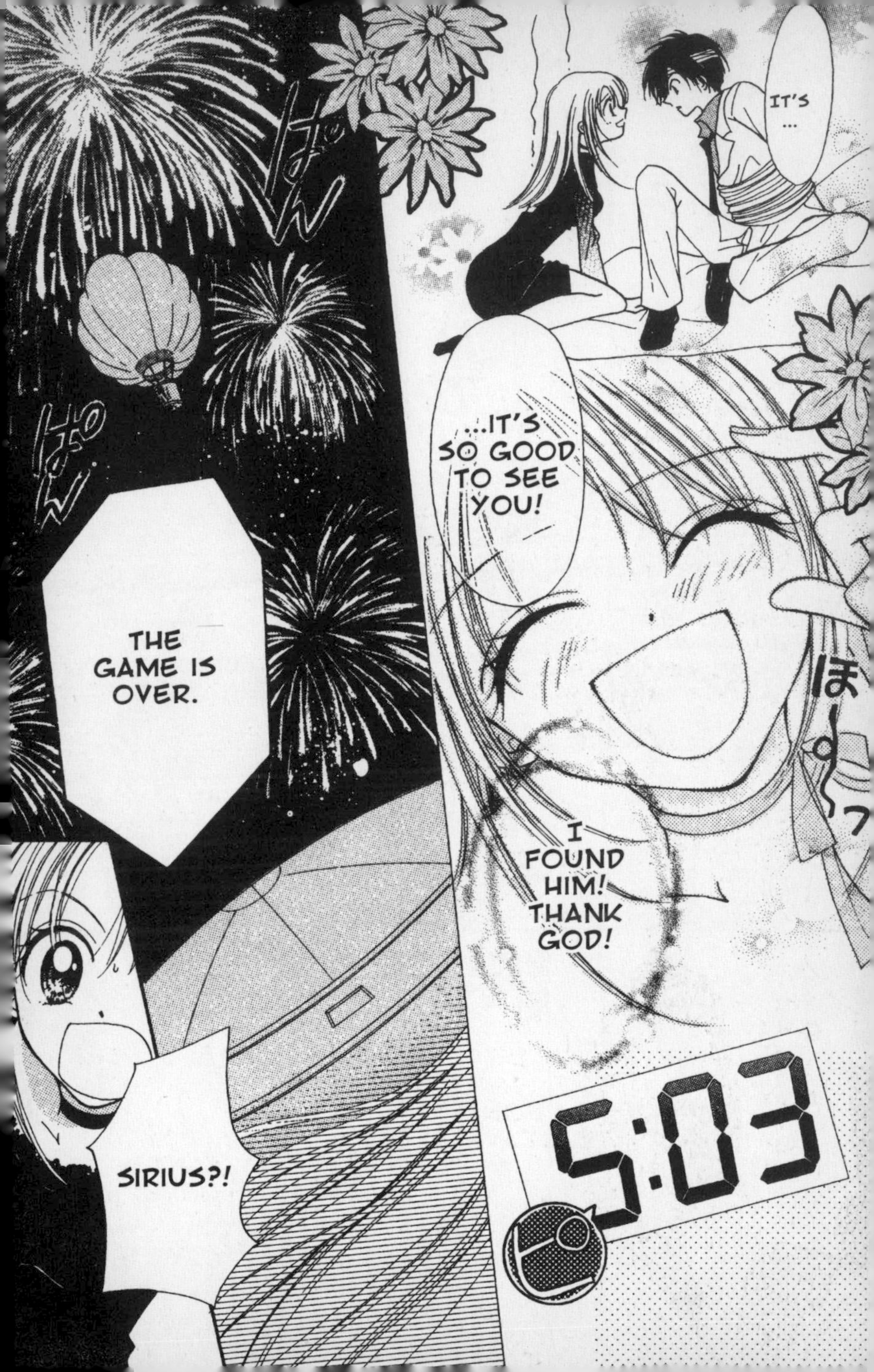
IT'S ...
...IT'S SO GOOD TO SEE YOU!
I FOUND HIM! THANK GOD!
5:03
THE GAME IS OVER.
SIRIUS?!

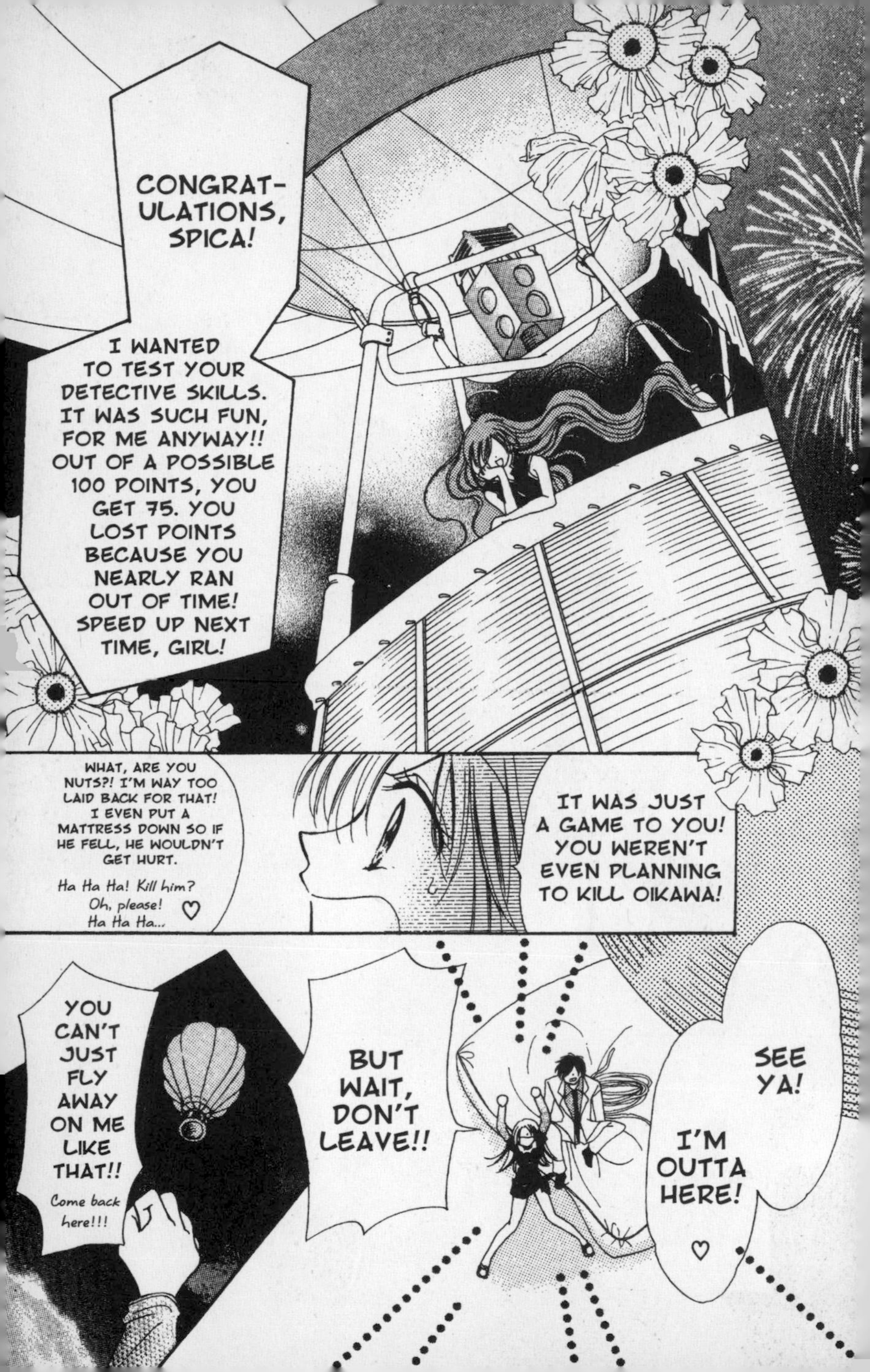
CONGRAT-ULATIONS, SPICA!
I WANTED TO TEST YOUR DETECTIVE SKILLS. IT WAS SUCH FUN, FOR ME ANYWAY!! OUT OF A POSSIBLE 100 POINTS, YOU GET 75. YOU LOST POINTS BECAUSE YOU NEARLY RAN OUT OF TIME! SPEED UP NEXT TIME, GIRL!
IT WAS JUST A GAME TO YOU! YOU WEREN'T EVEN PLANNING TO KILL OIKAWA!
WHAT, ARE YOU NUTS?! I'M WAY TOO LAID BACK FOR THAT! I EVEN PUT A MATTRESS DOWN SO IF HE FELL, HE WOULDN'T GET HURT.
Ha Ha Ha! Kill him? Oh, please! Ha Ha Ha... ♡
SEE YA!
I'M OUTTA HERE! ♡
BUT WAIT, DON'T LEAVE!!
YOU CAN'T JUST FLY AWAY ON ME LIKE THAT!!
Come back here!!!

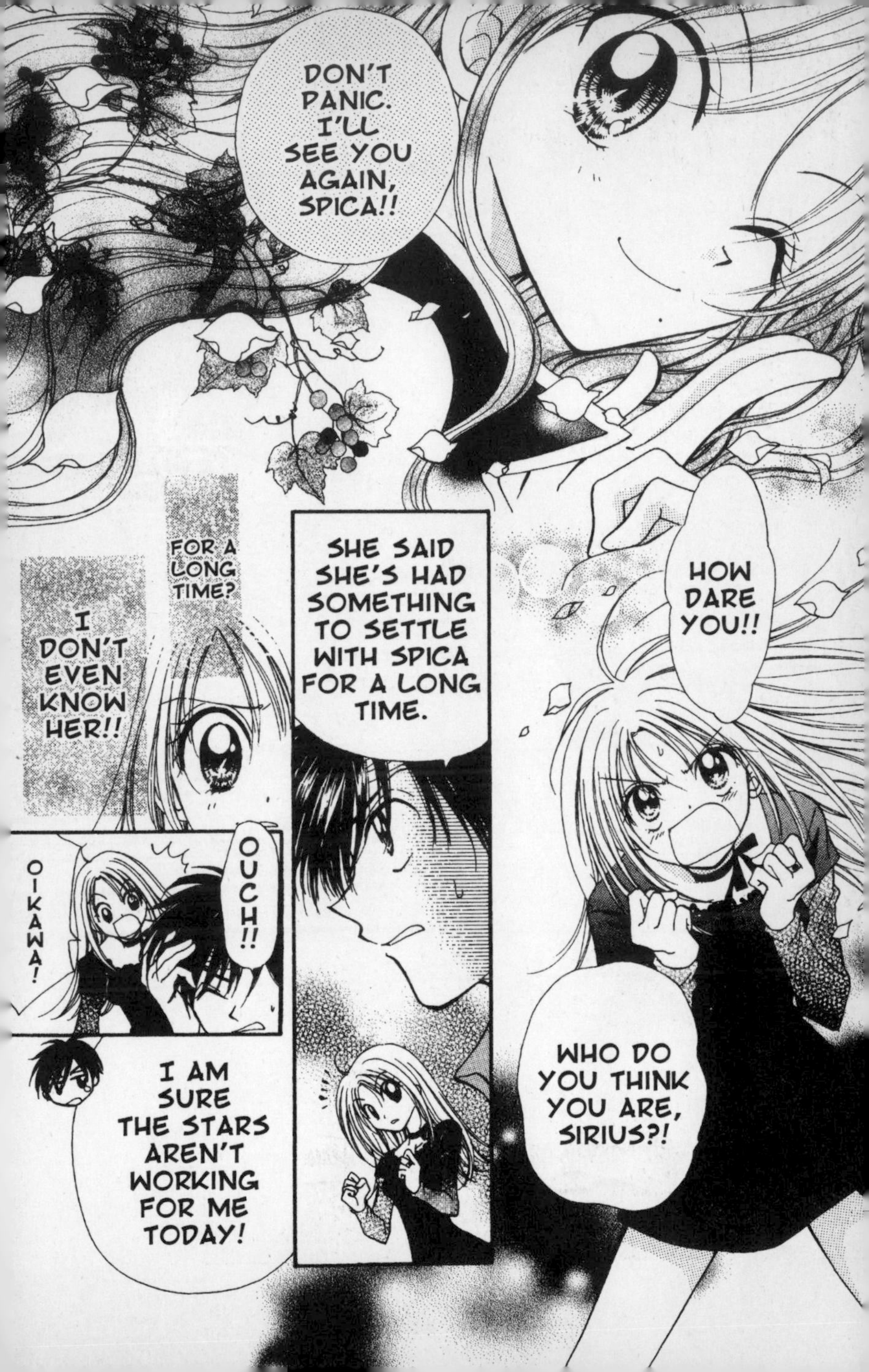
DON'T PANIC. I'LL SEE YOU AGAIN, SPICA!!
HOW DARE YOU!!
WHO DO YOU THINK YOU ARE, SIRIUS?!
SHE SAID SHE'S HAD SOMETHING TO SETTLE WITH SPICA FOR A LONG TIME.
FOR A LONG TIME?
I DON'T EVEN KNOW HER!!
OUCH!!
OIKAWA!
I AM SURE THE STARS AREN'T WORKING FOR ME TODAY!

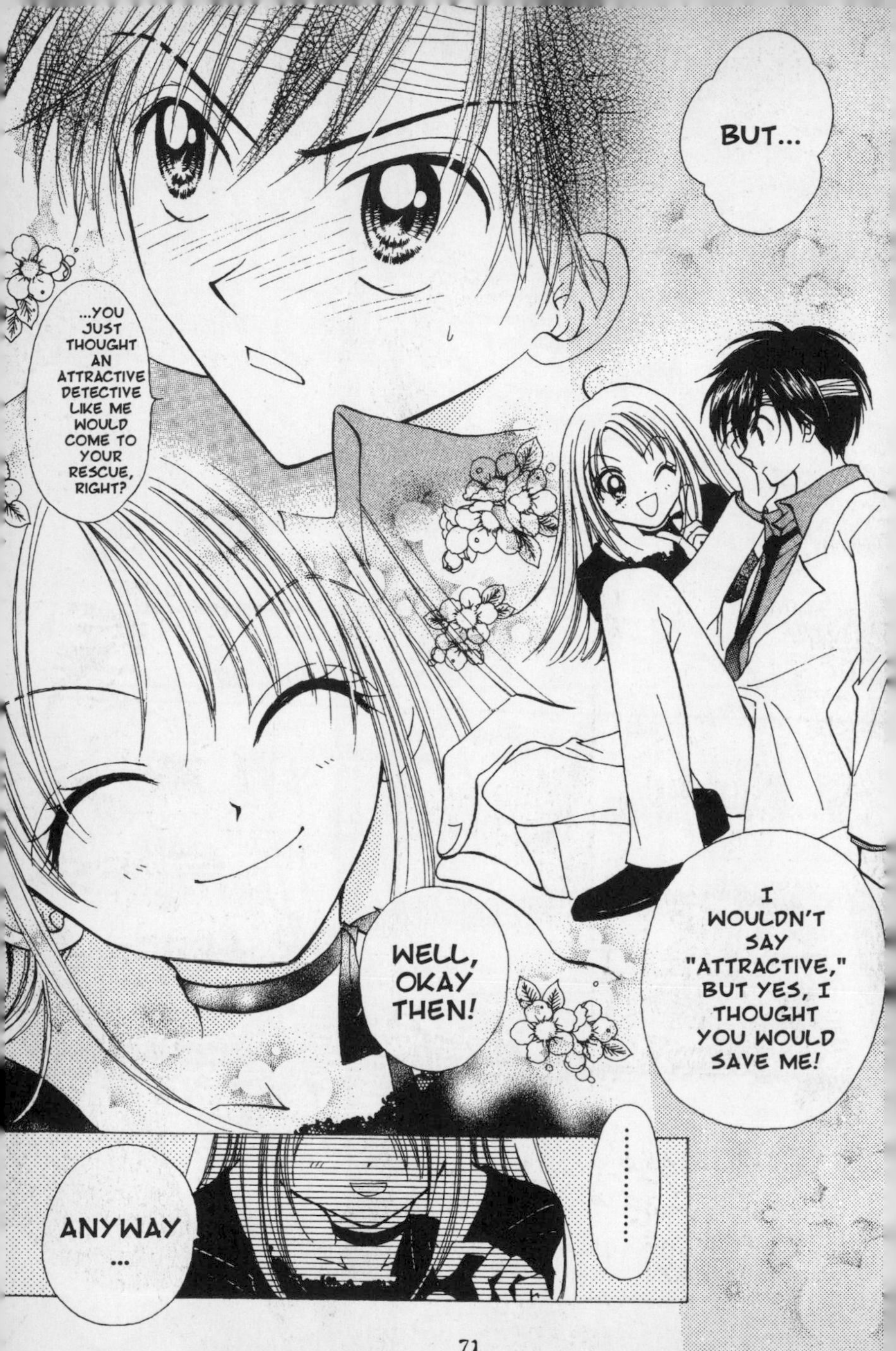
BUT...
...YOU JUST THOUGHT AN ATTRACTIVE DETECTIVE LIKE ME WOULD COME TO YOUR RESCUE, RIGHT?
I WOULDN'T SAY "ATTRACTIVE," BUT YES, I THOUGHT YOU WOULD SAVE ME!
WELL, OKAY THEN!
....
ANYWAY ...

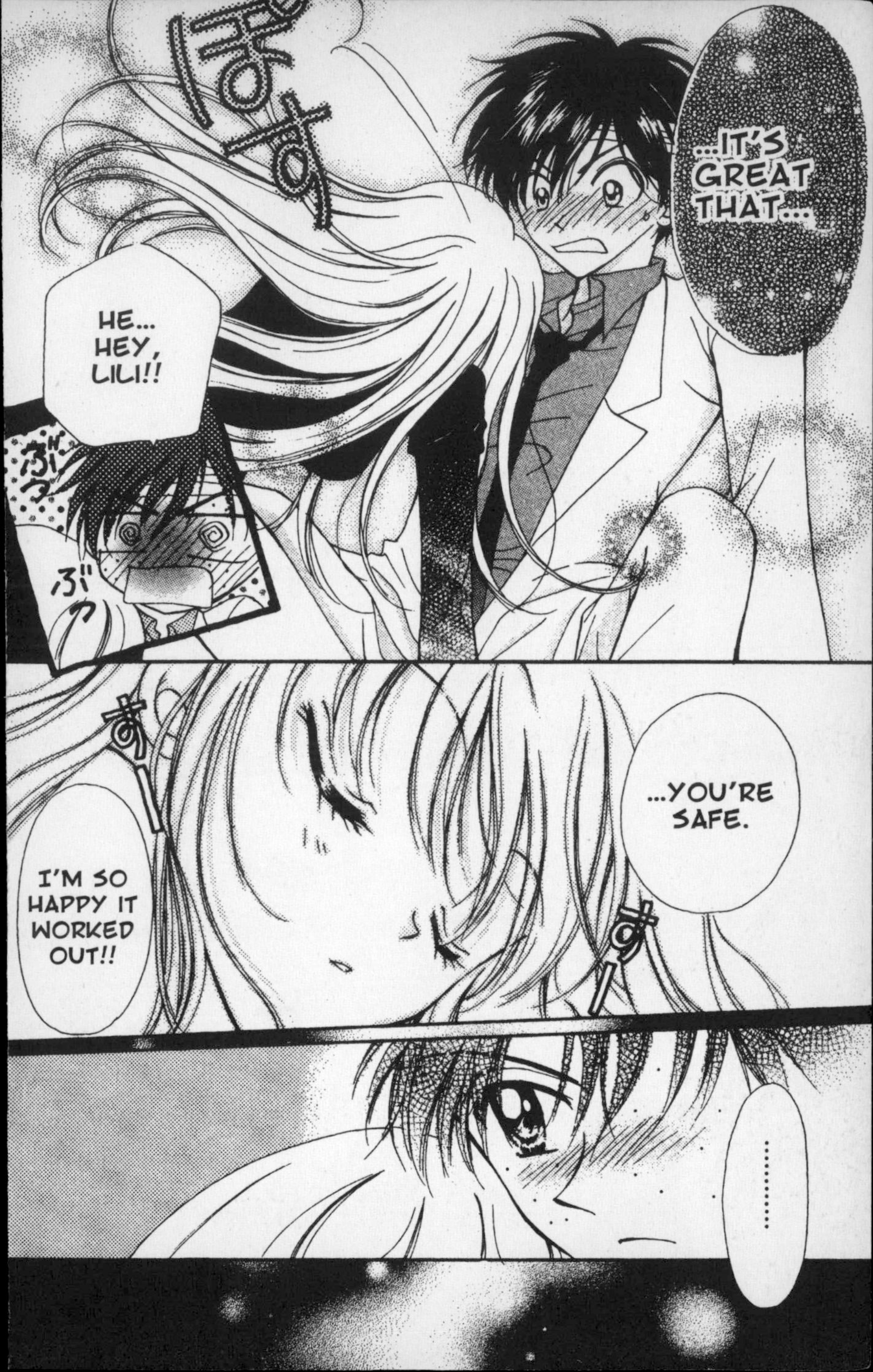
...IT'S GREAT THAT...
ぽすっ
HE... HEY, LILI!!
ぶっ
ぶっ
...YOU'RE SAFE.
I'M SO HAPPY IT WORKED OUT!!
......

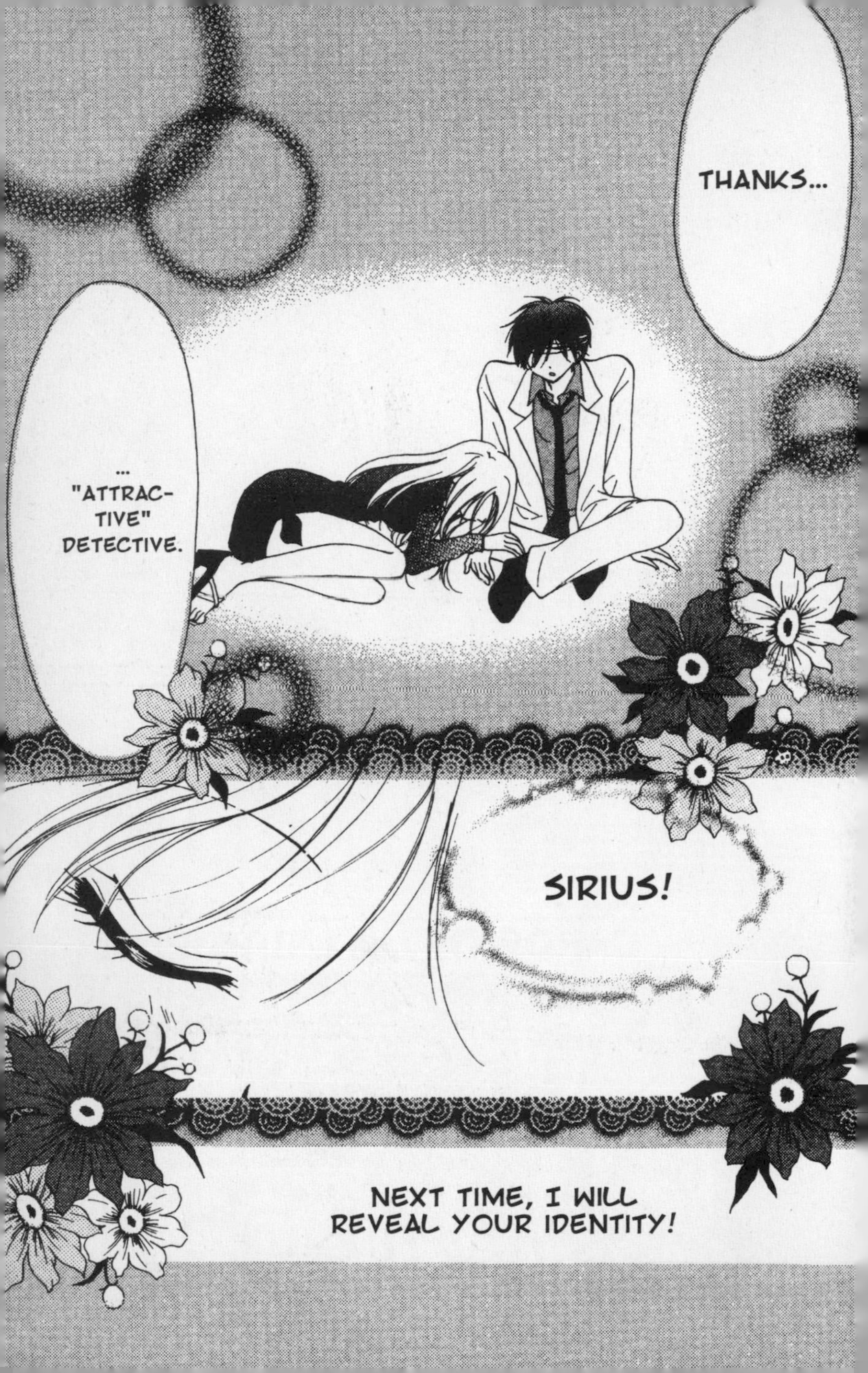
THANKS...
... "ATTRAC-TIVE" DETECTIVE.
SIRIUS!
NEXT TIME, I WILL REVEAL YOUR IDENTITY!

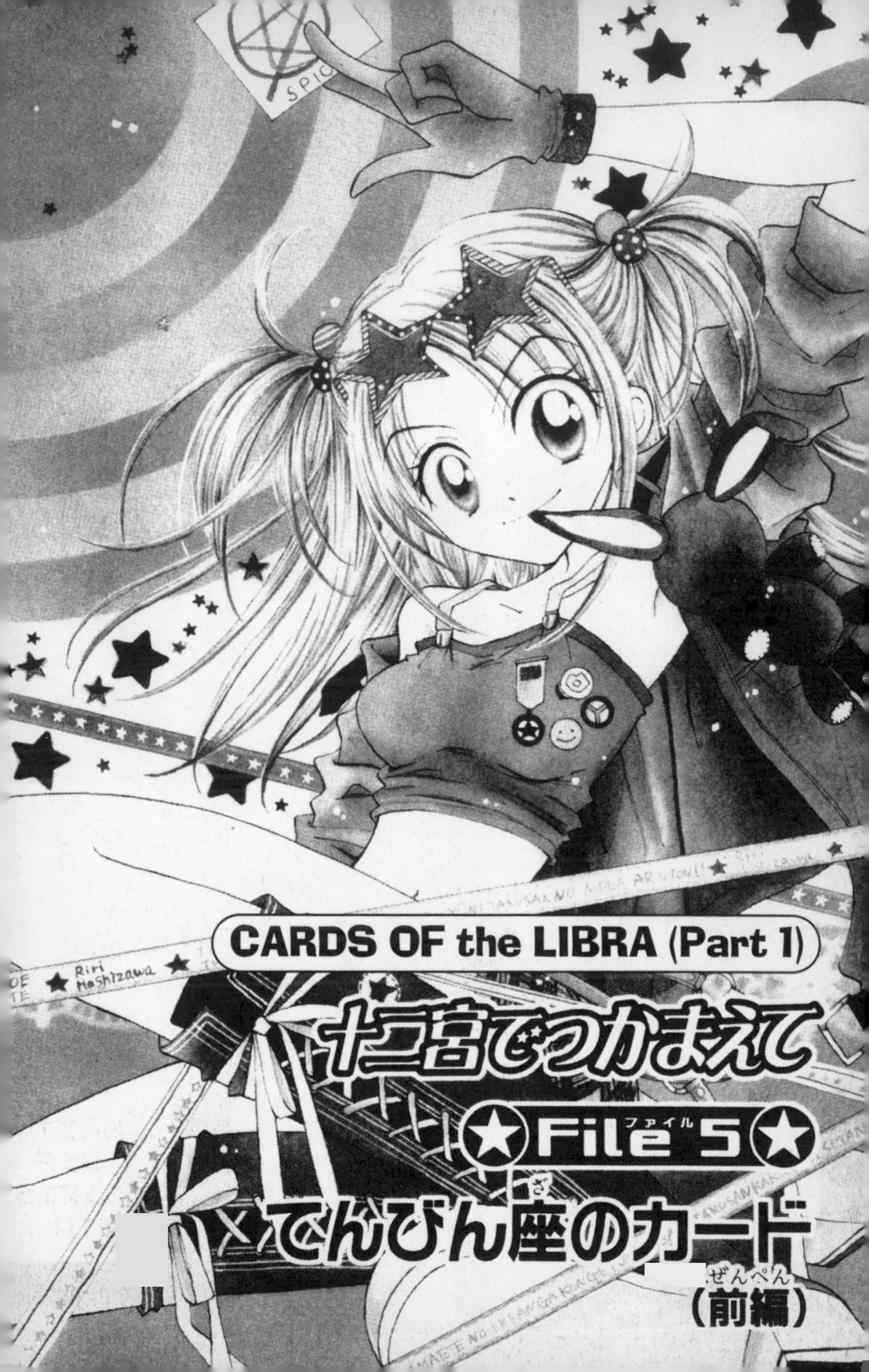
CARDS OF the LIBRA (Part 1)
十二宮でつかまえて
File 5
てんびん座のカード
(前編)
Riri Hoshizawa

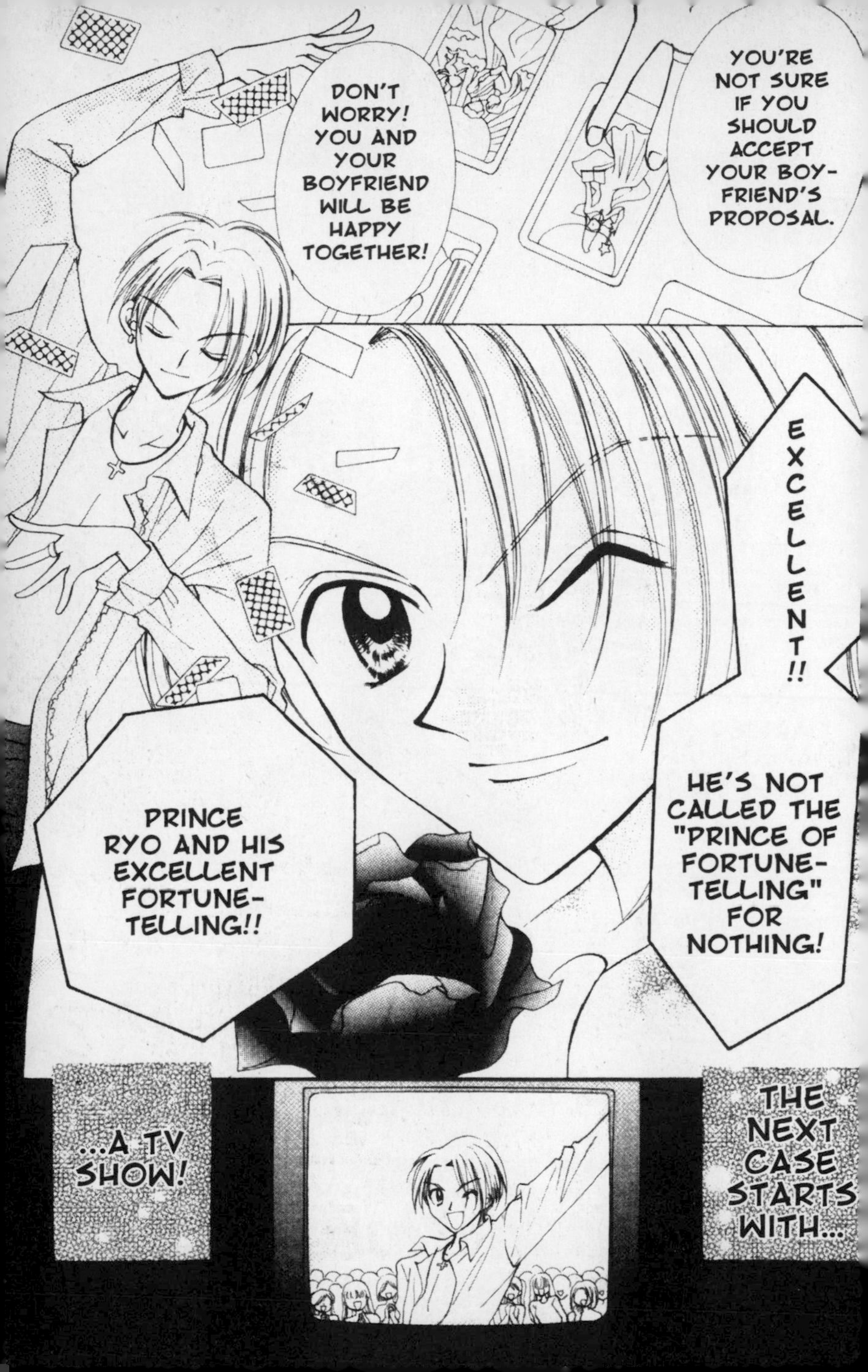
YOU'RE NOT SURE IF YOU SHOULD ACCEPT YOUR BOY-FRIEND'S PROPOSAL.
DON'T WORRY! YOU AND YOUR BOYFRIEND WILL BE HAPPY TOGETHER!
EXCELLENT!!
HE'S NOT CALLED THE "PRINCE OF FORTUNE-TELLING" FOR NOTHING!
PRINCE RYO AND HIS EXCELLENT FORTUNE-TELLING!!
THE NEXT CASE STARTS WITH...
...A TV SHOW!

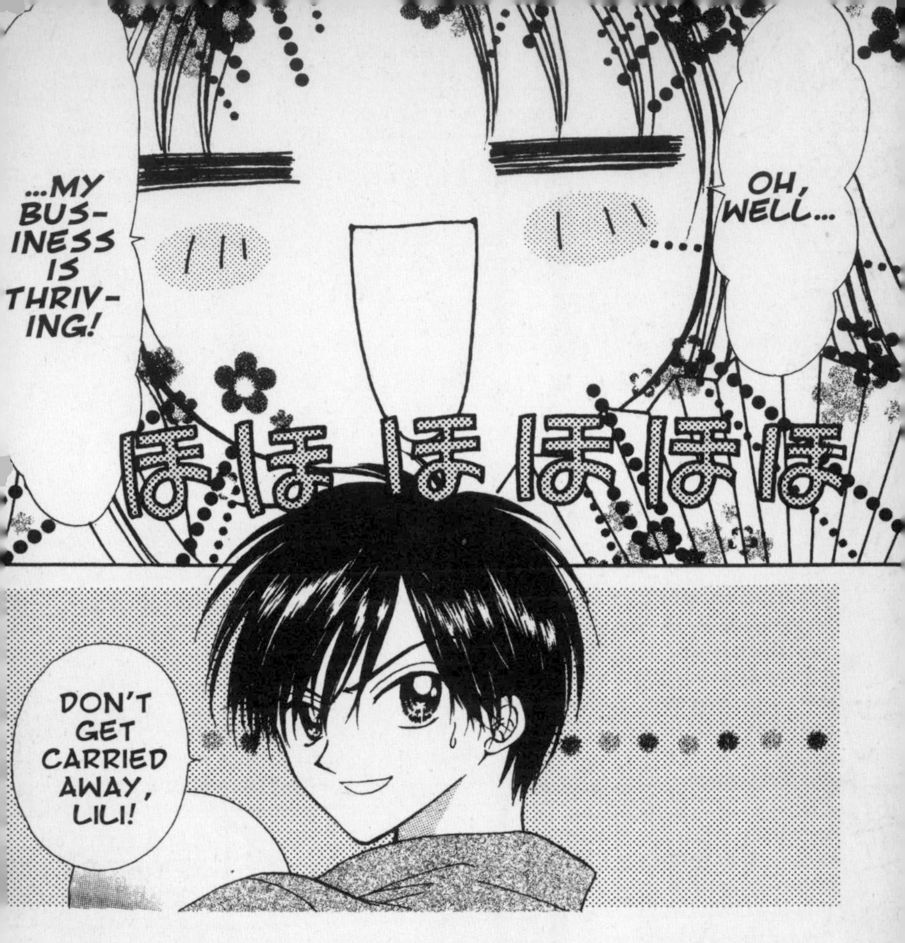
OH, WELL...
...MY BUSINESS IS THRIVING!
ほほほほほほ
DON'T GET CARRIED AWAY, LILI!

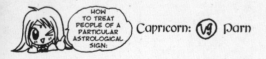

ademoiselle Lili's Astrology (7)

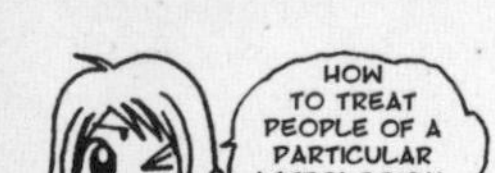
HOW TO TREAT PEOPLE OF A PARTICULAR ASTROLOGICAL SIGN:

Capricorn: ♑ Parn

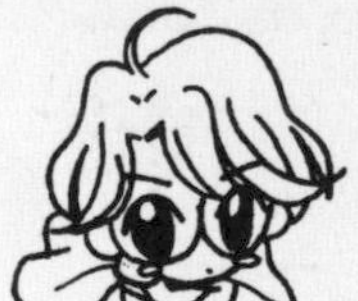

e day, Priest Parn was attacked by a monster. He tried to escape into a er by turning into a fish. However, he was in such a hurry that his nsformation didn't work quite right. He ended up being half-fish and half-it. Priest Parn is named after this character. He's always proper and ponsible. He appears formal, but he's really sweet. Capricorns are often e bloomers. Capricorn boys tend to keep their emotions deep inside and d it hard to confess their love. The Capricorn can be bitter and sarcastic vards girls he's attracted to.

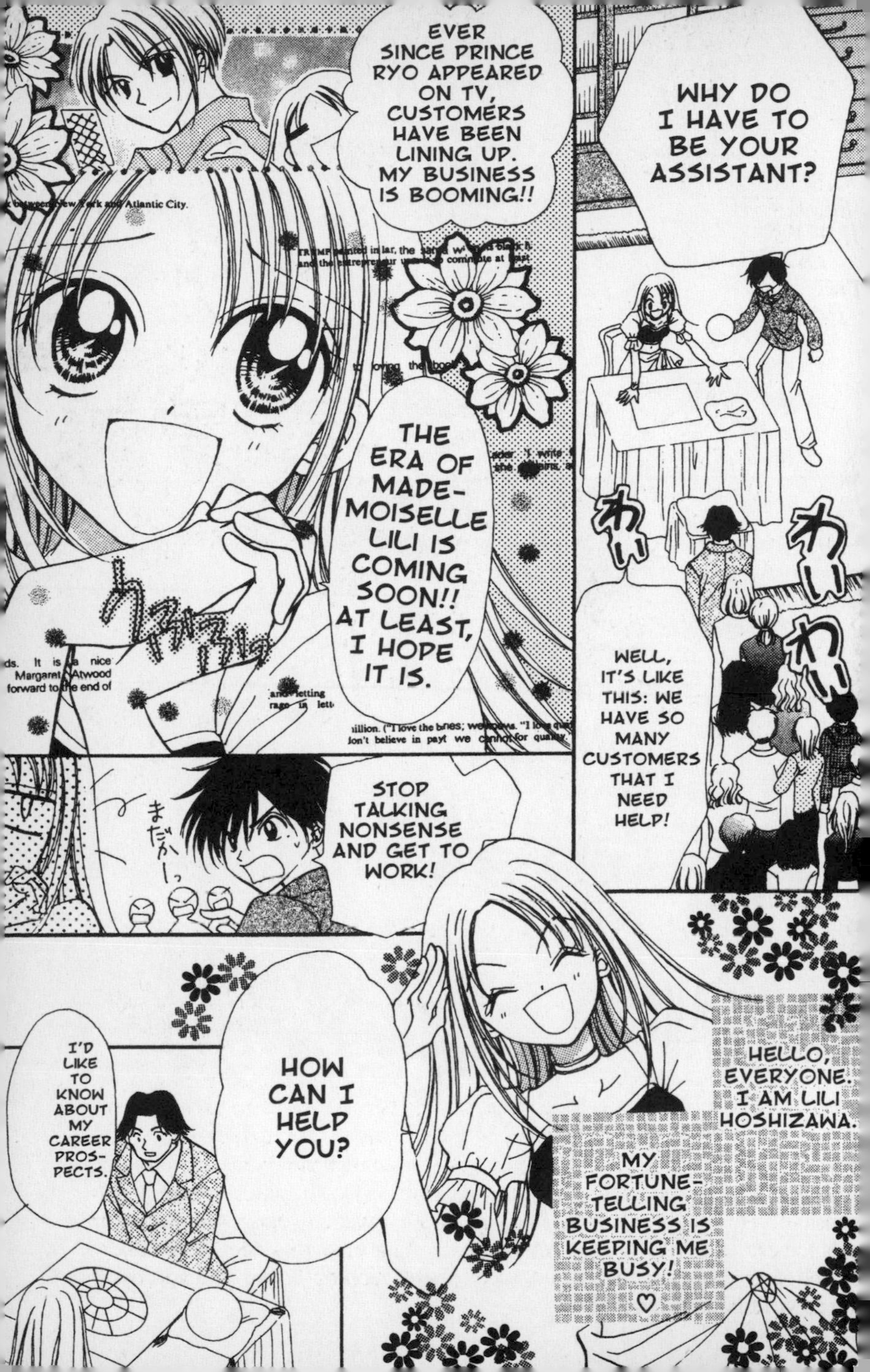

WHY DO I HAVE TO BE YOUR ASSISTANT?
わい わい
WELL, IT'S LIKE THIS: WE HAVE SO MANY CUSTOMERS THAT I NEED HELP!
EVER SINCE PRINCE RYO APPEARED ON TV, CUSTOMERS HAVE BEEN LINING UP. MY BUSINESS IS BOOMING!!
THE ERA OF MADE-MOISELLE LILI IS COMING SOON!! AT LEAST, I HOPE IT IS.
STOP TALKING NONSENSE AND GET TO WORK!
またかーっ
HELLO, EVERYONE. I AM LILI HOSHIZAWA.
MY FORTUNE-TELLING BUSINESS IS KEEPING ME BUSY! ♡
HOW CAN I HELP YOU?
I'D LIKE TO KNOW ABOUT MY CAREER PROS-PECTS.

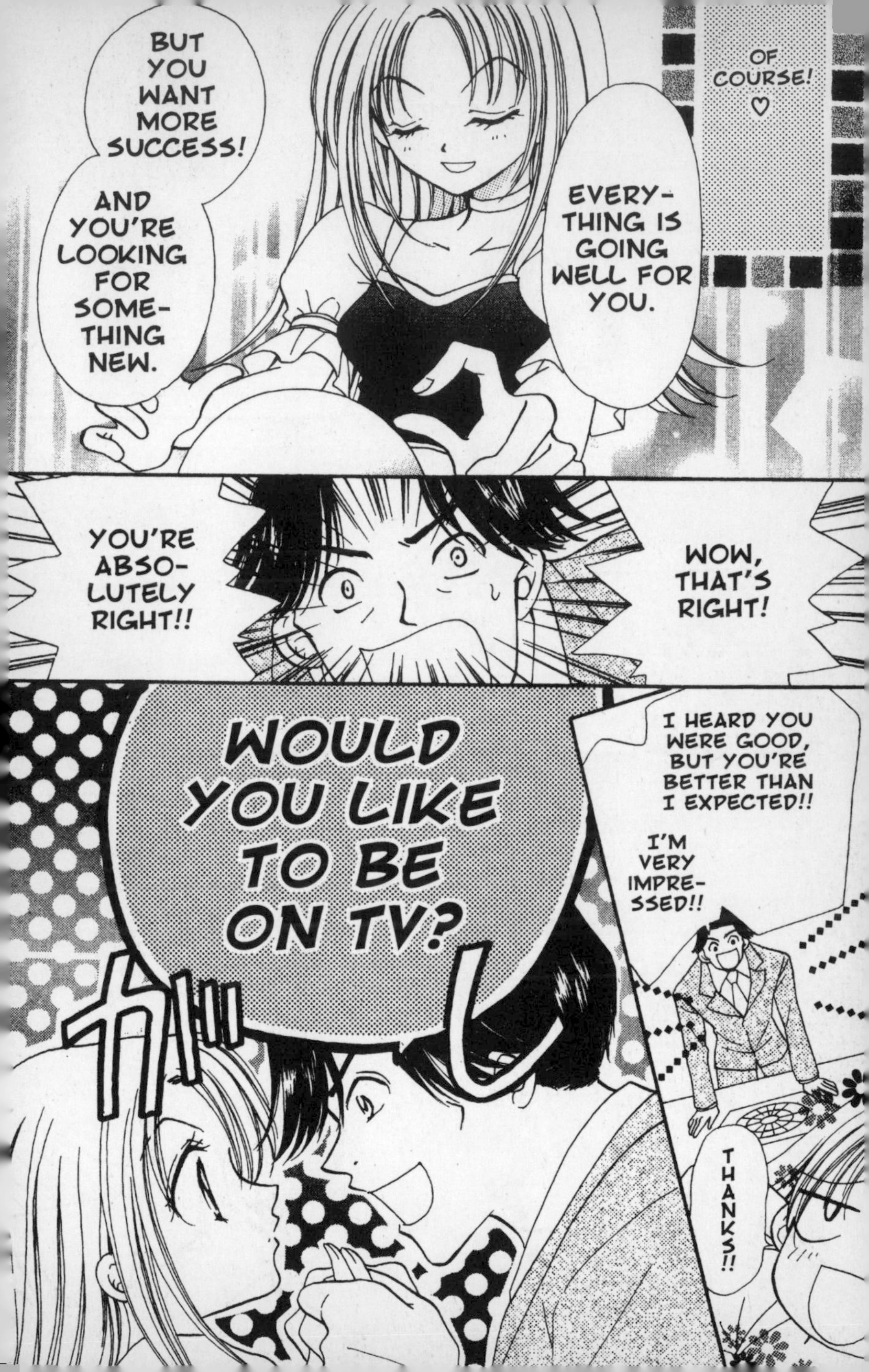
OF COURSE! ♡
EVERY-THING IS GOING WELL FOR YOU.
BUT YOU WANT MORE SUCCESS!
AND YOU'RE LOOKING FOR SOME-THING NEW.
WOW, THAT'S RIGHT!
YOU'RE ABSO-LUTELY RIGHT!!
I HEARD YOU WERE GOOD, BUT YOU'RE BETTER THAN I EXPECTED!!
I'M VERY IMPRE-SSED!!
THANKS!!
WOULD YOU LIKE TO BE ON TV?

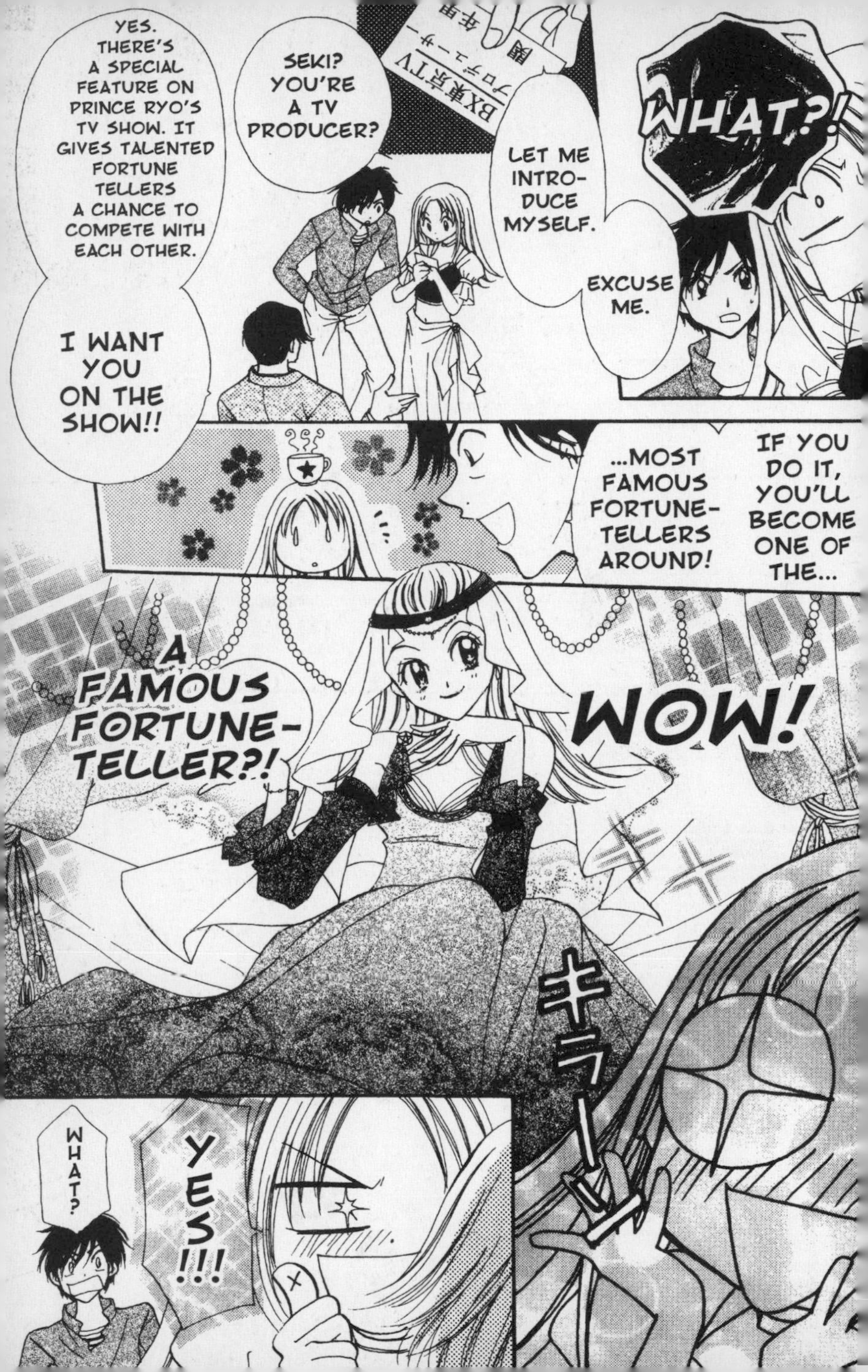
WHAT?!
EXCUSE ME.
LET ME INTRODUCE MYSELF.
BX東京TV
プロデューサー
SEKI? YOU'RE A TV PRODUCER?
YES. THERE'S A SPECIAL FEATURE ON PRINCE RYO'S TV SHOW. IT GIVES TALENTED FORTUNE TELLERS A CHANCE TO COMPETE WITH EACH OTHER.
I WANT YOU ON THE SHOW!!
IF YOU DO IT, YOU'LL BECOME ONE OF THE...
...MOST FAMOUS FORTUNE-TELLERS AROUND!
WOW!
A FAMOUS FORTUNE-TELLER?!
キラーン
YES!!!
WHAT?

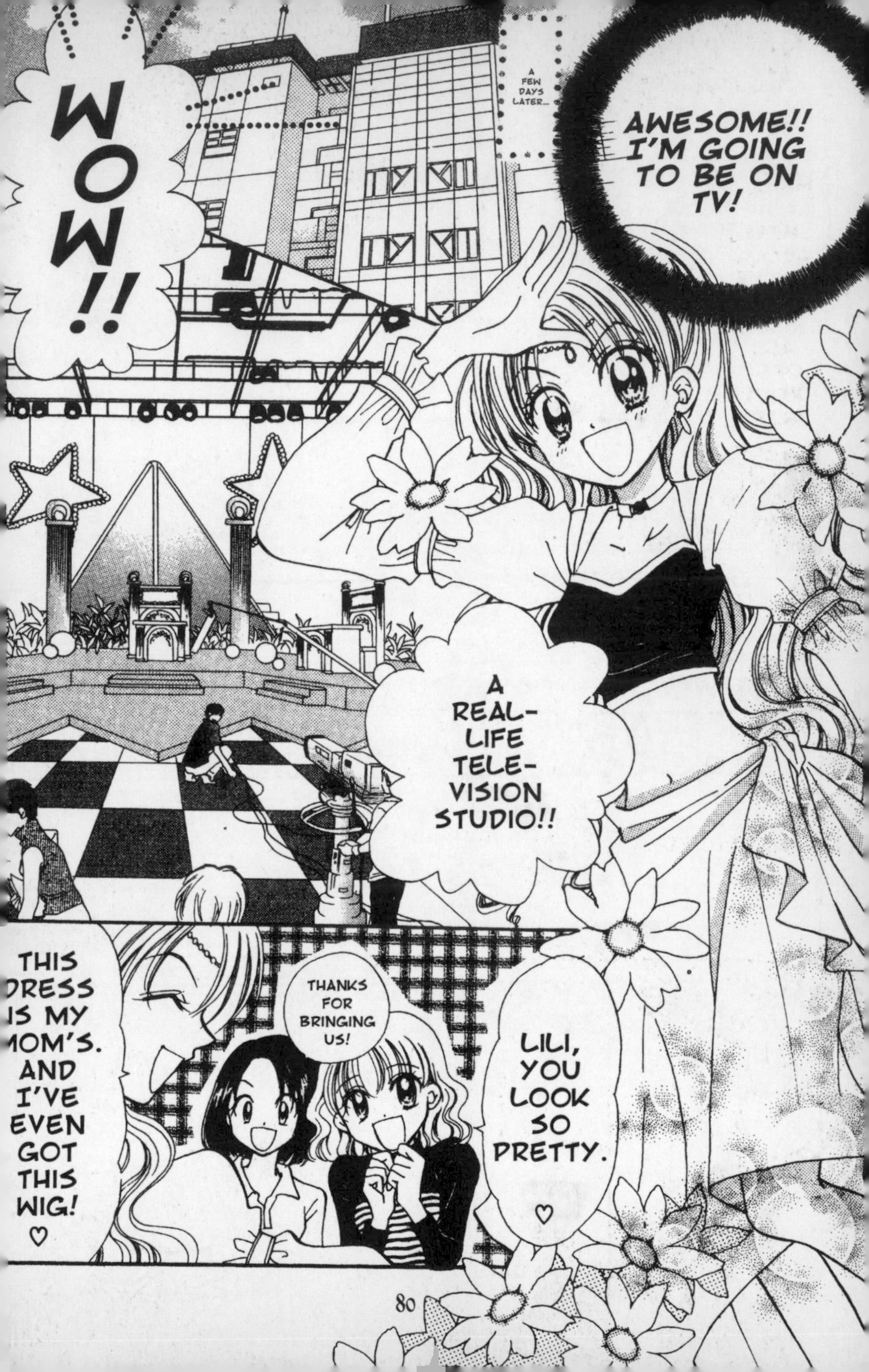
AWESOME!! I'M GOING TO BE ON TV!
A FEW DAYS LATER...
WOW!!
A REAL-LIFE TELE-VISION STUDIO!!
LILI, YOU LOOK SO PRETTY. ♡
THANKS FOR BRINGING US!
THIS DRESS IS MY MOM'S. AND I'VE EVEN GOT THIS WIG! ♡

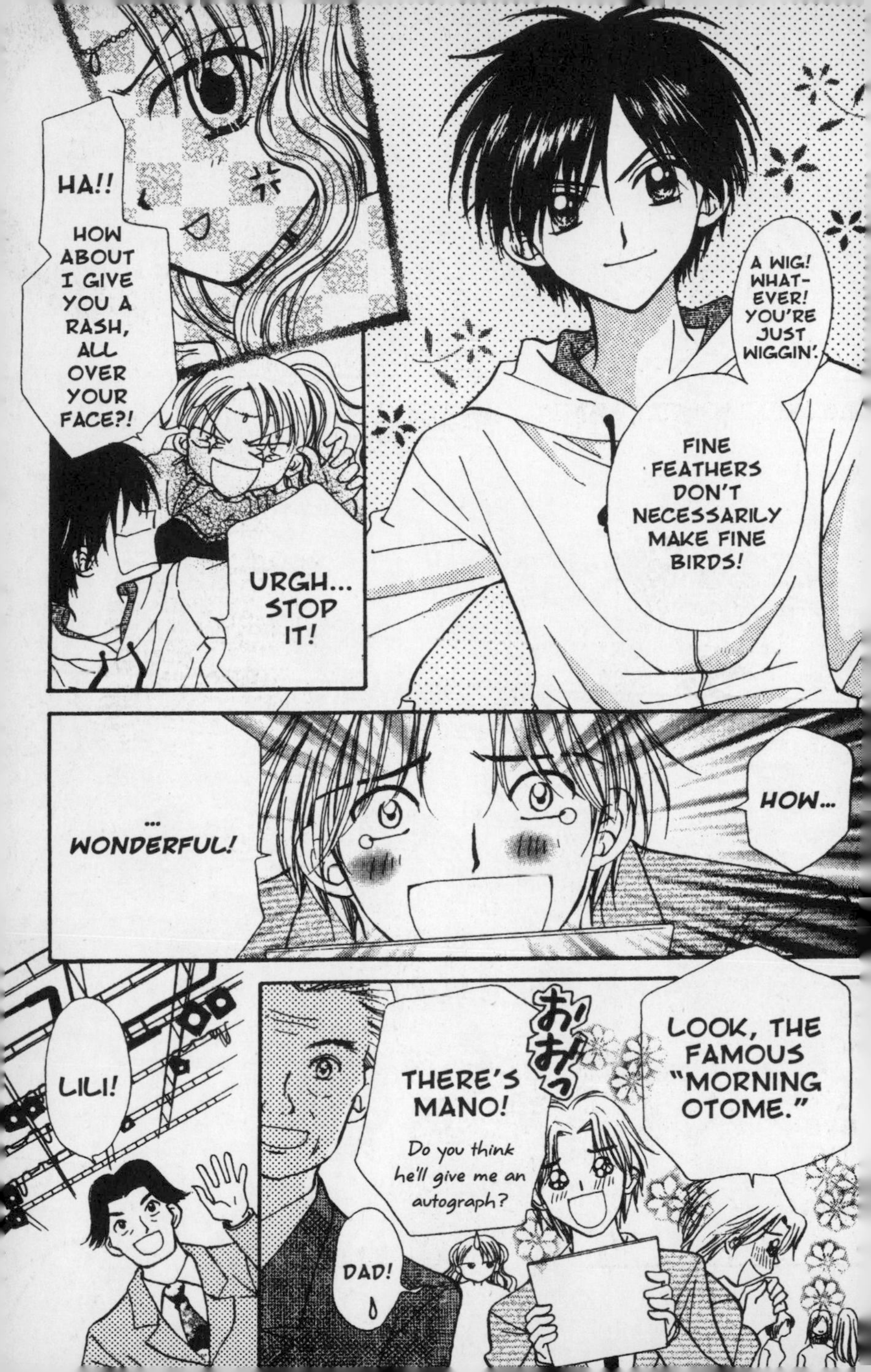
A WIG! WHATEVER! YOU'RE JUST WIGGIN'.
FINE FEATHERS DON'T NECESSARILY MAKE FINE BIRDS!
HA!!
HOW ABOUT I GIVE YOU A RASH, ALL OVER YOUR FACE?!
URGH... STOP IT!
HOW...
...WONDERFUL!
LOOK, THE FAMOUS "MORNING OTOME."
おおっ
THERE'S MANO!
Do you think he'll give me an autograph?
DAD!
LILI!

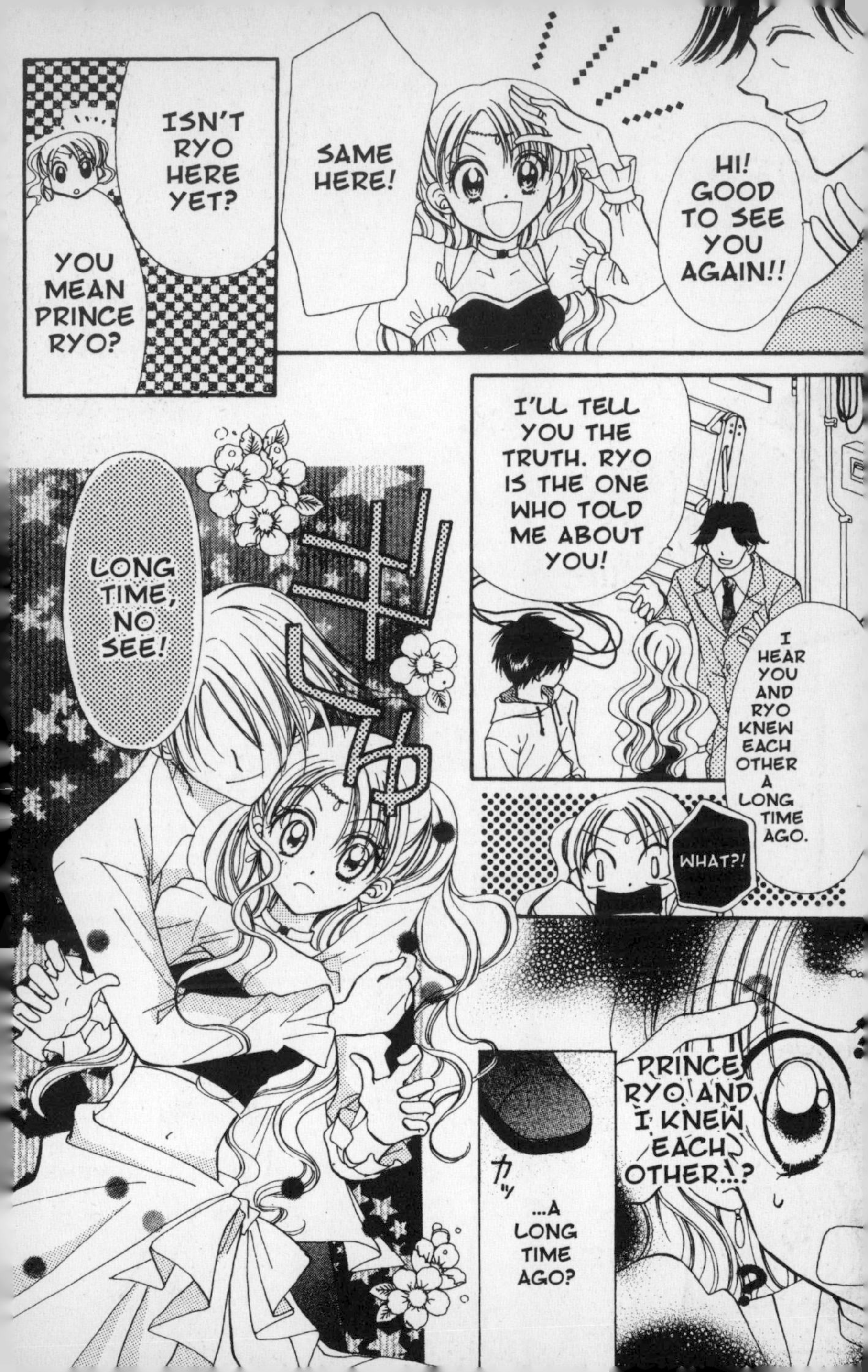
HI! GOOD TO SEE YOU AGAIN!!
SAME HERE!
ISN'T RYO HERE YET?
YOU MEAN PRINCE RYO?
I'LL TELL YOU THE TRUTH. RYO IS THE ONE WHO TOLD ME ABOUT YOU!
I HEAR YOU AND RYO KNEW EACH OTHER A LONG TIME AGO.
WHAT?!
PRINCE RYO AND I KNEW EACH OTHER...?
カッ
...A LONG TIME AGO?
LONG TIME, NO SEE!

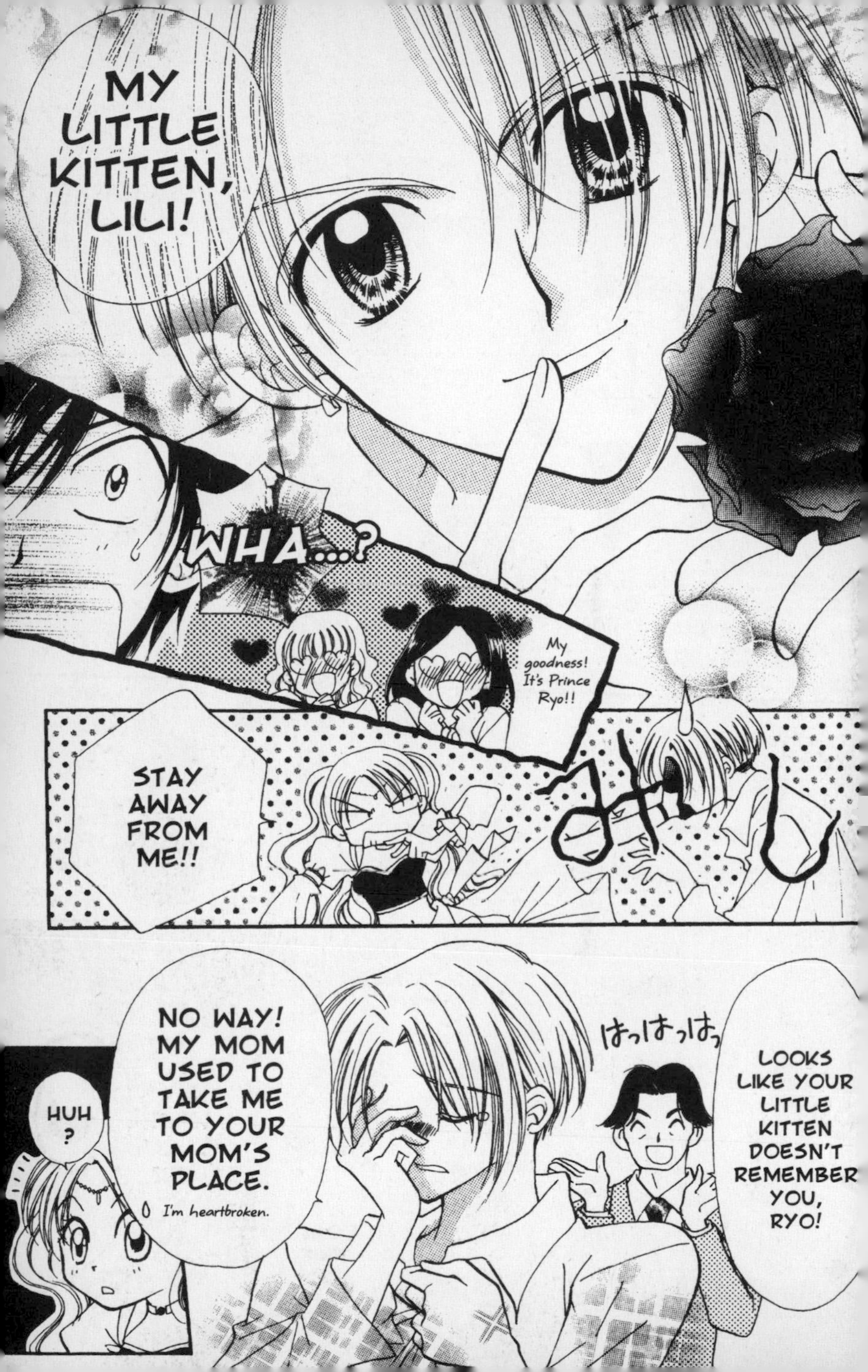
MY LITTLE KITTEN, LILI!
WHA...?
My goodness! It's Prince Ryo!!
STAY AWAY FROM ME!!
LOOKS LIKE YOUR LITTLE KITTEN DOESN'T REMEMBER YOU, RYO!
はっはっはっ
NO WAY! MY MOM USED TO TAKE ME TO YOUR MOM'S PLACE.
I'm heartbroken.
HUH?

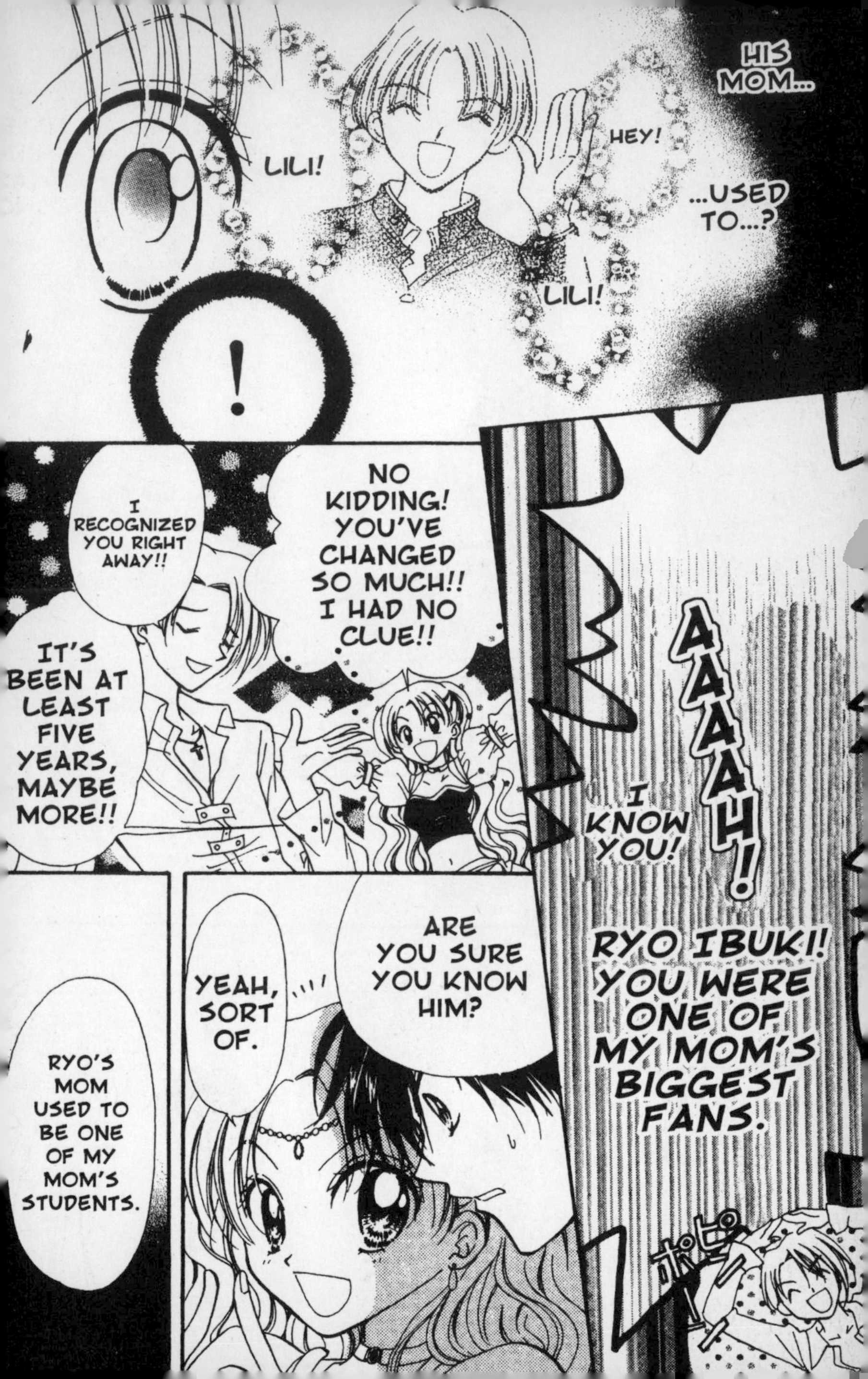
HIS MOM...
...USED TO...?
HEY!
LILI!
LILI!
!
AAAAH!
I KNOW YOU!
RYO IBUKI! YOU WERE ONE OF MY MOM'S BIGGEST FANS.
ポピ
NO KIDDING! YOU'VE CHANGED SO MUCH!! I HAD NO CLUE!!
I RECOGNIZED YOU RIGHT AWAY!!
IT'S BEEN AT LEAST FIVE YEARS, MAYBE MORE!!
ARE YOU SURE YOU KNOW HIM?
YEAH, SORT OF.
RYO'S MOM USED TO BE ONE OF MY MOM'S STUDENTS.

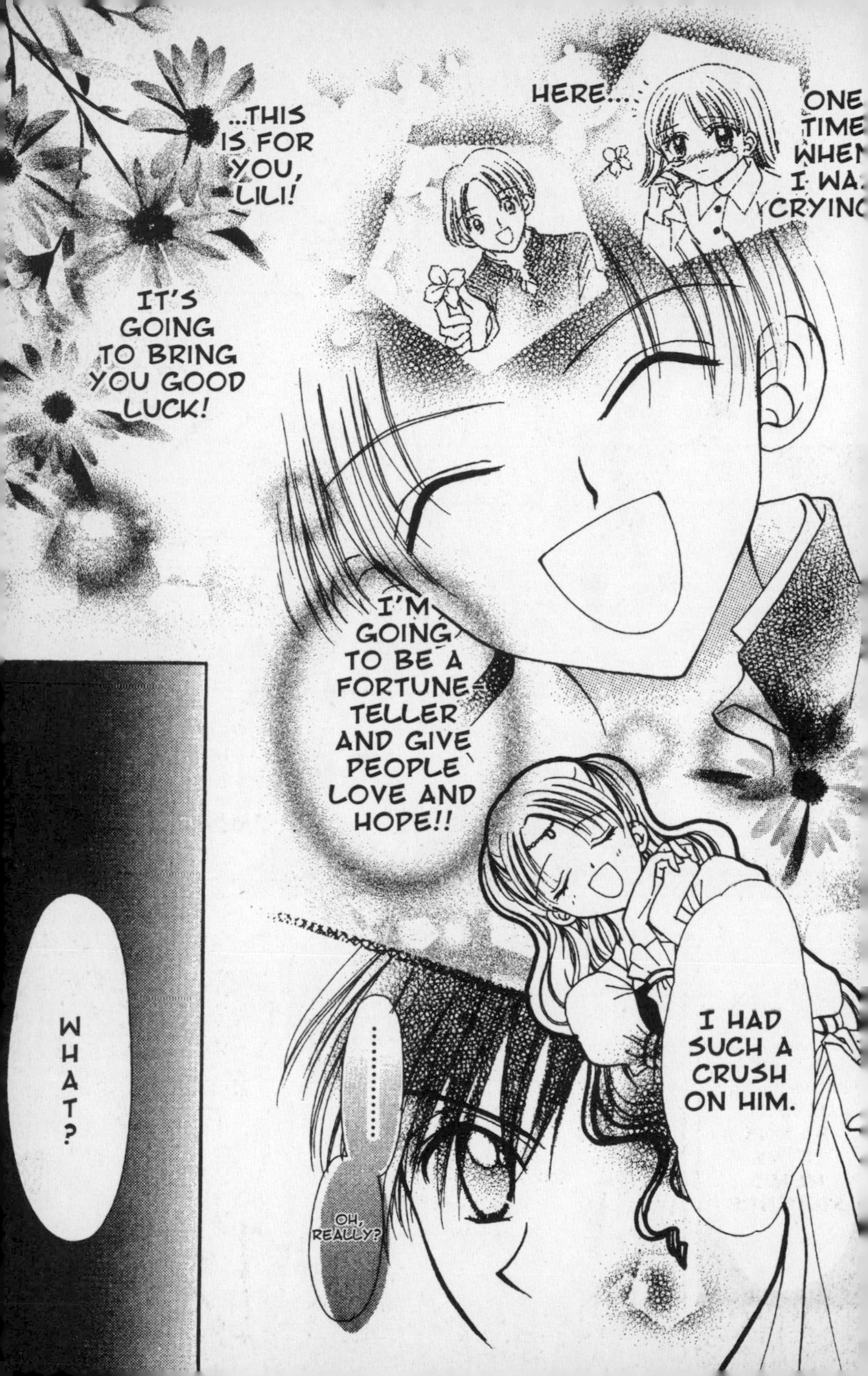
ONE TIME WHEN I WA CRYIN
HERE...
...THIS IS FOR YOU, LILI!
IT'S GOING TO BRING YOU GOOD LUCK!
I'M GOING TO BE A FORTUNE-TELLER AND GIVE PEOPLE LOVE AND HOPE!!
I HAD SUCH A CRUSH ON HIM.
......
OH, REALLY?
WHAT?

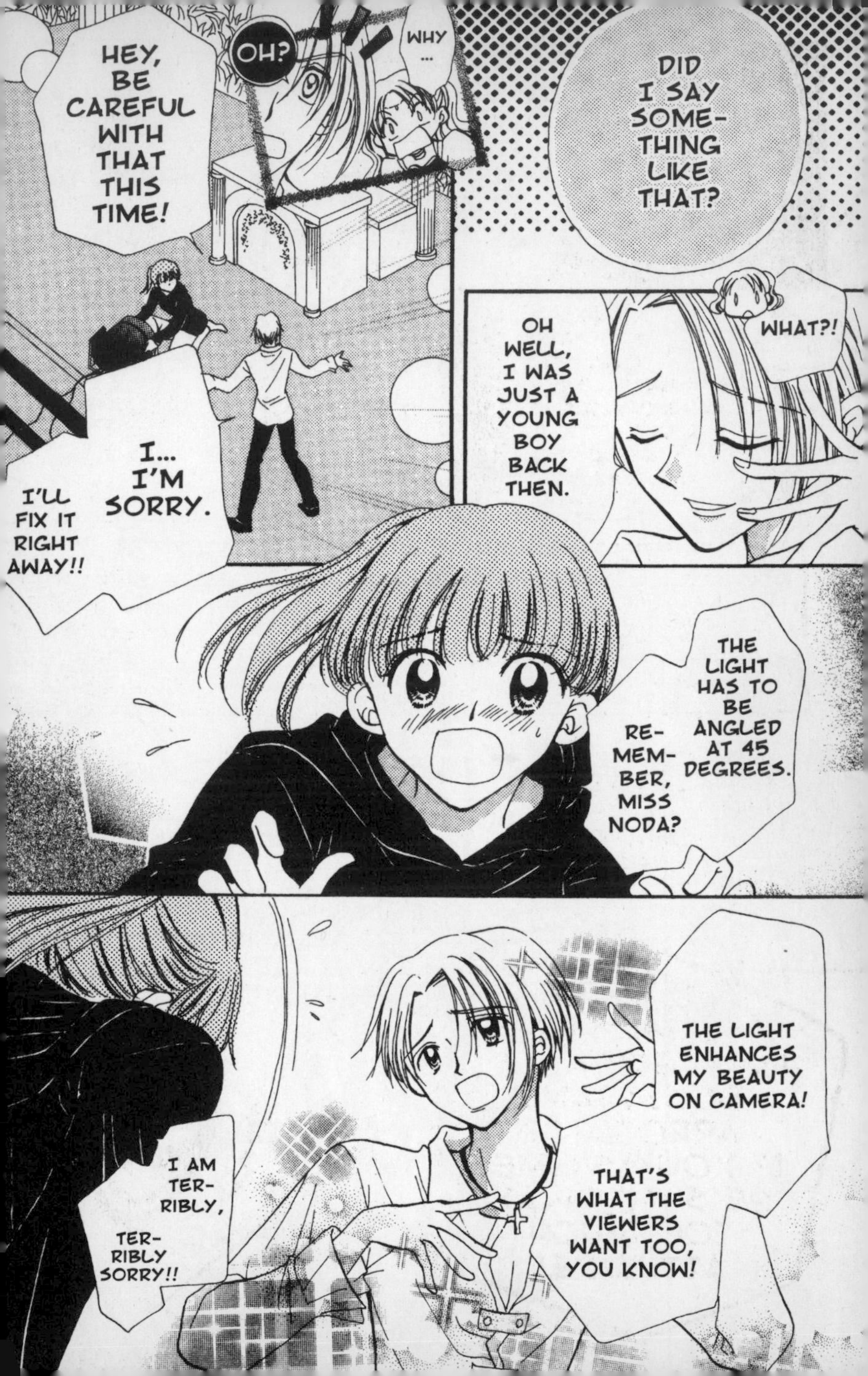
DID I SAY SOMETHING LIKE THAT?
WHAT?!
OH WELL, I WAS JUST A YOUNG BOY BACK THEN.
OH?
WHY...
HEY, BE CAREFUL WITH THAT THIS TIME!
I... I'M SORRY.
I'LL FIX IT RIGHT AWAY!!
THE LIGHT HAS TO BE ANGLED AT 45 DEGREES.
REMEMBER, MISS NODA?
THE LIGHT ENHANCES MY BEAUTY ON CAMERA!
THAT'S WHAT THE VIEWERS WANT TOO, YOU KNOW!
I AM TERRIBLY, TERRIBLY SORRY!!

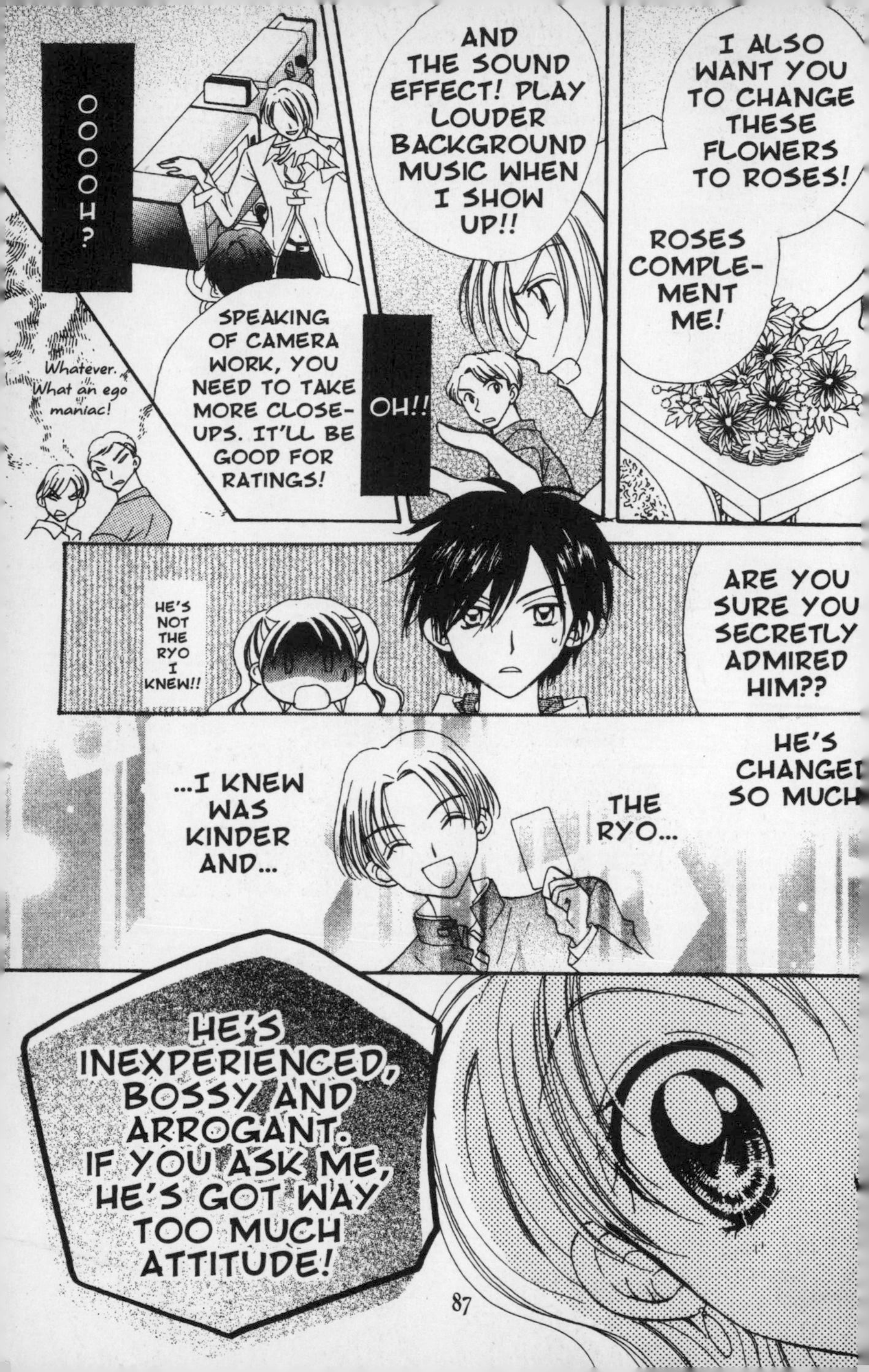
I ALSO WANT YOU TO CHANGE THESE FLOWERS TO ROSES!
ROSES COMPLEMENT ME!
AND THE SOUND EFFECT! PLAY LOUDER BACKGROUND MUSIC WHEN I SHOW UP!!
OH!!
SPEAKING OF CAMERA WORK, YOU NEED TO TAKE MORE CLOSE-UPS. IT'LL BE GOOD FOR RATINGS!
OOOOOH?
Whatever. What an ego maniac!
ARE YOU SURE YOU SECRETLY ADMIRED HIM??
HE'S NOT THE RYO I KNEW!!
HE'S CHANGED SO MUCH
THE RYO...
...I KNEW WAS KINDER AND...
HE'S INEXPERIENCED, BOSSY AND ARROGANT. IF YOU ASK ME, HE'S GOT WAY TOO MUCH ATTITUDE!

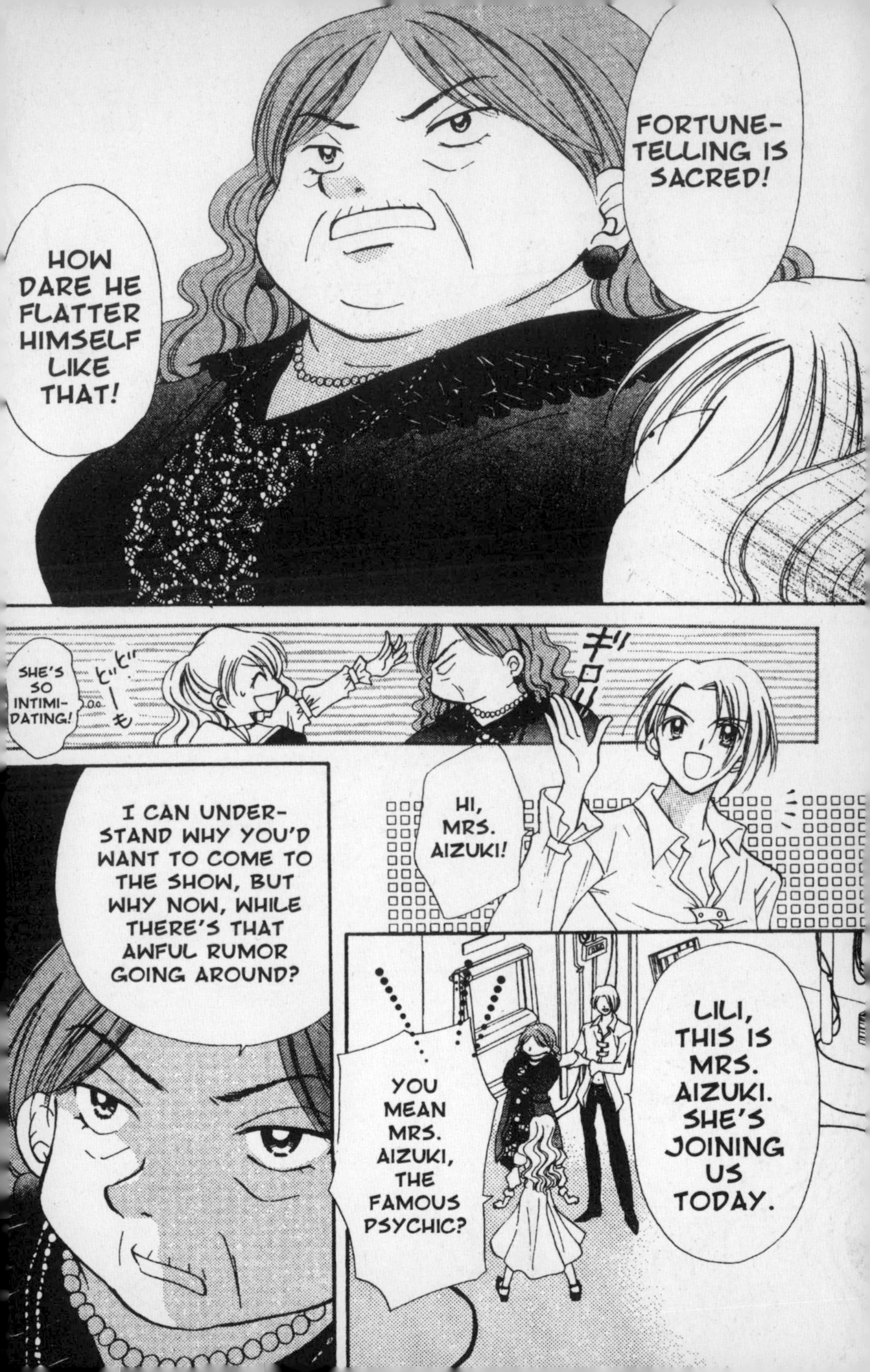
FORTUNE-TELLING IS SACRED!
HOW DARE HE FLATTER HIMSELF LIKE THAT!
ギロッ
SHE'S SO INTIMIDATING!
HI, MRS. AIZUKI!
LILI, THIS IS MRS. AIZUKI. SHE'S JOINING US TODAY.
YOU MEAN MRS. AIZUKI, THE FAMOUS PSYCHIC?
I CAN UNDERSTAND WHY YOU'D WANT TO COME TO THE SHOW, BUT WHY NOW, WHILE THERE'S THAT AWFUL RUMOR GOING AROUND?

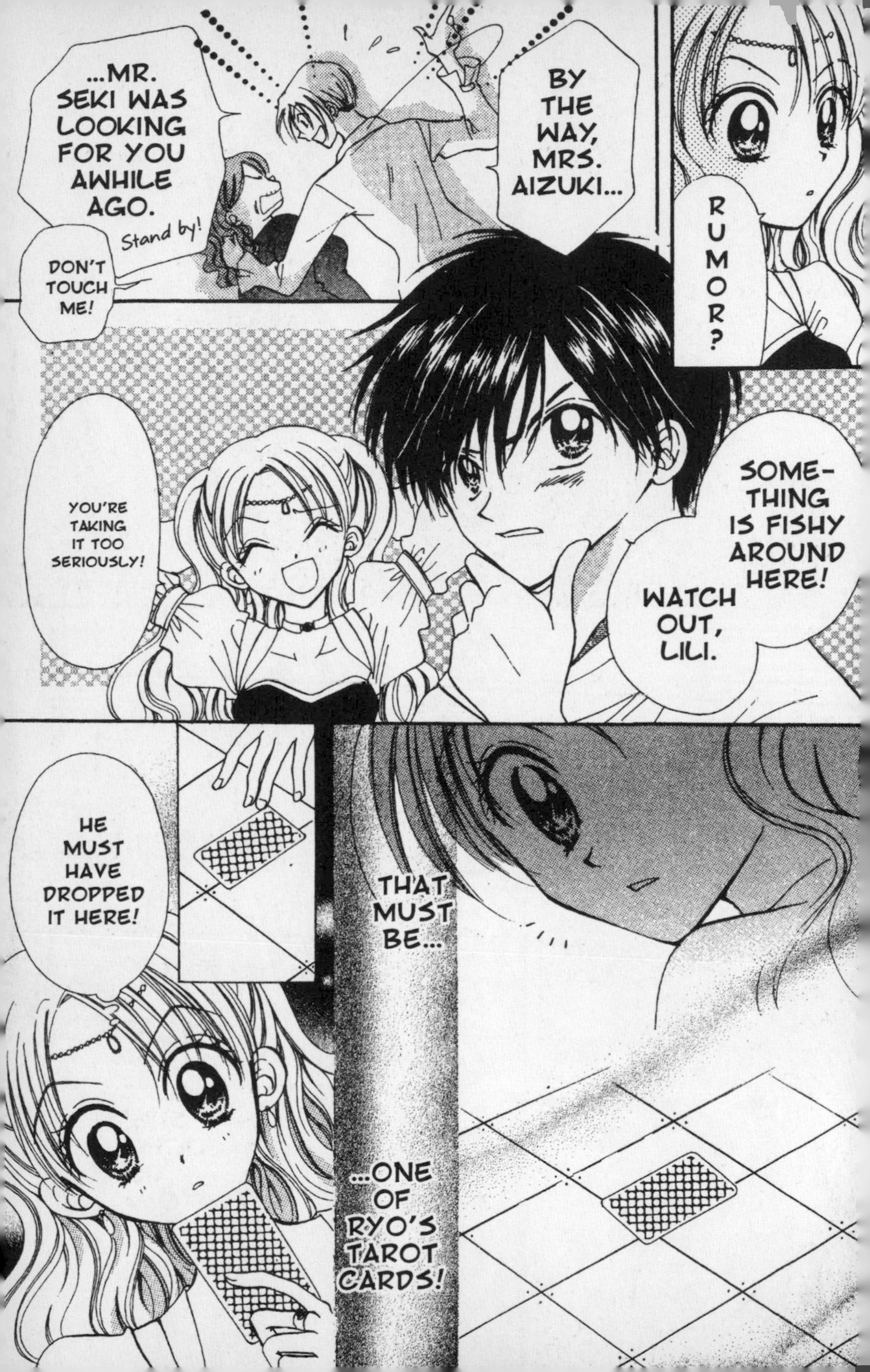
RUMOR?
BY THE WAY, MRS. AIZUKI...
...MR. SEKI WAS LOOKING FOR YOU AWHILE AGO.
Stand by!
DON'T TOUCH ME!
SOME-THING IS FISHY AROUND HERE!
WATCH OUT, LILI.
YOU'RE TAKING IT TOO SERIOUSLY!
THAT MUST BE...
...ONE OF RYO'S TAROT CARDS!
HE MUST HAVE DROPPED IT HERE!

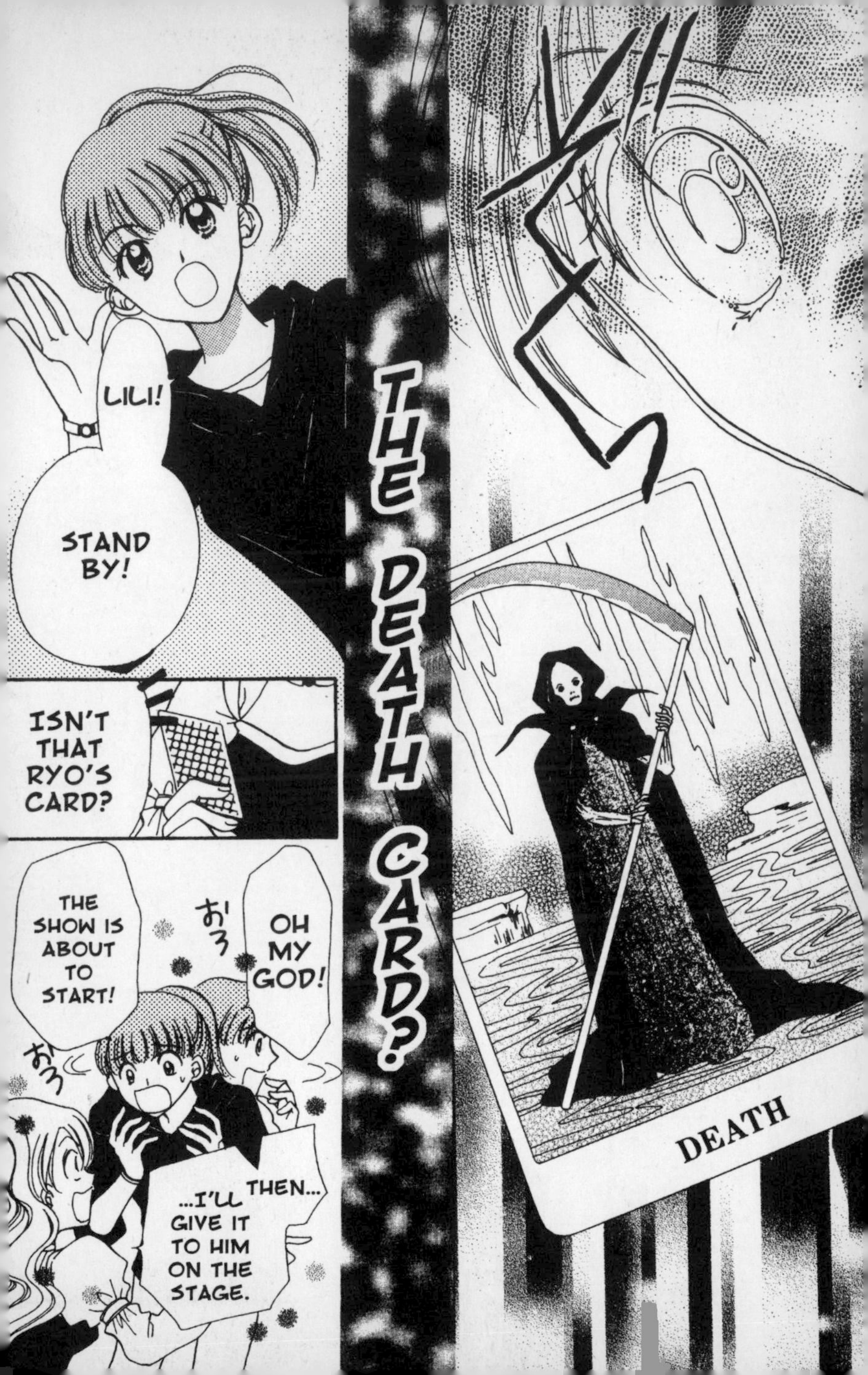

DEATH
THE DEATH CARD?
LILI!
STAND BY!
ISN'T THAT RYO'S CARD?
OH MY GOD!
おろ
THE SHOW IS ABOUT TO START!
おろ
THEN...
...I'LL GIVE IT TO HIM ON THE STAGE.

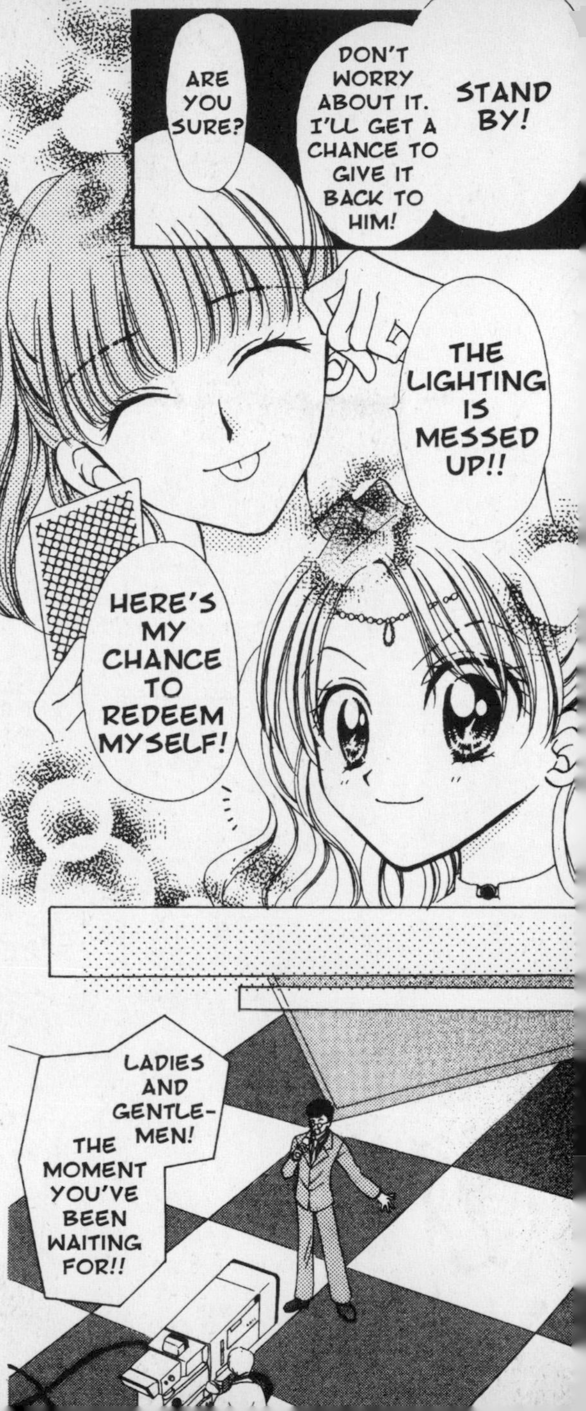
STAND BY!
DON'T WORRY ABOUT IT. I'LL GET A CHANCE TO GIVE IT BACK TO HIM!
ARE YOU SURE?
THE LIGHTING IS MESSED UP!!
HERE'S MY CHANCE TO REDEEM MYSELF!
LADIES AND GENTLEMEN!
THE MOMENT YOU'VE BEEN WAITING FOR!!

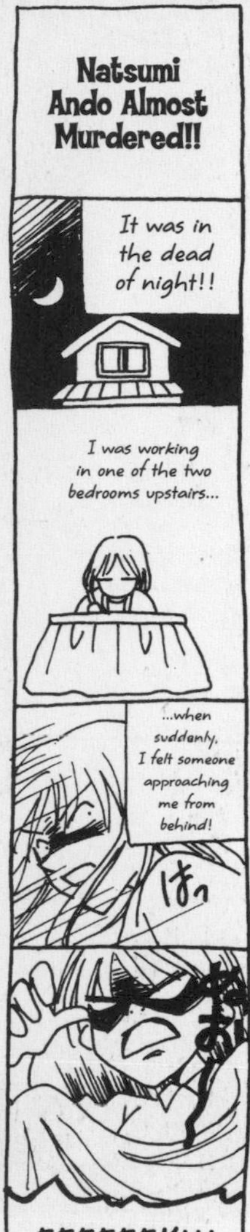
Natsumi Ando Almost Murdered!!
It was in the dead of night!!
I was working in one of the two bedrooms upstairs...
...when suddenly, I felt someone approaching me from behind!
EEEEEEK!!!
My sister was supposed to be sleeping in the other room!
Is Ando in danger?!
(To be continued.)

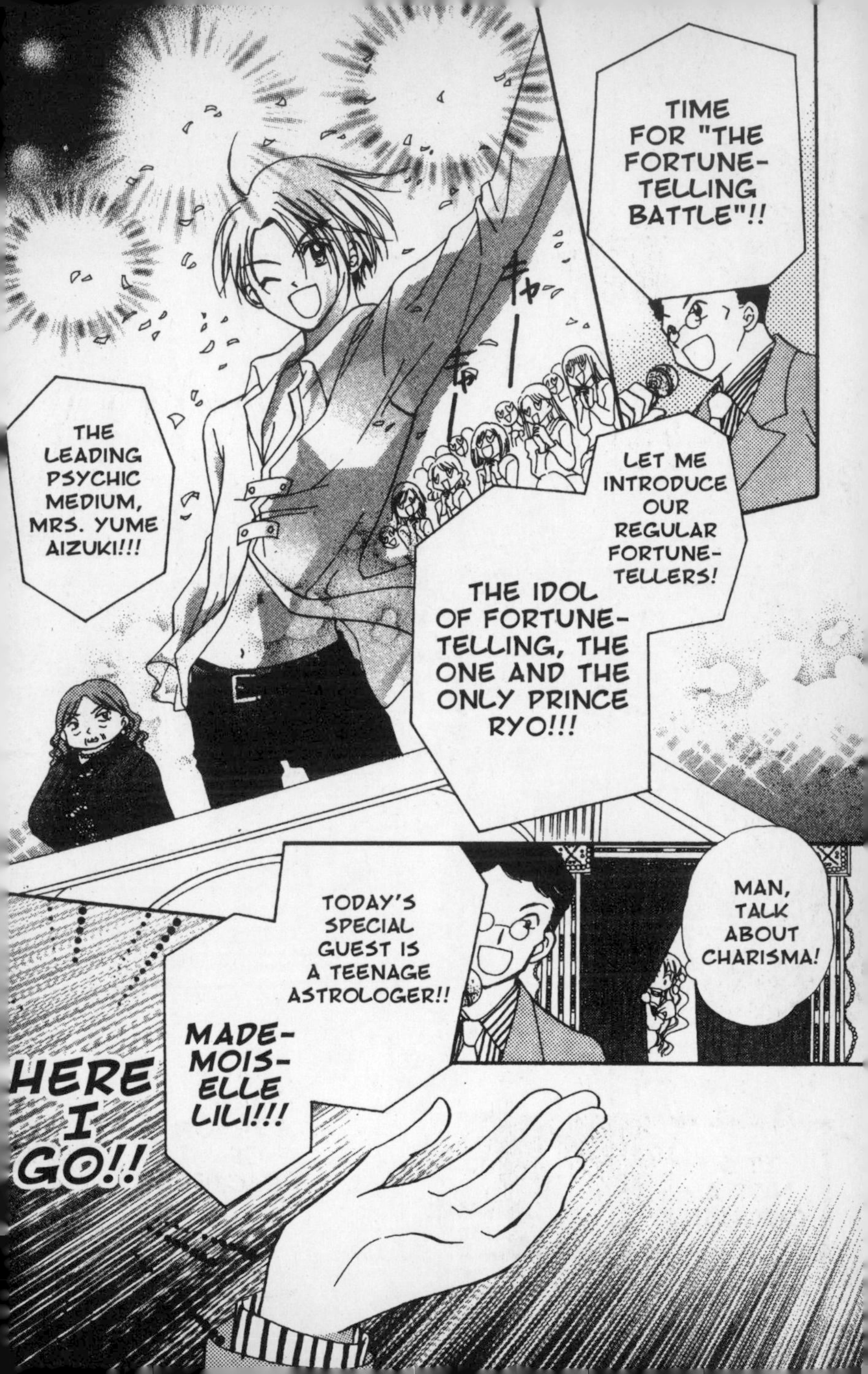
TIME FOR "THE FORTUNE-TELLING BATTLE"!!
キャー
キャー
LET ME INTRODUCE OUR REGULAR FORTUNE-TELLERS!
THE IDOL OF FORTUNE-TELLING, THE ONE AND THE ONLY PRINCE RYO!!!
THE LEADING PSYCHIC MEDIUM, MRS. YUME AIZUKI!!!
MAN, TALK ABOUT CHARISMA!
TODAY'S SPECIAL GUEST IS A TEENAGE ASTROLOGER!!
MADE-MOIS-ELLE LILI!!!
HERE I GO!!

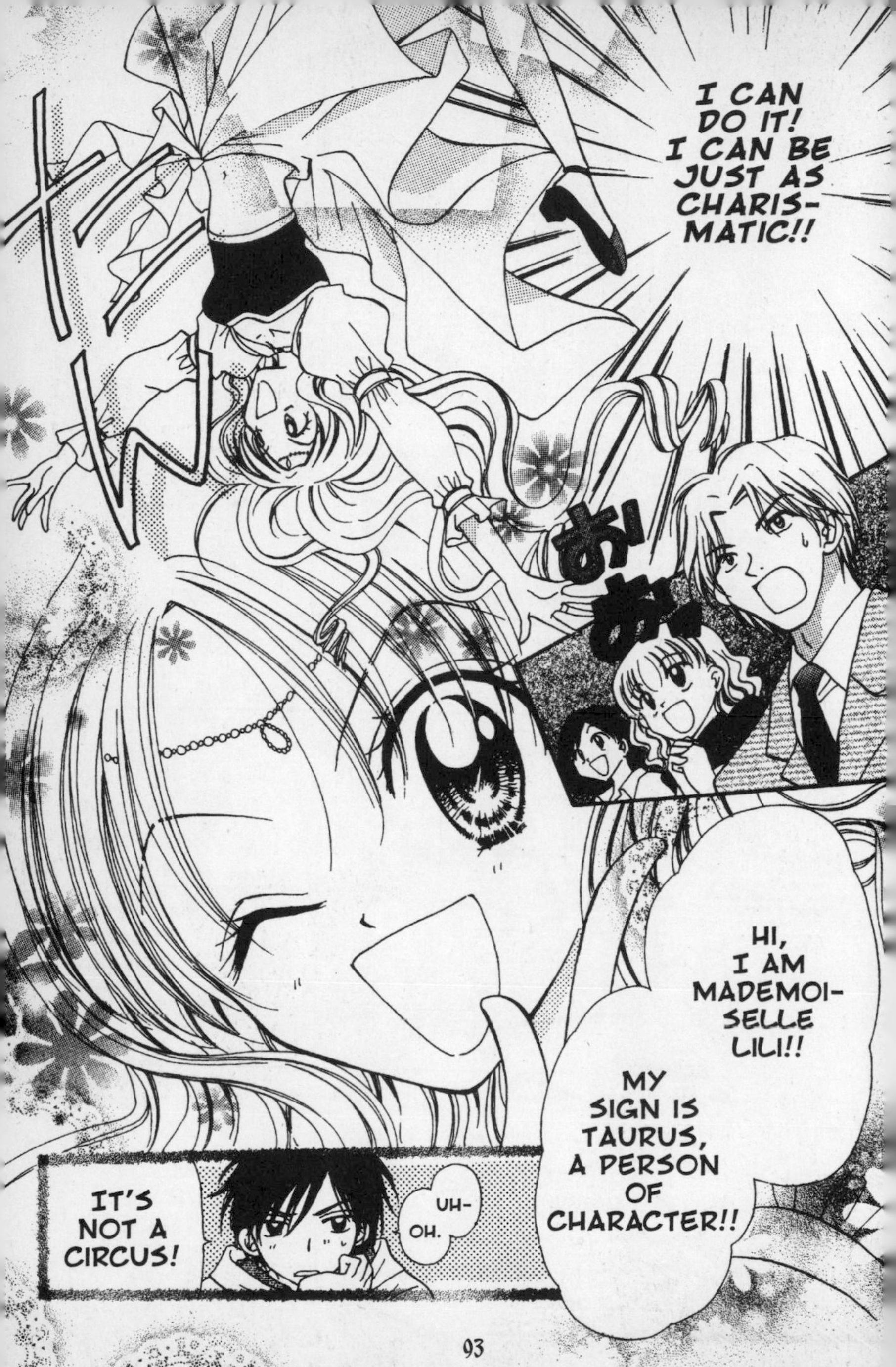
I CAN DO IT! I CAN BE JUST AS CHARIS-MATIC!!
おお
HI, I AM MADEMOI-SELLE LILI!!
MY SIGN IS TAURUS, A PERSON OF CHARACTER!!
UH-OH.
IT'S NOT A CIRCUS!

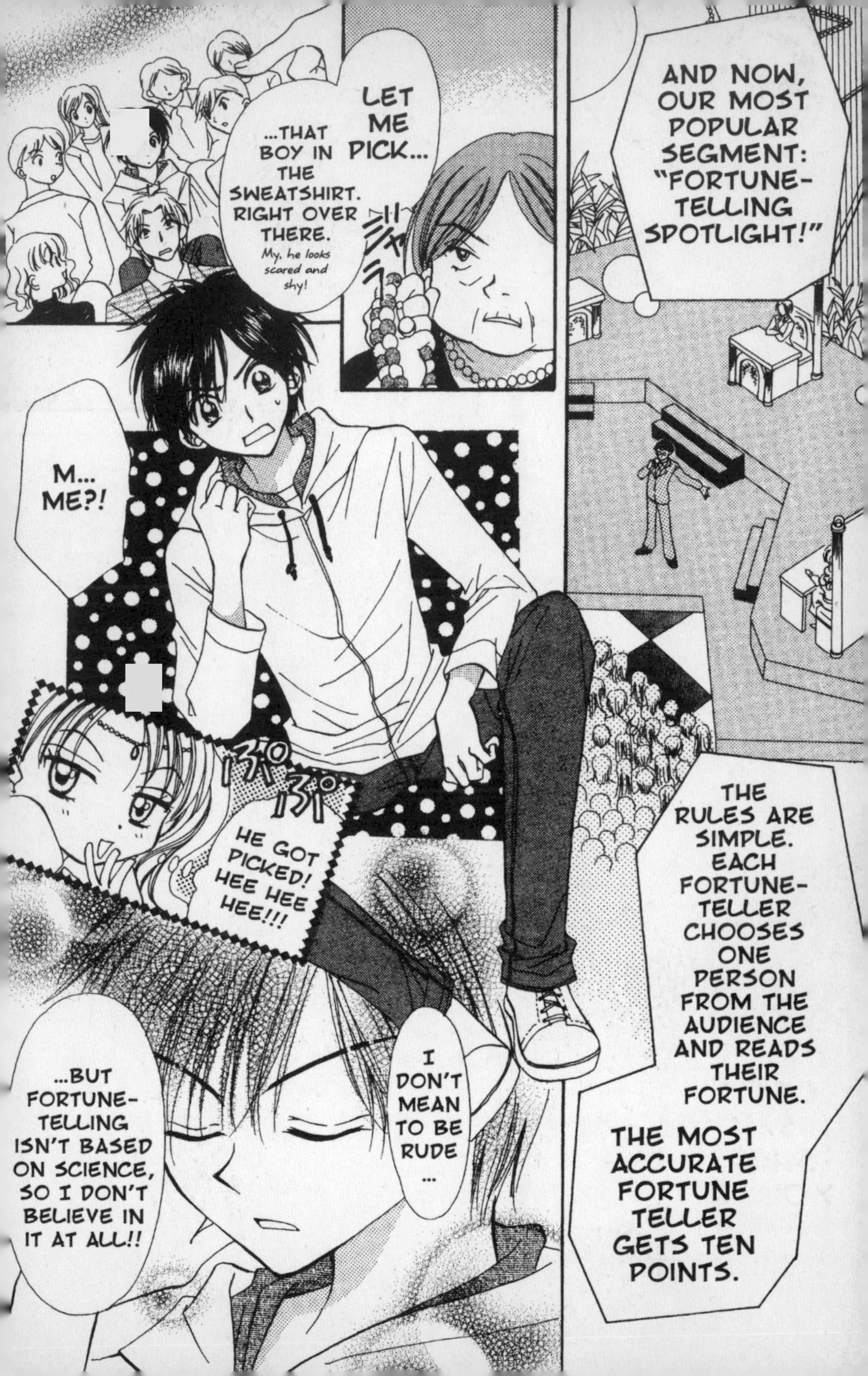

AND NOW, OUR MOST POPULAR SEGMENT: "FORTUNE-TELLING SPOTLIGHT!"
THE RULES ARE SIMPLE. EACH FORTUNE-TELLER CHOOSES ONE PERSON FROM THE AUDIENCE AND READS THEIR FORTUNE.
THE MOST ACCURATE FORTUNE TELLER GETS TEN POINTS.
LET ME PICK...
...THAT BOY IN THE SWEATSHIRT. RIGHT OVER THERE.
My, he looks scared and shy!
M... ME?!
HE GOT PICKED! HEE HEE HEE!!!
I DON'T MEAN TO BE RUDE ...
...BUT FORTUNE-TELLING ISN'T BASED ON SCIENCE, SO I DON'T BELIEVE IN IT AT ALL!!

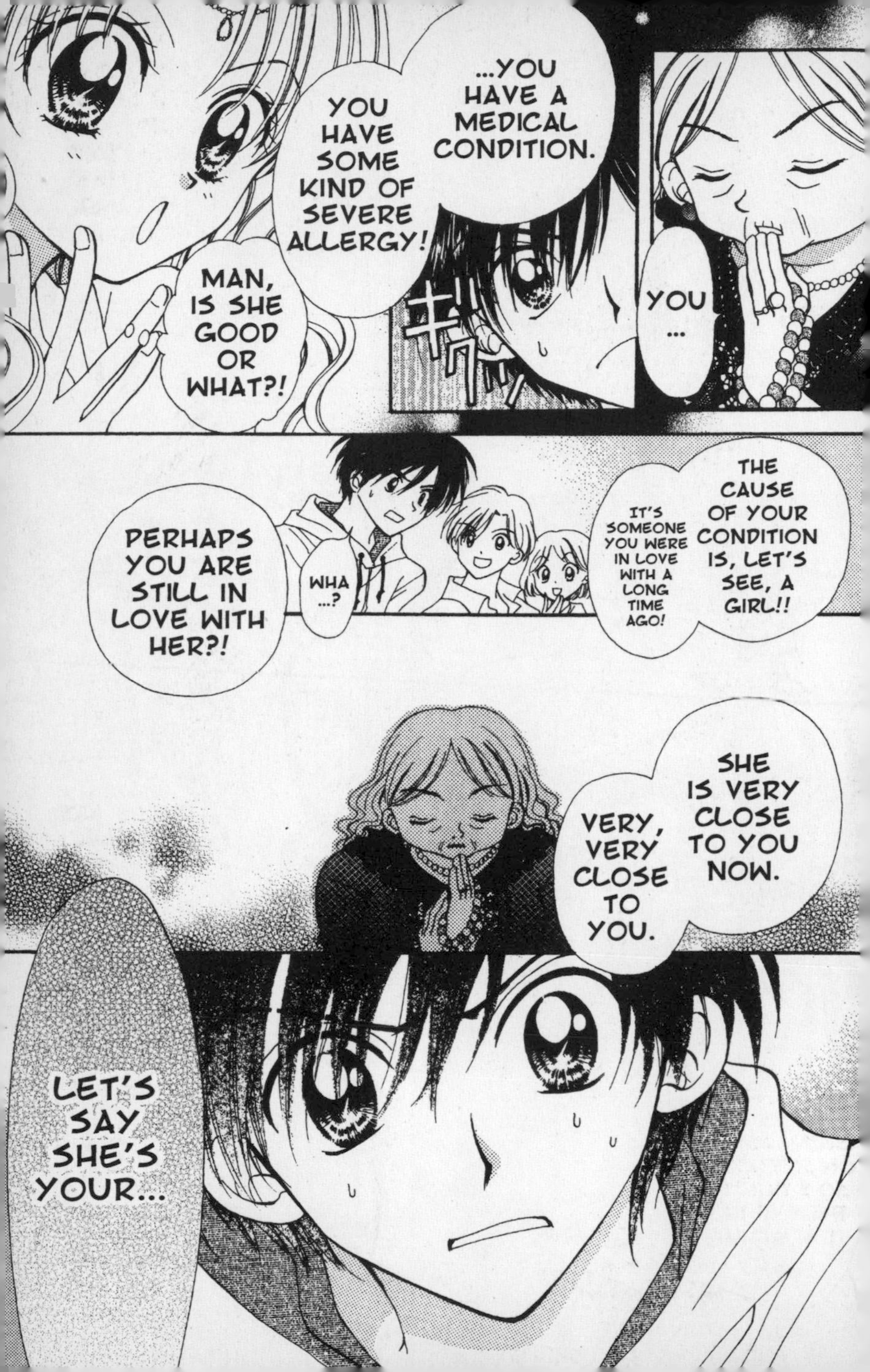
YOU ...
...YOU HAVE A MEDICAL CONDITION.
YOU HAVE SOME KIND OF SEVERE ALLERGY!
MAN, IS SHE GOOD OR WHAT?!
THE CAUSE OF YOUR CONDITION IS, LET'S SEE, A GIRL!!
IT'S SOMEONE YOU WERE IN LOVE WITH A LONG TIME AGO!
WHA ...?
PERHAPS YOU ARE STILL IN LOVE WITH HER?!
SHE IS VERY CLOSE TO YOU NOW.
VERY, VERY CLOSE TO YOU.
LET'S SAY SHE'S YOUR...

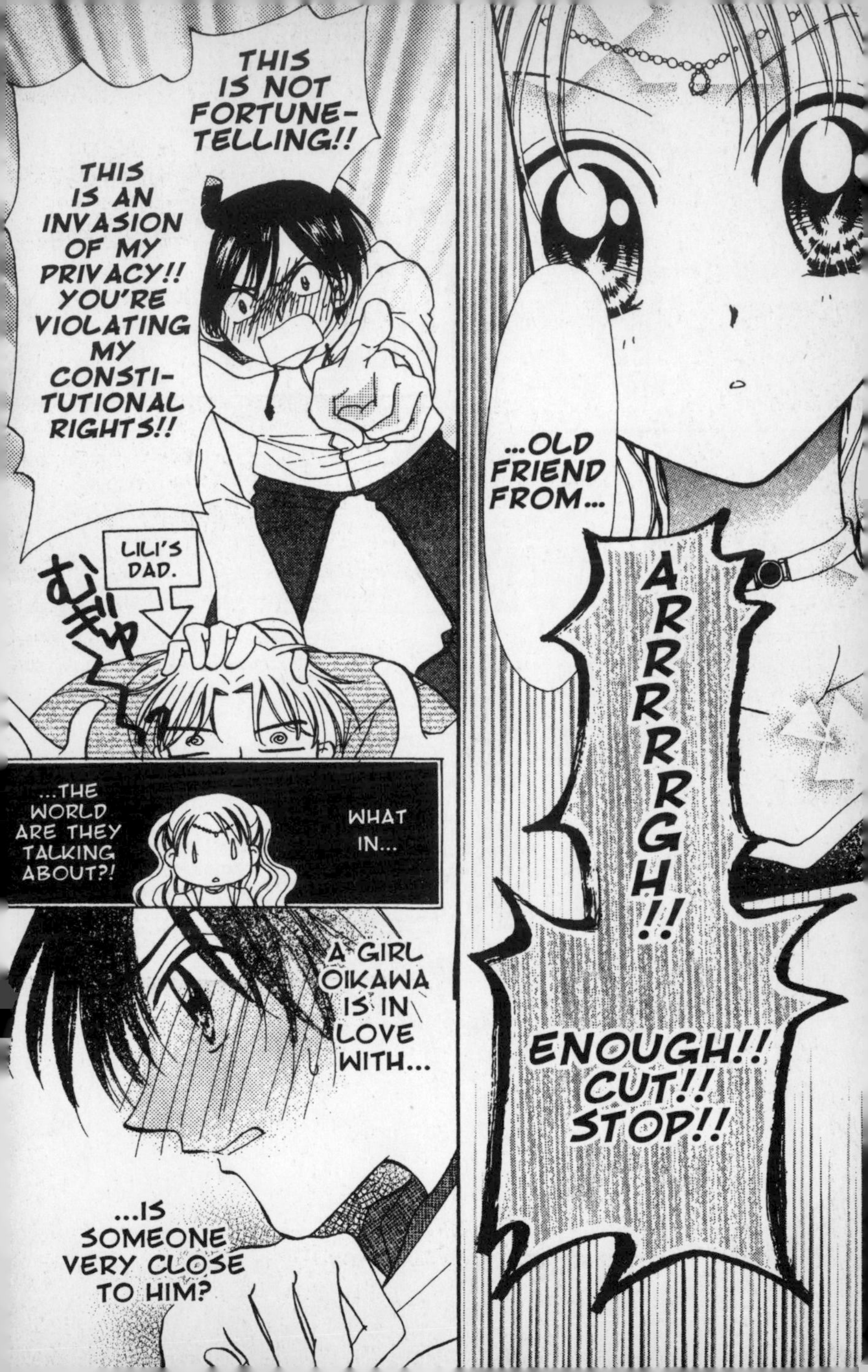
THIS IS NOT FORTUNE-TELLING!!
THIS IS AN INVASION OF MY PRIVACY!! YOU'RE VIOLATING MY CONSTITUTIONAL RIGHTS!!
LILI'S DAD.
むぎゅ
WHAT IN...
...THE WORLD ARE THEY TALKING ABOUT?!
A GIRL OIKAWA IS IN LOVE WITH...
...IS SOMEONE VERY CLOSE TO HIM?
...OLD FRIEND FROM...
ARRRRRGH!!
ENOUGH!! CUT!! STOP!!

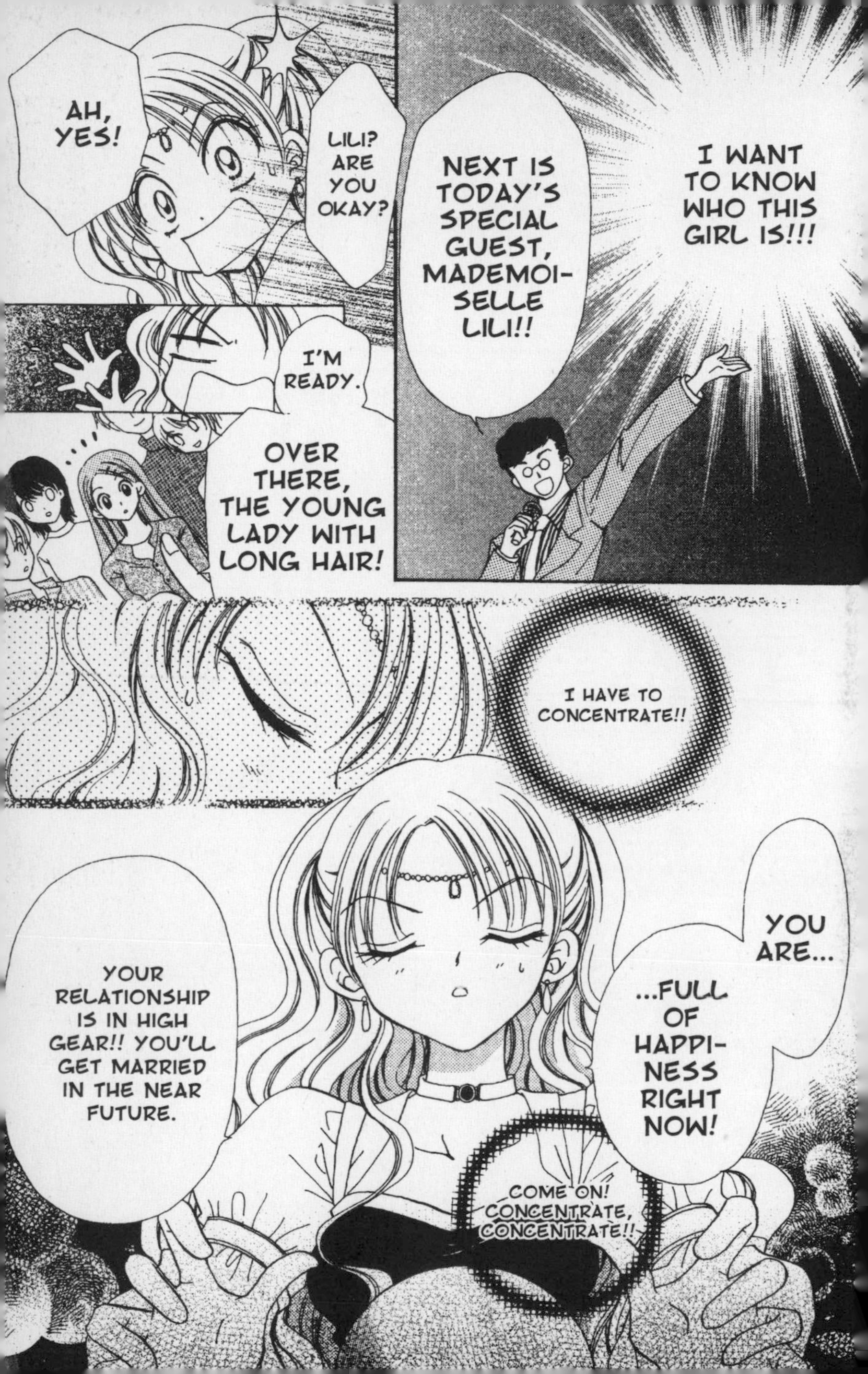
I WANT TO KNOW WHO THIS GIRL IS!!!
NEXT IS TODAY'S SPECIAL GUEST, MADEMOI-SELLE LILI!!
LILI? ARE YOU OKAY?
AH, YES!
I'M READY.
OVER THERE, THE YOUNG LADY WITH LONG HAIR!
...
I HAVE TO CONCENTRATE!!
YOU ARE...
...FULL OF HAPPI-NESS RIGHT NOW!
COME ON! CONCENTRATE, CONCENTRATE!!
YOUR RELATIONSHIP IS IN HIGH GEAR!! YOU'LL GET MARRIED IN THE NEAR FUTURE.

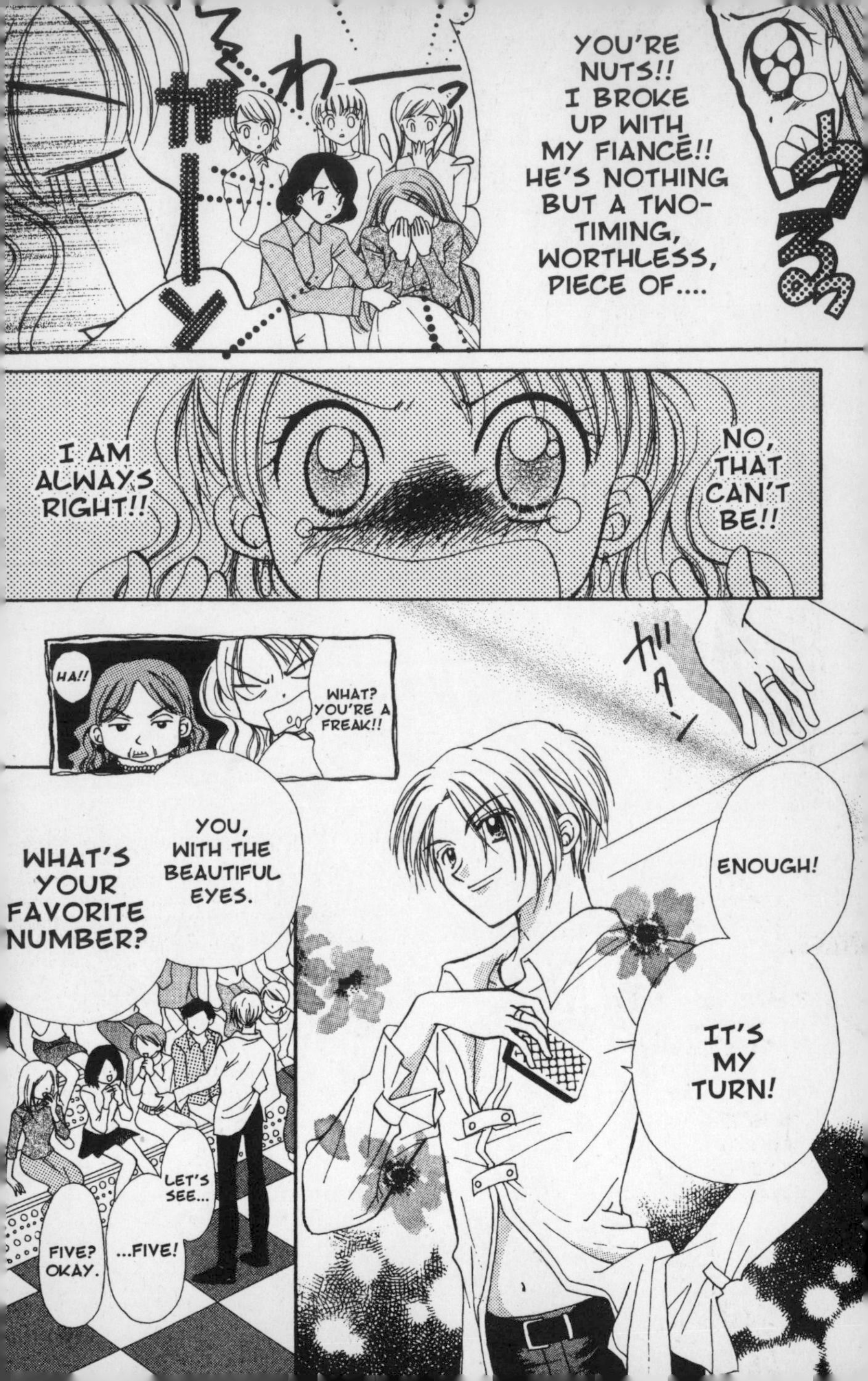
YOU'RE NUTS!! I BROKE UP WITH MY FIANCÉ!! HE'S NOTHING BUT A TWO-TIMING, WORTHLESS, PIECE OF....
NO, THAT CAN'T BE!!
I AM ALWAYS RIGHT!!
ENOUGH!
IT'S MY TURN!
WHAT? YOU'RE A FREAK!!
HA!!
YOU, WITH THE BEAUTIFUL EYES.
WHAT'S YOUR FAVORITE NUMBER?
LET'S SEE...
...FIVE!
FIVE? OKAY.

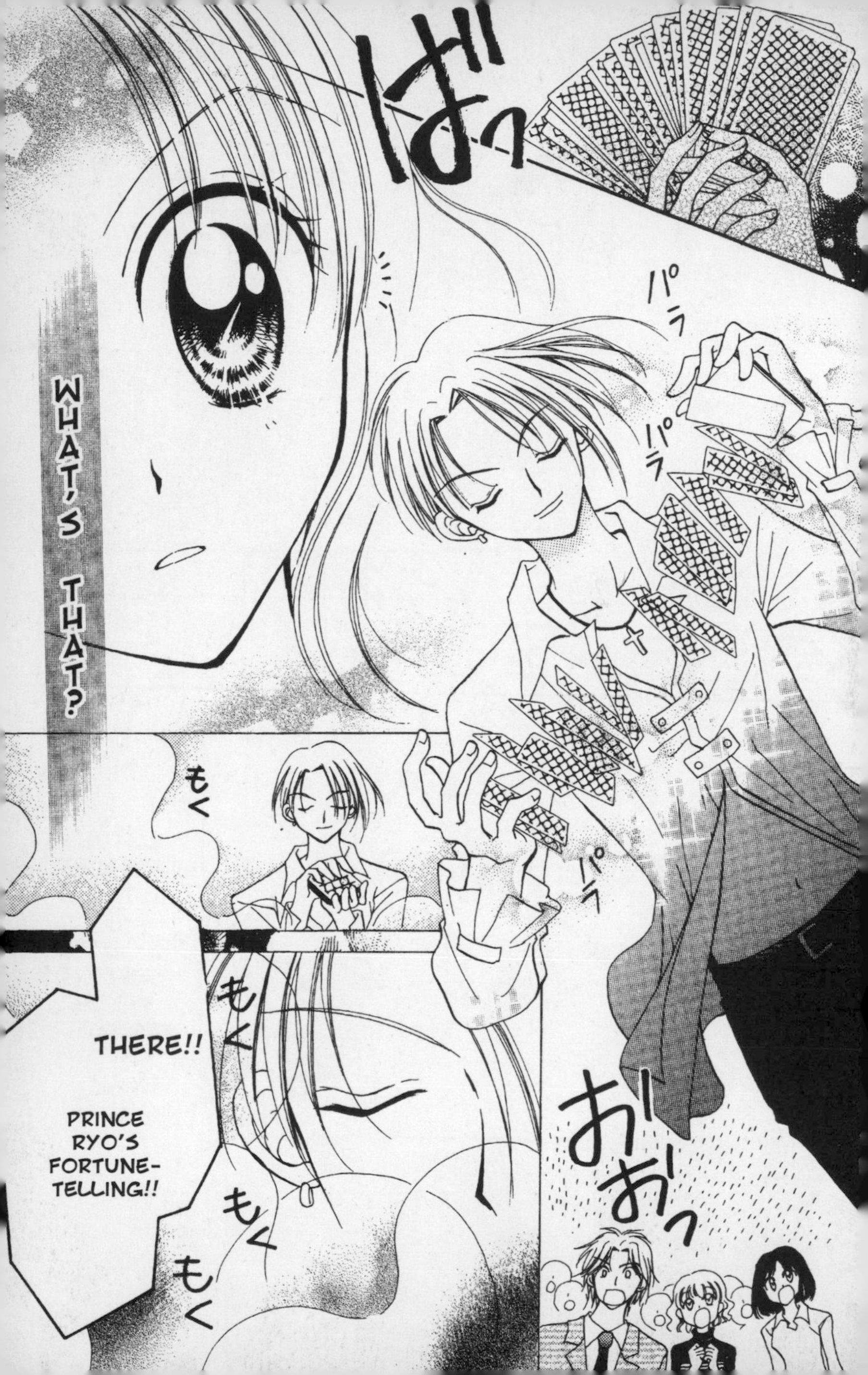
ばっ
パラ
パラ
WHAT'S THAT?
パラ
おおっ
もく
もく
もく
もく
THERE!!
PRINCE RYO'S FORTUNE-TELLING!!

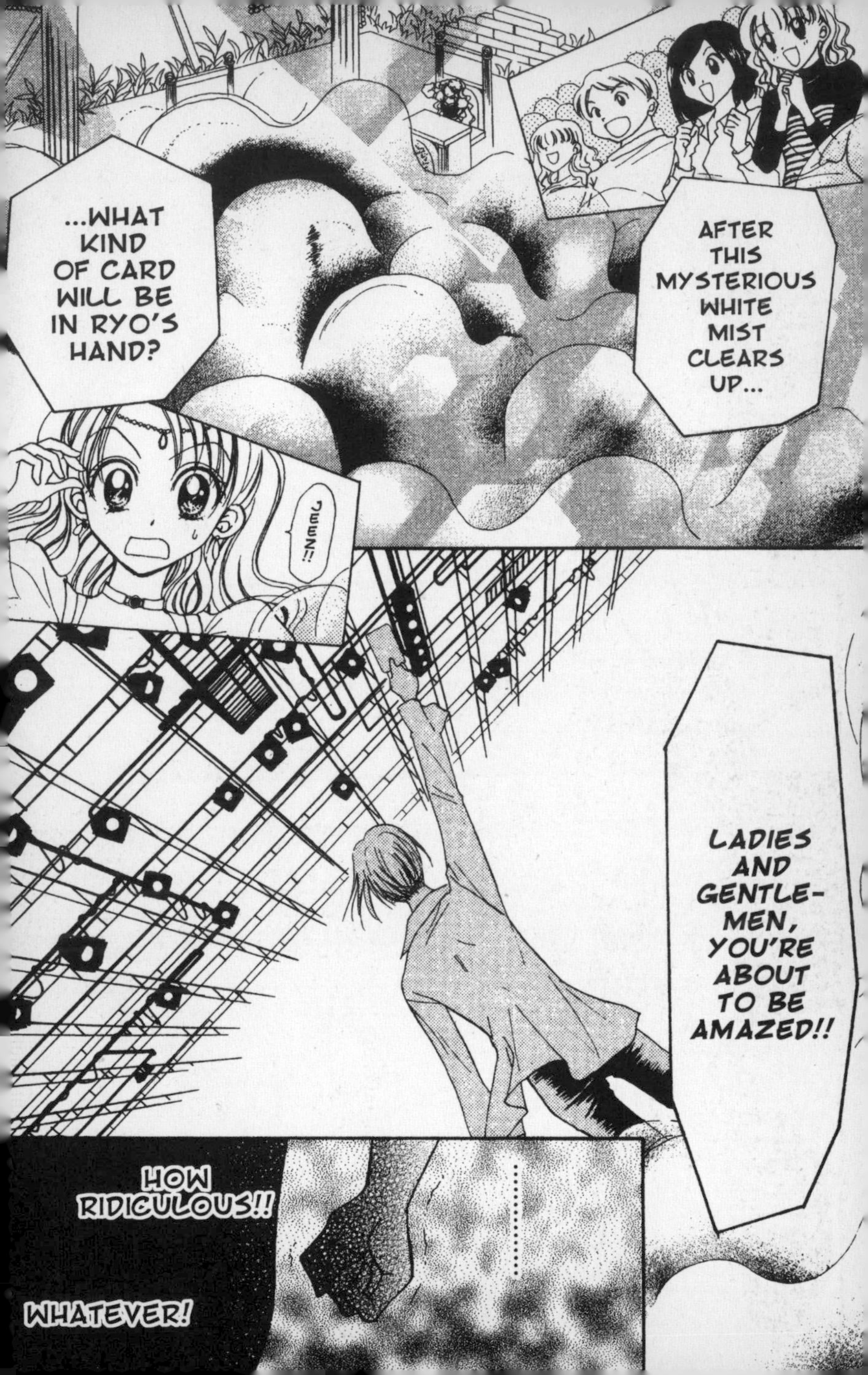
AFTER THIS MYSTERIOUS WHITE MIST CLEARS UP...
...WHAT KIND OF CARD WILL BE IN RYO'S HAND?
JEEN!!
LADIES AND GENTLE-MEN, YOU'RE ABOUT TO BE AMAZED!!
......
HOW RIDICULOUS!!
WHATEVER!

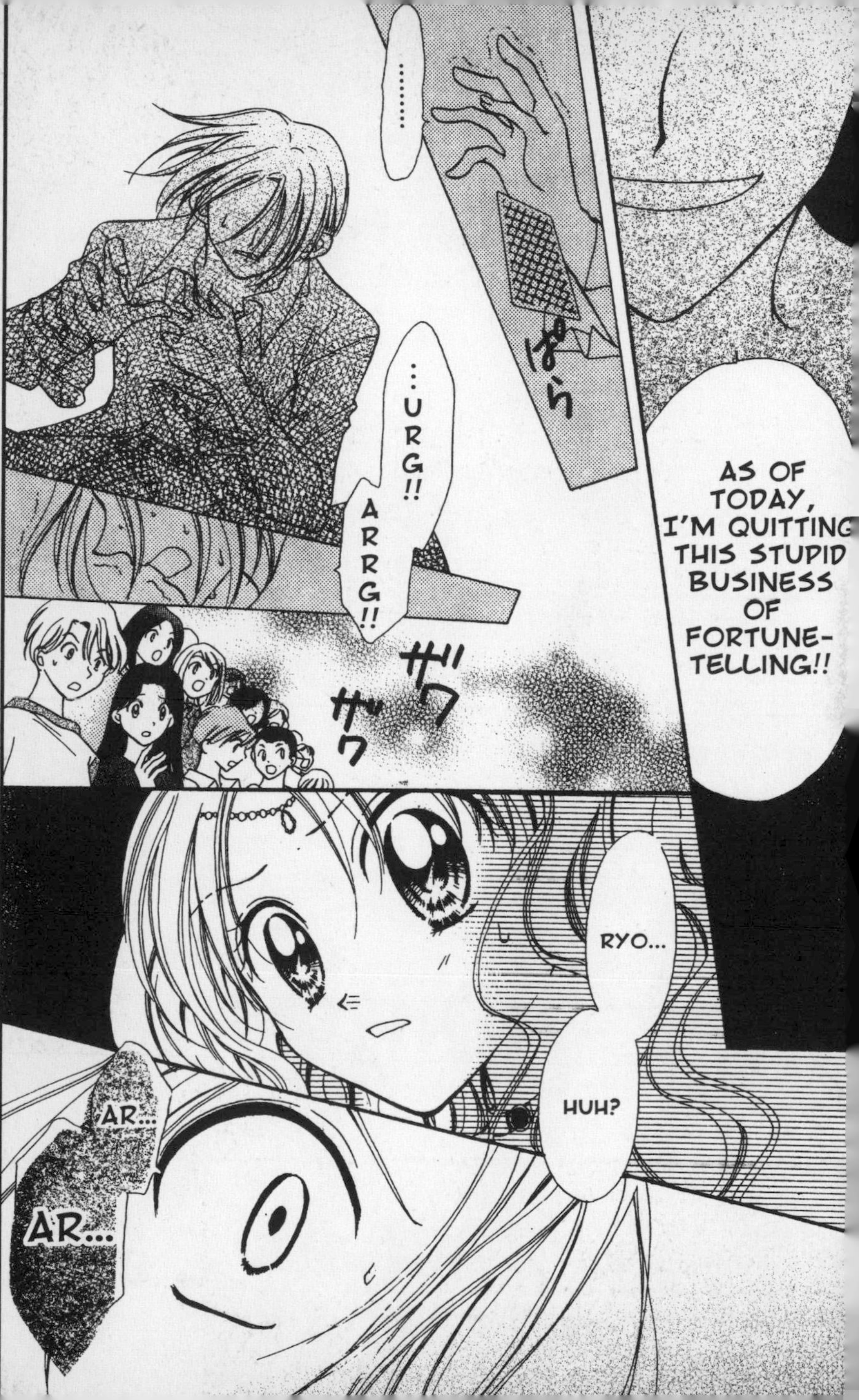

AS OF TODAY, I'M QUITTING THIS STUPID BUSINESS OF FORTUNE-TELLING!!
......
ぱら
...URG!! ARRG!!
ザワ
ザワ
RYO...
HUH?
AR...
AR...

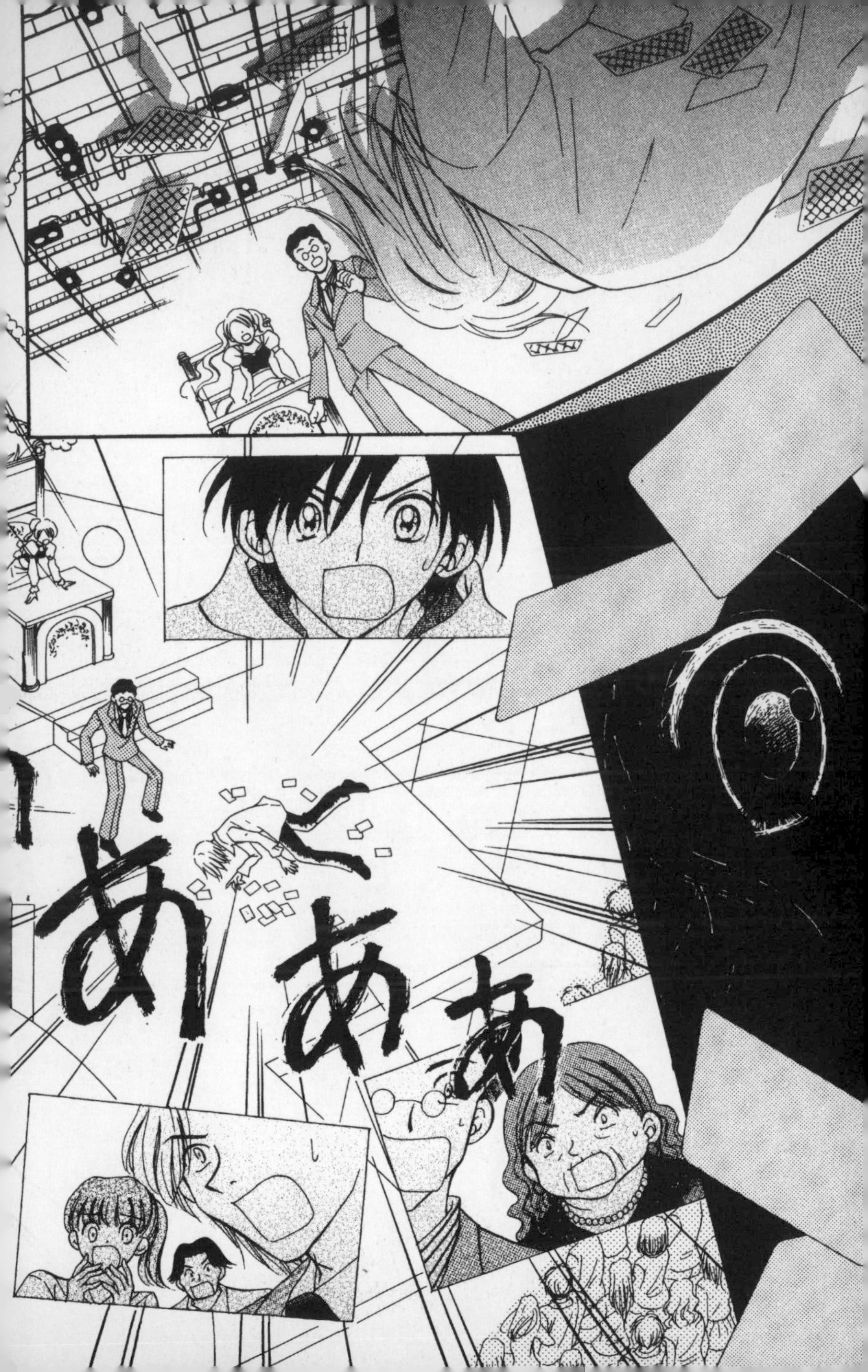
あああ

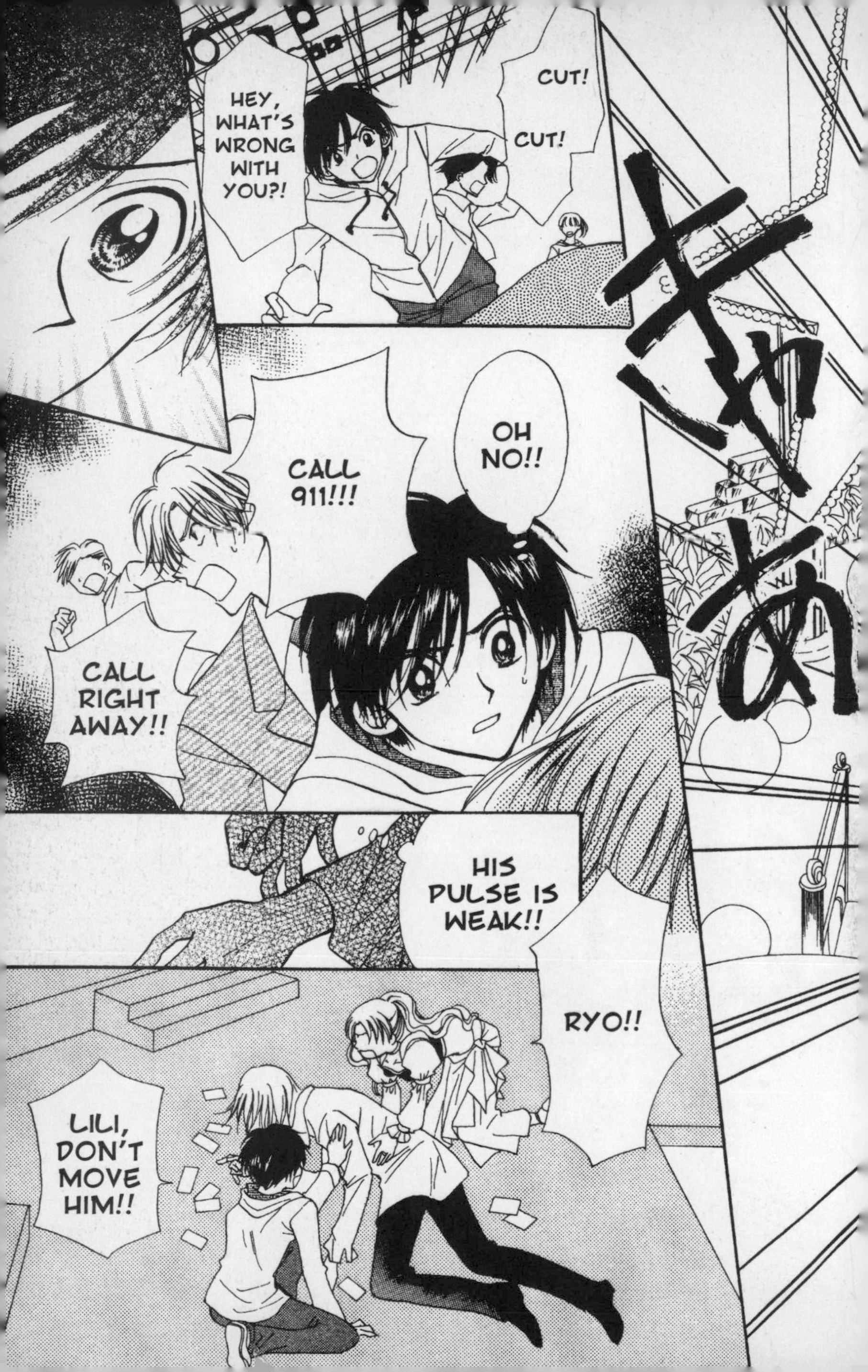
キゃあ
CUT!
CUT!
HEY, WHAT'S WRONG WITH YOU?!
OH NO!!
CALL 911!!!
CALL RIGHT AWAY!!
HIS PULSE IS WEAK!!
RYO!!
LILI, DON'T MOVE HIM!!

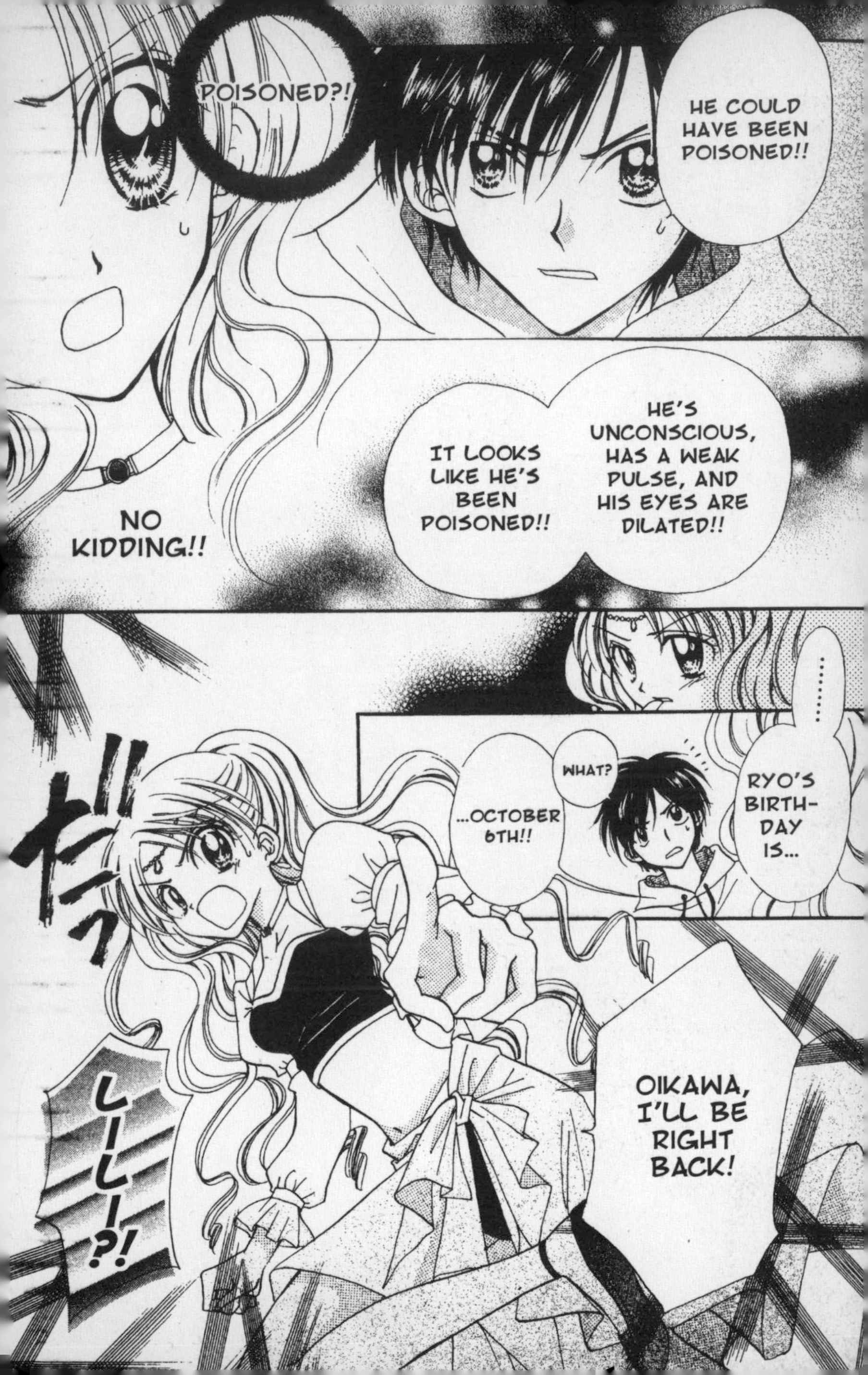
HE COULD HAVE BEEN POISONED!!
POISONED?!
HE'S UNCONSCIOUS, HAS A WEAK PULSE, AND HIS EYES ARE DILATED!!
IT LOOKS LIKE HE'S BEEN POISONED!!
NO KIDDING!!
......
RYO'S BIRTH-DAY IS...
WHAT?
...OCTOBER 6TH!!
OIKAWA, I'LL BE RIGHT BACK!
しししー?!

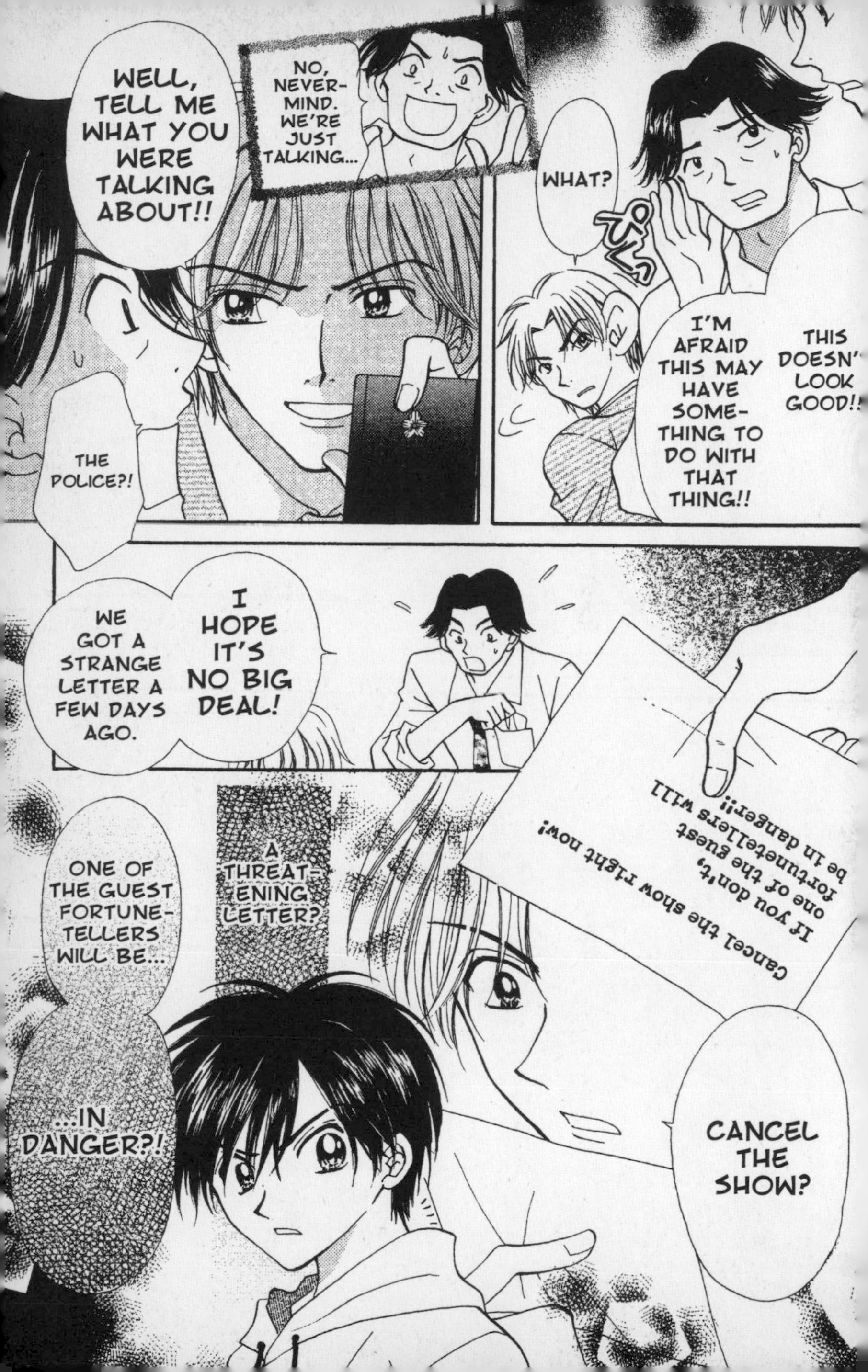
WHAT?
THIS DOESN' LOOK GOOD!!
I'M AFRAID THIS MAY HAVE SOME-THING TO DO WITH THAT THING!!
NO, NEVER-MIND. WE'RE JUST TALKING...
WELL, TELL ME WHAT YOU WERE TALKING ABOUT!!
THE POLICE?!
I HOPE IT'S NO BIG DEAL!
WE GOT A STRANGE LETTER A FEW DAYS AGO.
Cancel the show right now! If you don't, one of the guest fortunetellers will be in danger!!
CANCEL THE SHOW?
A THREAT-ENING LETTER?
ONE OF THE GUEST FORTUNE-TELLERS WILL BE...
...IN DANGER?!

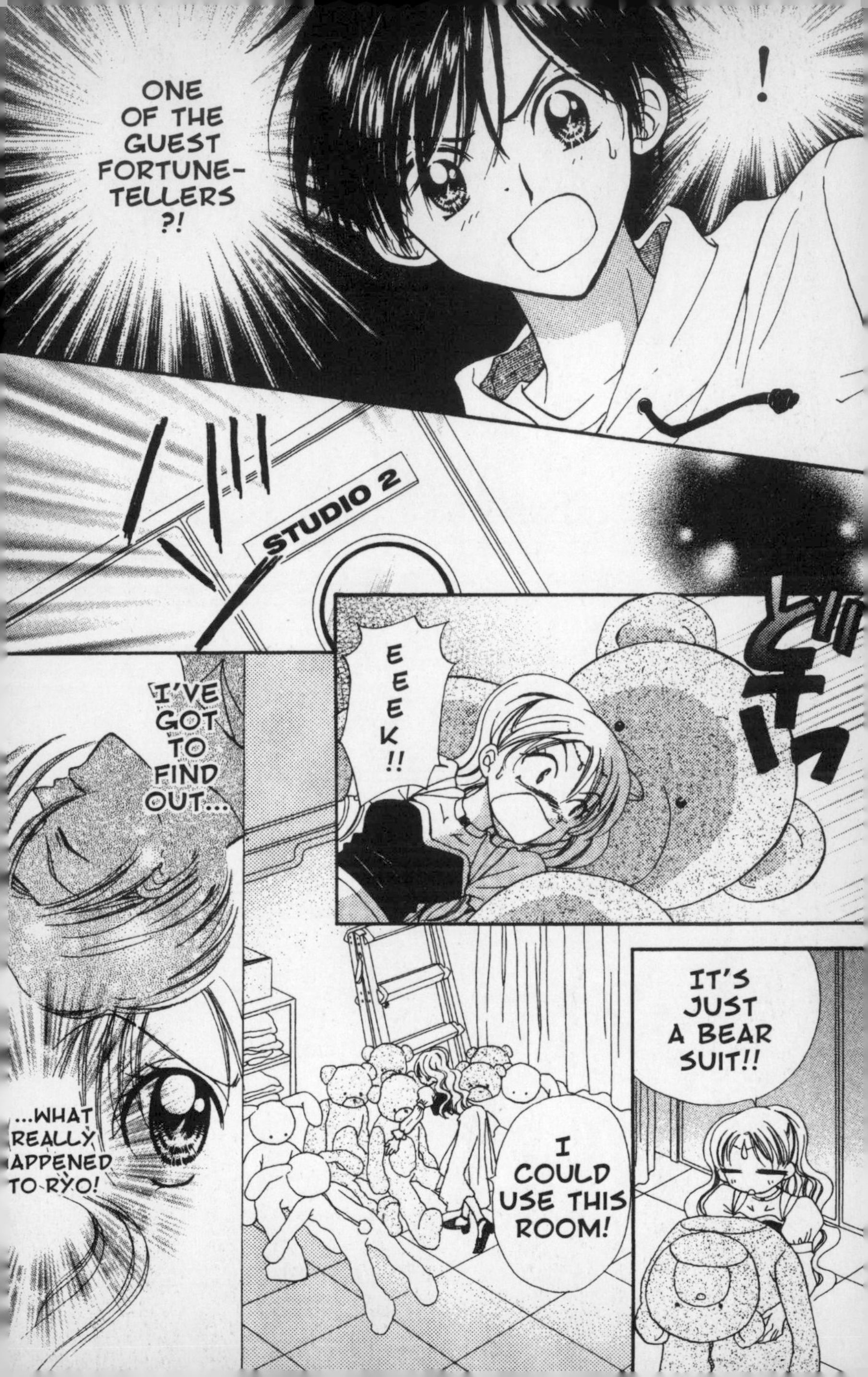
!
ONE OF THE GUEST FORTUNE-TELLERS ?!
STUDIO 2
EEEK!!
IT'S JUST A BEAR SUIT!!
I COULD USE THIS ROOM!
I'VE GOT TO FIND OUT...
...WHAT REALLY APPENED TO RYO!

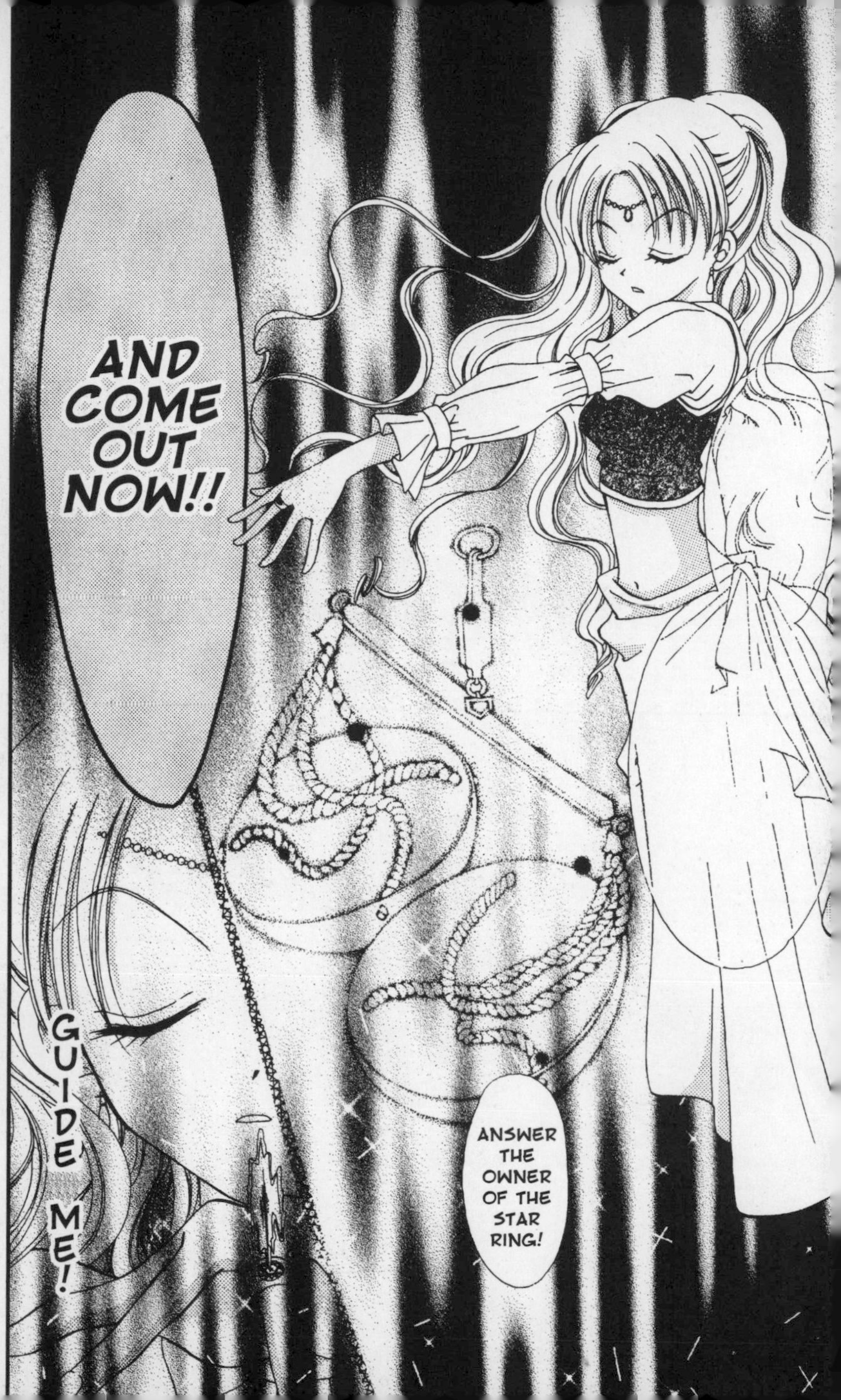
ANSWER THE OWNER OF THE STAR RING!
AND COME OUT NOW!!
GUIDE ME!

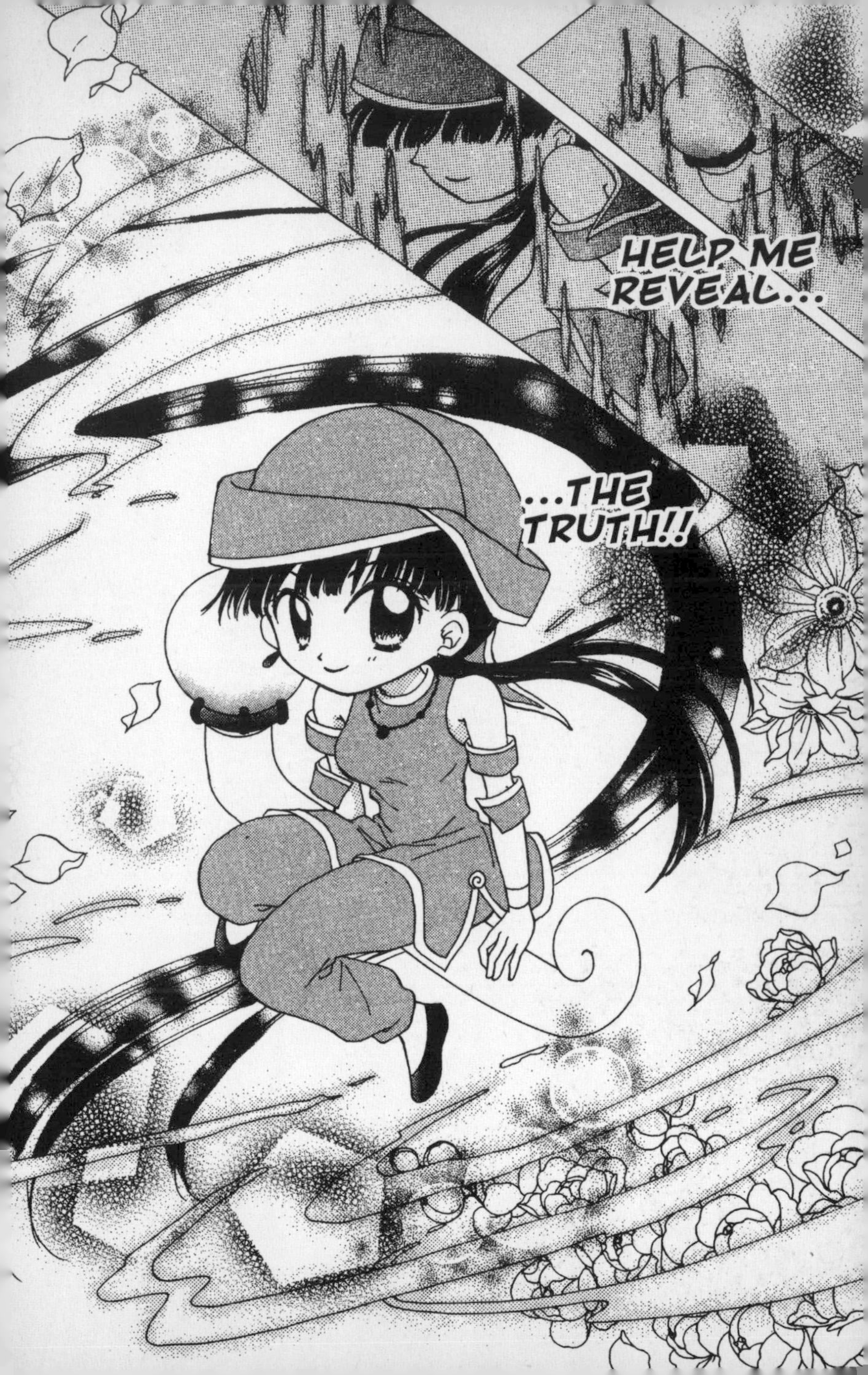
HELP ME REVEAL...
...THE TRUTH!!

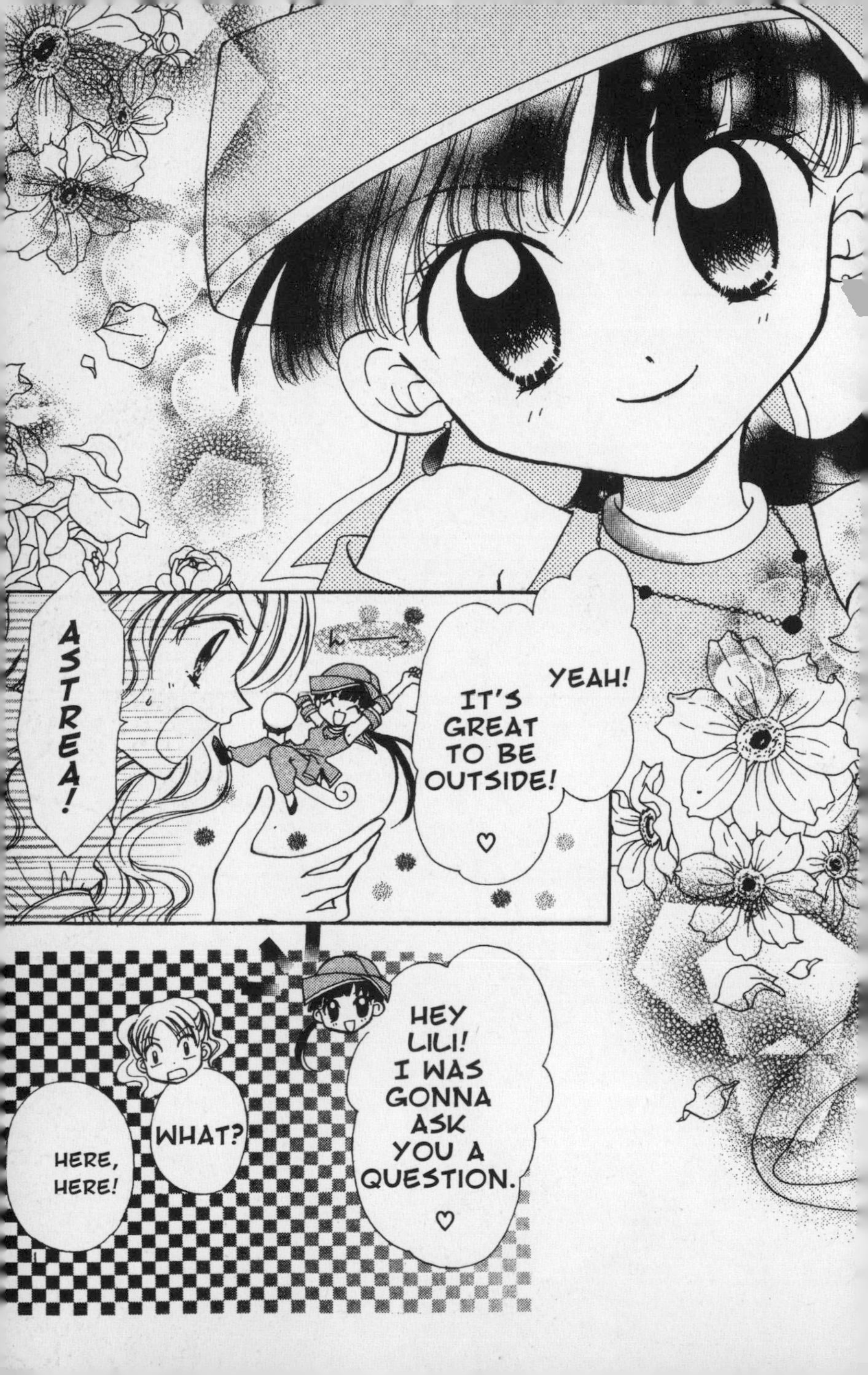
YEAH! IT'S GREAT TO BE OUTSIDE! ♡
ASTREA!
HEY LILI! I WAS GONNA ASK YOU A QUESTION. ♡
WHAT?
HERE, HERE!

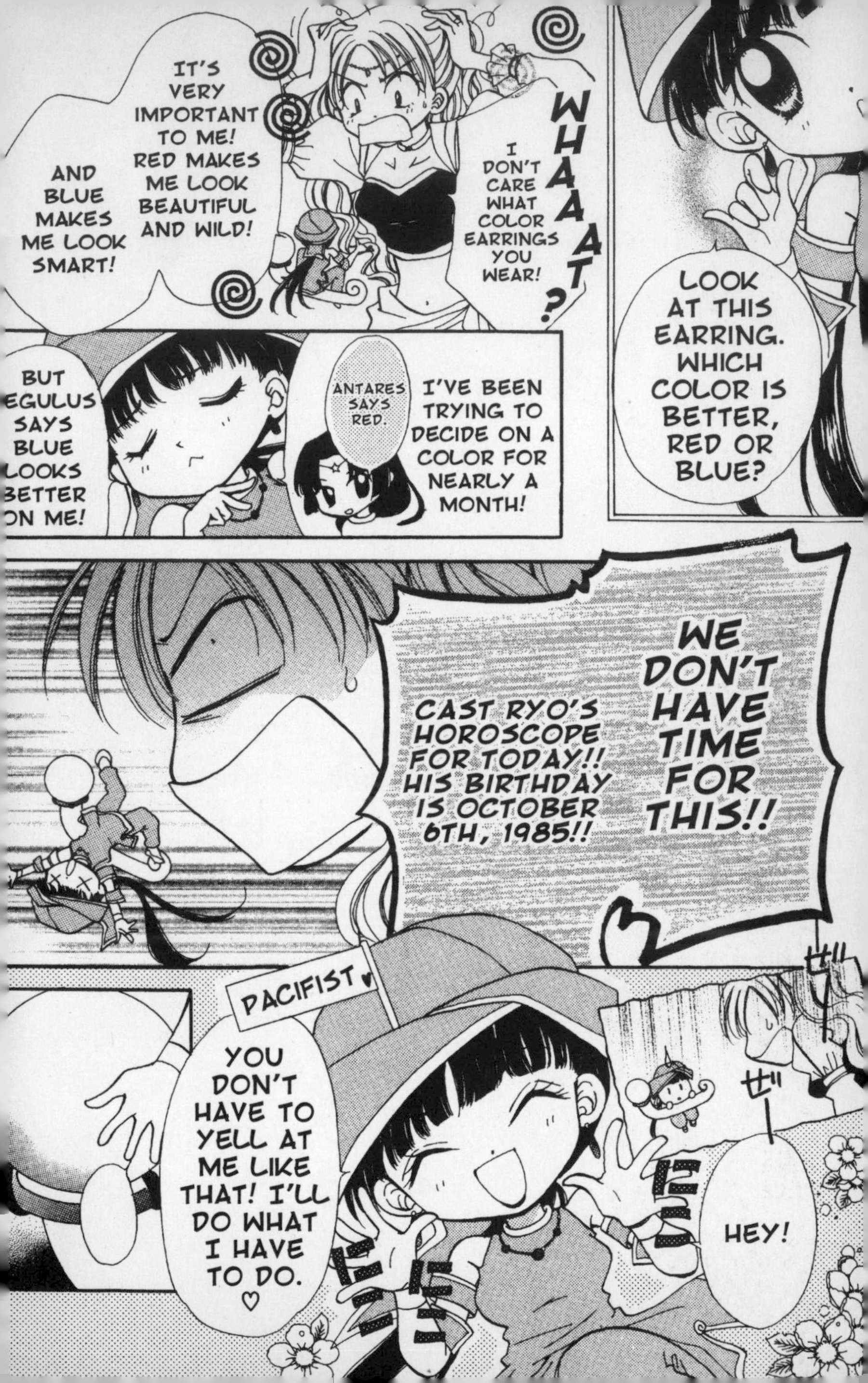
LOOK AT THIS EARRING. WHICH COLOR IS BETTER, RED OR BLUE?
WHAAAT?
I DON'T CARE WHAT COLOR EARRINGS YOU WEAR!
IT'S VERY IMPORTANT TO ME! RED MAKES ME LOOK BEAUTIFUL AND WILD!
AND BLUE MAKES ME LOOK SMART!
I'VE BEEN TRYING TO DECIDE ON A COLOR FOR NEARLY A MONTH!
ANTARES SAYS RED.
BUT EGULUS SAYS BLUE LOOKS BETTER ON ME!
WE DON'T HAVE TIME FOR THIS!!
CAST RYO'S HOROSCOPE FOR TODAY!! HIS BIRTHDAY IS OCTOBER 6TH, 1985!!
HEY!
PACIFIST ♥
YOU DON'T HAVE TO YELL AT ME LIKE THAT! I'LL DO WHAT I HAVE TO DO. ♡

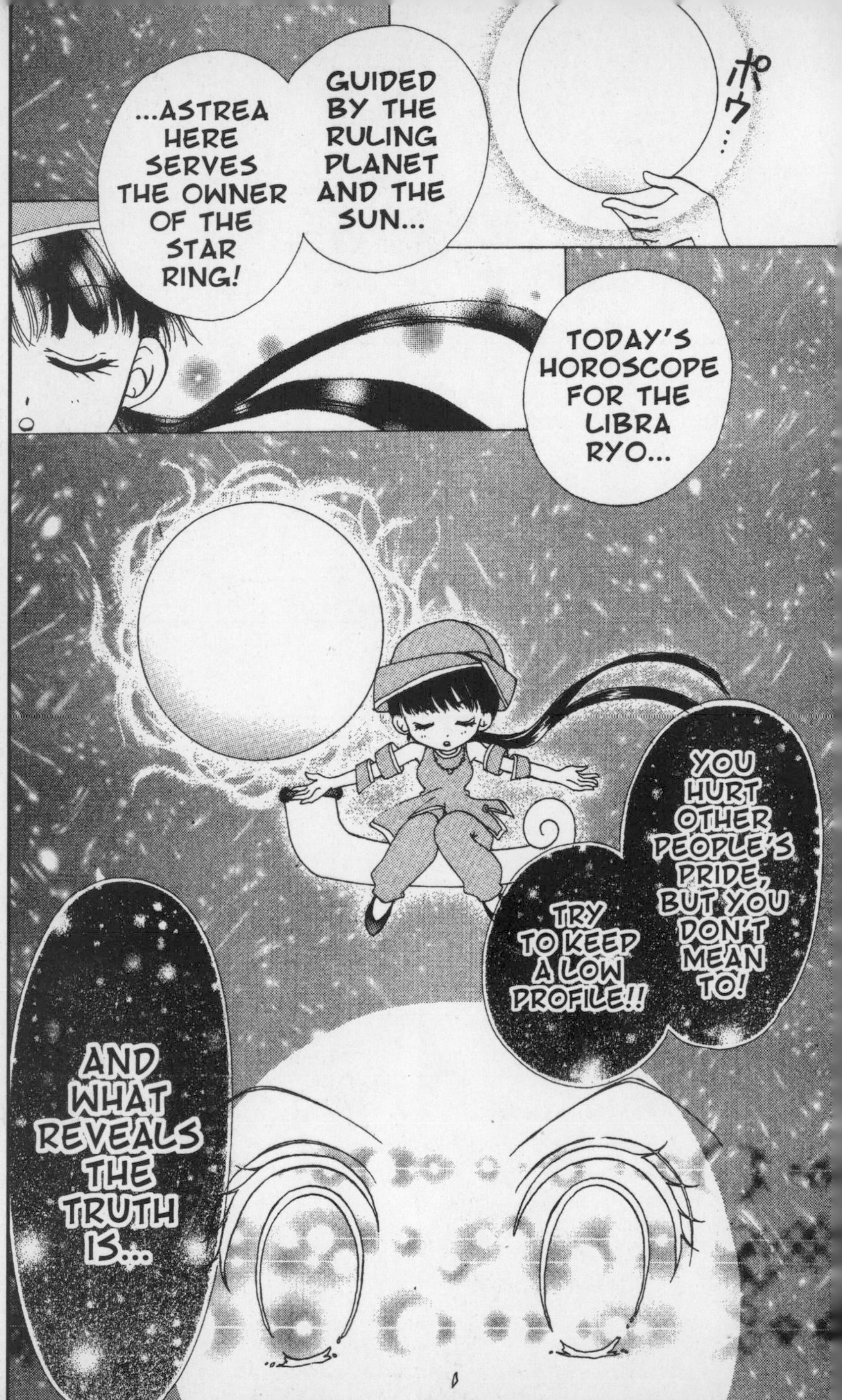
ポウ…
GUIDED BY THE RULING PLANET AND THE SUN...
...ASTREA HERE SERVES THE OWNER OF THE STAR RING!
TODAY'S HOROSCOPE FOR THE LIBRA RYO...
YOU HURT OTHER PEOPLE'S PRIDE, BUT YOU DON'T MEAN TO!
TRY TO KEEP A LOW PROFILE!!
AND WHAT REVEALS THE TRUTH IS...

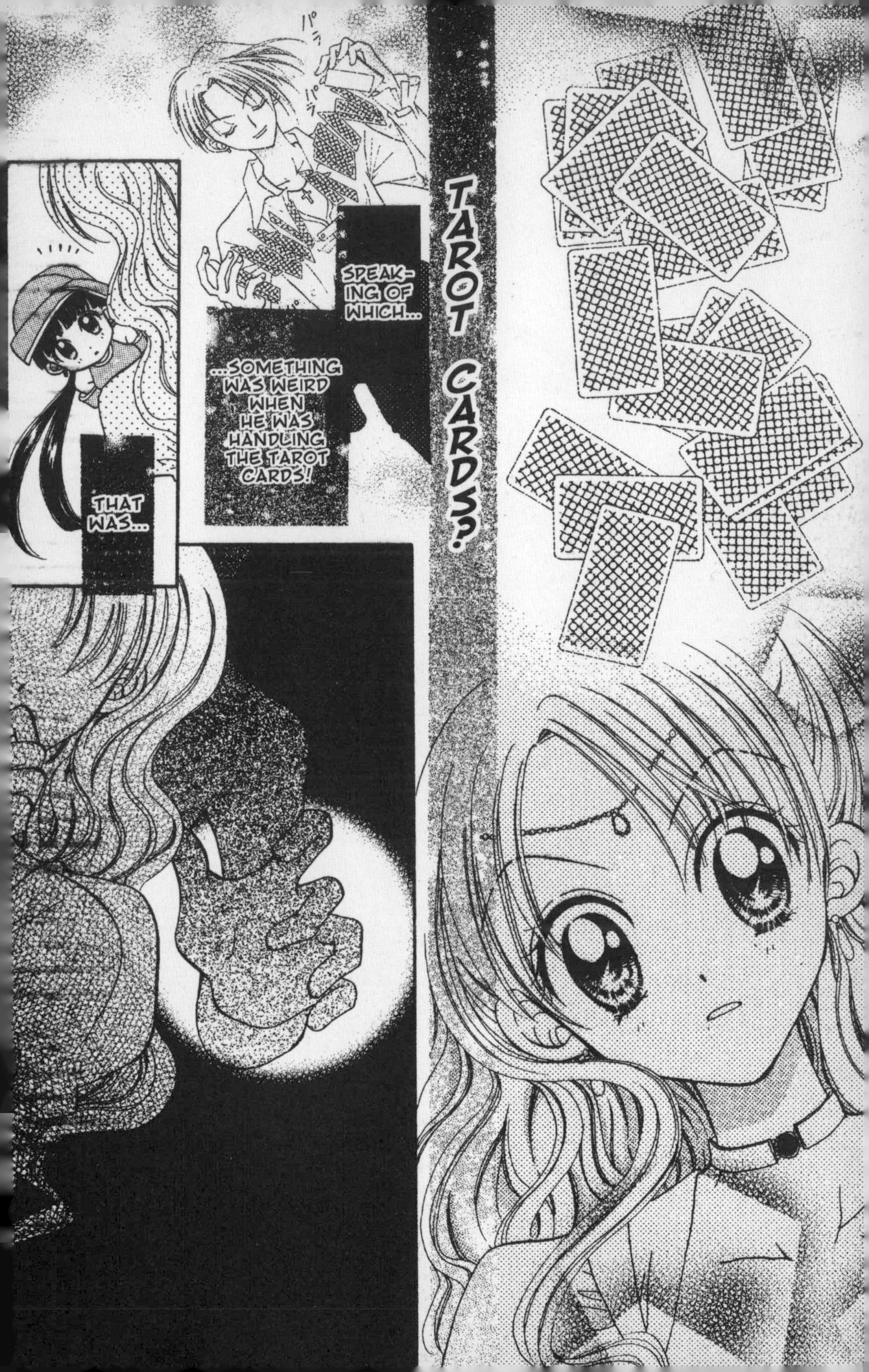
TAROT CARDS?
SPEAK-ING OF WHICH...
...SOMETHING WAS WEIRD WHEN HE WAS HANDLING THE TAROT CARDS!
THAT WAS...

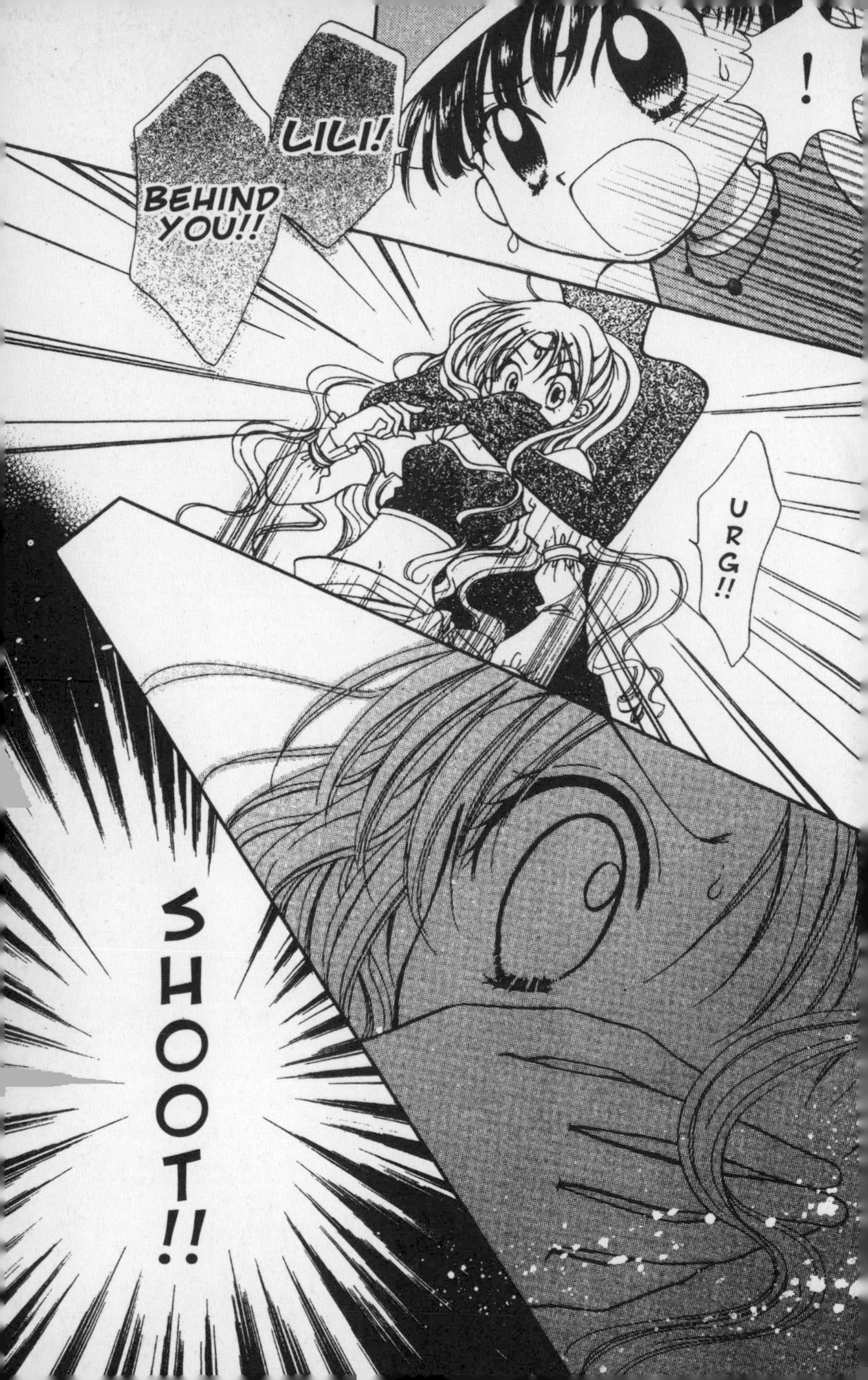
!
LILI!
BEHIND YOU!!
URG!!
SHOOT!!

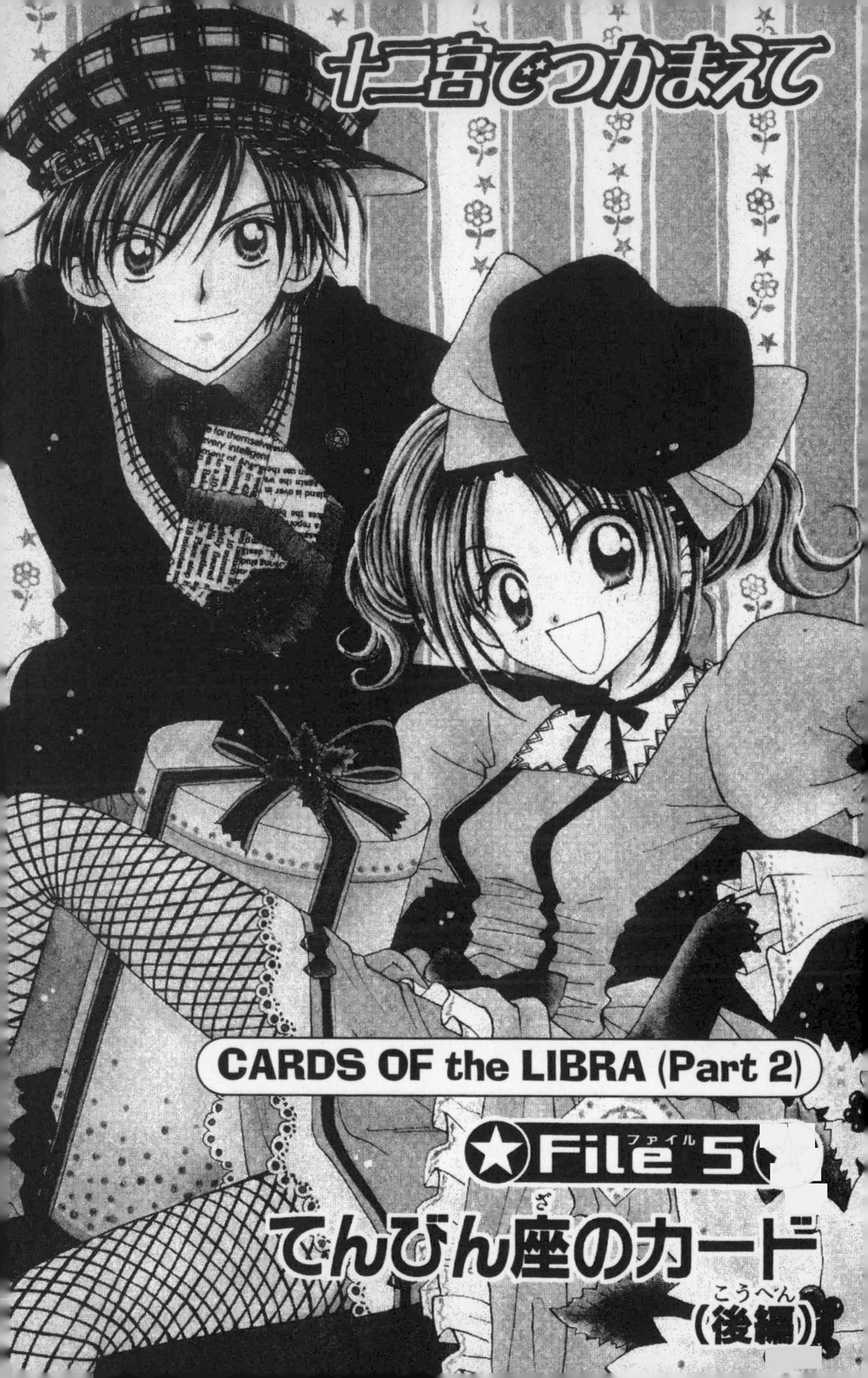
十二宮でつかまえて
CARDS OF the LIBRA (Part 2)
File 5
てんびん座のカード
(後編)

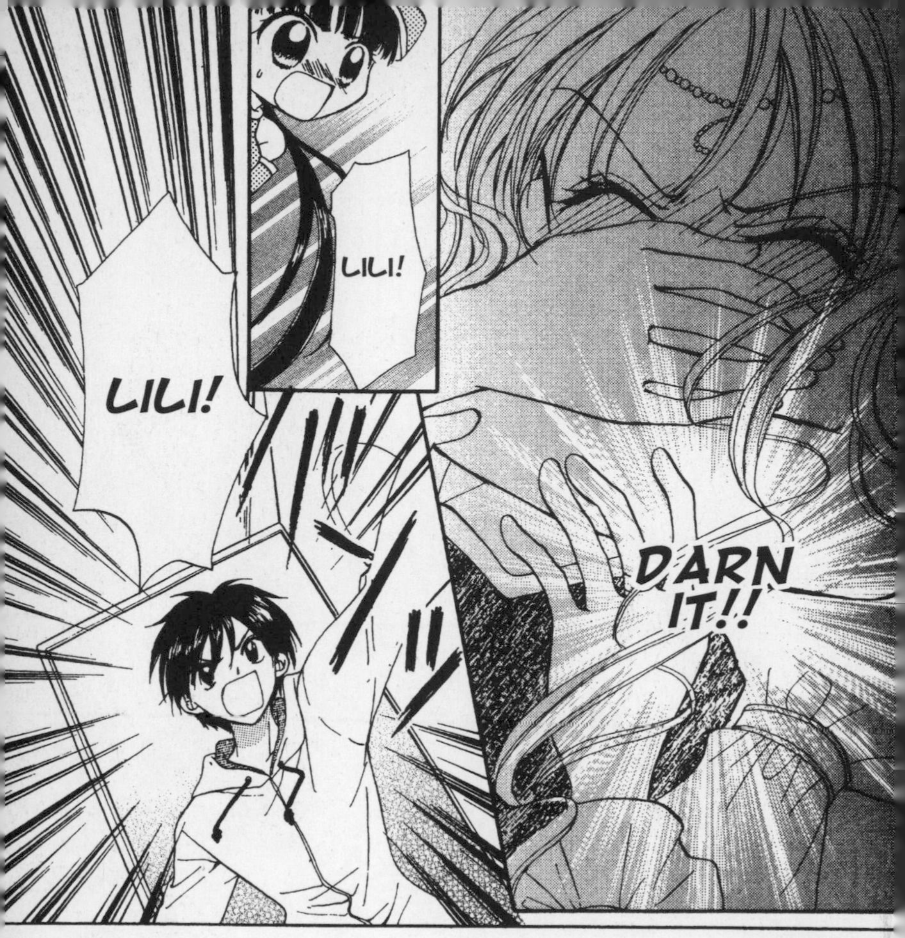
DARN IT!!
LILI!
LILI!

Mademoiselle Lili's Astrology (8)

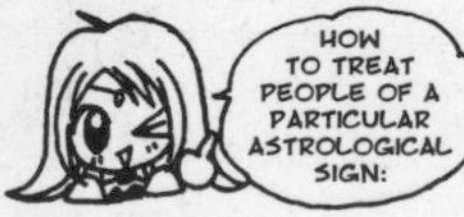
HOW TO TREAT PEOPLE OF A PARTICULAR ASTROLOGICAL SIGN:

Libra: ♎ Astrea

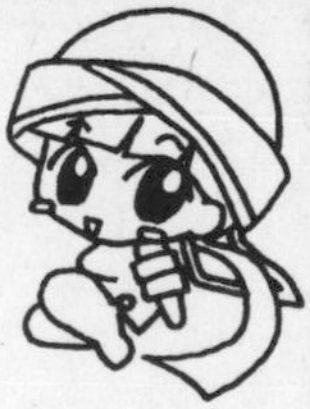

Astrea is the Goddess of Justice and holds the scale, the symbol of Libra, in her hand. Some believe the constellation Virgo actually has the shape of Astrea, but I used her name for the astral spirit of Libra. Astrea is an elegant, attractive, and smart individual with a great aesthetic sense. She treats everyone equally. Although she appears impeccable, she tends to be too self-conscious. Libra boys like curious and cheerful mates. Because they are kind to everyone, misunderstandings in relationships can result.

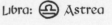

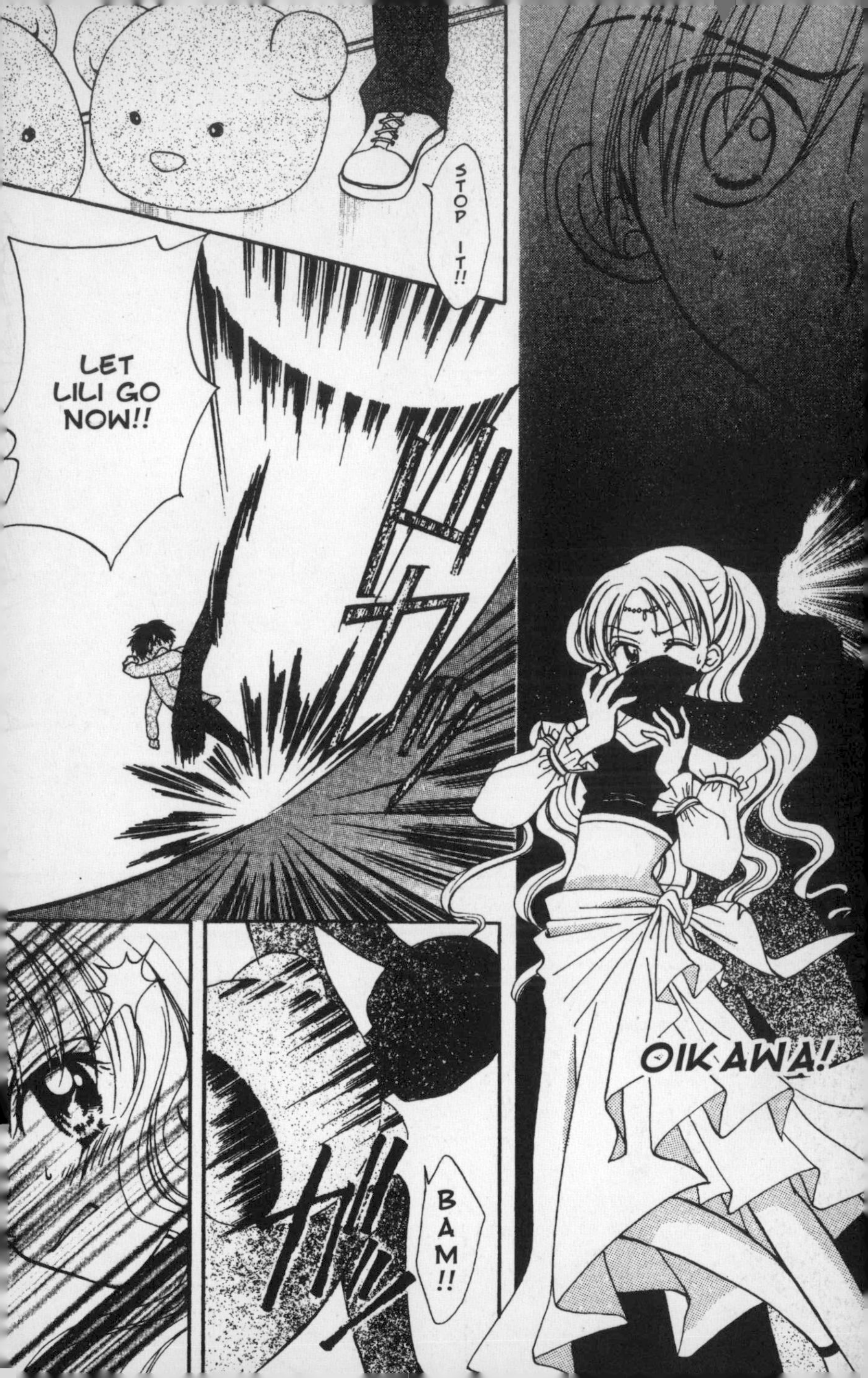
STOP IT!!
LET LILI GO NOW!!
BAM!!
OIKAWA!

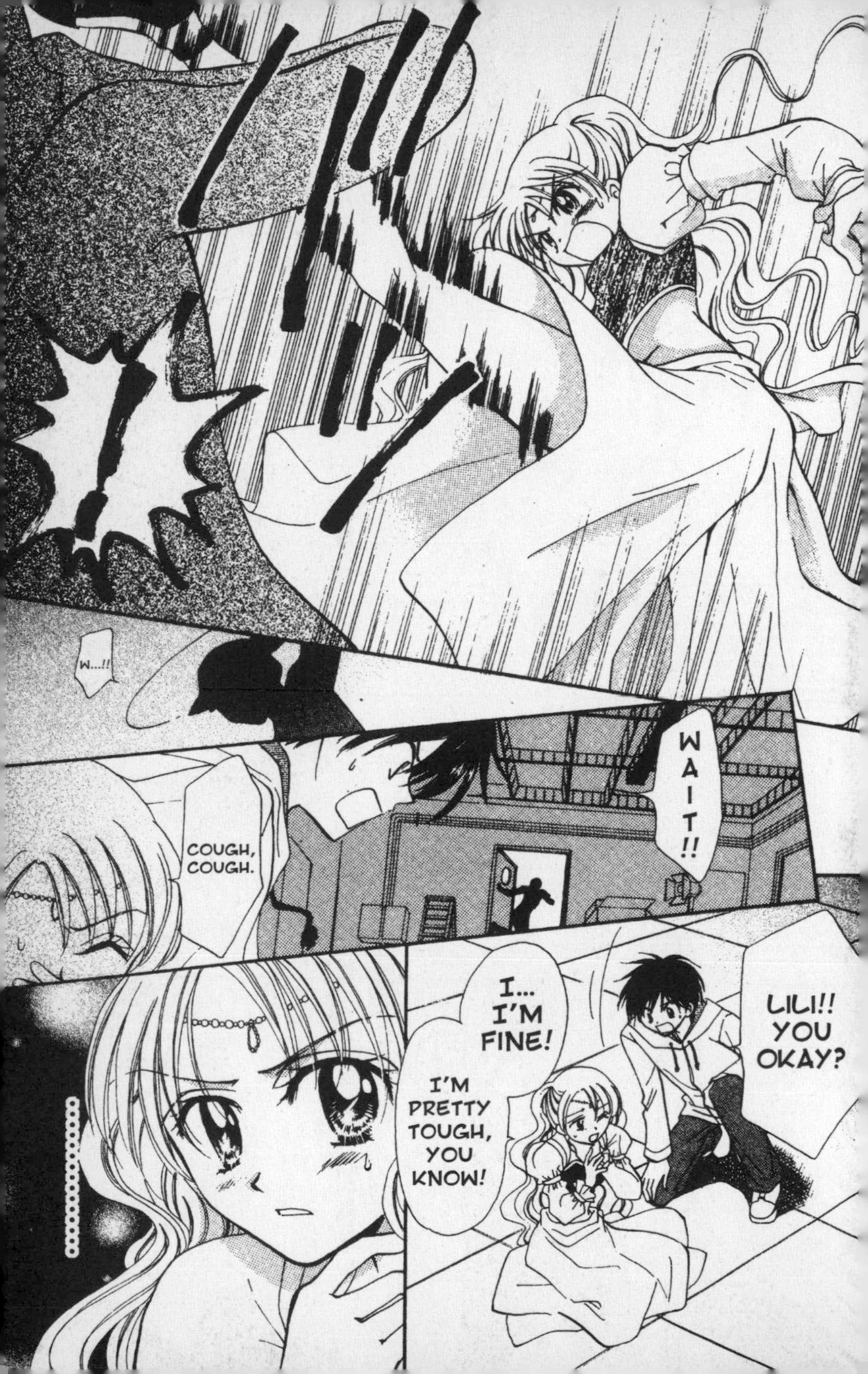
W...!!
WAIT!!
COUGH, COUGH.
LILI!! YOU OKAY?
I... I'M FINE!
I'M PRETTY TOUGH, YOU KNOW!

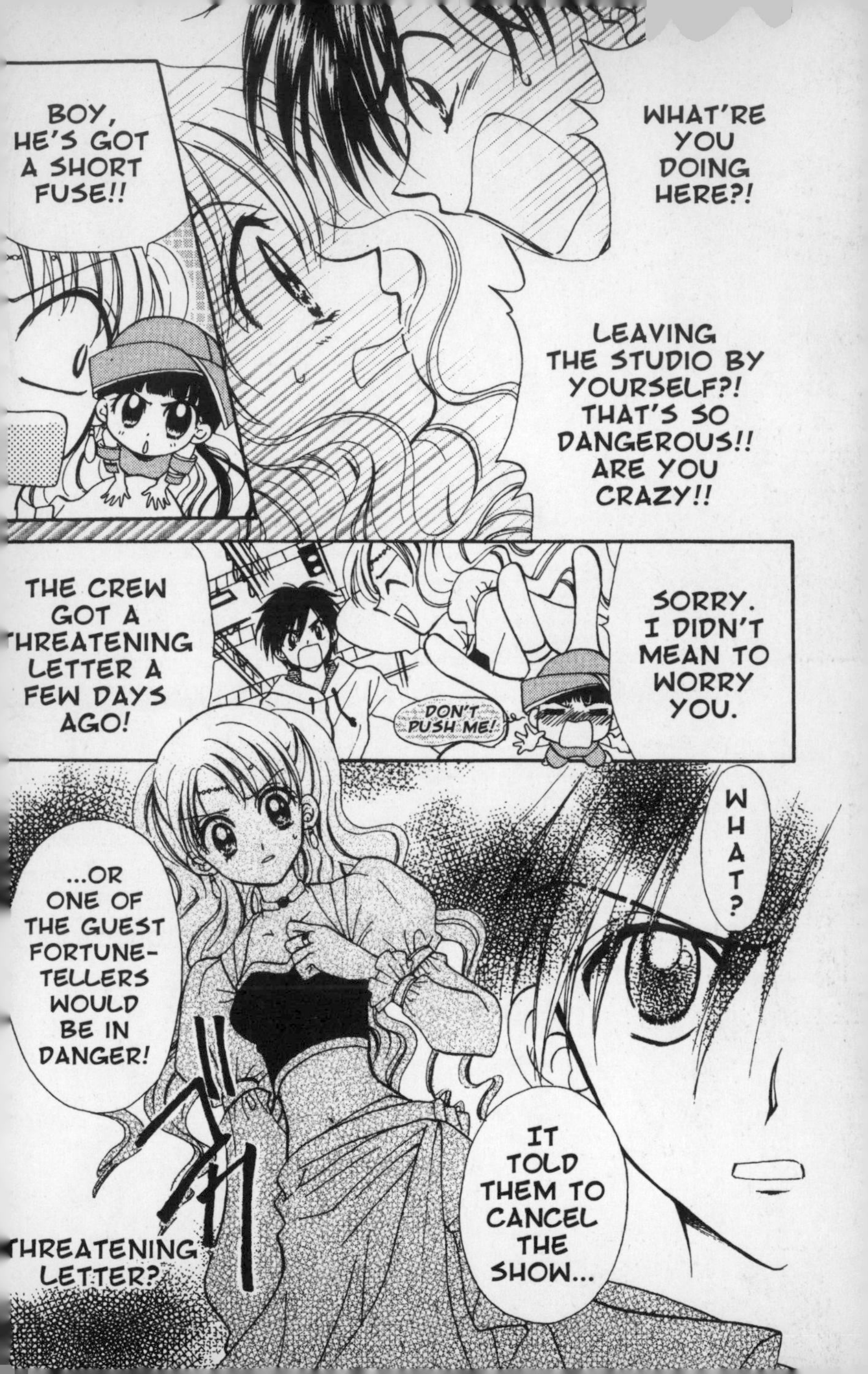
WHAT'RE YOU DOING HERE?!
LEAVING THE STUDIO BY YOURSELF?! THAT'S SO DANGEROUS!! ARE YOU CRAZY!!
BOY, HE'S GOT A SHORT FUSE!!
SORRY. I DIDN'T MEAN TO WORRY YOU.
DON'T PUSH ME!
THE CREW GOT A THREATENING LETTER A FEW DAYS AGO!
WHAT?
IT TOLD THEM TO CANCEL THE SHOW...
...OR ONE OF THE GUEST FORTUNE-TELLERS WOULD BE IN DANGER!
THREATENING LETTER?

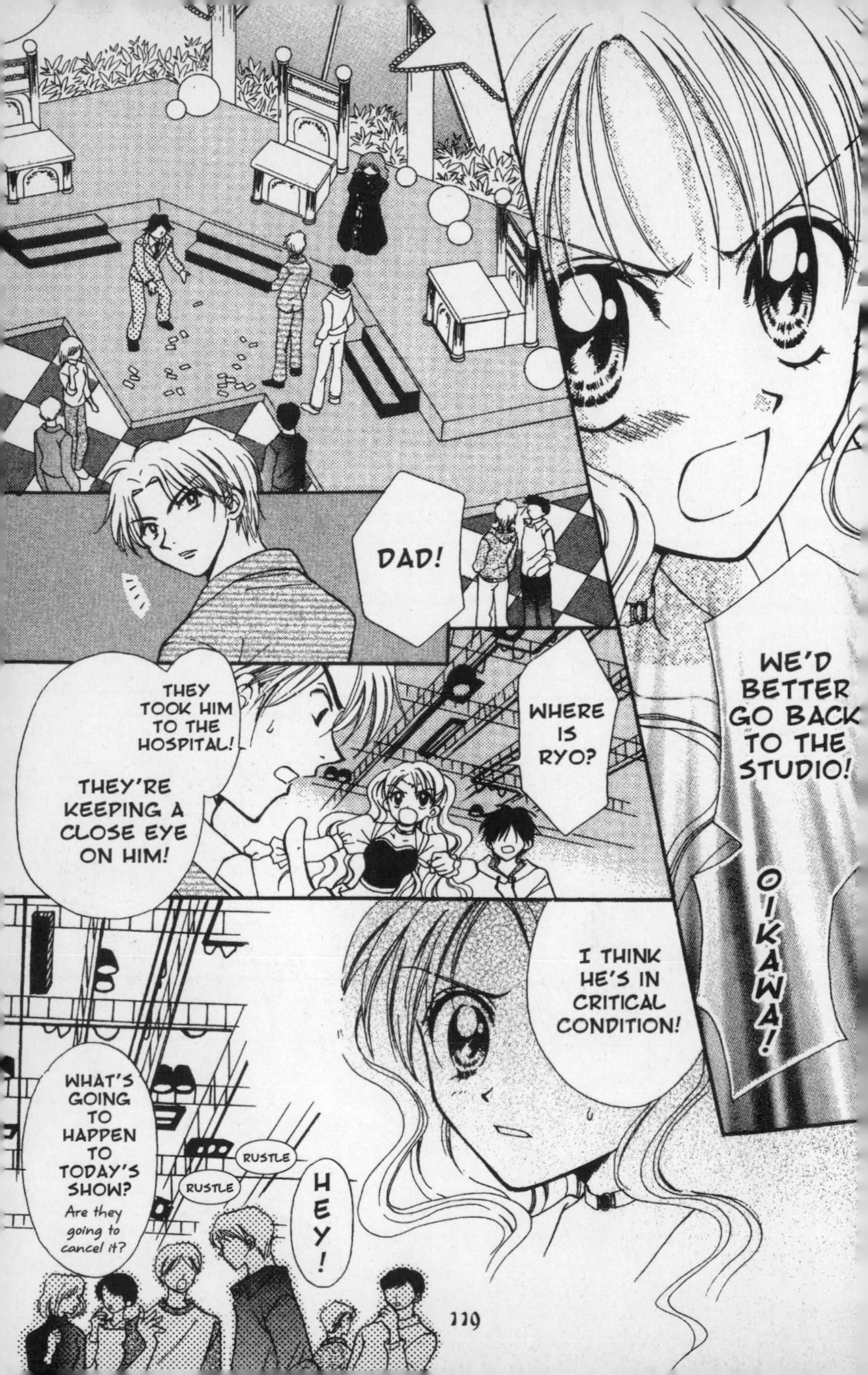
WE'D BETTER GO BACK TO THE STUDIO!
OIKAWA!
DAD!
WHERE IS RYO?
THEY TOOK HIM TO THE HOSPITAL!
THEY'RE KEEPING A CLOSE EYE ON HIM!
I THINK HE'S IN CRITICAL CONDITION!
HEY!
RUSTLE
RUSTLE
WHAT'S GOING TO HAPPEN TO TODAY'S SHOW?
Are they going to cancel it?

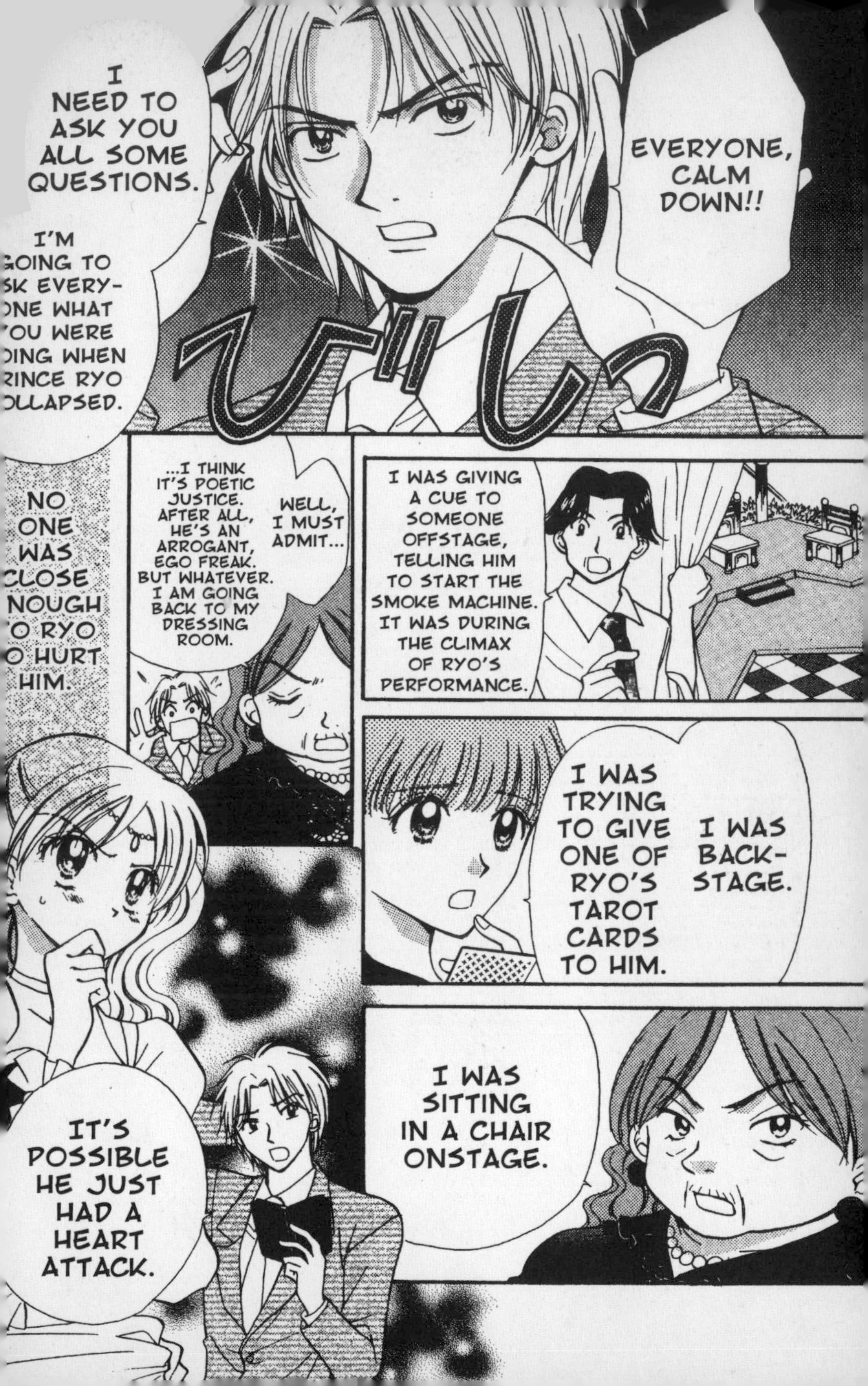
EVERYONE, CALM DOWN!!
I NEED TO ASK YOU ALL SOME QUESTIONS.
I'M GOING TO SK EVERY-ONE WHAT OU WERE OING WHEN RINCE RYO OLLAPSED.
I WAS GIVING A CUE TO SOMEONE OFFSTAGE, TELLING HIM TO START THE SMOKE MACHINE. IT WAS DURING THE CLIMAX OF RYO'S PERFORMANCE.
WELL, I MUST ADMIT...
...I THINK IT'S POETIC JUSTICE. AFTER ALL, HE'S AN ARROGANT, EGO FREAK. BUT WHATEVER. I AM GOING BACK TO MY DRESSING ROOM.
NO ONE WAS CLOSE NOUGH O RYO O HURT HIM.
I WAS BACK-STAGE.
I WAS TRYING TO GIVE ONE OF RYO'S TAROT CARDS TO HIM.
I WAS SITTING IN A CHAIR ONSTAGE.
IT'S POSSIBLE HE JUST HAD A HEART ATTACK.

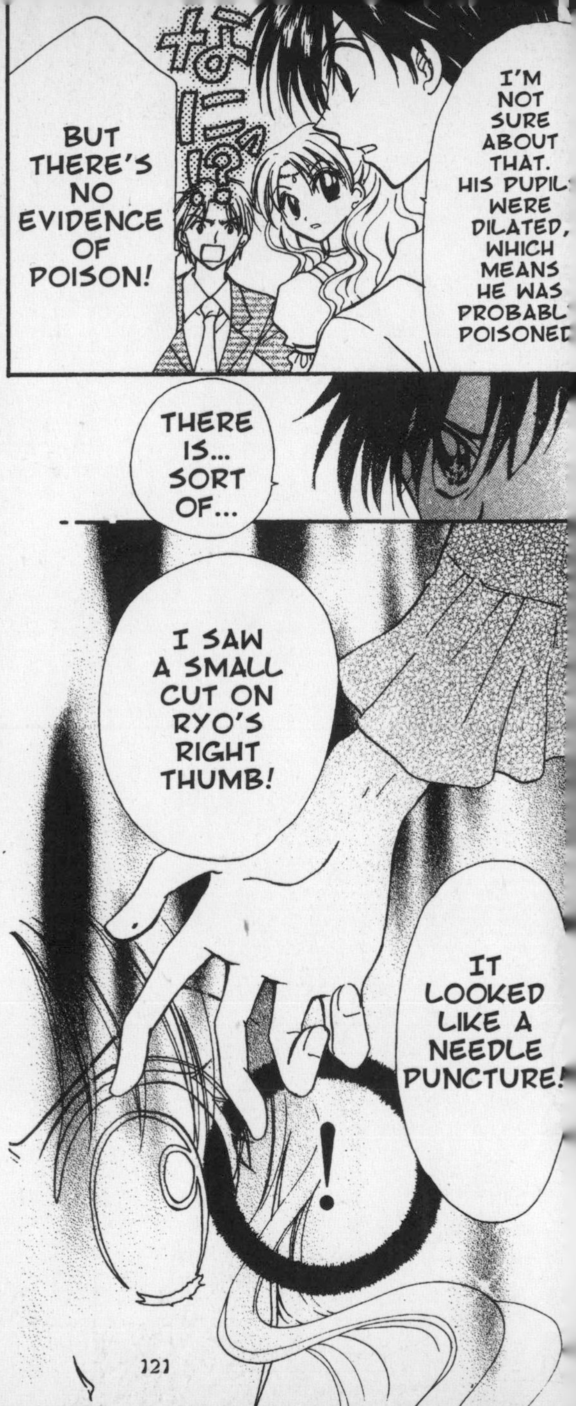
I'M NOT SURE ABOUT THAT. HIS PUPIL[S] WERE DILATED, WHICH MEANS HE WAS PROBABL[Y] POISONED
BUT THERE'S NO EVIDENCE OF POISON!
THERE IS... SORT OF...
I SAW A SMALL CUT ON RYO'S RIGHT THUMB!
IT LOOKED LIKE A NEEDLE PUNCTURE!
!

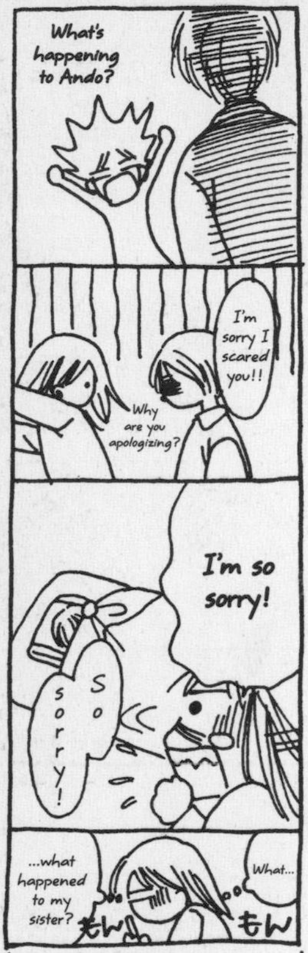
What's happening to Ando?
I'm sorry I scared you!!
Why are you apologizing?
I'm so sorry!
So sorry!
What...
...what happened to my sister?

The next day I asked my sister what really happened the night before. She lives by herself in an apartment, but on that night, she happened to be staying at my parents' house. She woke up in the middle of the night thinking she was by herself in her apartment. She got scared because she heard noises from the room next door. She decided to go and investigate the strange noises. She ended up in my room where I was working.

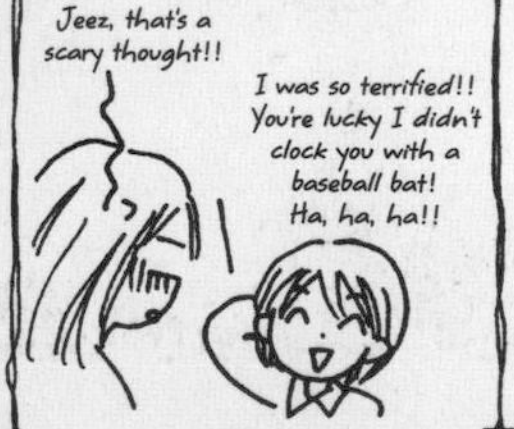
Jeez, that's a scary thought!!
I was so terrified!! You're lucky I didn't clock you with a baseball bat! Ha, ha, ha!!

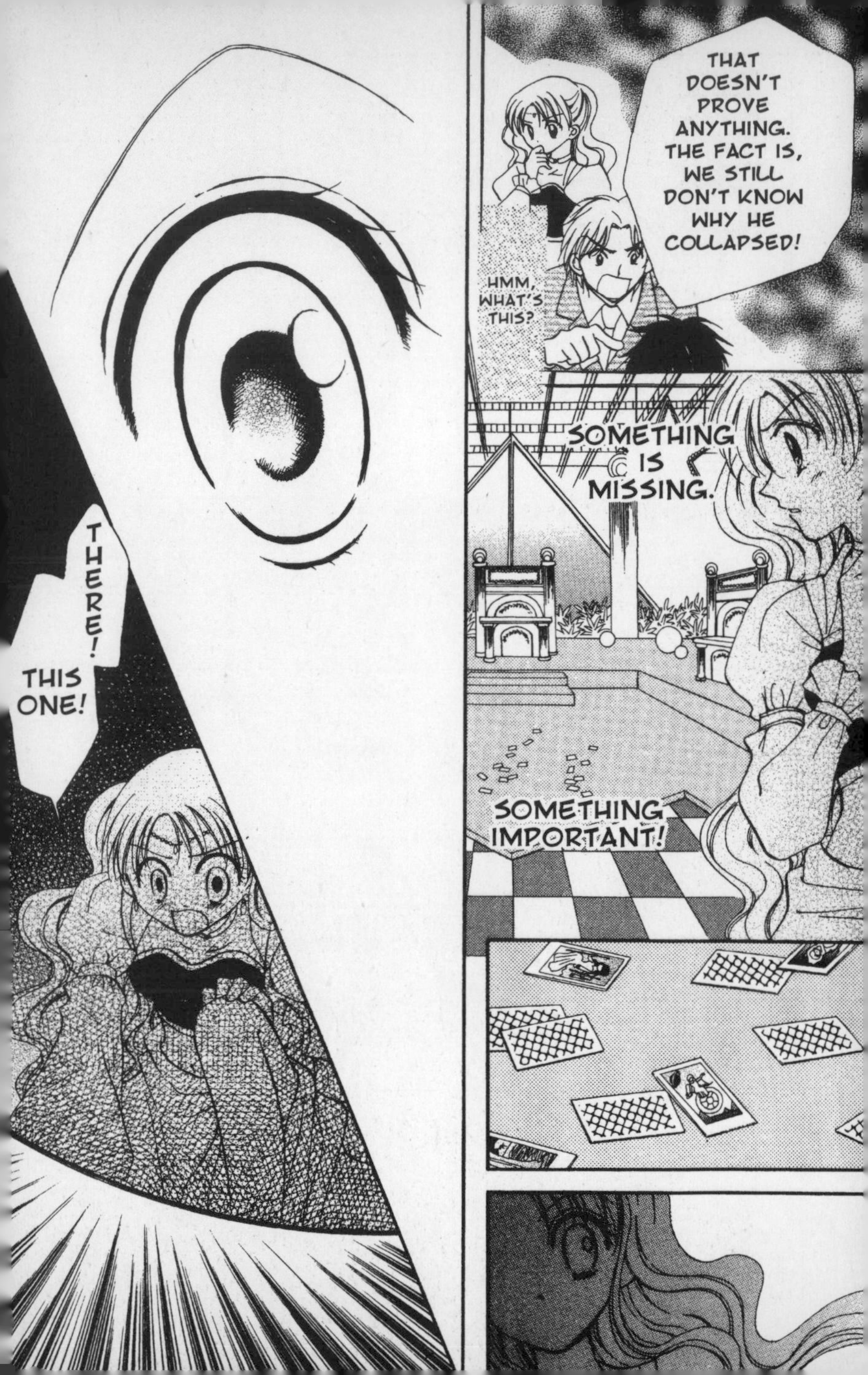
THAT DOESN'T PROVE ANYTHING. THE FACT IS, WE STILL DON'T KNOW WHY HE COLLAPSED!
HMM, WHAT'S THIS?
SOMETHING IS MISSING.
SOMETHING IMPORTANT!
THERE!
THIS ONE!

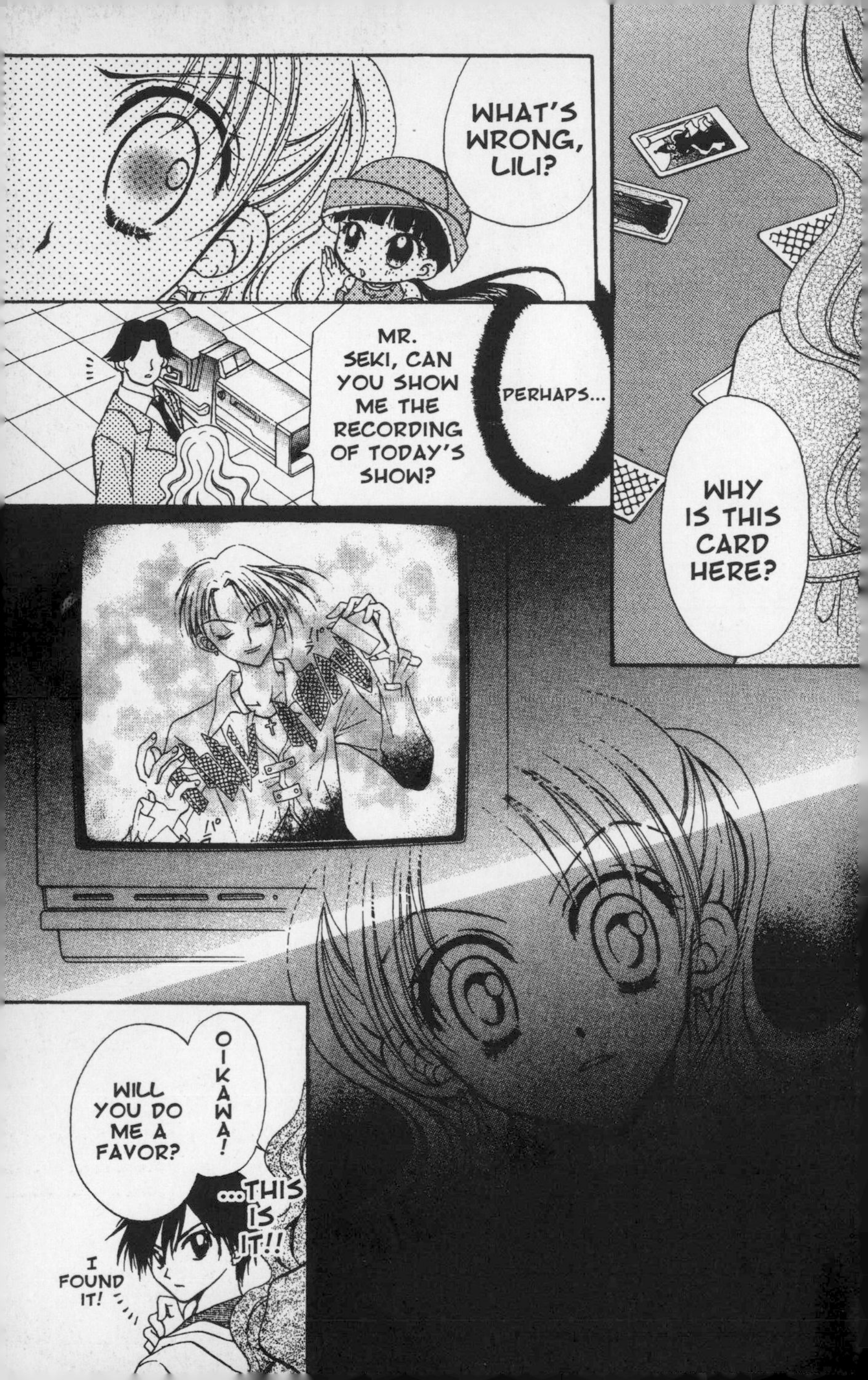
WHY IS THIS CARD HERE?
WHAT'S WRONG, LILI?
PERHAPS...
MR. SEKI, CAN YOU SHOW ME THE RECORDING OF TODAY'S SHOW?
...THIS IS IT!!
OIKAWA!
WILL YOU DO ME A FAVOR?
I FOUND IT!

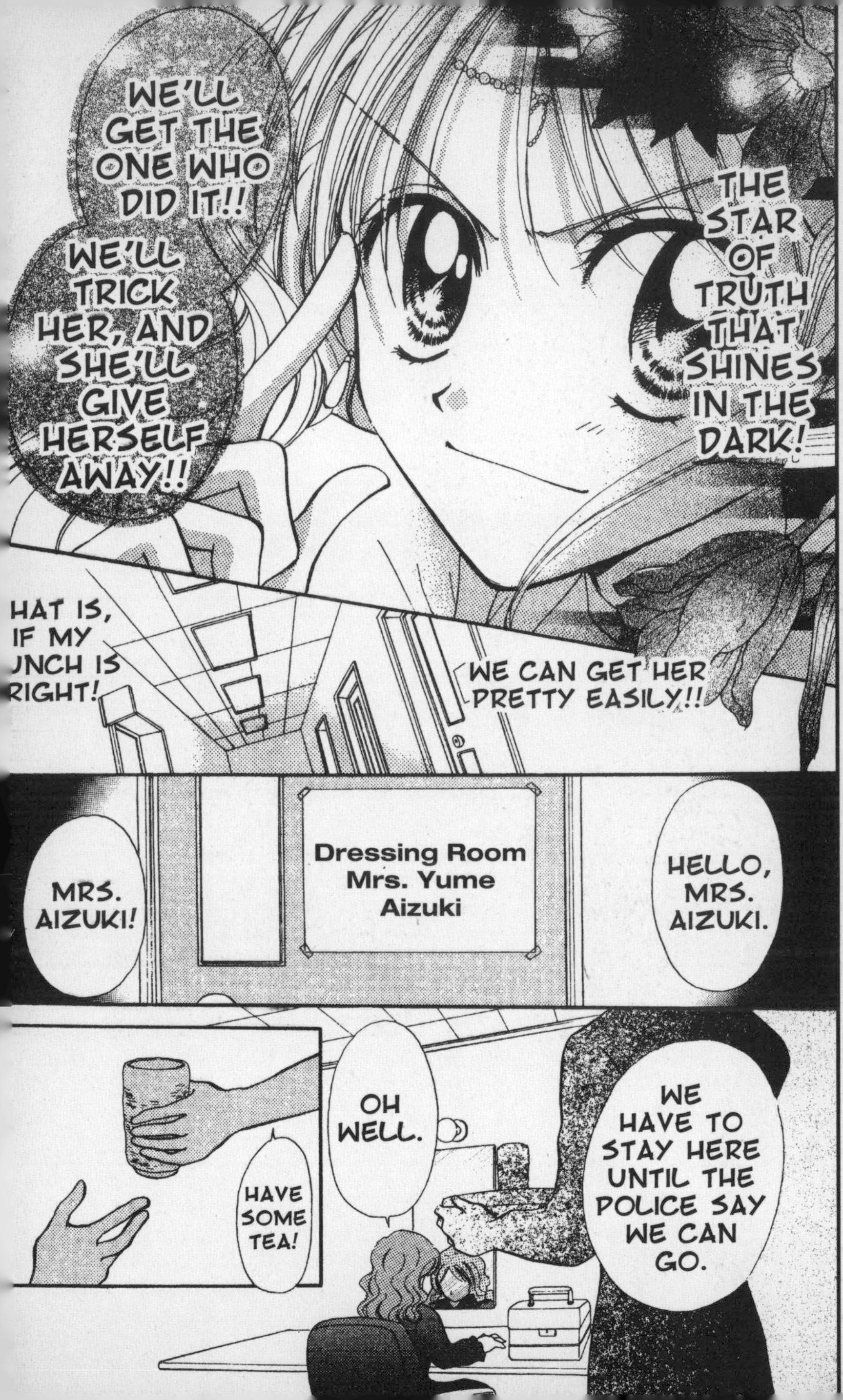
THE STAR OF TRUTH THAT SHINES IN THE DARK!
WE'LL GET THE ONE WHO DID IT!!
WE'LL TRICK HER, AND SHE'LL GIVE HERSELF AWAY!!
WE CAN GET HER PRETTY EASILY!!
HAT IS, IF MY UNCH IS RIGHT!
HELLO, MRS. AIZUKI.
Dressing Room Mrs. Yume Aizuki
MRS. AIZUKI!
WE HAVE TO STAY HERE UNTIL THE POLICE SAY WE CAN GO.
OH WELL.
HAVE SOME TEA!

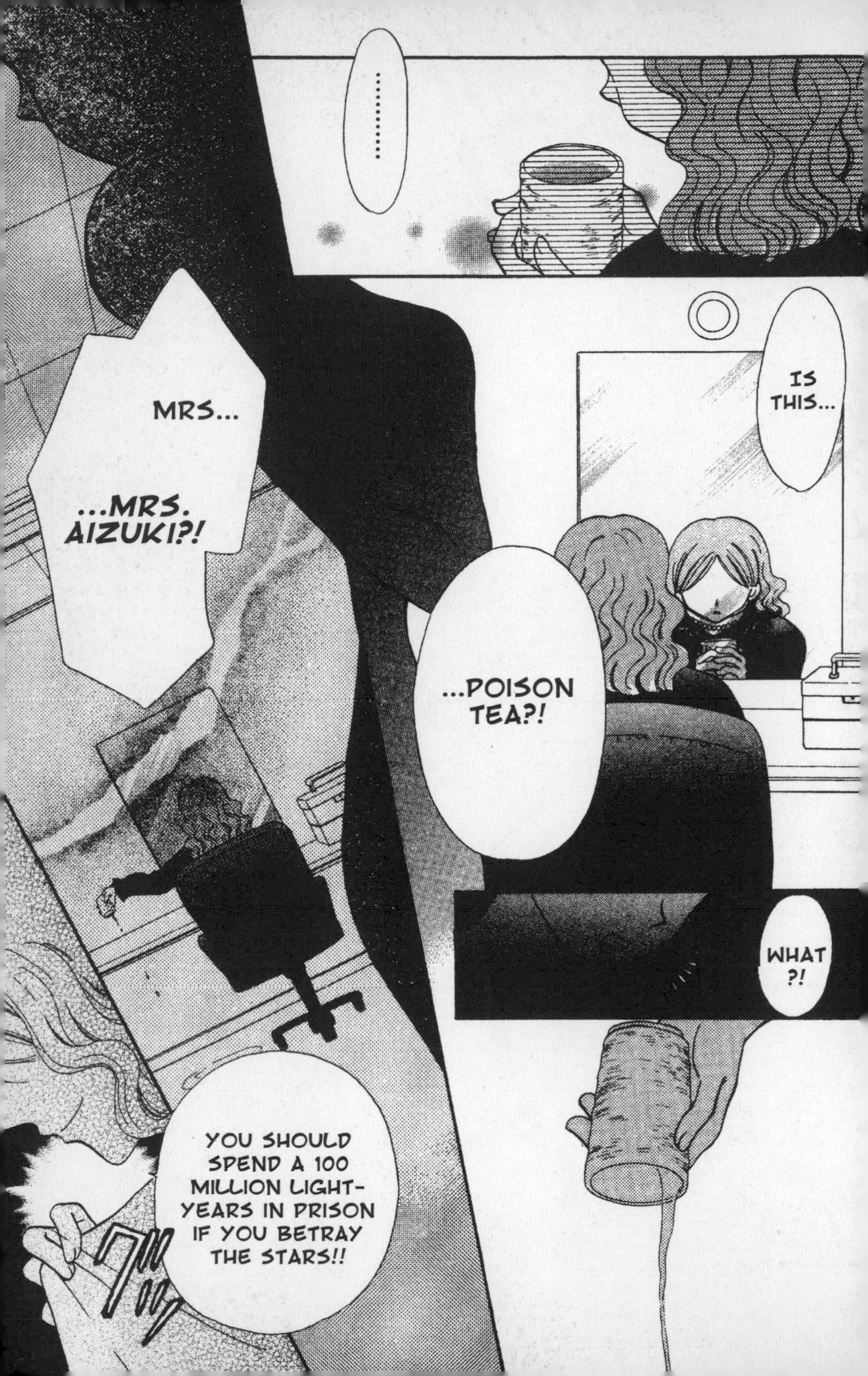
......
IS THIS...
...POISON TEA?!
WHAT ?!
MRS...
...MRS. AIZUKI?!
YOU SHOULD SPEND A 100 MILLION LIGHT-YEARS IN PRISON IF YOU BETRAY THE STARS!!

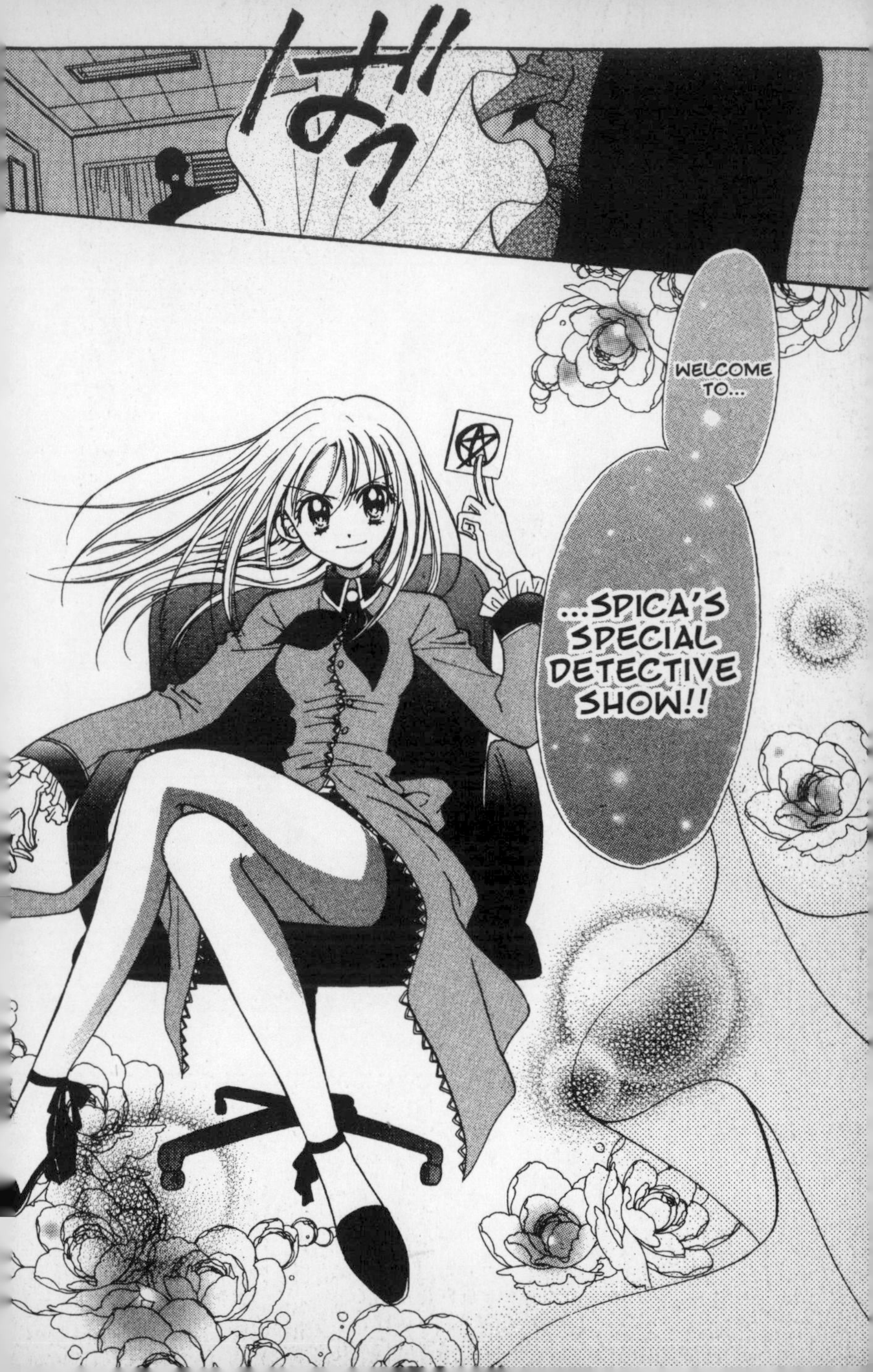
ばっ
WELCOME TO...
...SPICA'S SPECIAL DETECTIVE SHOW!!

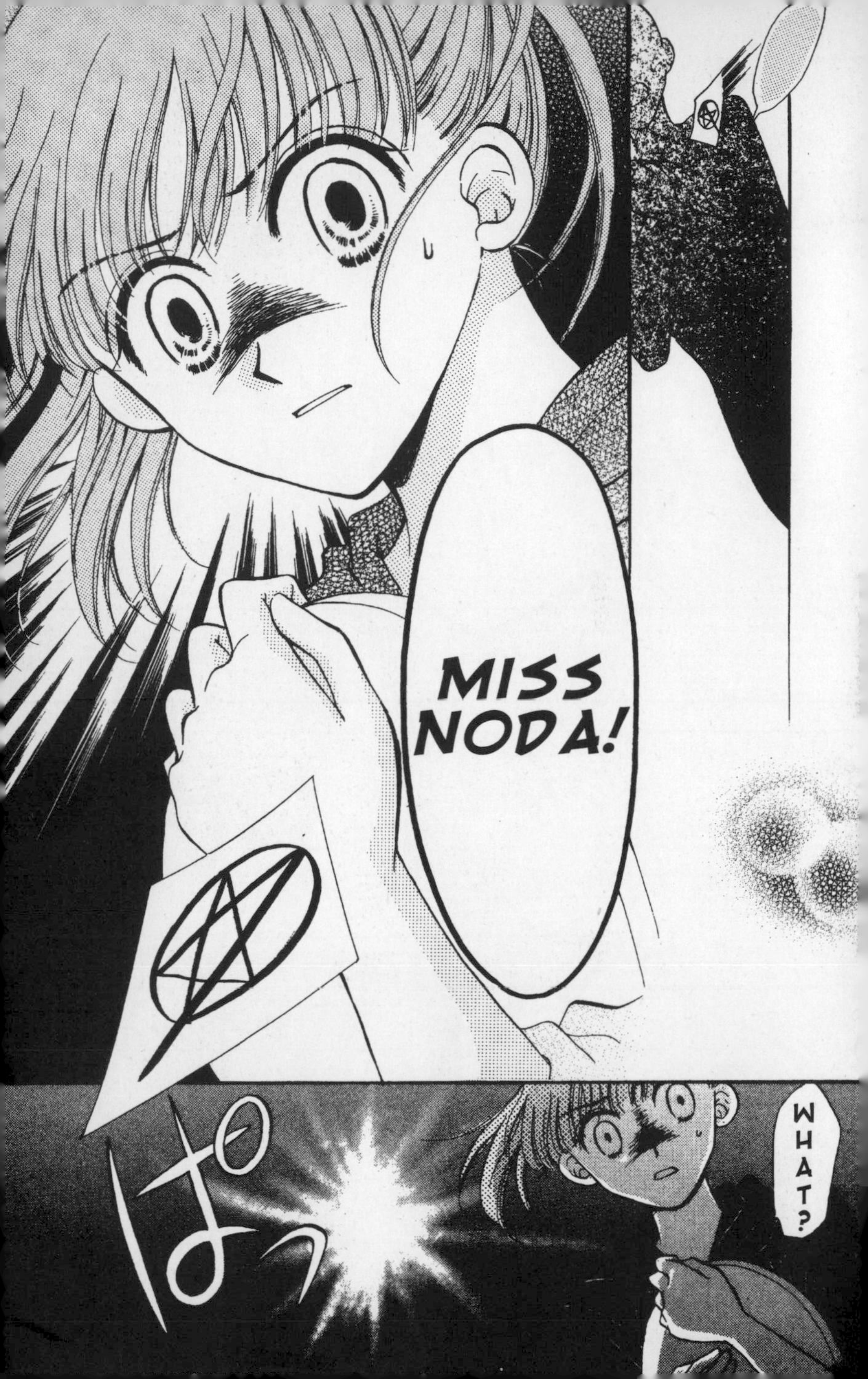
MISS NODA!
WHAT?
ぱっ

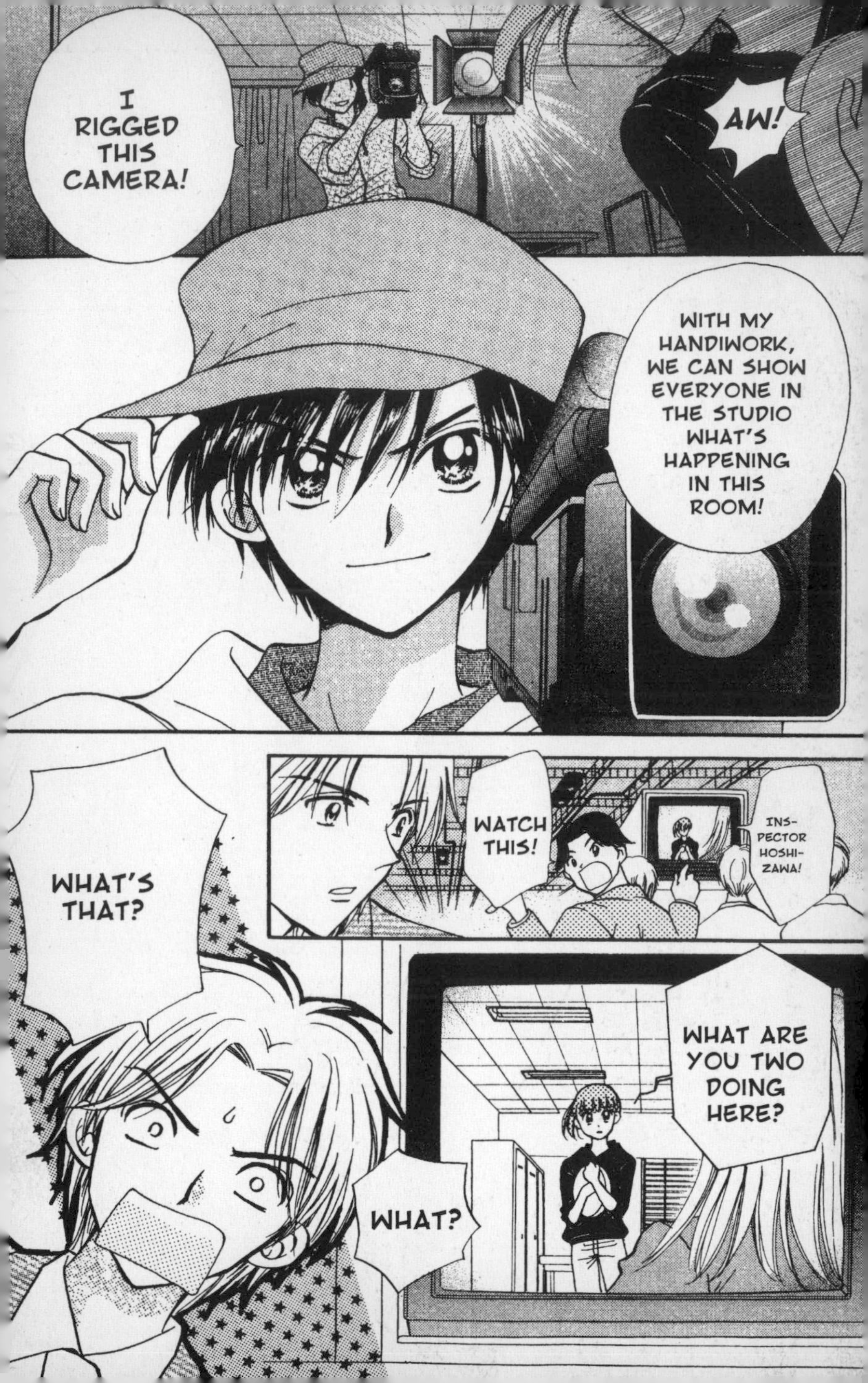
AW!
I RIGGED THIS CAMERA!
WITH MY HANDIWORK, WE CAN SHOW EVERYONE IN THE STUDIO WHAT'S HAPPENING IN THIS ROOM!
INSPECTOR HOSHIZAWA!
WATCH THIS!
WHAT ARE YOU TWO DOING HERE?
WHAT'S THAT?
WHAT?

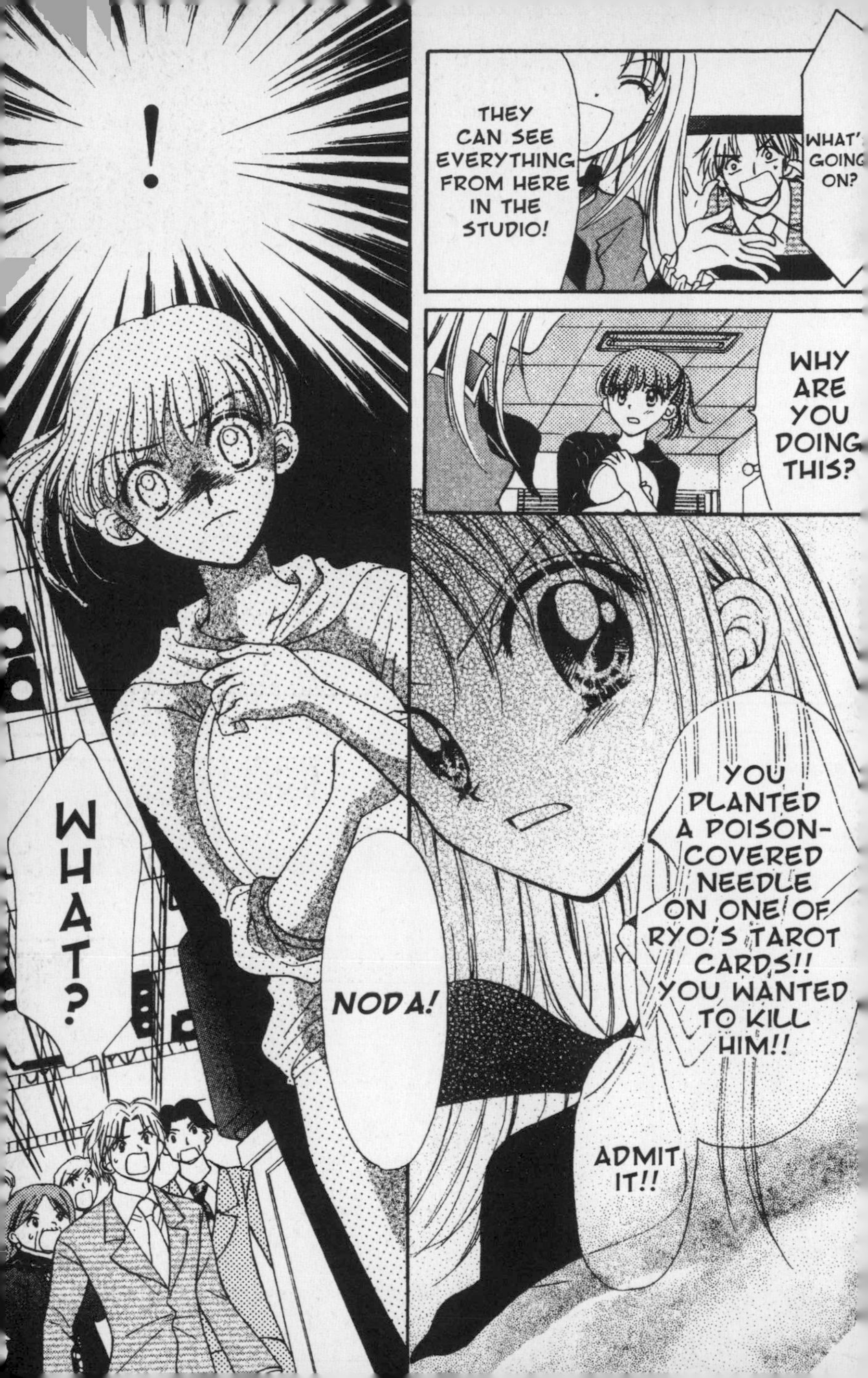
THEY CAN SEE EVERYTHING FROM HERE IN THE STUDIO!
WHAT'S GOING ON?
WHY ARE YOU DOING THIS?
YOU PLANTED A POISON-COVERED NEEDLE ON ONE OF RYO'S TAROT CARDS!! YOU WANTED TO KILL HIM!!
ADMIT IT!!
NODA!
!
WHAT?

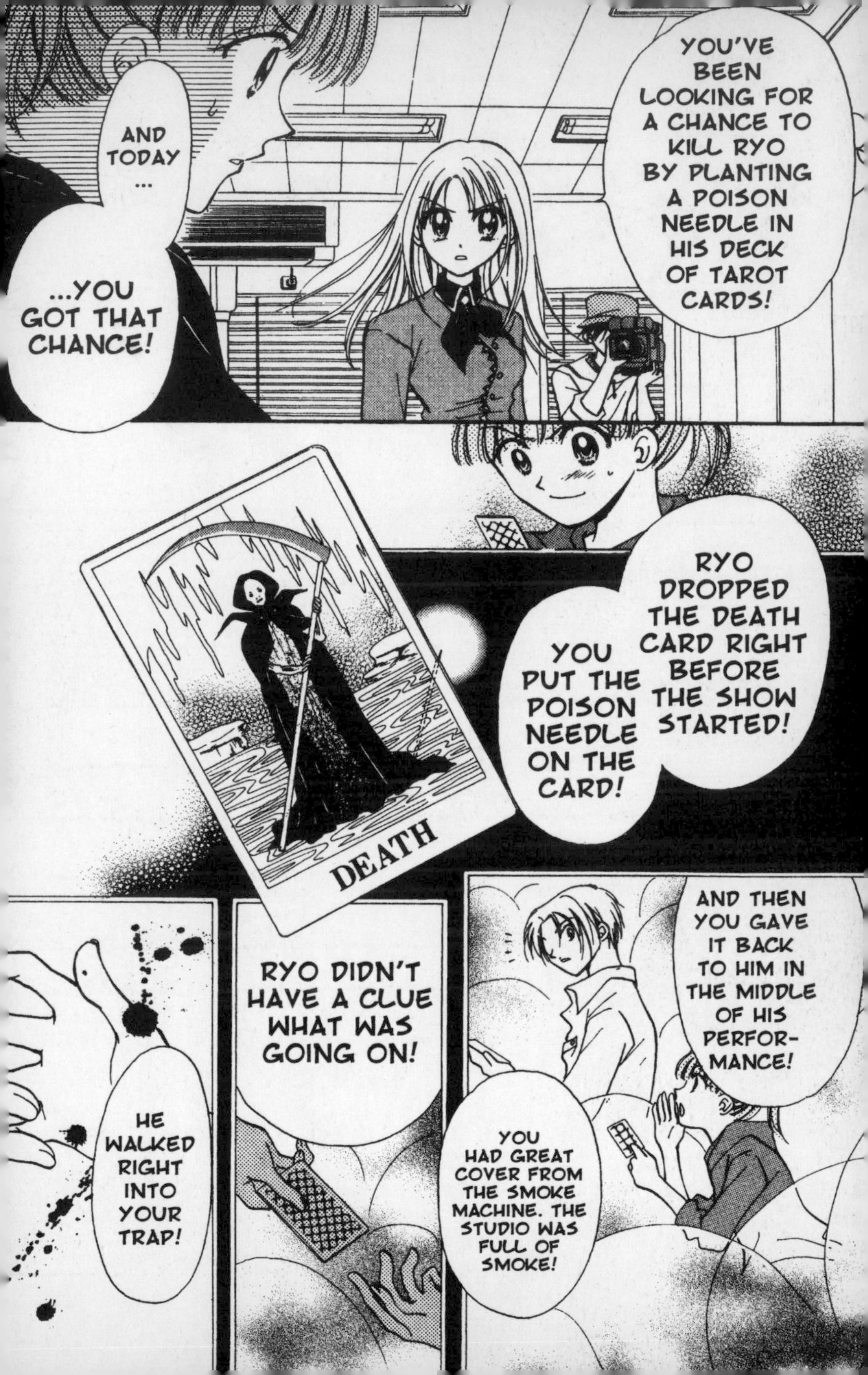
YOU'VE BEEN LOOKING FOR A CHANCE TO KILL RYO BY PLANTING A POISON NEEDLE IN HIS DECK OF TAROT CARDS!
AND TODAY ...
...YOU GOT THAT CHANCE!
RYO DROPPED THE DEATH CARD RIGHT BEFORE THE SHOW STARTED!
YOU PUT THE POISON NEEDLE ON THE CARD!
DEATH
AND THEN YOU GAVE IT BACK TO HIM IN THE MIDDLE OF HIS PERFOR-MANCE!
YOU HAD GREAT COVER FROM THE SMOKE MACHINE. THE STUDIO WAS FULL OF SMOKE!
RYO DIDN'T HAVE A CLUE WHAT WAS GOING ON!
HE WALKED RIGHT INTO YOUR TRAP!

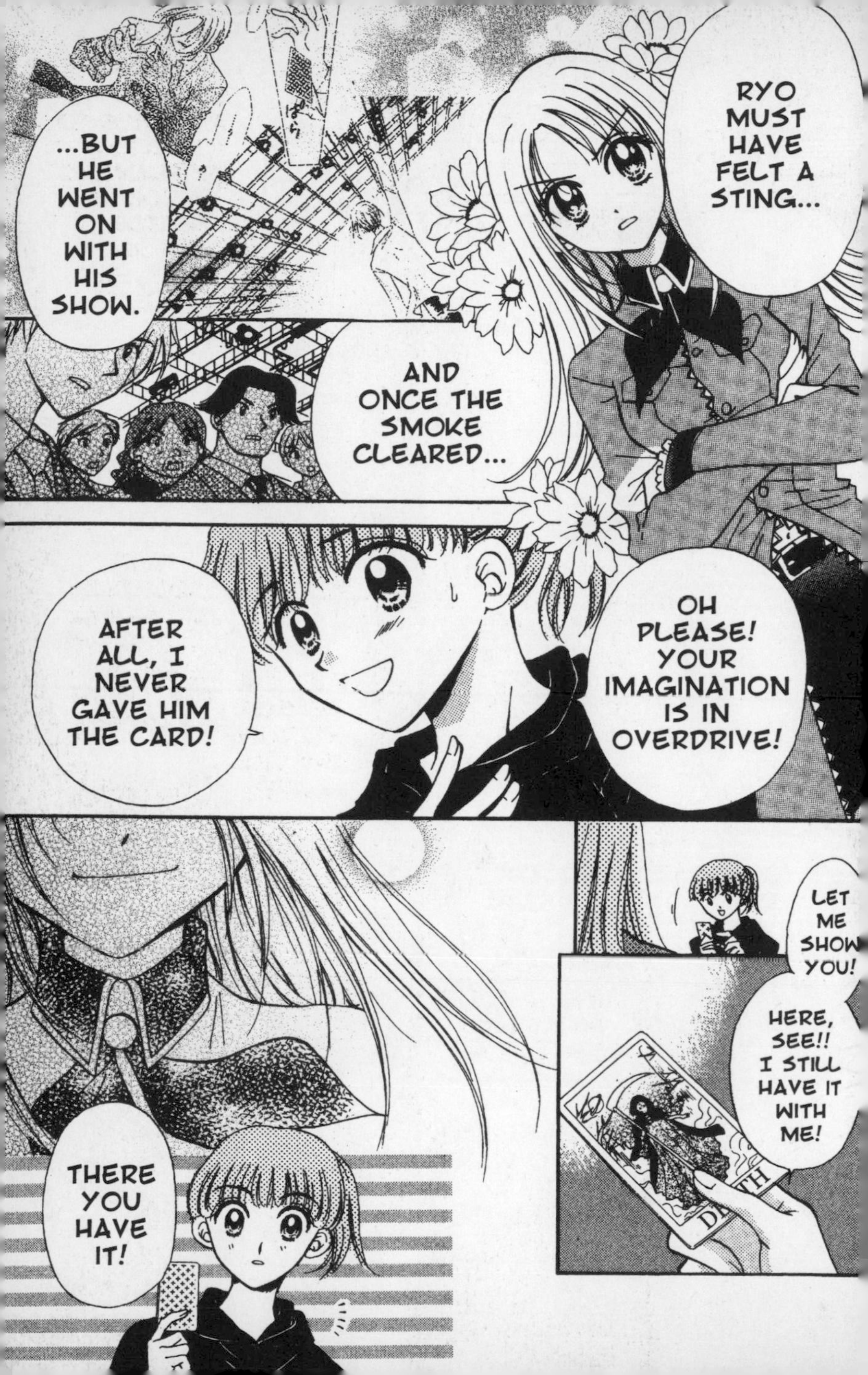
RYO MUST HAVE FELT A STING...
...BUT HE WENT ON WITH HIS SHOW.
AND ONCE THE SMOKE CLEARED...
OH PLEASE! YOUR IMAGINATION IS IN OVERDRIVE!
AFTER ALL, I NEVER GAVE HIM THE CARD!
LET ME SHOW YOU!
HERE, SEE!! I STILL HAVE IT WITH ME!
THERE YOU HAVE IT!

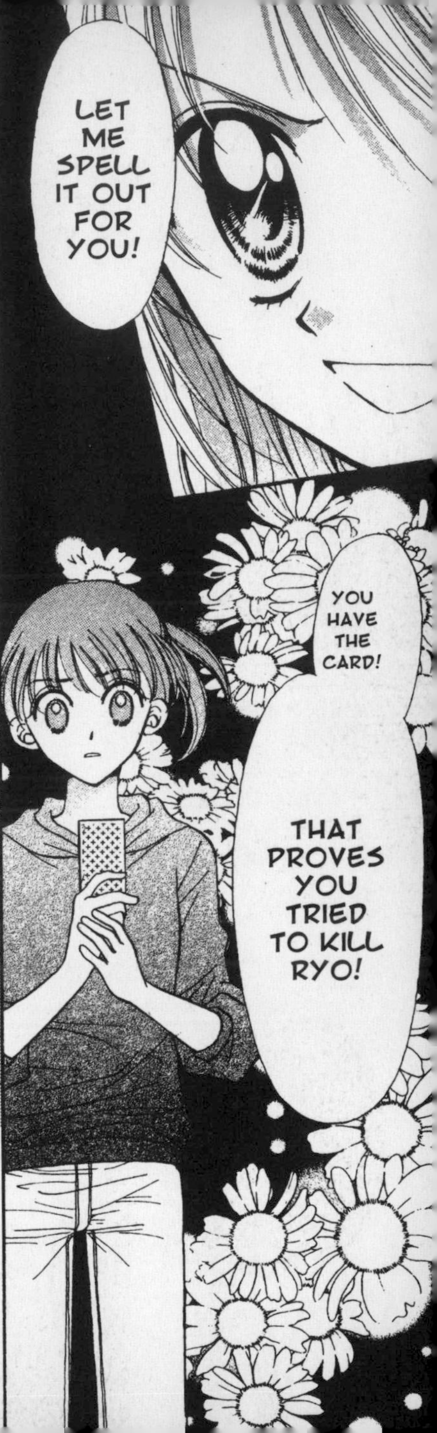
LET ME SPELL IT OUT FOR YOU!
YOU HAVE THE CARD!
THAT PROVES YOU TRIED TO KILL RYO!

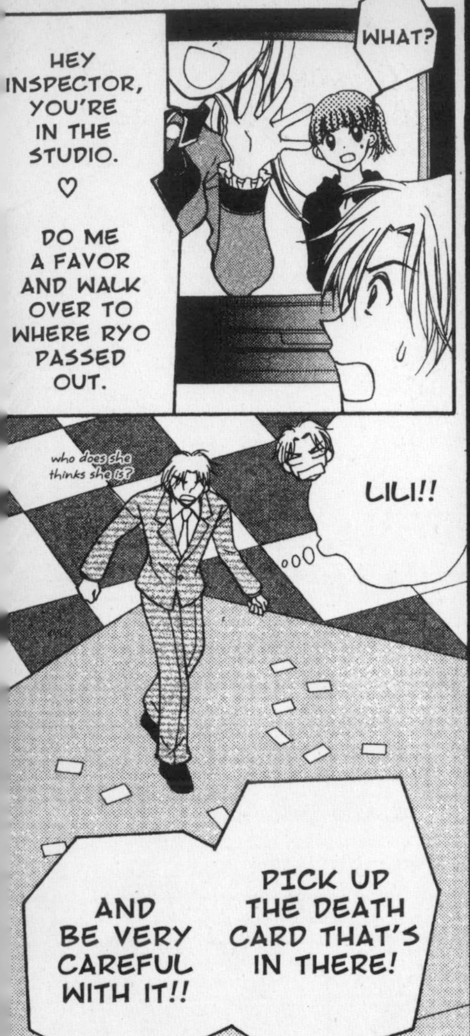
WHAT?
HEY INSPECTOR, YOU'RE IN THE STUDIO. ♡
DO ME A FAVOR AND WALK OVER TO WHERE RYO PASSED OUT.
LILI!!
who does she thinks she is?
PICK UP THE DEATH CARD THAT'S IN THERE!
AND BE VERY CAREFUL WITH IT!!
THERE'S NO WAY HE'LL FIND IT!

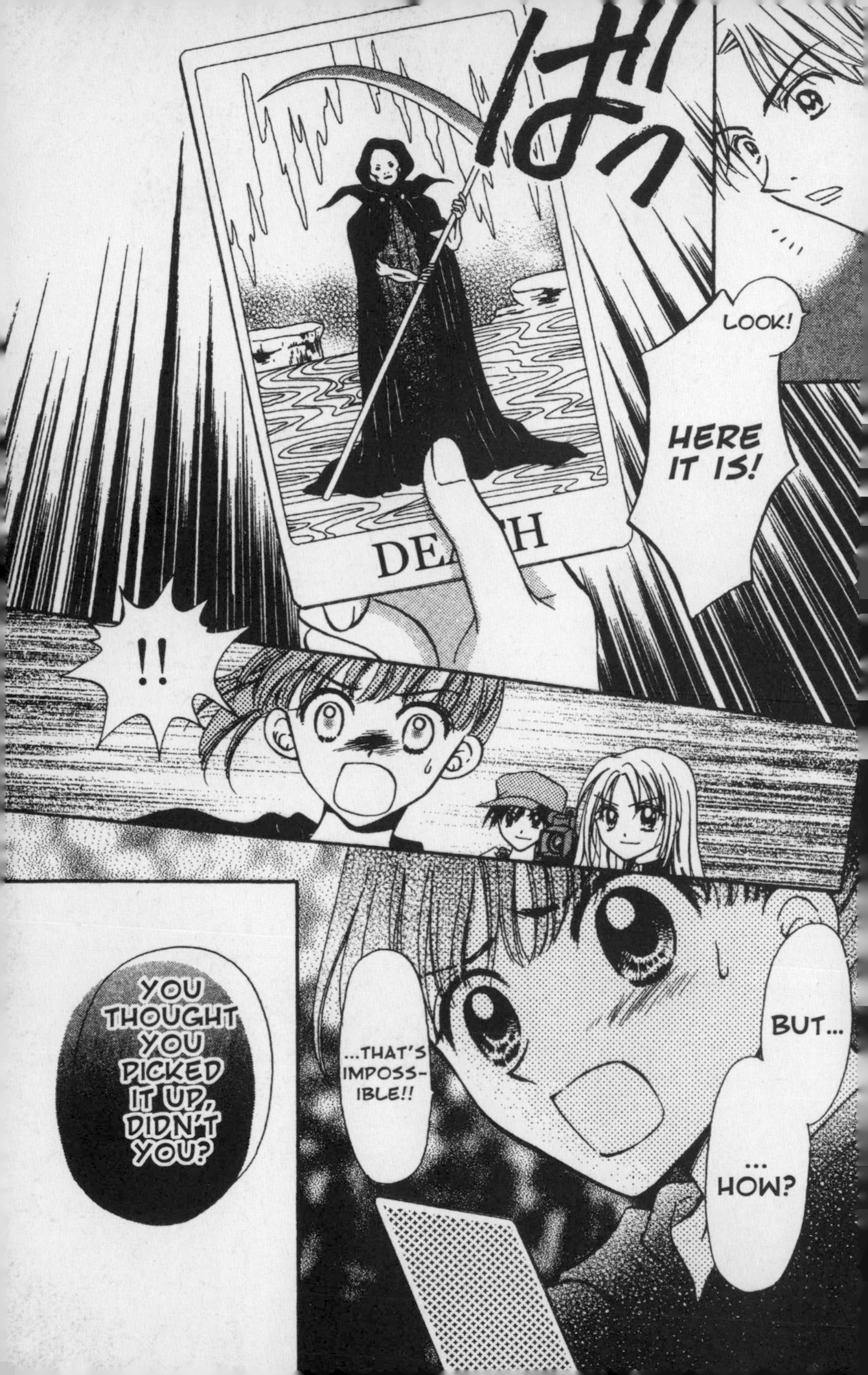
LOOK!
HERE IT IS!
ぱっ
!!
BUT...
...HOW?
...THAT'S IMPOSS-IBLE!!
YOU THOUGHT YOU PICKED IT UP, DIDN'T YOU?

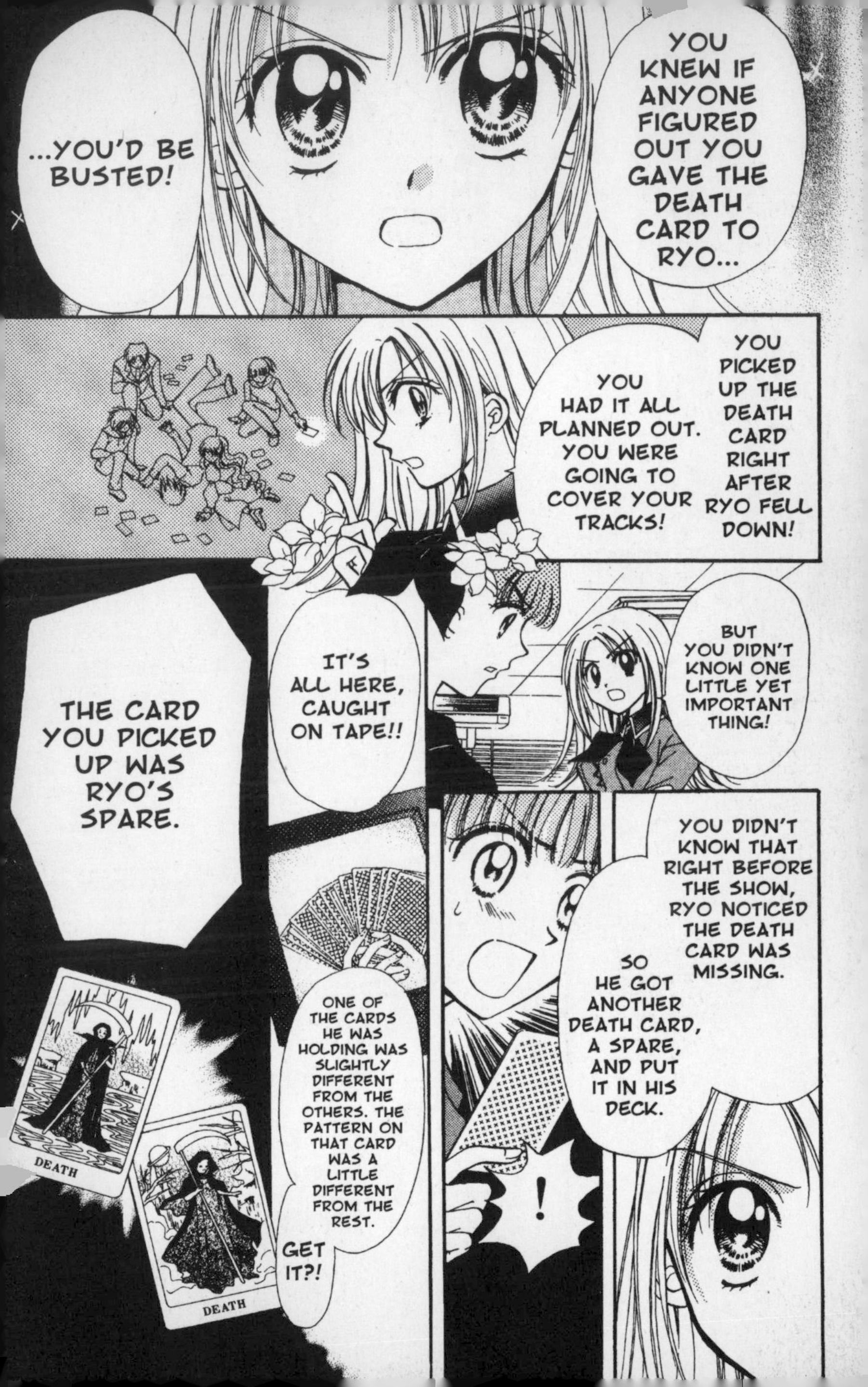

YOU KNEW IF ANYONE FIGURED OUT YOU GAVE THE DEATH CARD TO RYO...
...YOU'D BE BUSTED!
YOU PICKED UP THE DEATH CARD RIGHT AFTER RYO FELL DOWN!
YOU HAD IT ALL PLANNED OUT. YOU WERE GOING TO COVER YOUR TRACKS!
BUT YOU DIDN'T KNOW ONE LITTLE YET IMPORTANT THING!
IT'S ALL HERE, CAUGHT ON TAPE!!
YOU DIDN'T KNOW THAT RIGHT BEFORE THE SHOW, RYO NOTICED THE DEATH CARD WAS MISSING.
SO HE GOT ANOTHER DEATH CARD, A SPARE, AND PUT IT IN HIS DECK.
!
ONE OF THE CARDS HE WAS HOLDING WAS SLIGHTLY DIFFERENT FROM THE OTHERS. THE PATTERN ON THAT CARD WAS A LITTLE DIFFERENT FROM THE REST.
GET IT?!
THE CARD YOU PICKED UP WAS RYO'S SPARE.
DEATH
DEATH

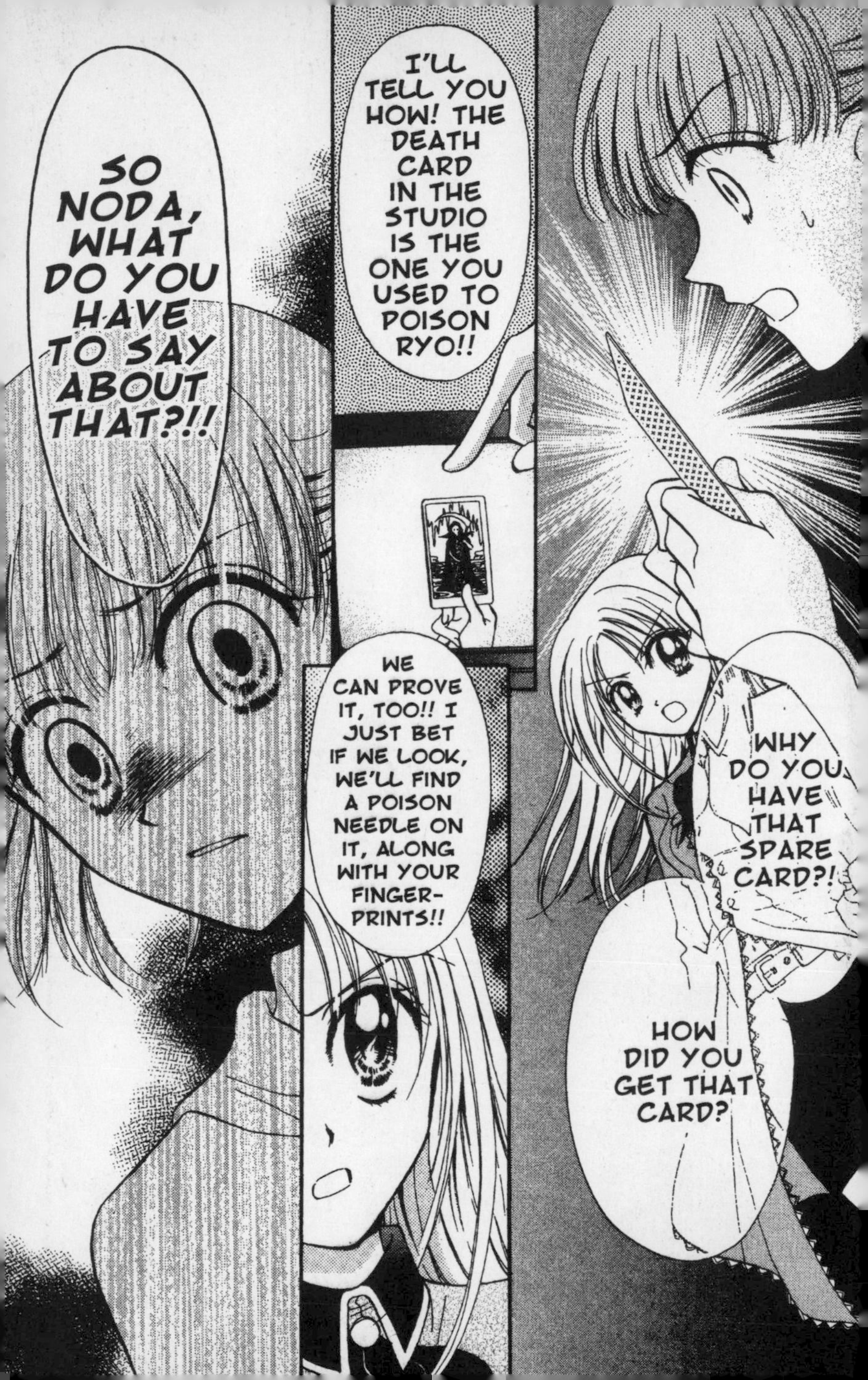
WHY DO YOU HAVE THAT SPARE CARD?!
HOW DID YOU GET THAT CARD?
I'LL TELL YOU HOW! THE DEATH CARD IN THE STUDIO IS THE ONE YOU USED TO POISON RYO!!
WE CAN PROVE IT, TOO!! I JUST BET IF WE LOOK, WE'LL FIND A POISON NEEDLE ON IT, ALONG WITH YOUR FINGER-PRINTS!!
SO NODA, WHAT DO YOU HAVE TO SAY ABOUT THAT?!!

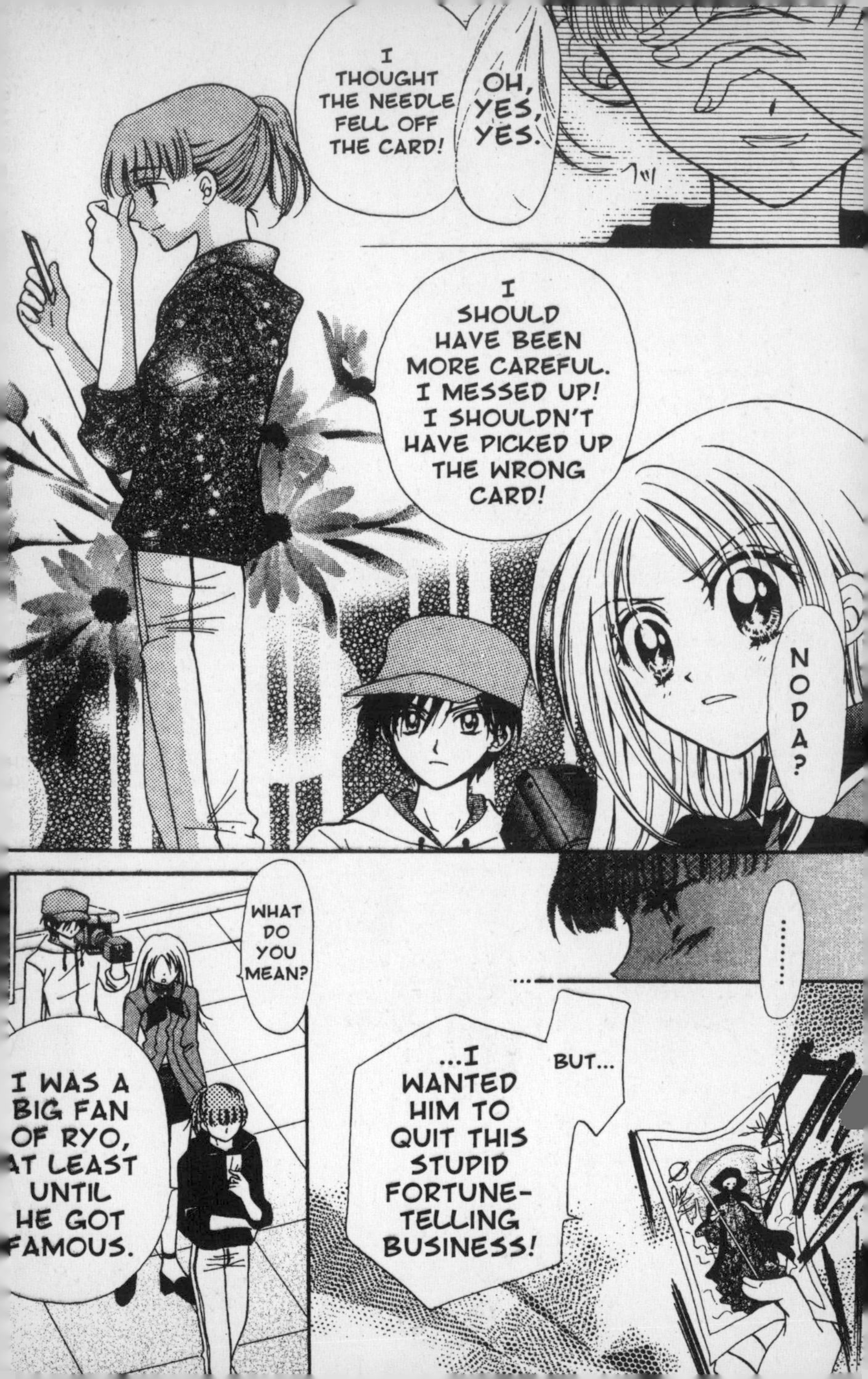
OH, YES, YES.
I THOUGHT THE NEEDLE FELL OFF THE CARD!
I SHOULD HAVE BEEN MORE CAREFUL. I MESSED UP! I SHOULDN'T HAVE PICKED UP THE WRONG CARD!
NODA?
......
...
BUT...
...I WANTED HIM TO QUIT THIS STUPID FORTUNE-TELLING BUSINESS!
WHAT DO YOU MEAN?
I WAS A BIG FAN OF RYO, AT LEAST UNTIL HE GOT FAMOUS.

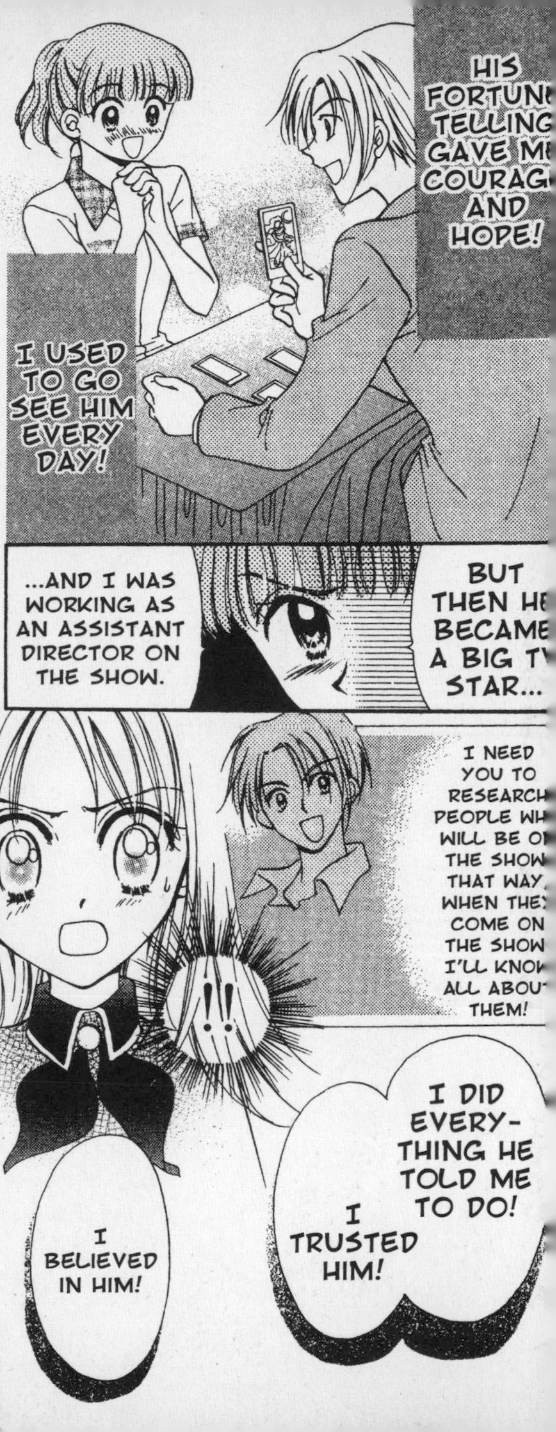
HIS FORTUN TELLING GAVE M COURAG AND HOPE!
I USED TO GO SEE HIM EVERY DAY!
BUT THEN HE BECAME A BIG T STAR...
...AND I WAS WORKING AS AN ASSISTANT DIRECTOR ON THE SHOW.
I NEED YOU TO RESEARCH PEOPLE WH WILL BE O THE SHOW THAT WAY, WHEN THE COME ON THE SHOW I'LL KNOW ALL ABOU THEM!
!!
I DID EVERY-THING HE TOLD ME TO DO!
I TRUSTED HIM!
I BELIEVED IN HIM!

Kyoto

I went to Kyoto to gather material to write File 6. I go to Kyoto all the time, so it wasn't a big deal. When I was in grade school, I went to Kyoto on class picnics. I got so tired of visiting temples and shrines. But now that I'm an adult, I really like seeing the sites there.

My favorite place is Gion City. Time seems to stop when I'm there. There was a great shop there that sold green tea. I'd like to go there again-!

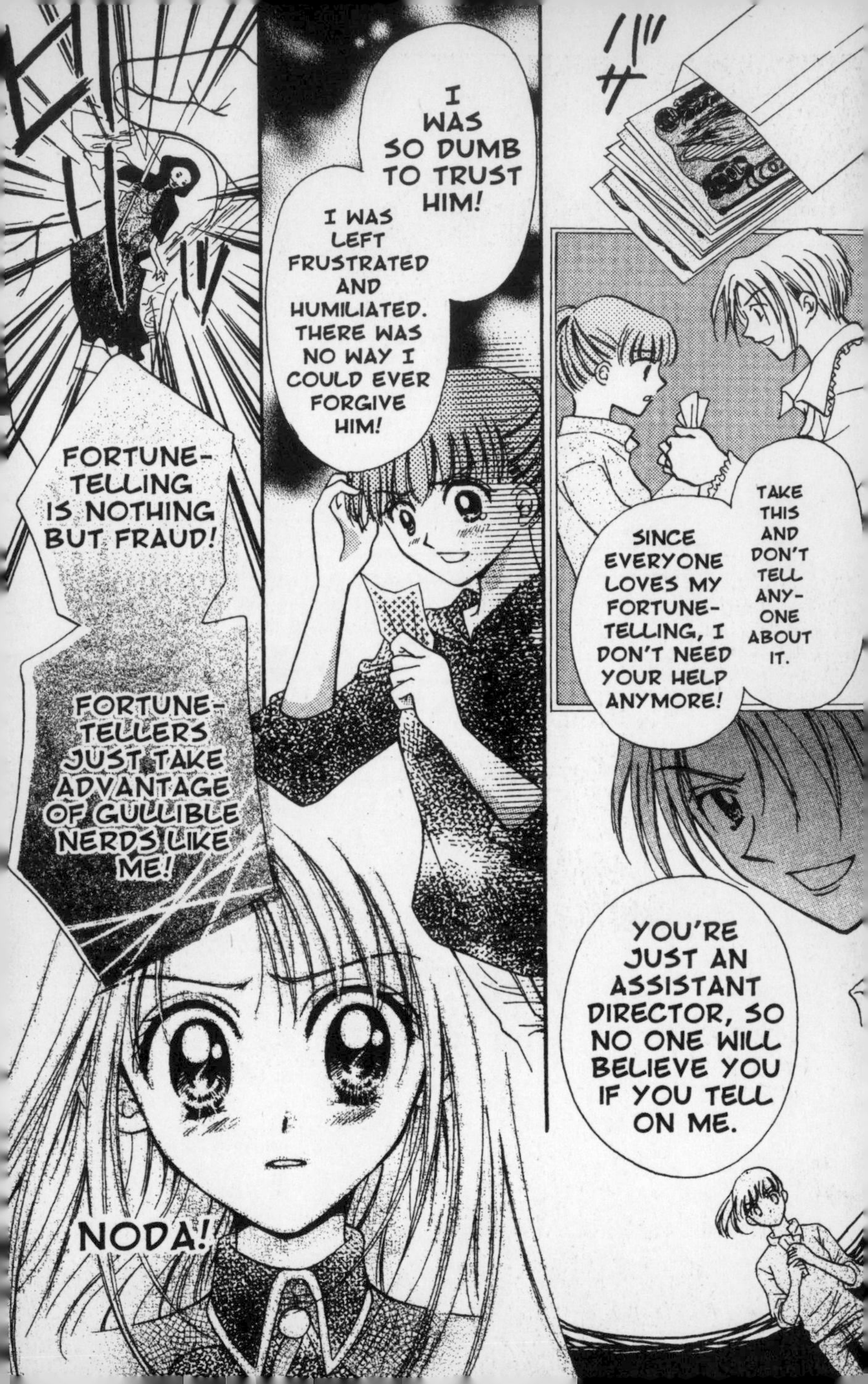
TAKE THIS AND DON'T TELL ANY-ONE ABOUT IT.
SINCE EVERYONE LOVES MY FORTUNE-TELLING, I DON'T NEED YOUR HELP ANYMORE!
YOU'RE JUST AN ASSISTANT DIRECTOR, SO NO ONE WILL BELIEVE YOU IF YOU TELL ON ME.
I WAS SO DUMB TO TRUST HIM!
I WAS LEFT FRUSTRATED AND HUMILIATED. THERE WAS NO WAY I COULD EVER FORGIVE HIM!
FORTUNE-TELLING IS NOTHING BUT FRAUD!
FORTUNE-TELLERS JUST TAKE ADVANTAGE OF GULLIBLE NERDS LIKE ME!
NODA!

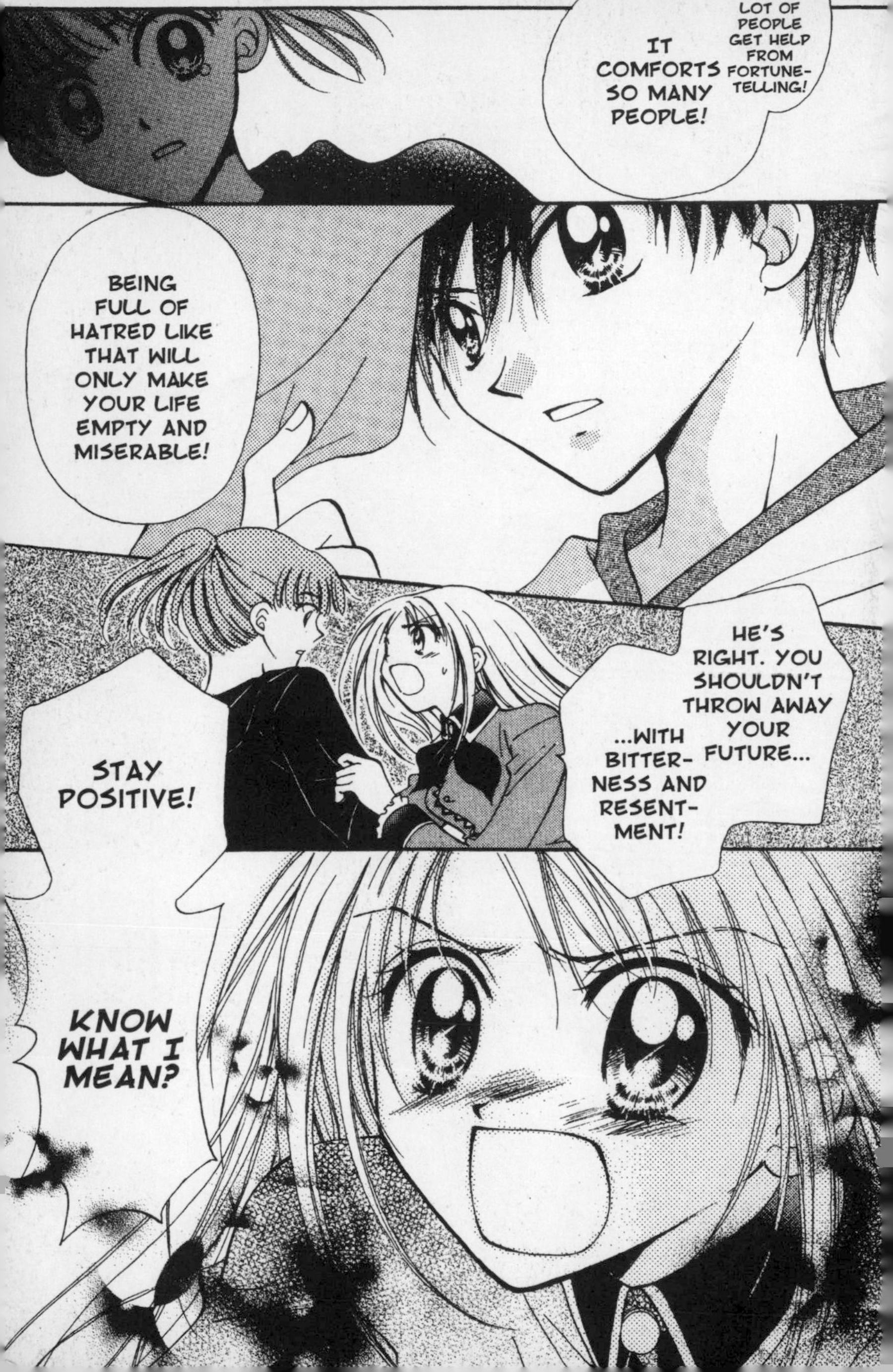
BUT A LOT OF PEOPLE GET HELP FROM FORTUNE-TELLING!
IT COMFORTS SO MANY PEOPLE!
BEING FULL OF HATRED LIKE THAT WILL ONLY MAKE YOUR LIFE EMPTY AND MISERABLE!
HE'S RIGHT. YOU SHOULDN'T THROW AWAY YOUR FUTURE...
...WITH BITTER-NESS AND RESENT-MENT!
STAY POSITIVE!
KNOW WHAT I MEAN?

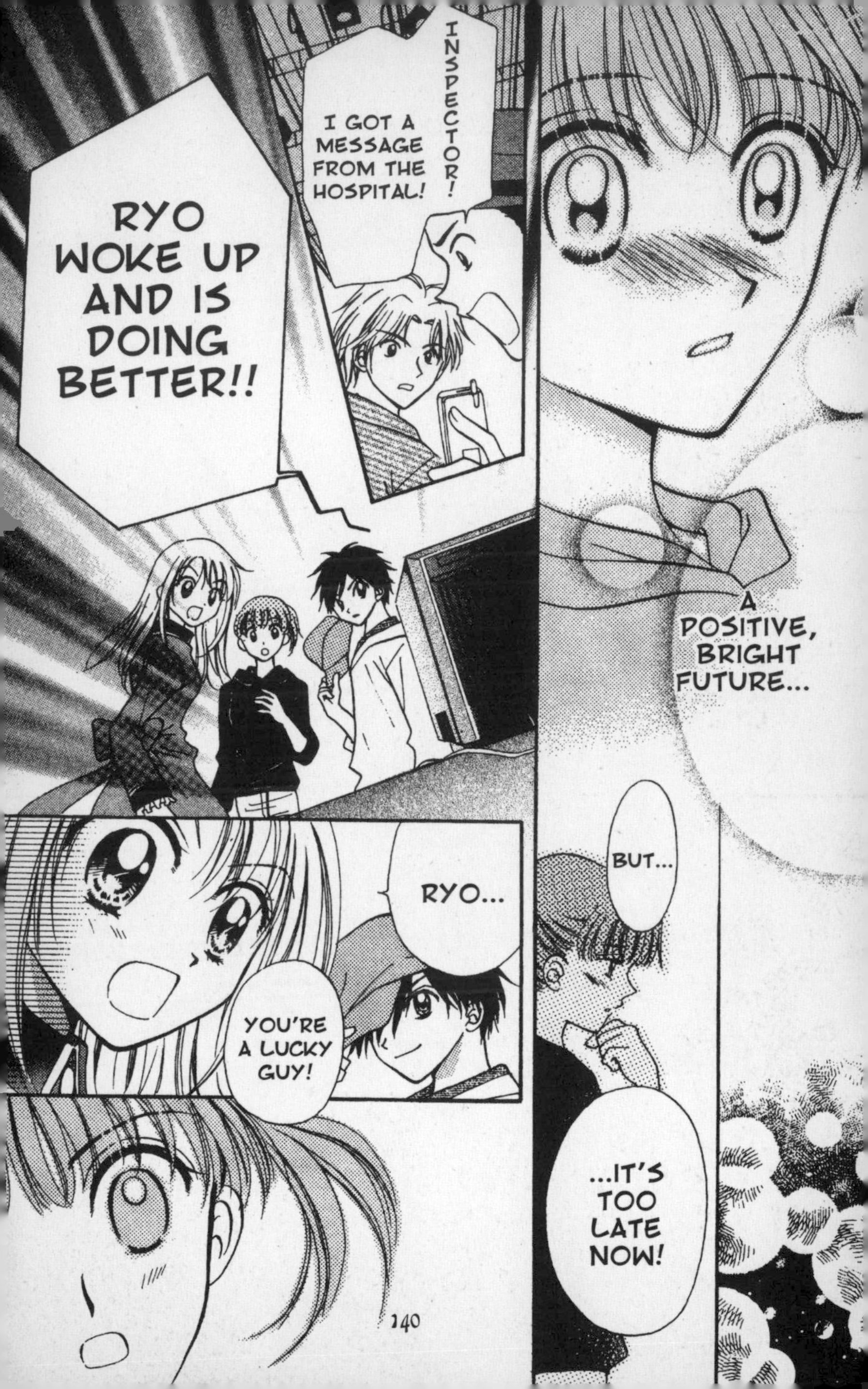
A POSITIVE, BRIGHT FUTURE...
BUT...
...IT'S TOO LATE NOW!
INSPECTOR!
I GOT A MESSAGE FROM THE HOSPITAL!
RYO WOKE UP AND IS DOING BETTER!!
RYO...
YOU'RE A LUCKY GUY!

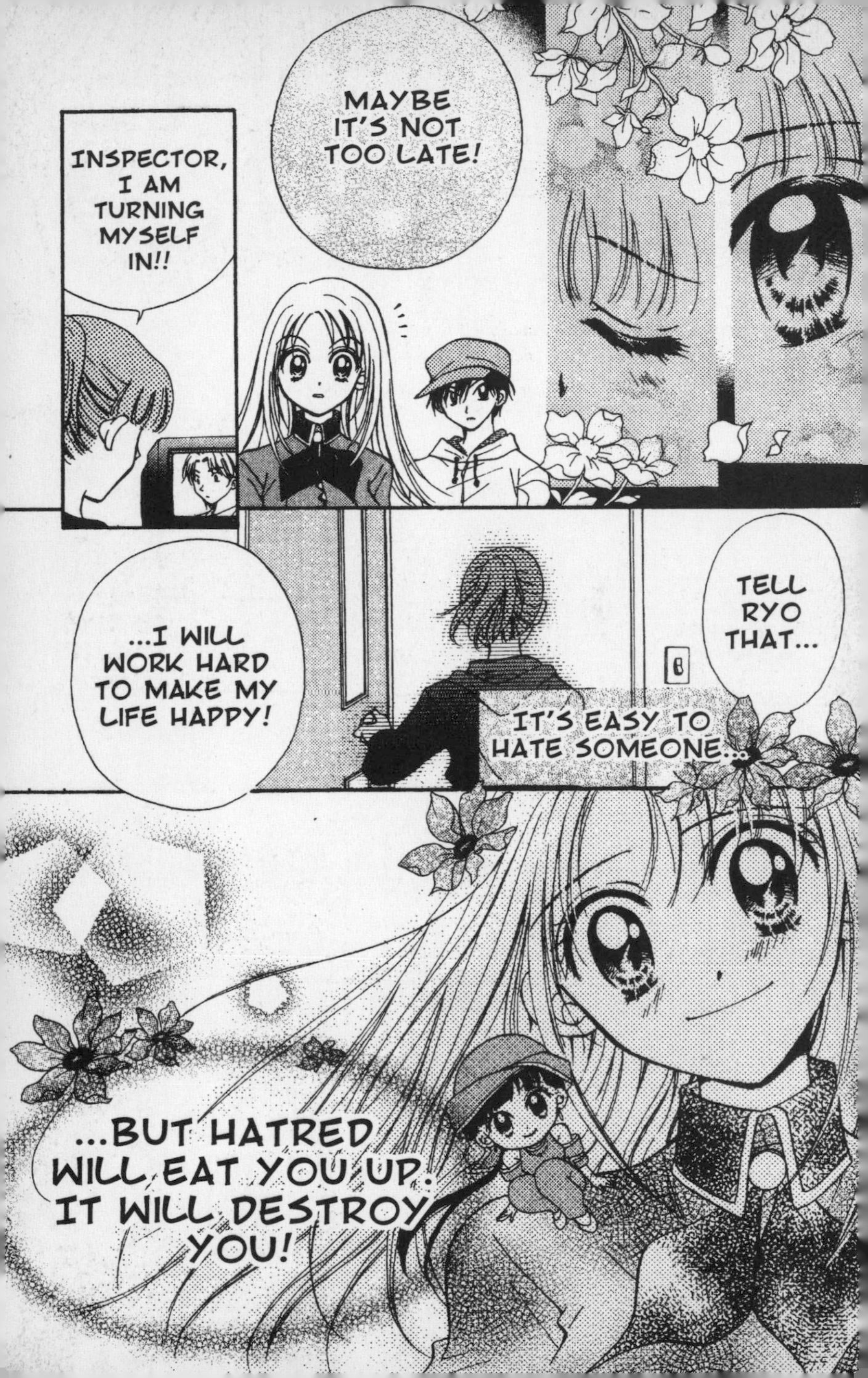
MAYBE IT'S NOT TOO LATE!
INSPECTOR, I AM TURNING MYSELF IN!!
TELL RYO THAT...
...I WILL WORK HARD TO MAKE MY LIFE HAPPY!
IT'S EASY TO HATE SOMEONE...
...BUT HATRED WILL EAT YOU UP. IT WILL DESTROY YOU!

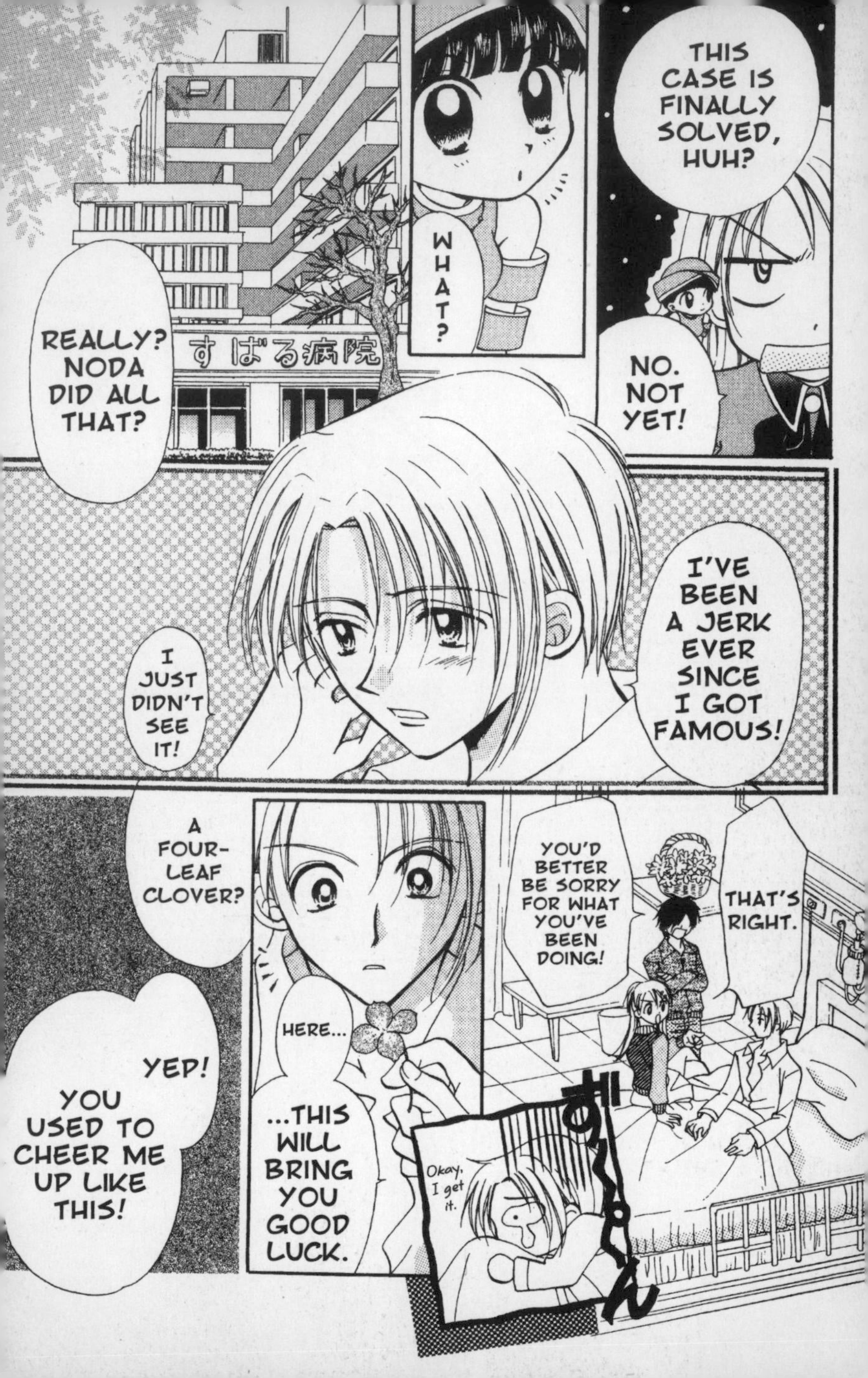
THIS CASE IS FINALLY SOLVED, HUH?
NO. NOT YET!
WHAT?
すばる病院
REALLY? NODA DID ALL THAT?
I'VE BEEN A JERK EVER SINCE I GOT FAMOUS!
I JUST DIDN'T SEE IT!
YOU'D BETTER BE SORRY FOR WHAT YOU'VE BEEN DOING!
THAT'S RIGHT.
Okay, I get it.
A FOUR-LEAF CLOVER?
HERE...
...THIS WILL BRING YOU GOOD LUCK.
YEP!
YOU USED TO CHEER ME UP LIKE THIS!

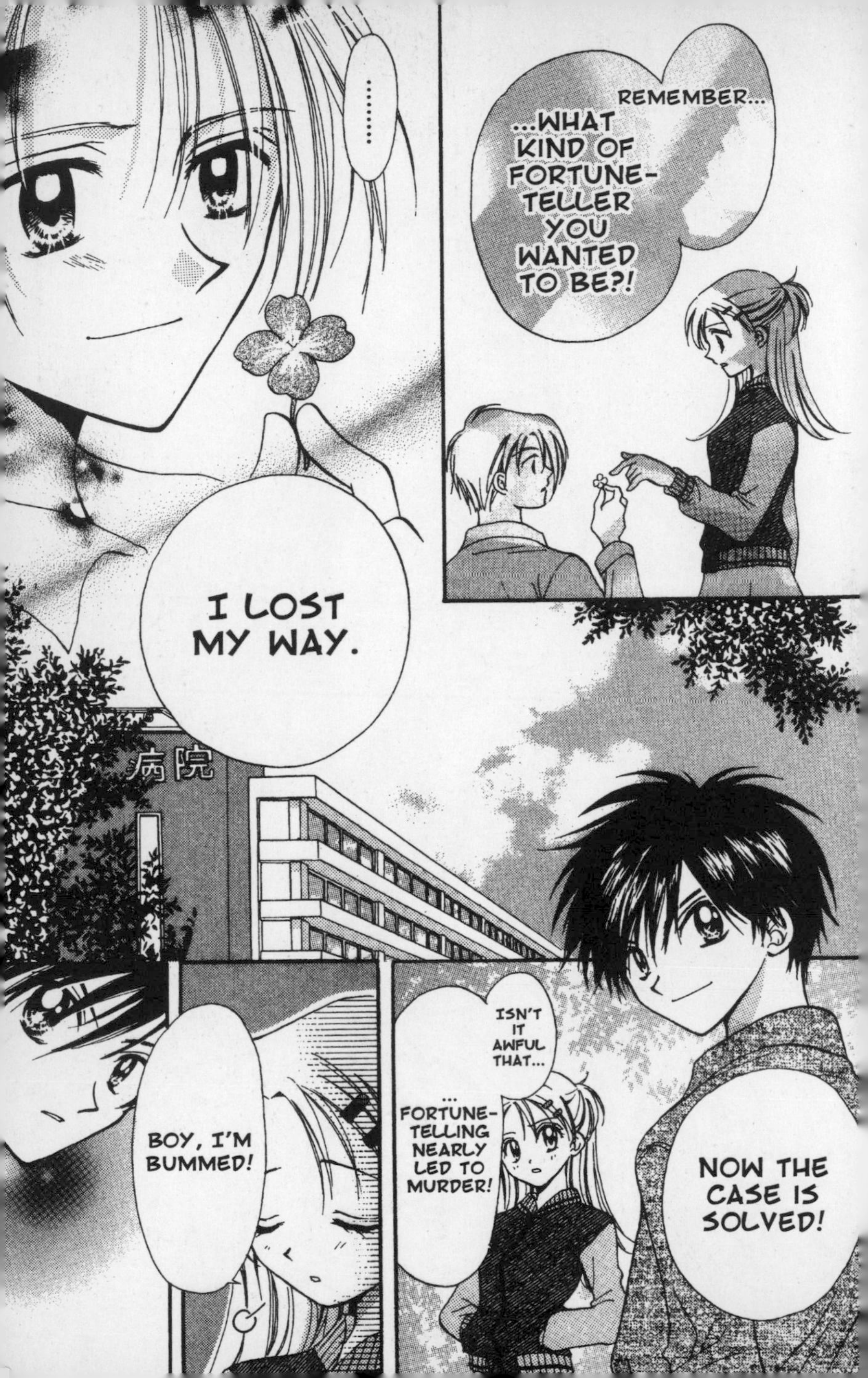
REMEMBER... ...WHAT KIND OF FORTUNE-TELLER YOU WANTED TO BE?!
....
I LOST MY WAY.
病院
NOW THE CASE IS SOLVED!
ISN'T IT AWFUL THAT...
...FORTUNE-TELLING NEARLY LED TO MURDER!
BOY, I'M BUMMED!

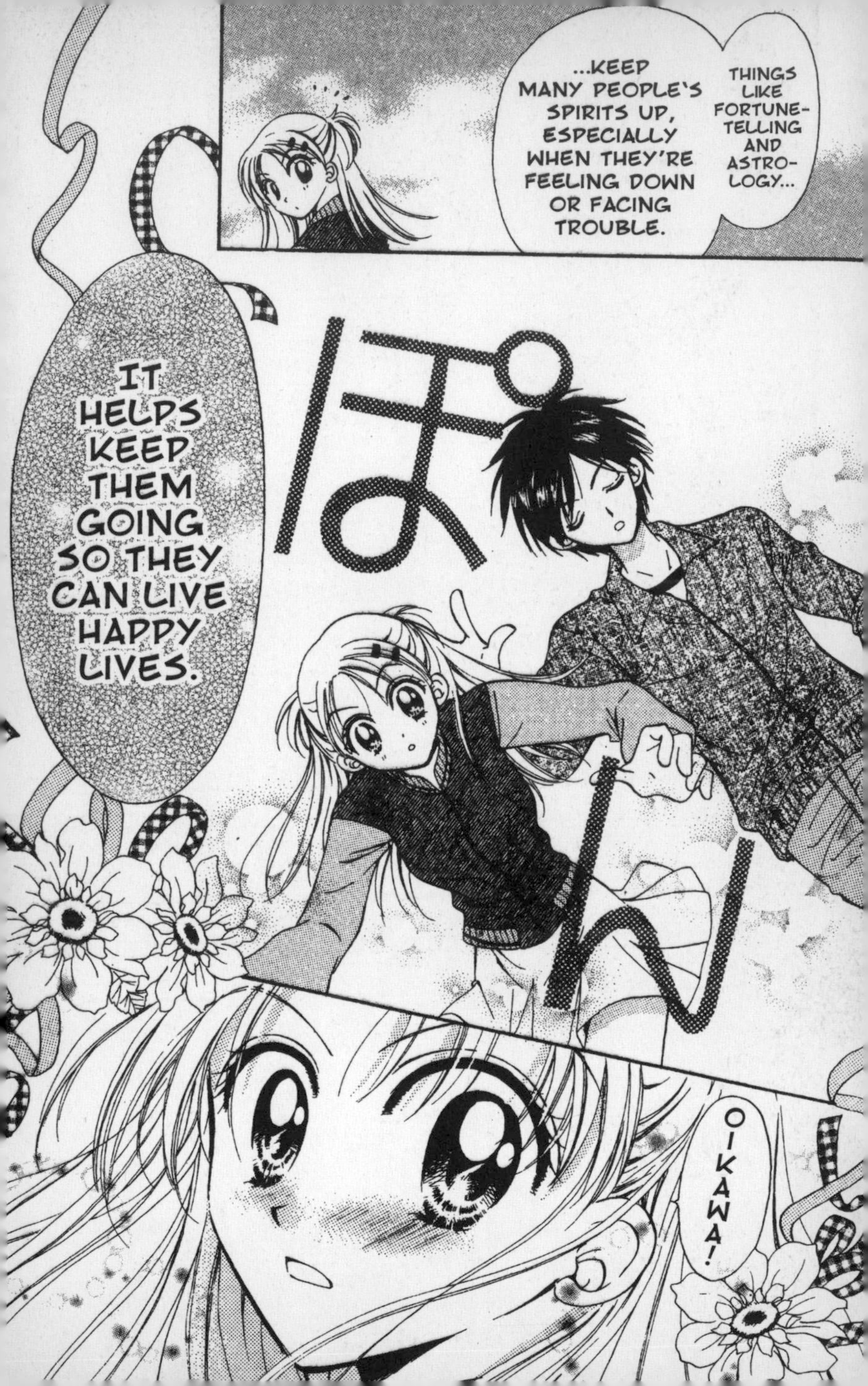
THINGS LIKE FORTUNE-TELLING AND ASTROLOGY...
...KEEP MANY PEOPLE'S SPIRITS UP, ESPECIALLY WHEN THEY'RE FEELING DOWN OR FACING TROUBLE.
IT HELPS KEEP THEM GOING SO THEY CAN LIVE HAPPY LIVES.
ぽん
OIKAWA!

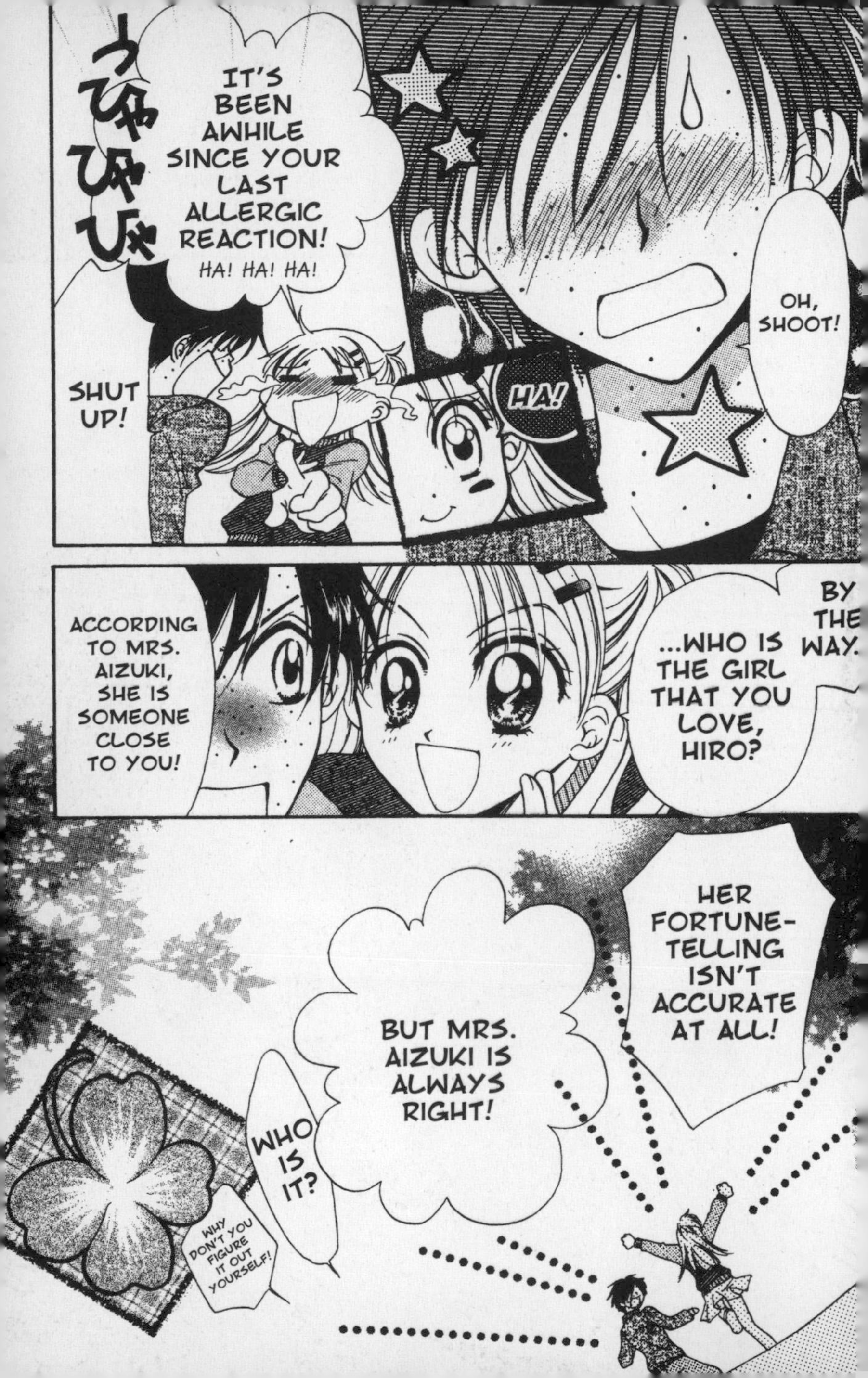
OH, SHOOT!
HA!
IT'S BEEN AWHILE SINCE YOUR LAST ALLERGIC REACTION!
HA! HA! HA!
うひゃひゃひゃ
SHUT UP!
BY THE WAY.
...WHO IS THE GIRL THAT YOU LOVE, HIRO?
ACCORDING TO MRS. AIZUKI, SHE IS SOMEONE CLOSE TO YOU!
HER FORTUNE-TELLING ISN'T ACCURATE AT ALL!
BUT MRS. AIZUKI IS ALWAYS RIGHT!
WHO IS IT?
WHY DON'T YOU FIGURE IT OUT YOURSELF!

Astrea, the astral spirit who appears in File 5, is a first-place winner of the Astral Spirit Design Contest. The submitted works were all impressive - and I had the hardest time choosing the winner. I remember not being able to decide until the last minute. All the contestants were talented. I could tell that all of them did their very best!

Many of them created female characters and added a comment that said "This astral spirit loves Regulus the Leo." Regulus, you are the most popular, hottest male character! (Ha ha!) To my surprise, the most popular signs were Pisces, Cancer and Libra. One of the characteristics of Cancer is "home-loving". There was an astral spirit of Cancer who was a domestic mom with an apron. It really cracked me up! What a great sense of humor!!

I would like to thank all of those who participated in the contest!

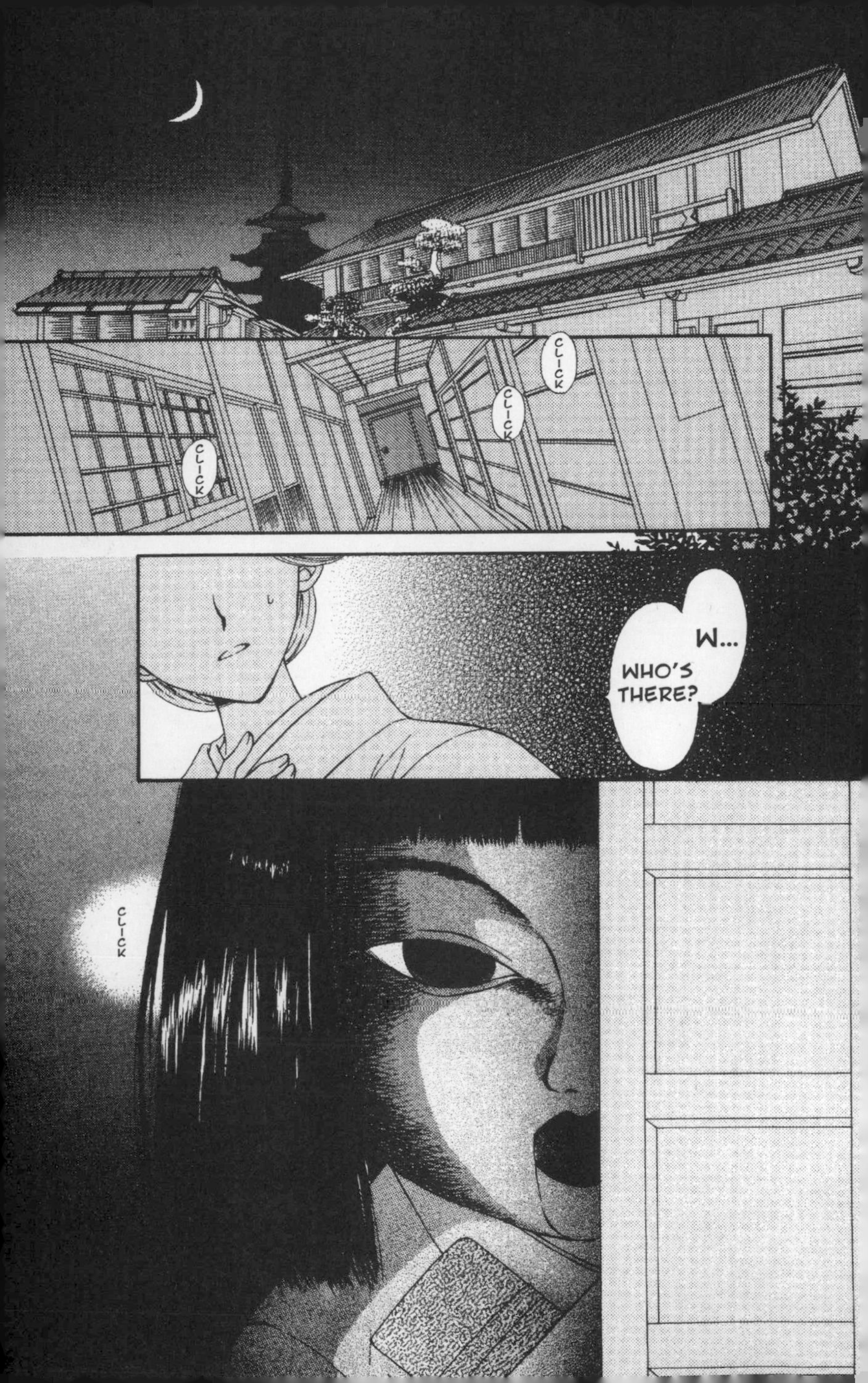

CLICK
CLICK
CLICK
W...
WHO'S THERE?
CLICK

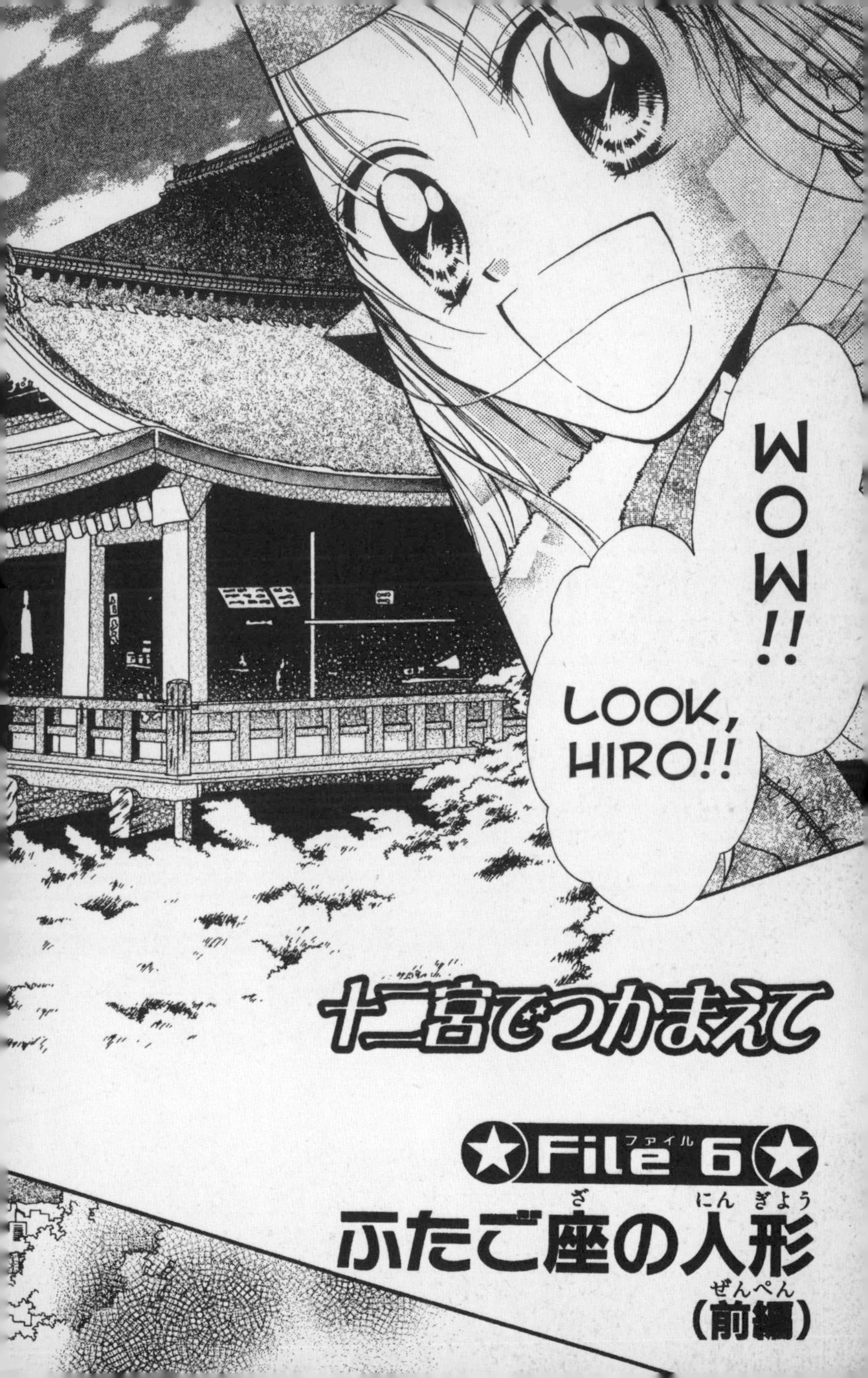
WOW!!
LOOK, HIRO!!
十二宮でつかまえて
☆File 6☆
ふたご座の人形
(前編)

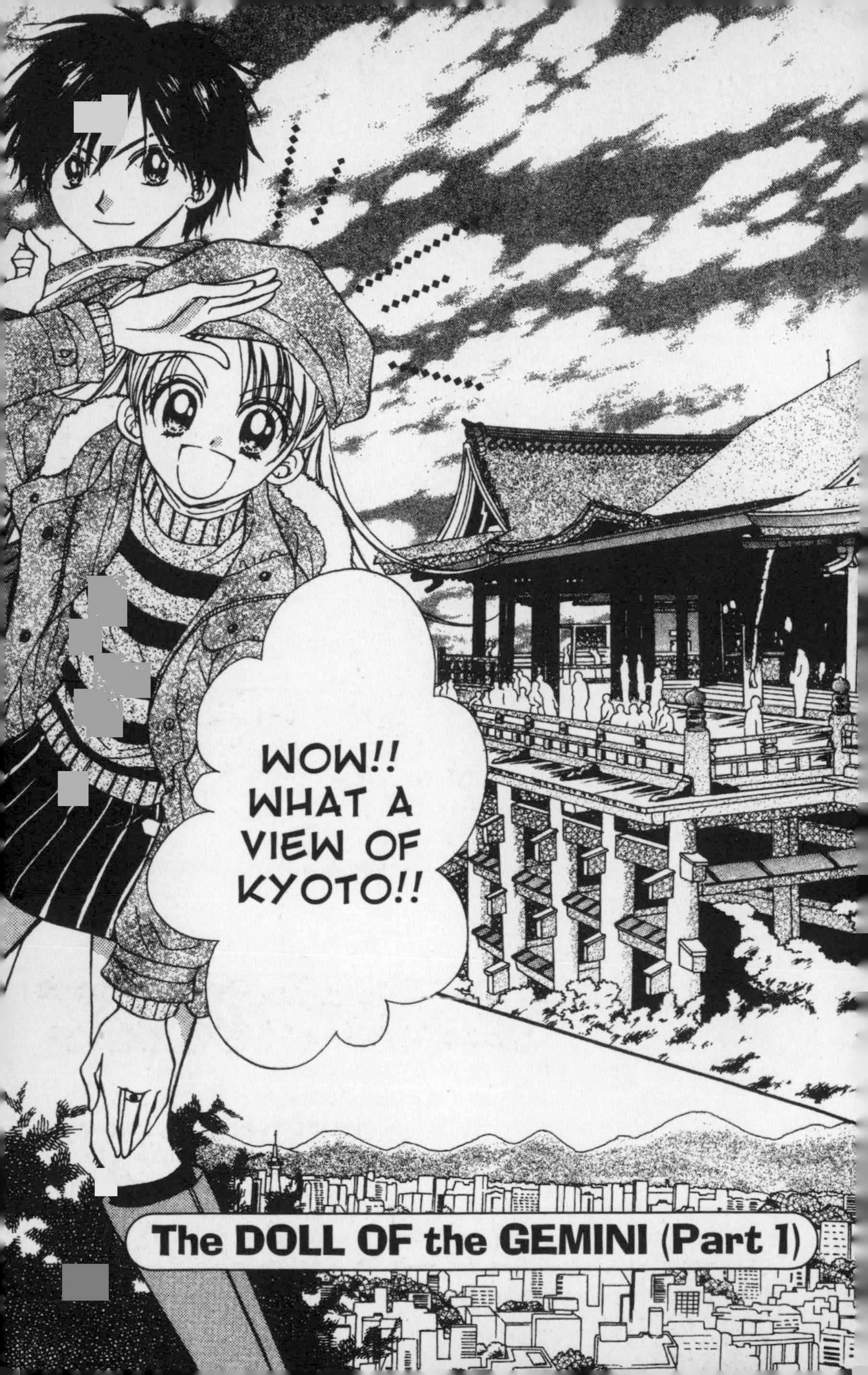
WOW!! WHAT A VIEW OF KYOTO!!
The DOLL OF the GEMINI (Part 1)

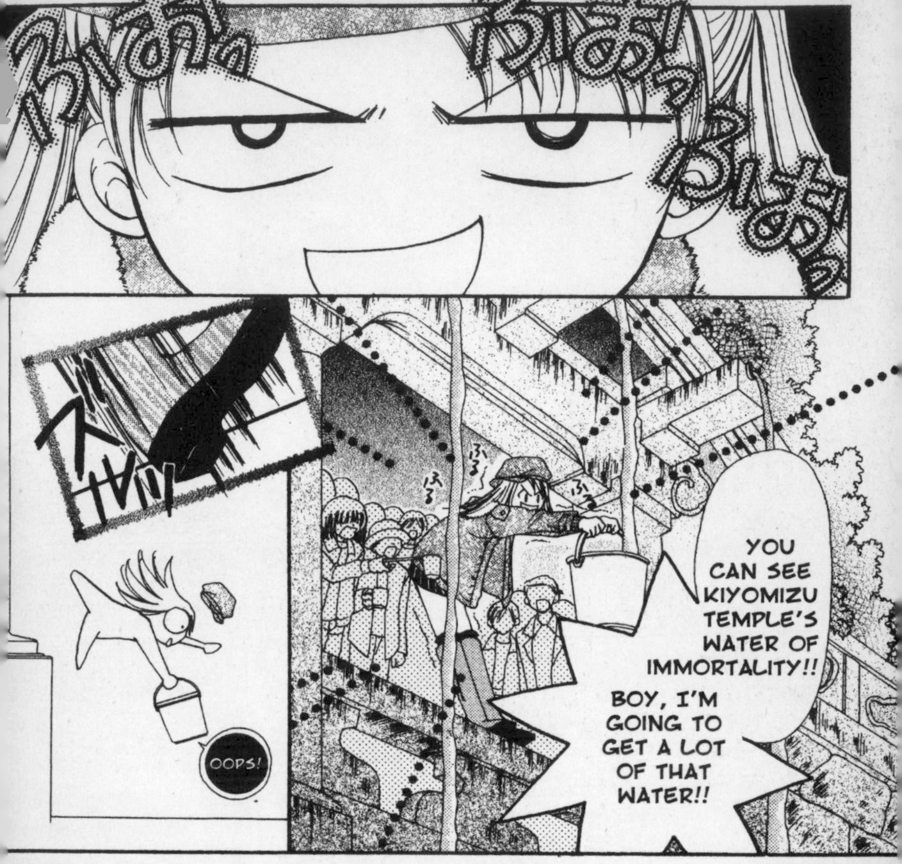
YOU CAN SEE KIYOMIZU TEMPLE'S WATER OF IMMORTALITY!!
BOY, I'M GOING TO GET A LOT OF THAT WATER!!
OOPS!

ademoiselle Lili's Astrology (9)

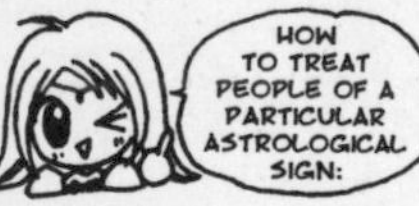
HOW TO TREAT PEOPLE OF A PARTICULAR ASTROLOGICAL SIGN:

Gemini: ♊ Castor and Pollux

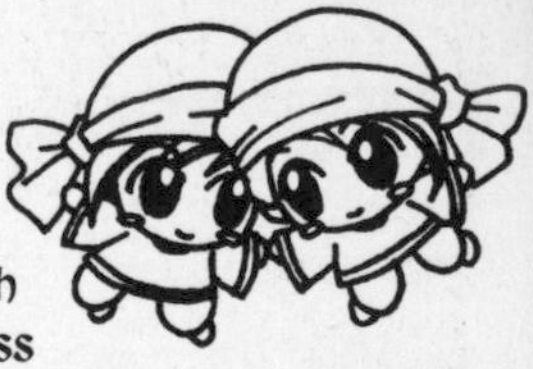

astor and Pollux are twins who were very close to each her. Their brother-in-law was jealous of their closeness d killed Castor. Pollux wanted to follow his twin brother, but he could not because he was immortal. He was later transformed into stars and joined brother as the constellation. It's a very sad story. Castor and Pollux are eerful, talkative and romantic. They are very friendly and easily make new iends. They also tend to get bored easily and give up on relationships easily. ey don't like girls who are too dependent. Gemini boys love challenges. ey are playboys who are good at coming up with cool pick-up lines.

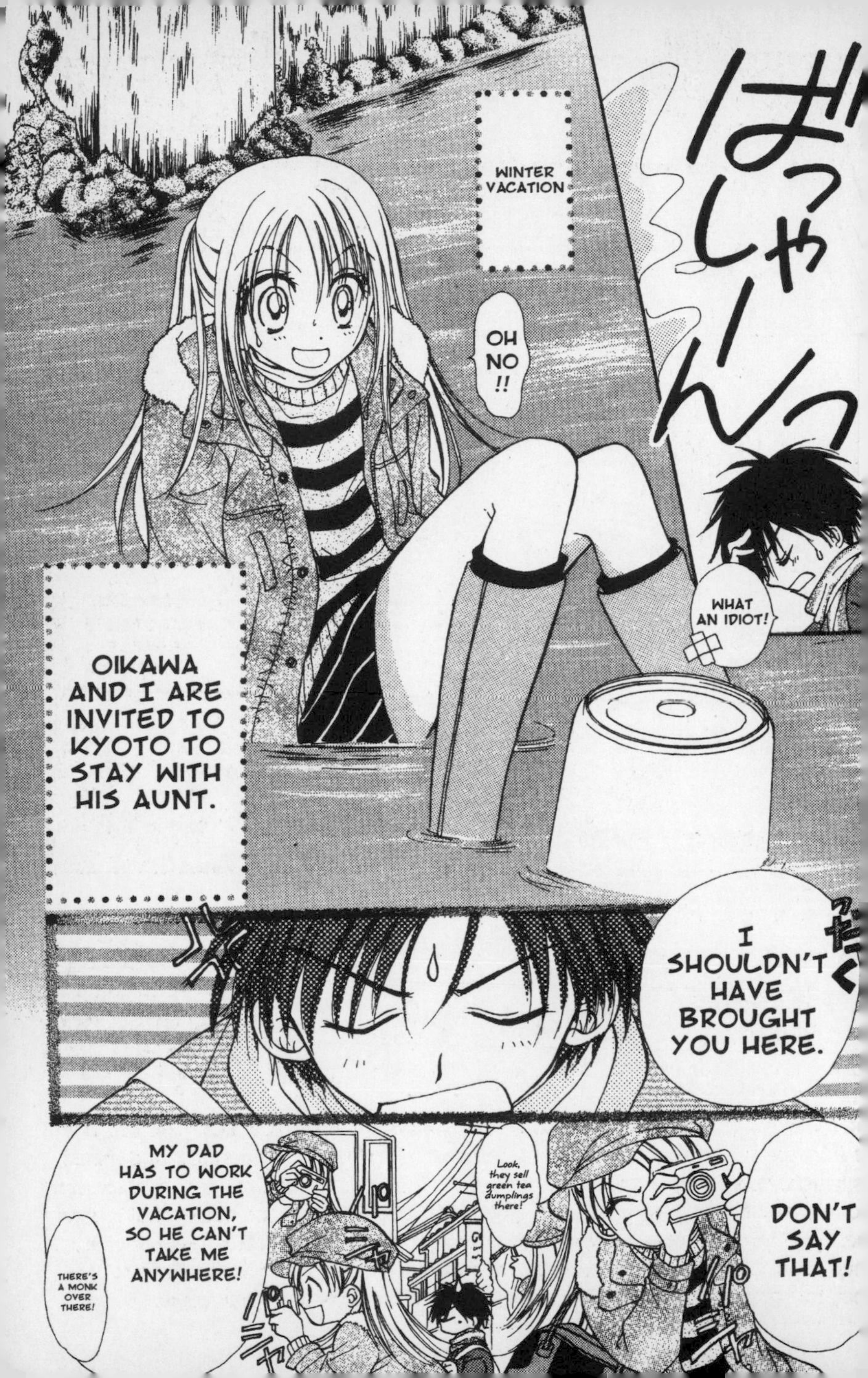
ぼっしゃーんっ
WINTER VACATION
OH NO !!
WHAT AN IDIOT!
OIKAWA AND I ARE INVITED TO KYOTO TO STAY WITH HIS AUNT.
I SHOULDN'T HAVE BROUGHT YOU HERE.
DON'T SAY THAT!
Look, they sell green tea dumplings there!
MY DAD HAS TO WORK DURING THE VACATION, SO HE CAN'T TAKE ME ANYWHERE!
THERE'S A MONK OVER THERE!

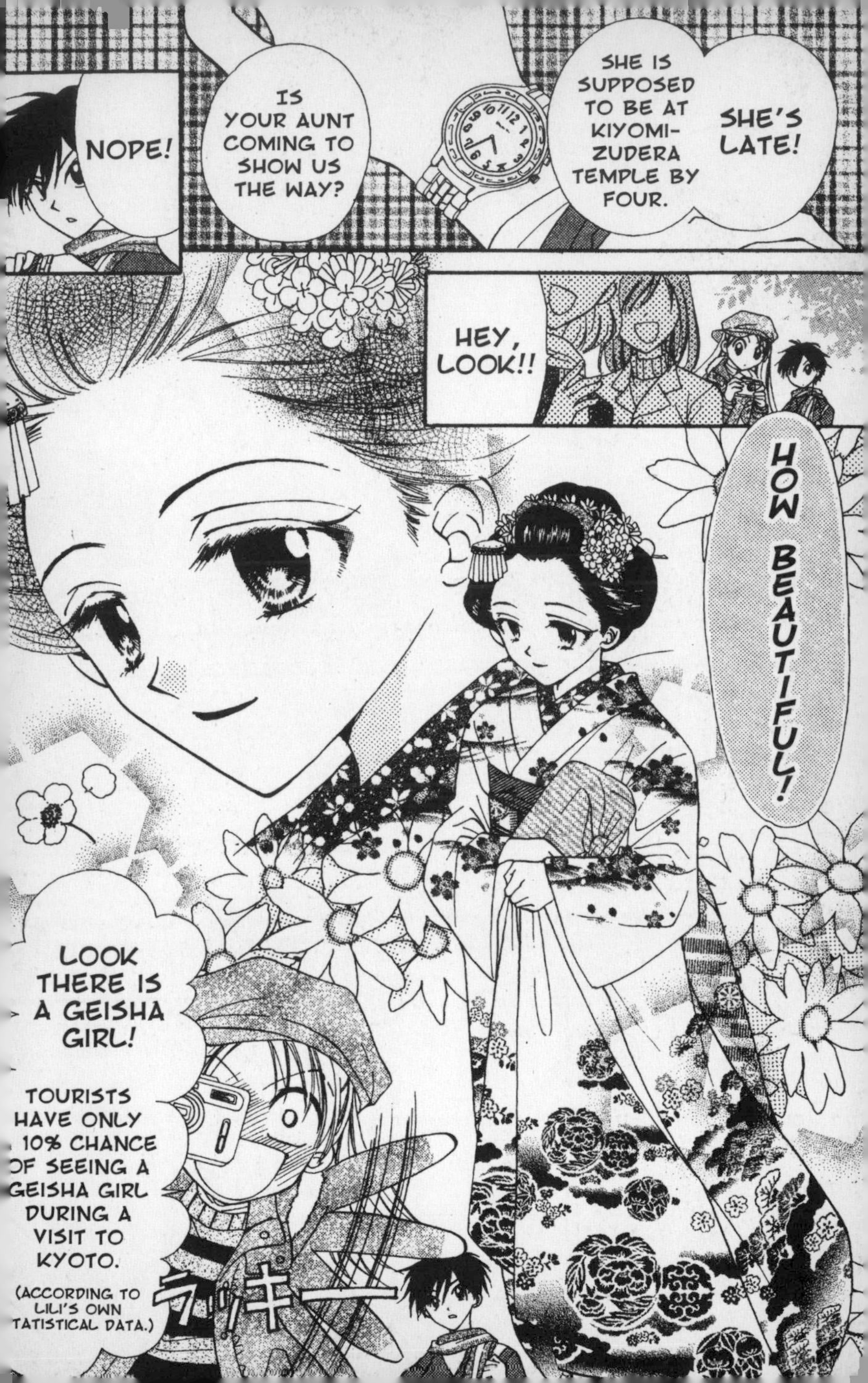

SHE'S LATE!
SHE IS SUPPOSED TO BE AT KIYOMI-ZUDERA TEMPLE BY FOUR.
IS YOUR AUNT COMING TO SHOW US THE WAY?
NOPE!
HEY, LOOK!!
HOW BEAUTIFUL!
LOOK THERE IS A GEISHA GIRL!
TOURISTS HAVE ONLY 10% CHANCE OF SEEING A GEISHA GIRL DURING A VISIT TO KYOTO.
(ACCORDING TO LILI'S OWN TATISTICAL DATA.)
ラッキー

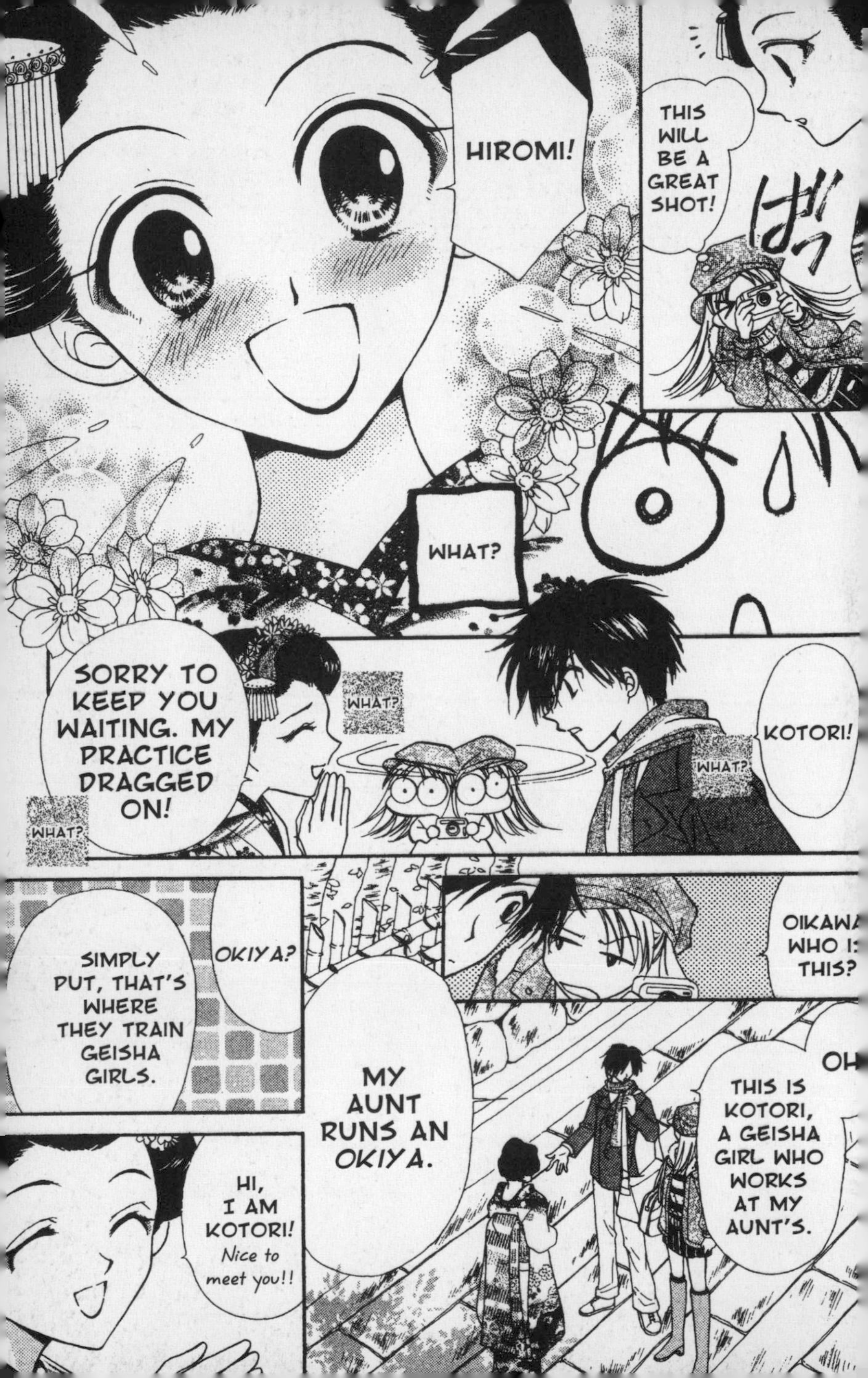
THIS WILL BE A GREAT SHOT!
ぱっ
HIROMI!
WHAT?
KOTORI!
WHAT?
WHAT?
SORRY TO KEEP YOU WAITING. MY PRACTICE DRAGGED ON!
WHAT?
OIKAWA WHO I THIS?
OH
THIS IS KOTORI, A GEISHA GIRL WHO WORKS AT MY AUNT'S.
MY AUNT RUNS AN OKIYA.
OKIYA?
SIMPLY PUT, THAT'S WHERE THEY TRAIN GEISHA GIRLS.
HI, I AM KOTORI! Nice to meet you!!

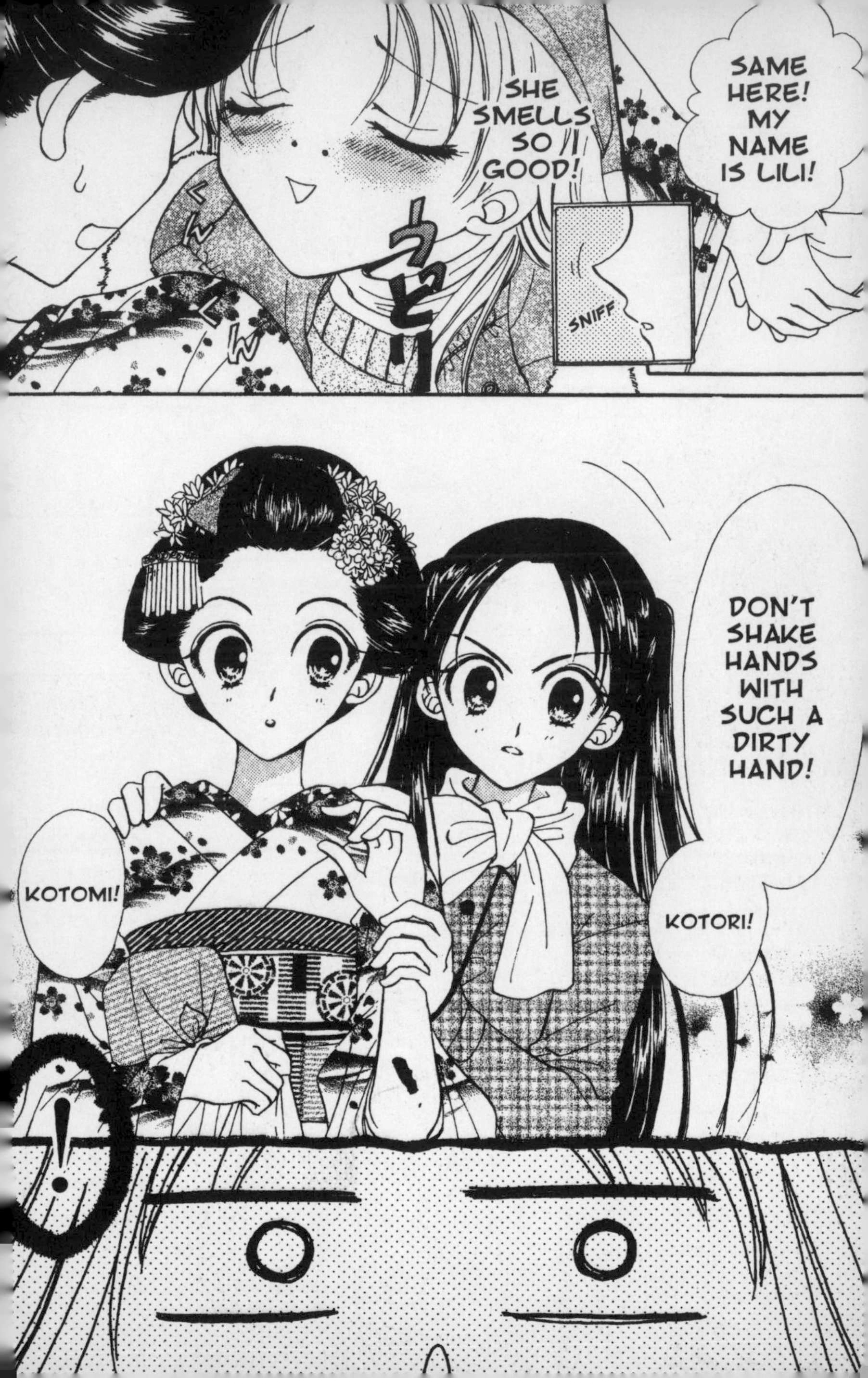
SAME HERE! MY NAME IS LILI!
SNIFF
SHE SMELLS SO GOOD!
うっとり
くんくん
DON'T SHAKE HANDS WITH SUCH A DIRTY HAND!
KOTORI!
KOTOMI!
!

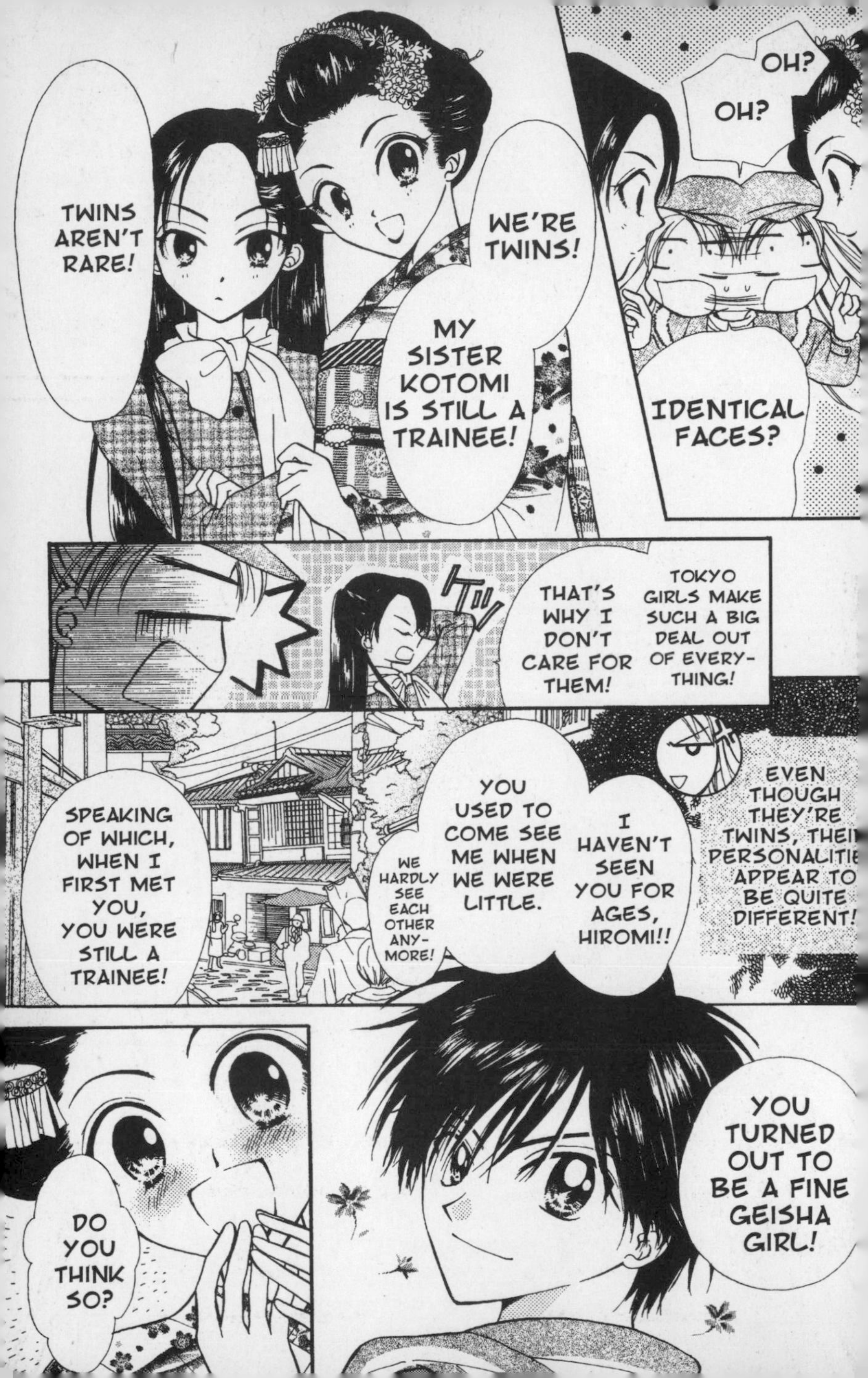

OH?
OH?
IDENTICAL FACES?
WE'RE TWINS!
MY SISTER KOTOMI IS STILL A TRAINEE!
TWINS AREN'T RARE!
TOKYO GIRLS MAKE SUCH A BIG DEAL OUT OF EVERY-THING!
THAT'S WHY I DON'T CARE FOR THEM!
EVEN THOUGH THEY'RE TWINS, THEI PERSONALITIE APPEAR TO BE QUITE DIFFERENT!
I HAVEN'T SEEN YOU FOR AGES, HIROMI!!
YOU USED TO COME SEE ME WHEN WE WERE LITTLE.
WE HARDLY SEE EACH OTHER ANY-MORE!
SPEAKING OF WHICH, WHEN I FIRST MET YOU, YOU WERE STILL A TRAINEE!
YOU TURNED OUT TO BE A FINE GEISHA GIRL!
DO YOU THINK SO?

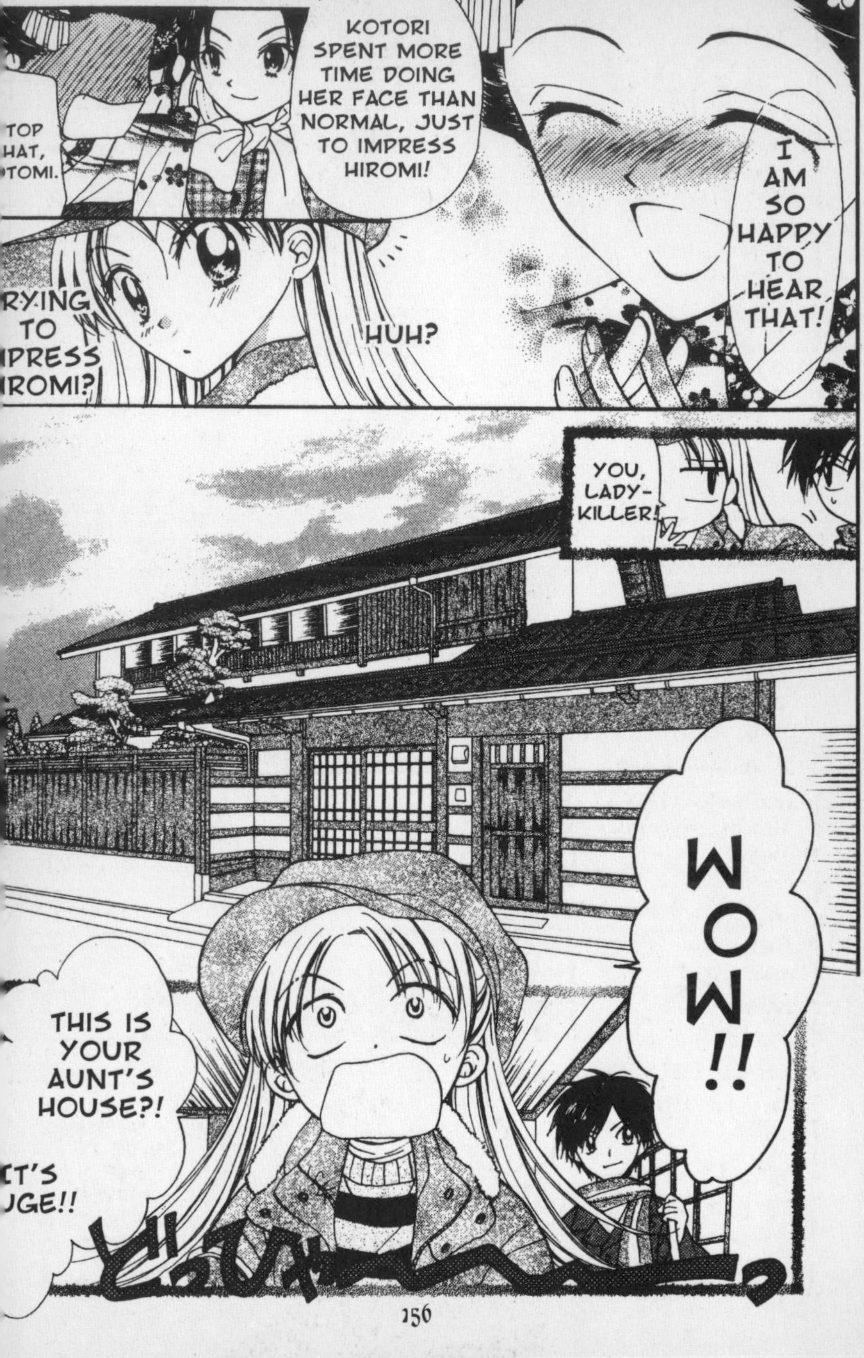
KOTORI SPENT MORE TIME DOING HER FACE THAN NORMAL, JUST TO IMPRESS HIROMI!
I AM SO HAPPY TO HEAR THAT!
TOP HAT, TOMI.
HUH?
RYING TO IPRESS IROMI?
YOU, LADY-KILLER!
WOW!!
THIS IS YOUR AUNT'S HOUSE?!
IT'S UGE!!

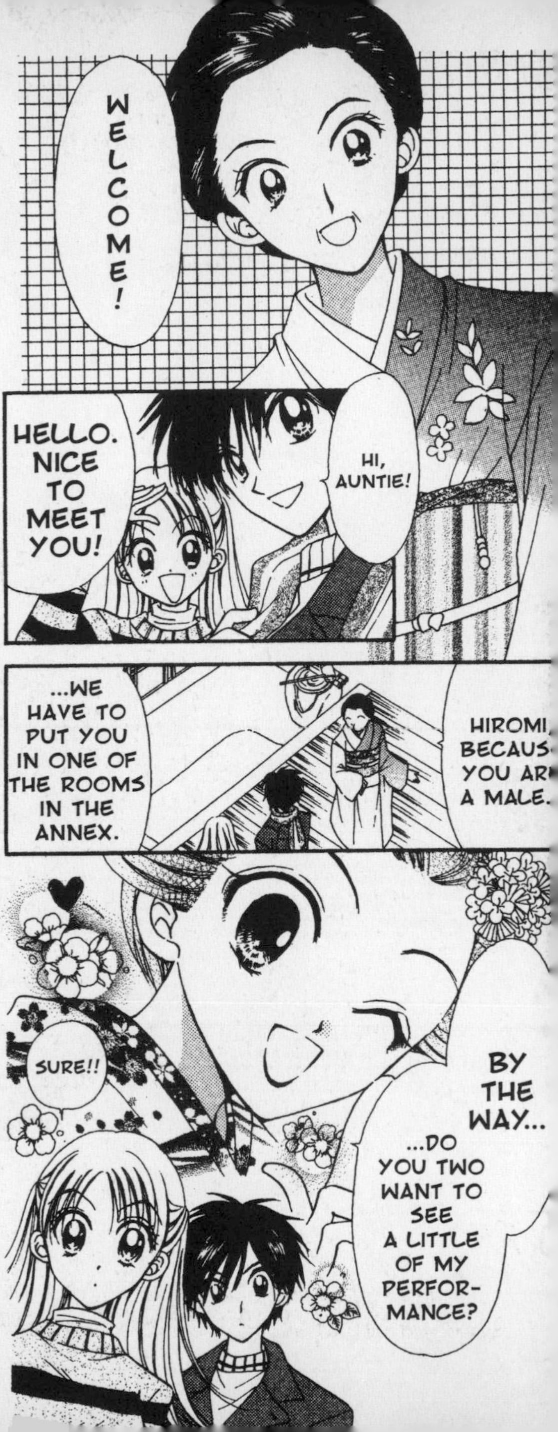

WELCOME!
HI, AUNTIE!
HELLO. NICE TO MEET YOU!
HIROMI, BECAUS YOU AR A MALE.
...WE HAVE TO PUT YOU IN ONE OF THE ROOMS IN THE ANNEX.
BY THE WAY...
...DO YOU TWO WANT TO SEE A LITTLE OF MY PERFORMANCE?
SURE!!

Big things:
I love to see big things in nature, like the sky, the ocean, the universe and the desert. When I see them, I feel like the mistakes I've made are trivial and forgivable. I can be optimistic again. I am not a bad person or anything.

Special thanks to:
Ms. Mika Murase
(She's a good artist.)

Ms. Sachiyo Murase
(She does fine screen tone work for me.)

Ms. Marimo Shirasawa
(She drew the Kiyomizudera Temple.)

Ms. Gomi and Ms. Zushi
Dear readers and fans, I will see you all again very soon!

Write to me!

Natsumi Ando
Nakayoshi
Editorial Office
PO BOX 91
Akasaka Post Office
Tokyo, Japan 107-8652
or
TOKYOPOP
5900 Wilshire Blvd.
Suite 2000
Los Angeles, CA 90036

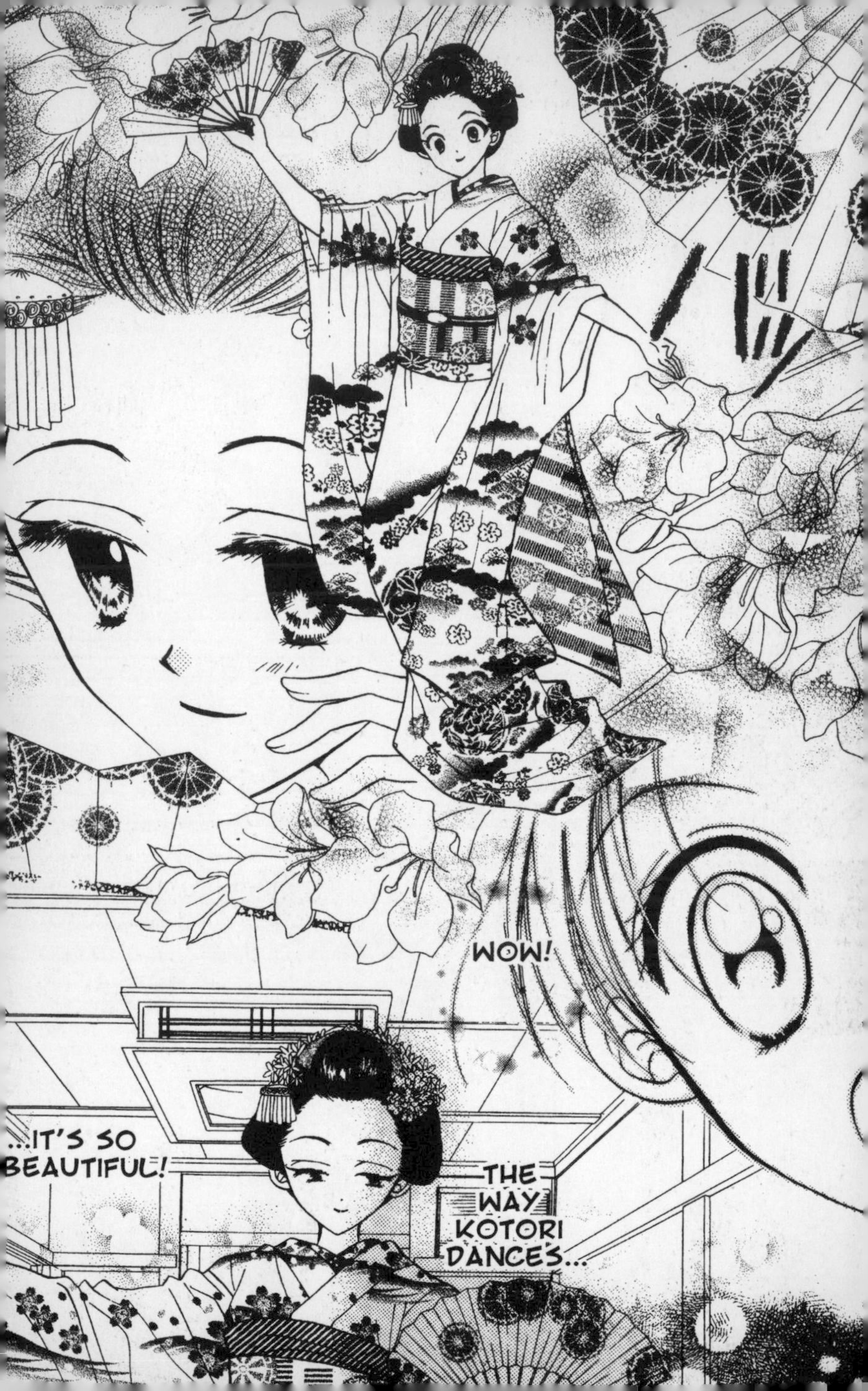
WOW!
THE WAY KOTORI DANCES...
...IT'S SO BEAUTIFUL!

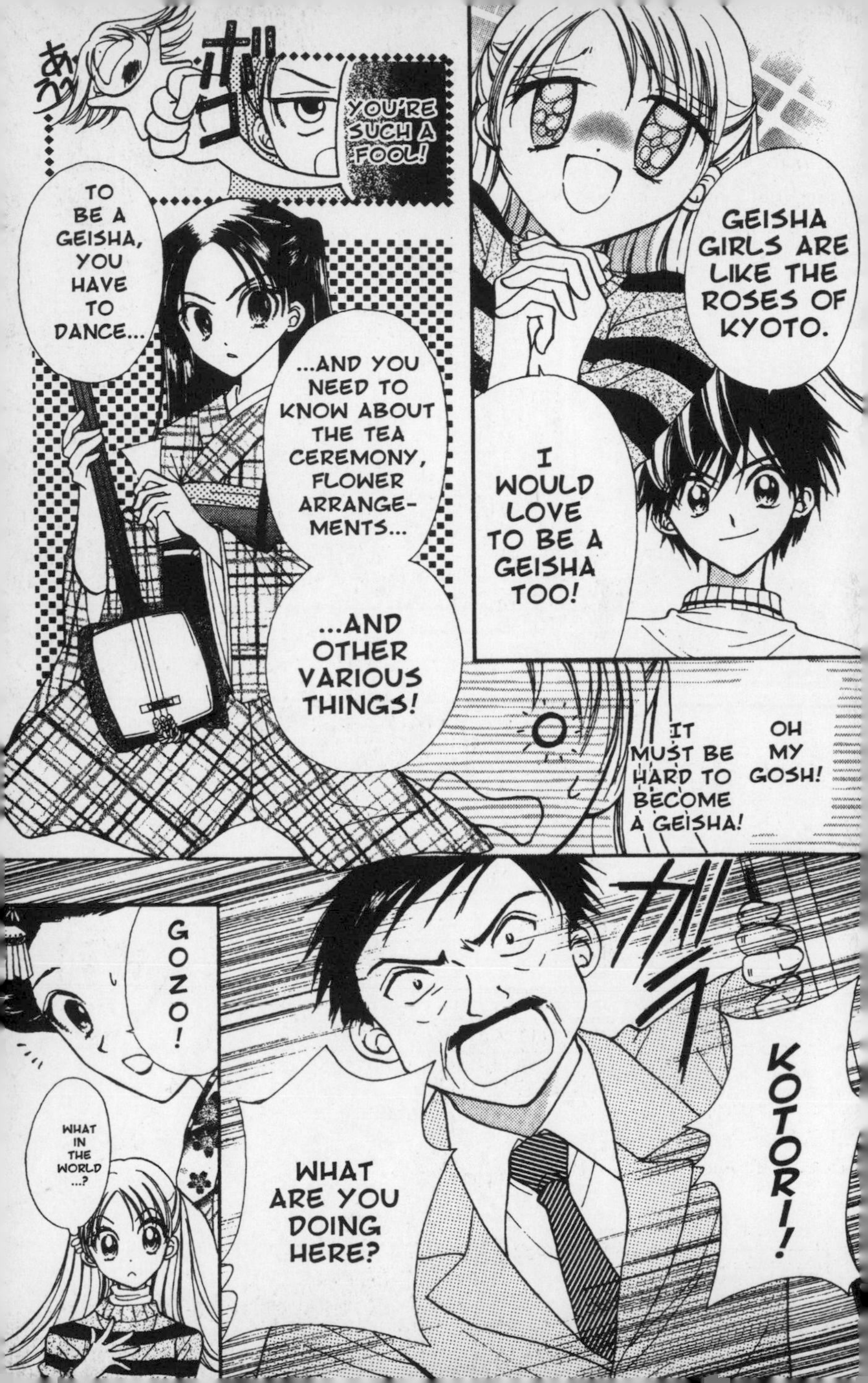
GEISHA GIRLS ARE LIKE THE ROSES OF KYOTO.
I WOULD LOVE TO BE A GEISHA TOO!
OH MY GOSH!
IT MUST BE HARD TO BECOME A GEISHA!
YOU'RE SUCH A FOOL!
TO BE A GEISHA, YOU HAVE TO DANCE...
...AND YOU NEED TO KNOW ABOUT THE TEA CEREMONY, FLOWER ARRANGE-MENTS...
...AND OTHER VARIOUS THINGS!
KOTORI!
WHAT ARE YOU DOING HERE?
GOZO!
WHAT IN THE WORLD ...?

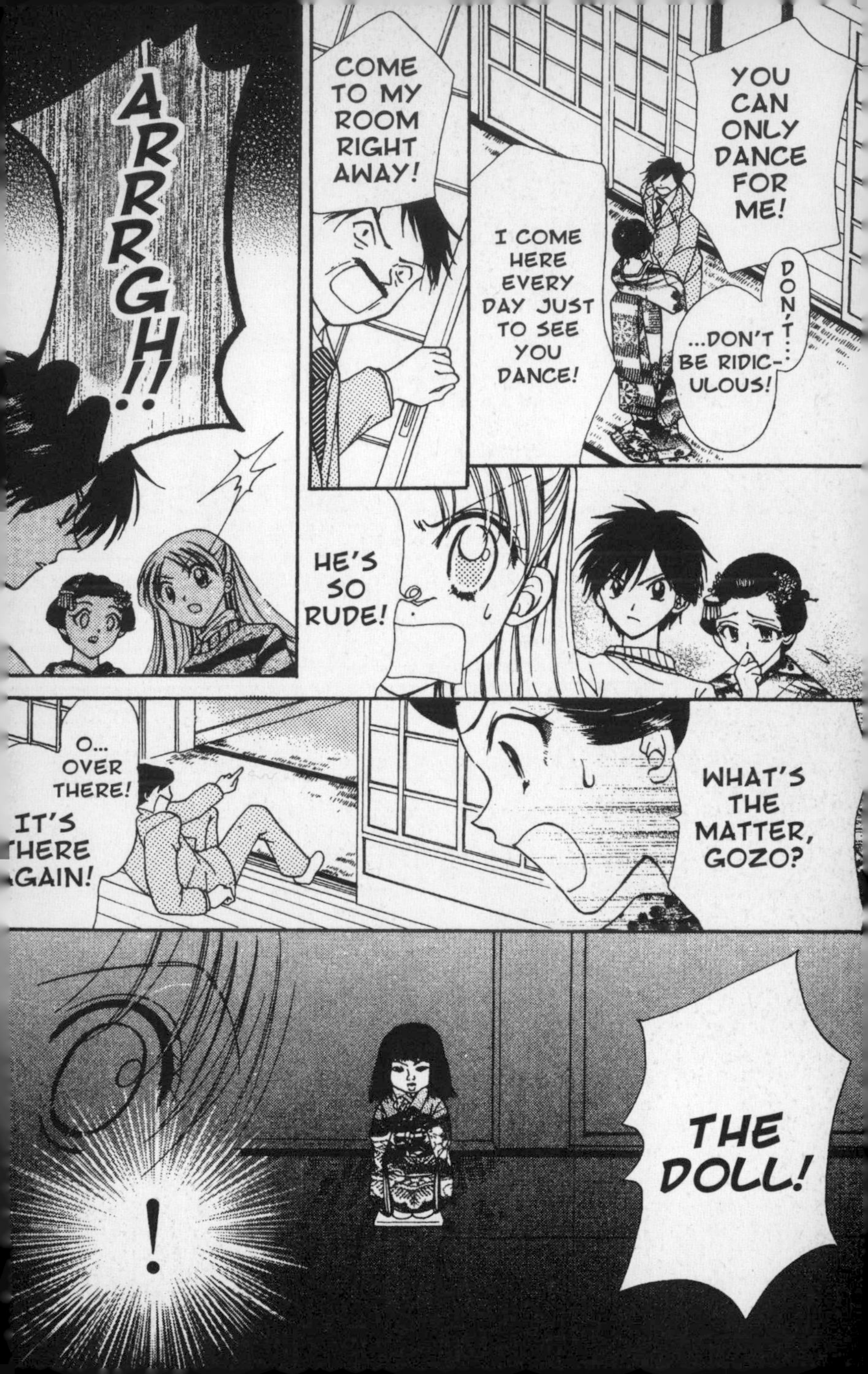
YOU CAN ONLY DANCE FOR ME!
I COME HERE EVERY DAY JUST TO SEE YOU DANCE!
DON'T...
...DON'T BE RIDICULOUS!
COME TO MY ROOM RIGHT AWAY!
HE'S SO RUDE!
ARRRGH!!
WHAT'S THE MATTER, GOZO?
O... OVER THERE!
IT'S THERE AGAIN!
THE DOLL!
!

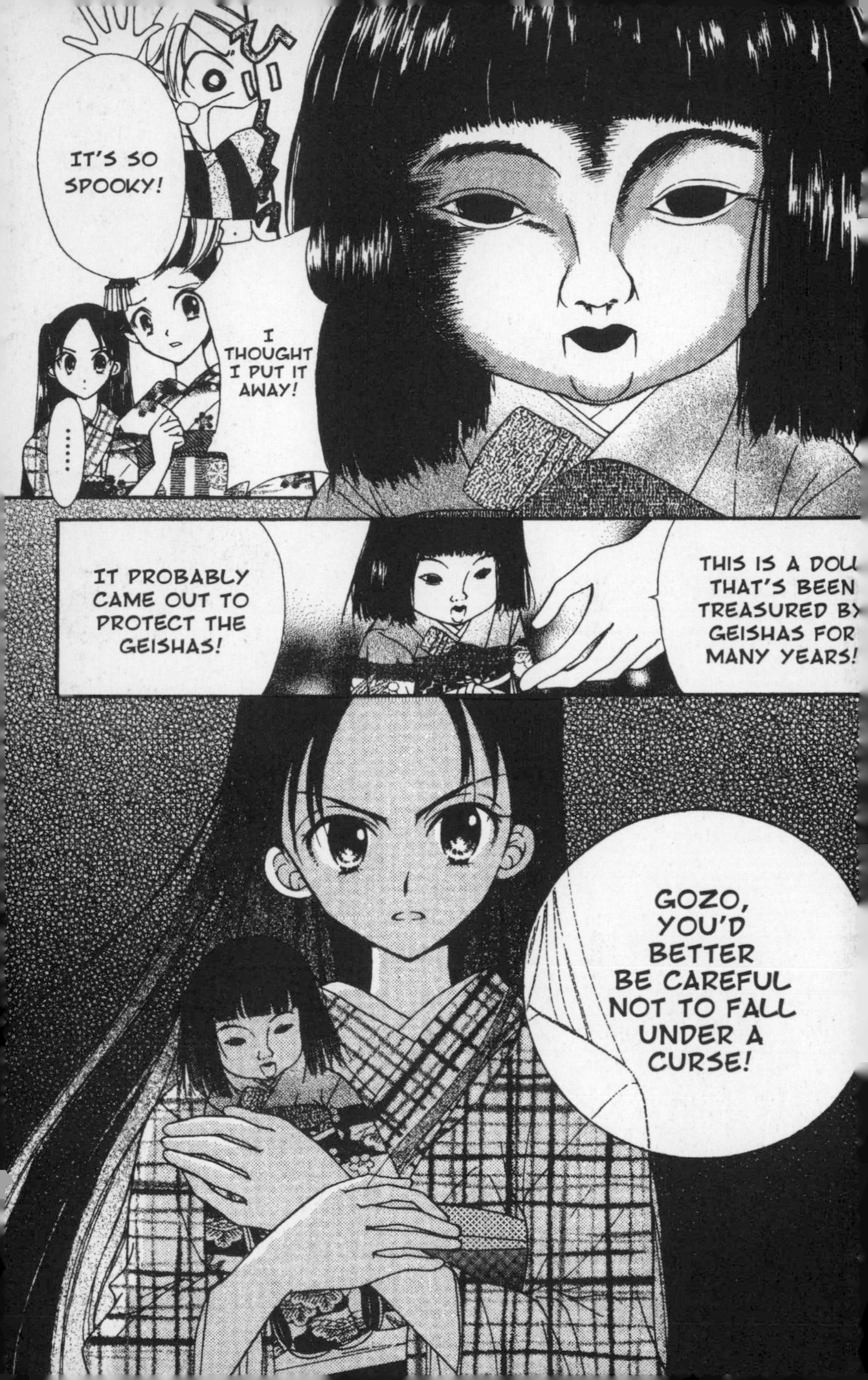
IT'S SO SPOOKY!
I THOUGHT I PUT IT AWAY!
......
THIS IS A DOLL THAT'S BEEN TREASURED BY GEISHAS FOR MANY YEARS!
IT PROBABLY CAME OUT TO PROTECT THE GEISHAS!
GOZO, YOU'D BETTER BE CAREFUL NOT TO FALL UNDER A CURSE!

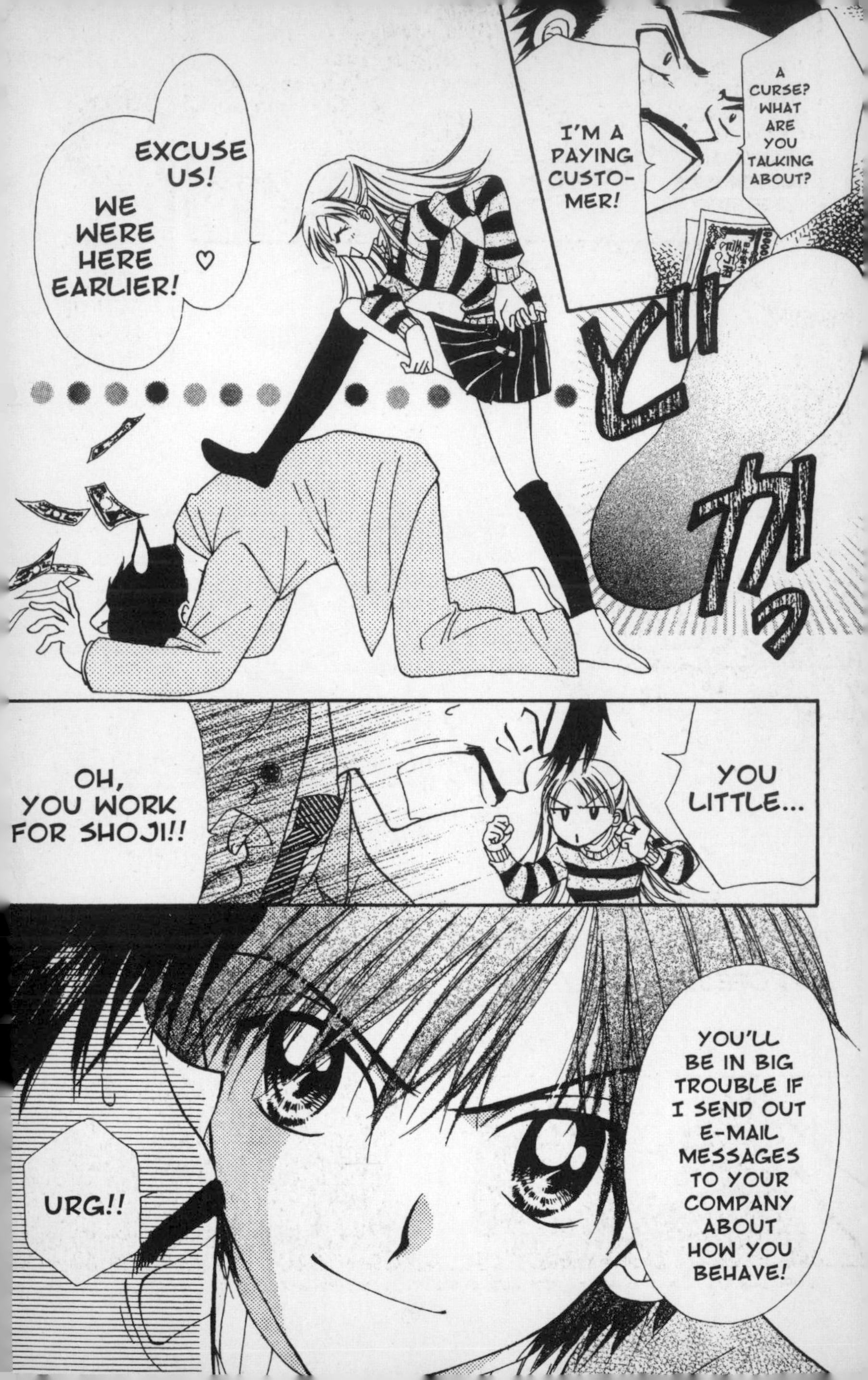
A CURSE? WHAT ARE YOU TALKING ABOUT?
I'M A PAYING CUSTO-MER!
EXCUSE US! WE WERE HERE EARLIER! ♡
YOU LITTLE...
OH, YOU WORK FOR SHOJI!!
YOU'LL BE IN BIG TROUBLE IF I SEND OUT E-MAIL MESSAGES TO YOUR COMPANY ABOUT HOW YOU BEHAVE!
URG!!

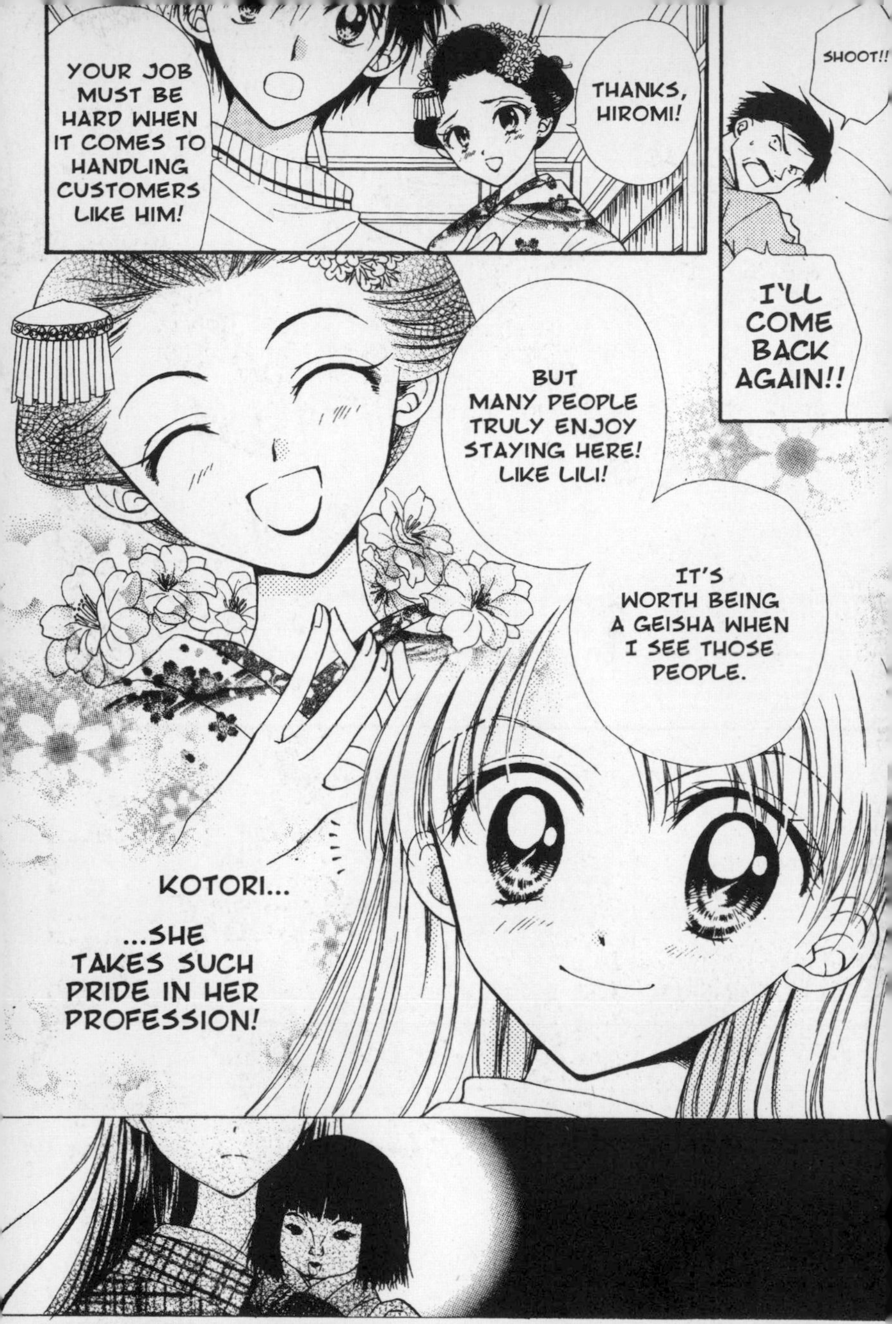
SHOOT!!
I'LL COME BACK AGAIN!!
YOUR JOB MUST BE HARD WHEN IT COMES TO HANDLING CUSTOMERS LIKE HIM!
THANKS, HIROMI!
BUT MANY PEOPLE TRULY ENJOY STAYING HERE! LIKE LILI!
IT'S WORTH BEING A GEISHA WHEN I SEE THOSE PEOPLE.
KOTORI...
...SHE TAKES SUCH PRIDE IN HER PROFESSION!

PUBLISHED IN "NAKAYOSHI" SEPTEMBER, OCTOBER, AND DECEMBER, 2001 - FEBRUARY 2002 ISSUE

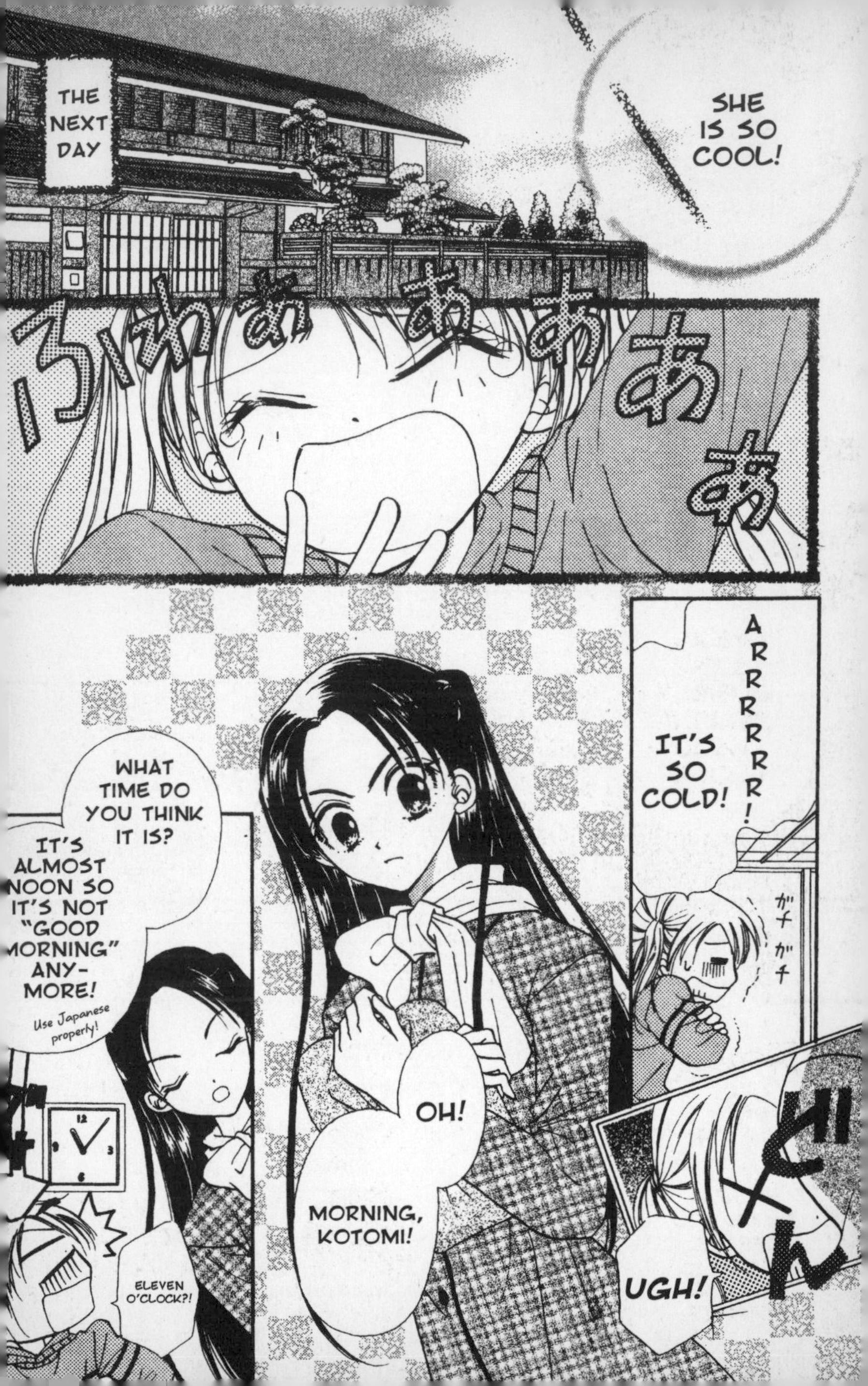
SHE IS SO COOL!
THE NEXT DAY
ふわああああ
ARRRRRR!
IT'S SO COLD!
ガチ ガチ
びくん
UGH!
OH!
MORNING, KOTOMI!
WHAT TIME DO YOU THINK IT IS?
IT'S ALMOST NOON SO IT'S NOT "GOOD MORNING" ANYMORE!
Use Japanese properly!
ELEVEN O'CLOCK?!

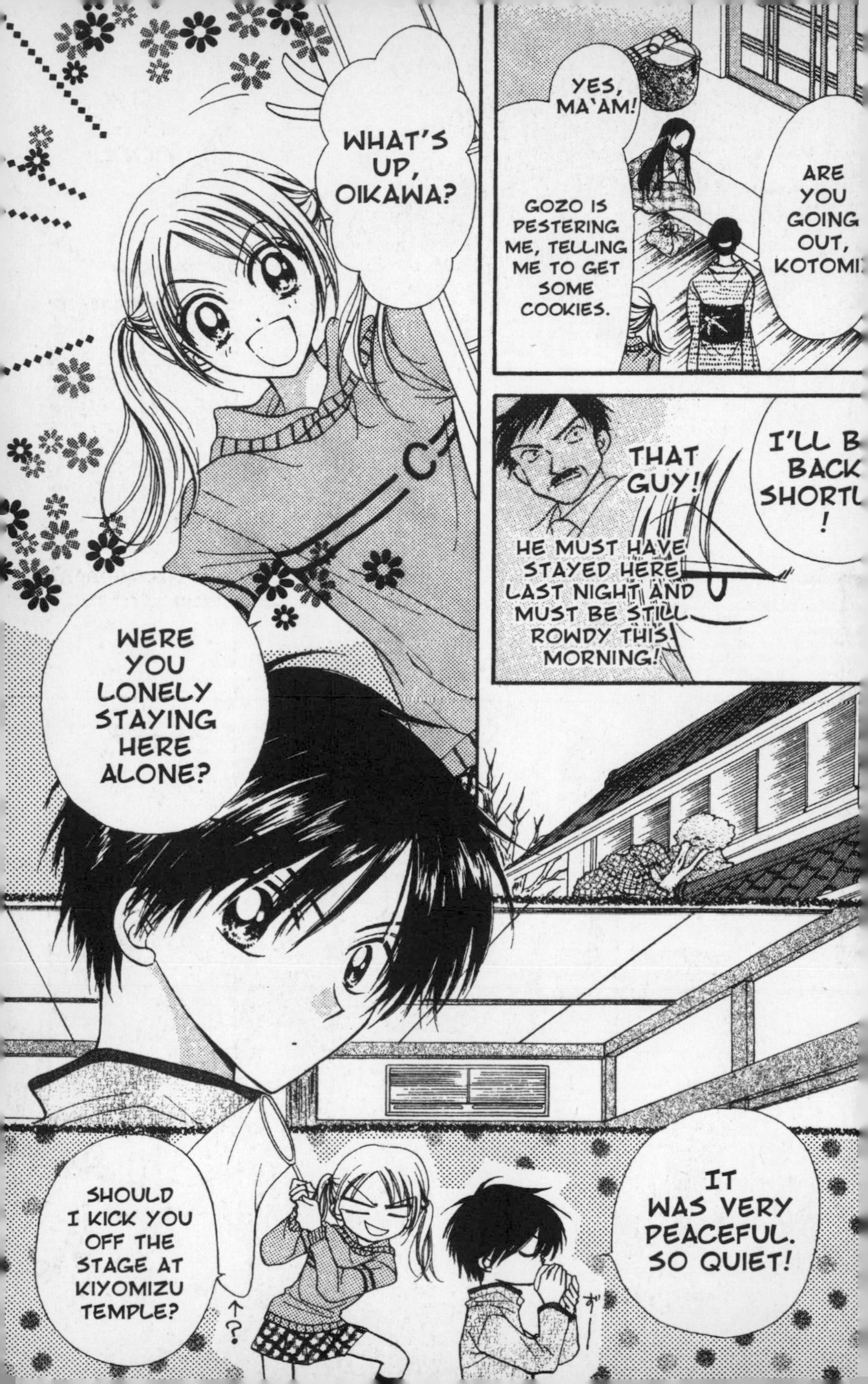
ARE YOU GOING OUT, KOTOMI
YES, MA'AM!
GOZO IS PESTERING ME, TELLING ME TO GET SOME COOKIES.
I'LL B BACK SHORTL !
THAT GUY!
HE MUST HAVE STAYED HERE LAST NIGHT AND MUST BE STILL ROWDY THIS MORNING!
WHAT'S UP, OIKAWA?
WERE YOU LONELY STAYING HERE ALONE?
IT WAS VERY PEACEFUL. SO QUIET!
ずー
SHOULD I KICK YOU OFF THE STAGE AT KIYOMIZU TEMPLE?
?

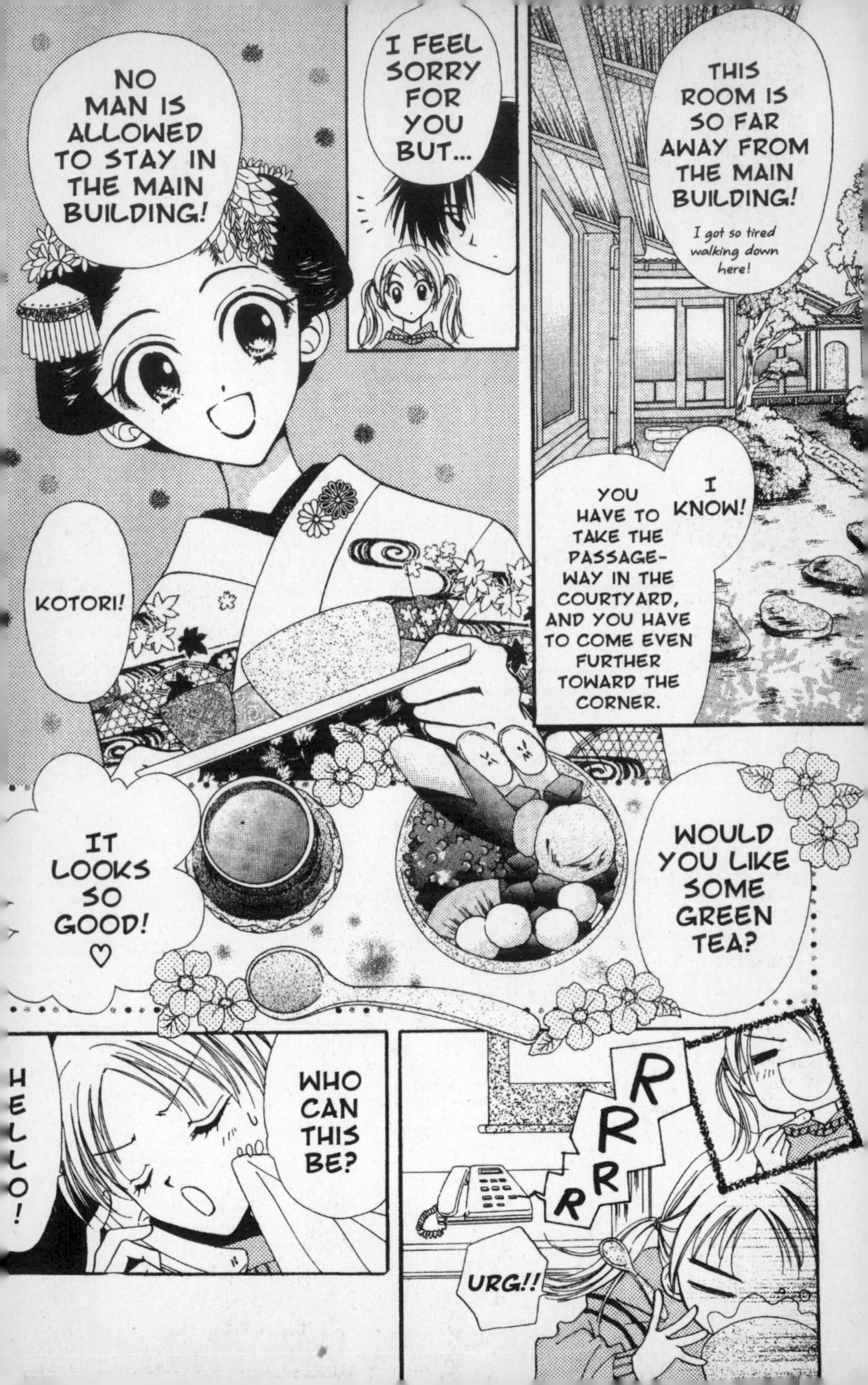
THIS ROOM IS SO FAR AWAY FROM THE MAIN BUILDING!
I got so tired walking down here!
I KNOW!
YOU HAVE TO TAKE THE PASSAGEWAY IN THE COURTYARD, AND YOU HAVE TO COME EVEN FURTHER TOWARD THE CORNER.
I FEEL SORRY FOR YOU BUT...
NO MAN IS ALLOWED TO STAY IN THE MAIN BUILDING!
KOTORI!
WOULD YOU LIKE SOME GREEN TEA?
IT LOOKS SO GOOD! ♡
RRRR
URG!!
WHO CAN THIS BE?
HELLO!

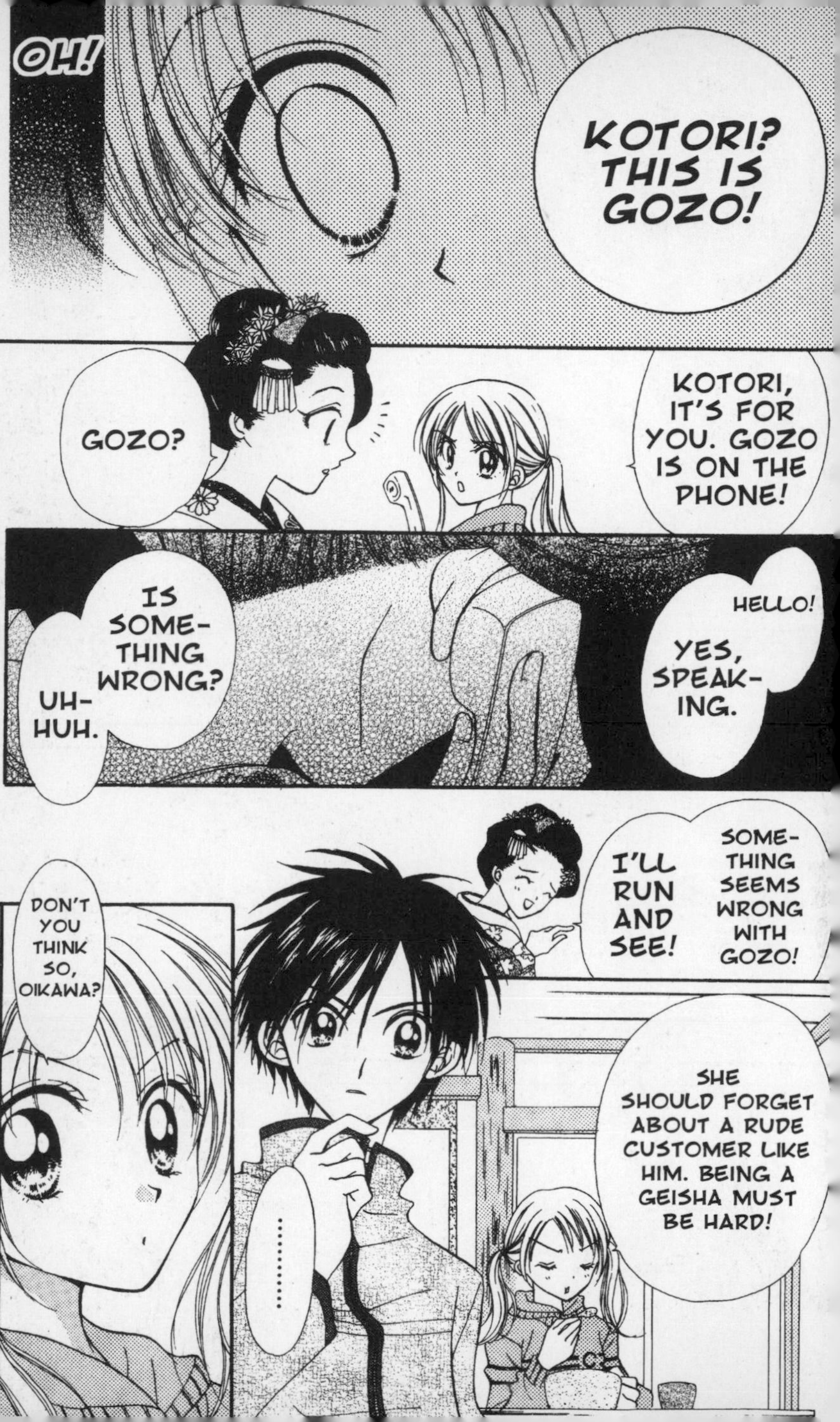
KOTORI? THIS IS GOZO!
OH!
KOTORI, IT'S FOR YOU. GOZO IS ON THE PHONE!
GOZO?
HELLO!
YES, SPEAK-ING.
IS SOME-THING WRONG?
UH-HUH.
SOME-THING SEEMS WRONG WITH GOZO!
I'LL RUN AND SEE!
SHE SHOULD FORGET ABOUT A RUDE CUSTOMER LIKE HIM. BEING A GEISHA MUST BE HARD!
DON'T YOU THINK SO, OIKAWA?
......

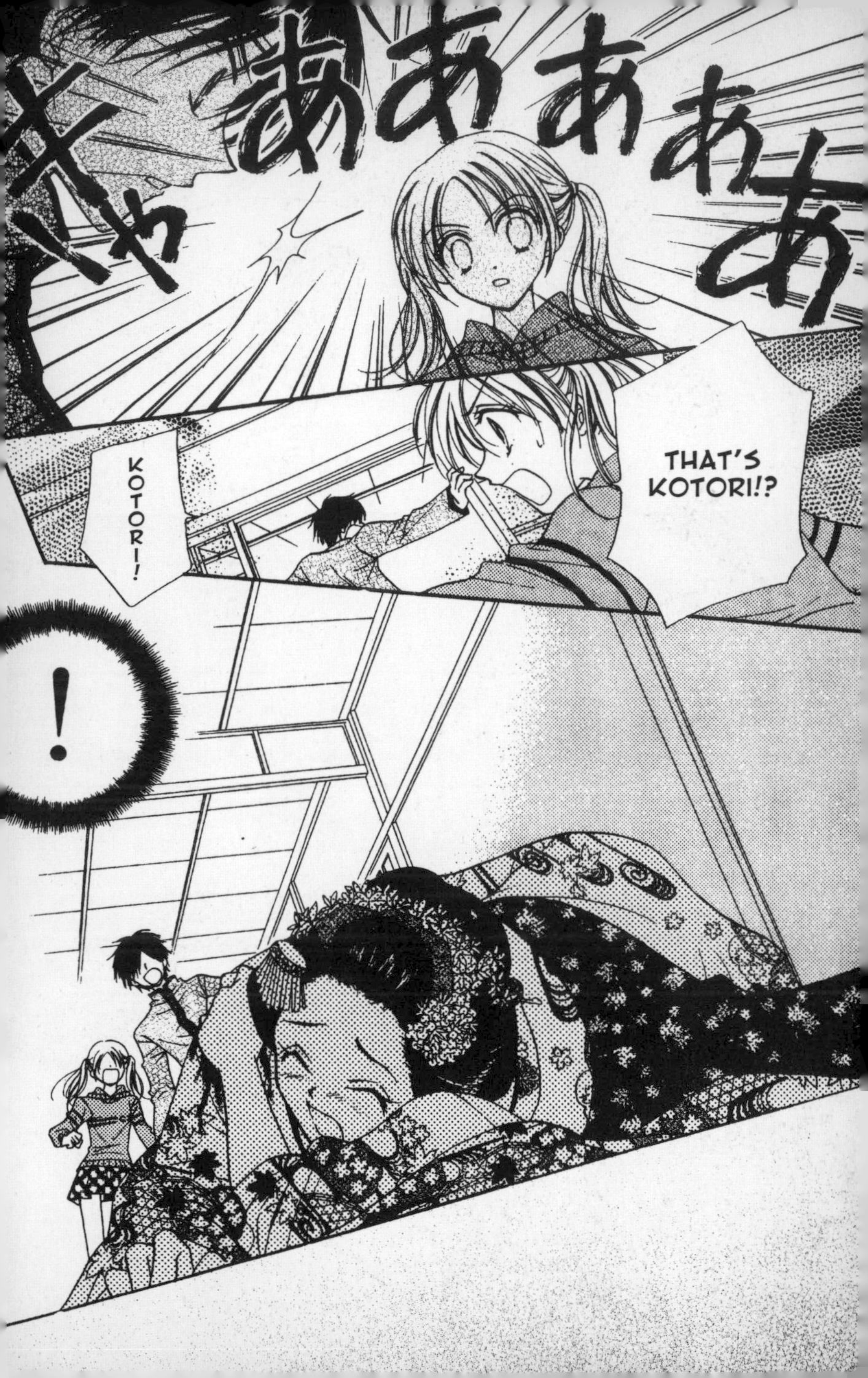
ギャあああああ
THAT'S KOTORI!?
KOTORI!
!

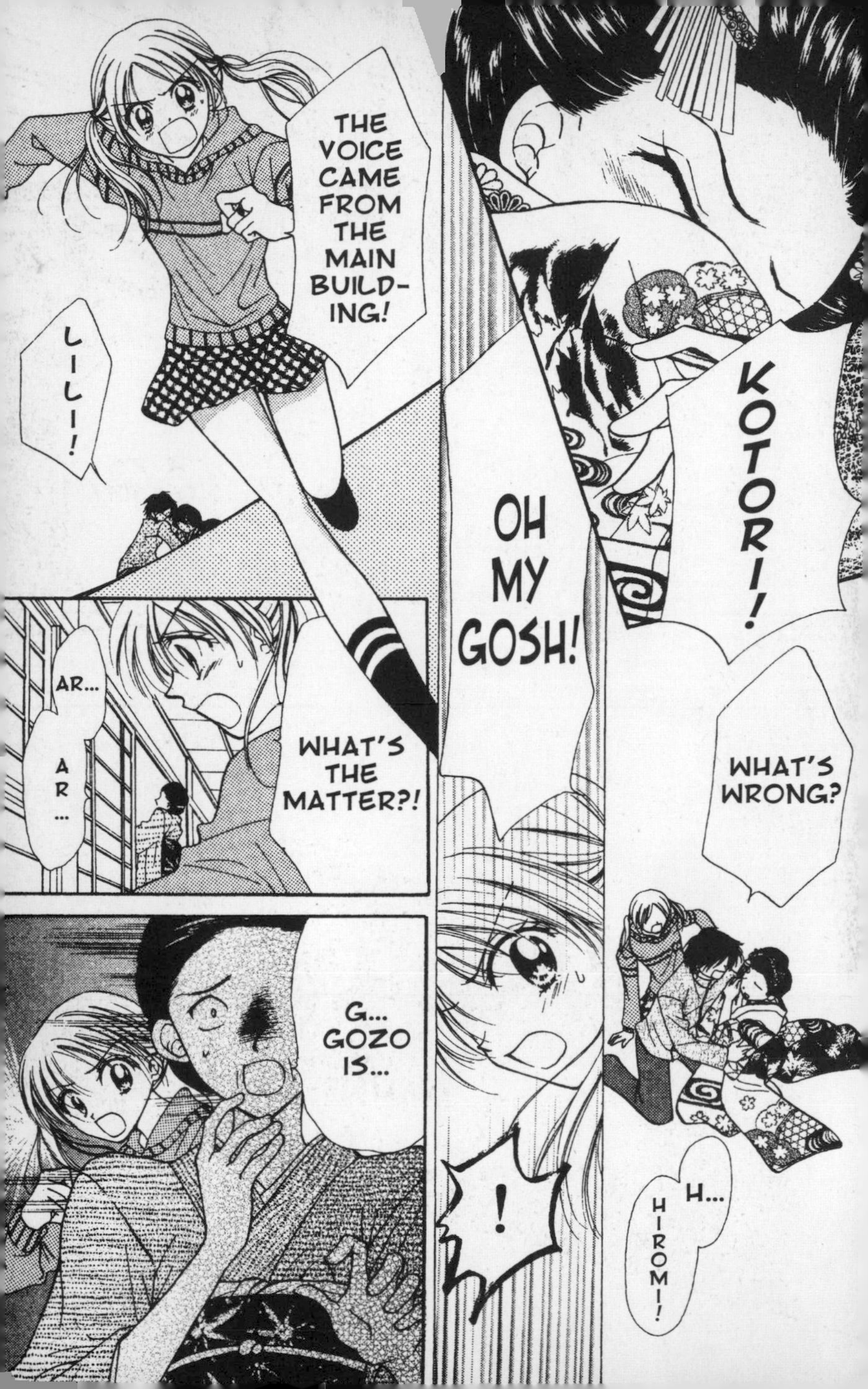
KOTORI!
OH MY GOSH!
WHAT'S WRONG?
!
H... HIROMI!
THE VOICE CAME FROM THE MAIN BUILD-ING!
LILI!
WHAT'S THE MATTER?!
AR... AR...
G... GOZO IS...

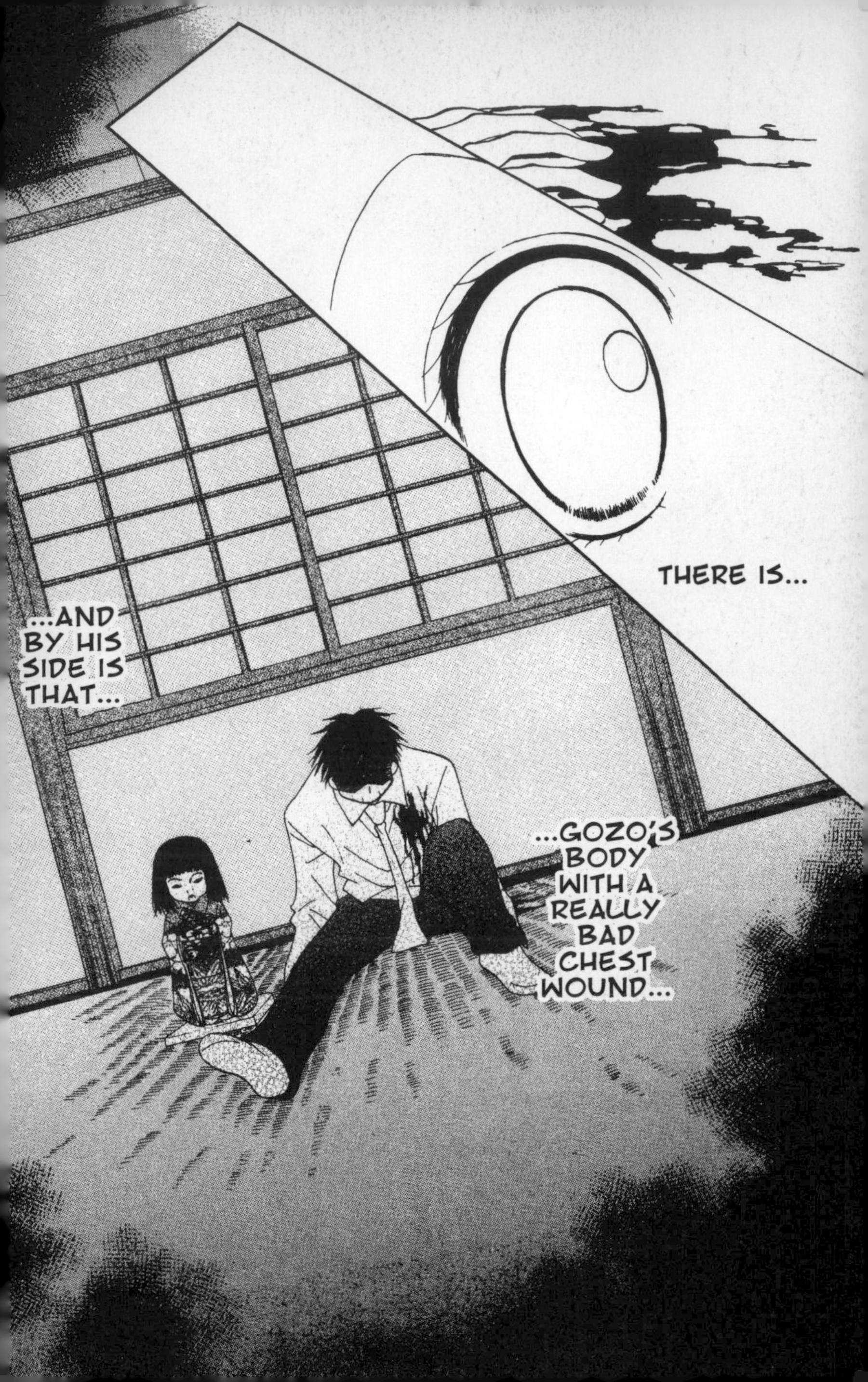
THERE IS...
...GOZO'S BODY WITH A REALLY BAD CHEST WOUND...
...AND BY HIS SIDE IS THAT...

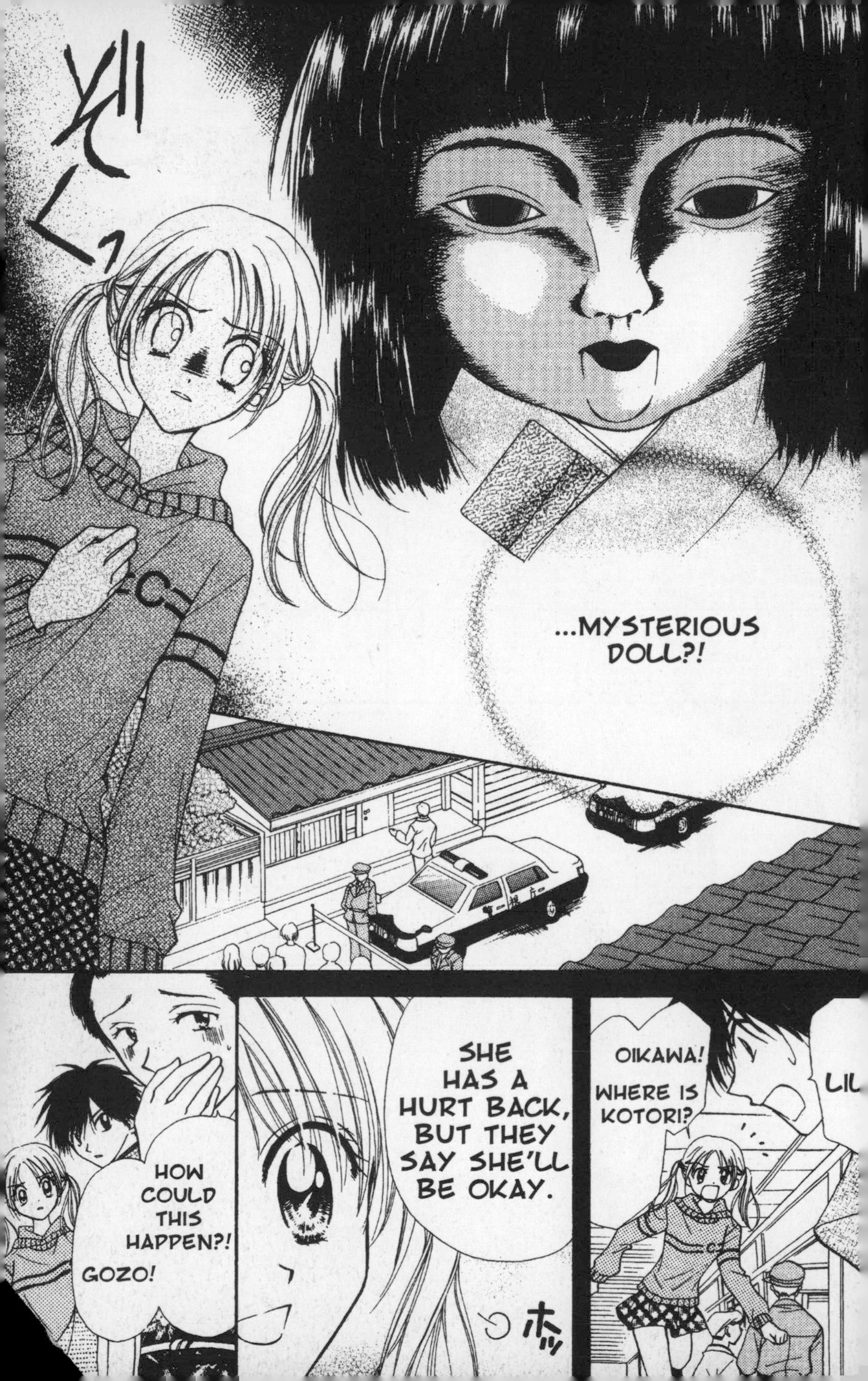
ぞくっ
...MYSTERIOUS DOLL?!
LIL
OIKAWA!
WHERE IS KOTORI?
SHE HAS A HURT BACK, BUT THEY SAY SHE'LL BE OKAY.
ホッ
HOW COULD THIS HAPPEN?!
GOZO!

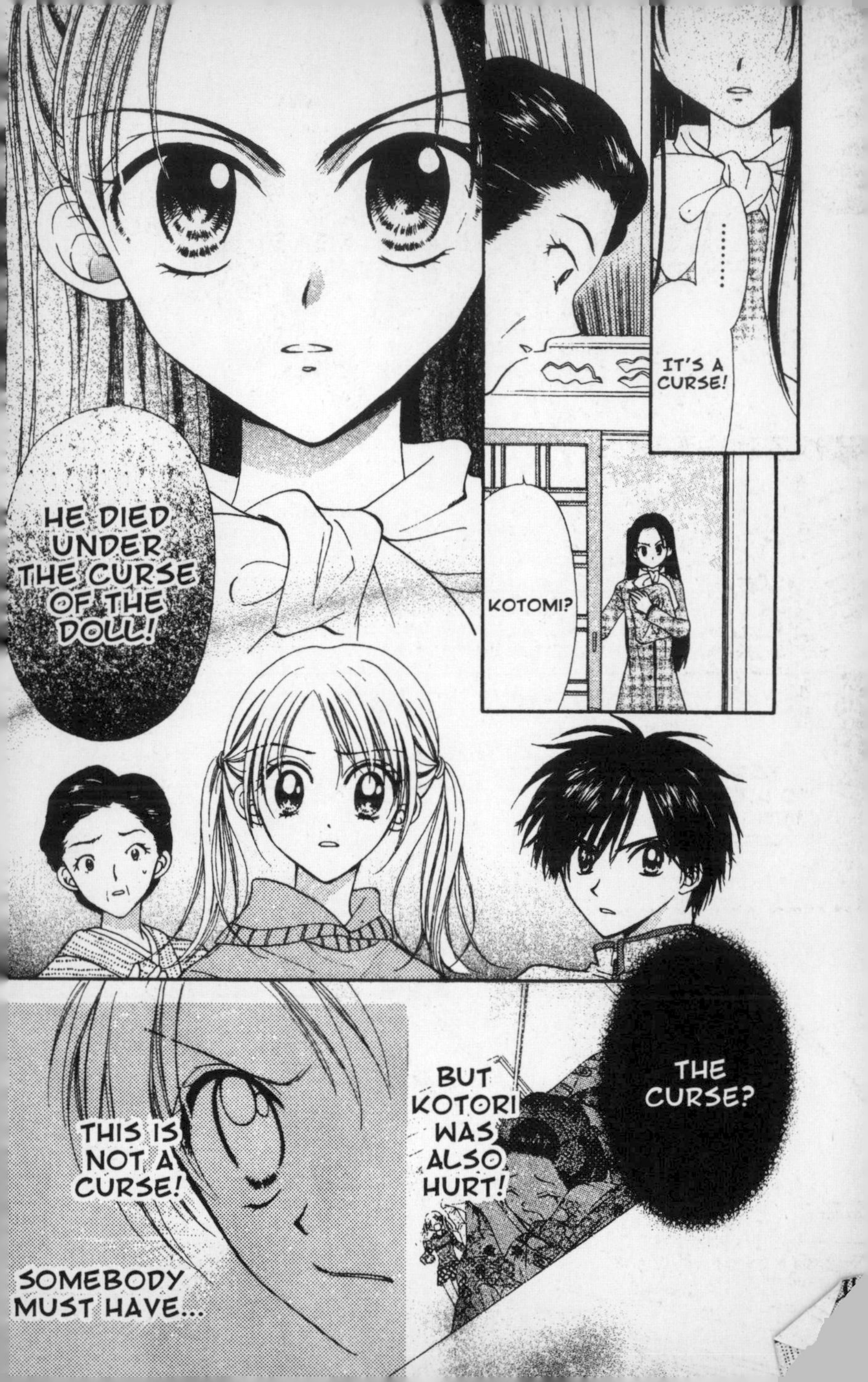
......
IT'S A CURSE!
KOTOMI?
HE DIED UNDER THE CURSE OF THE DOLL!
THE CURSE?
BUT KOTORI WAS ALSO HURT!
THIS IS NOT A CURSE!
SOMEBODY MUST HAVE...

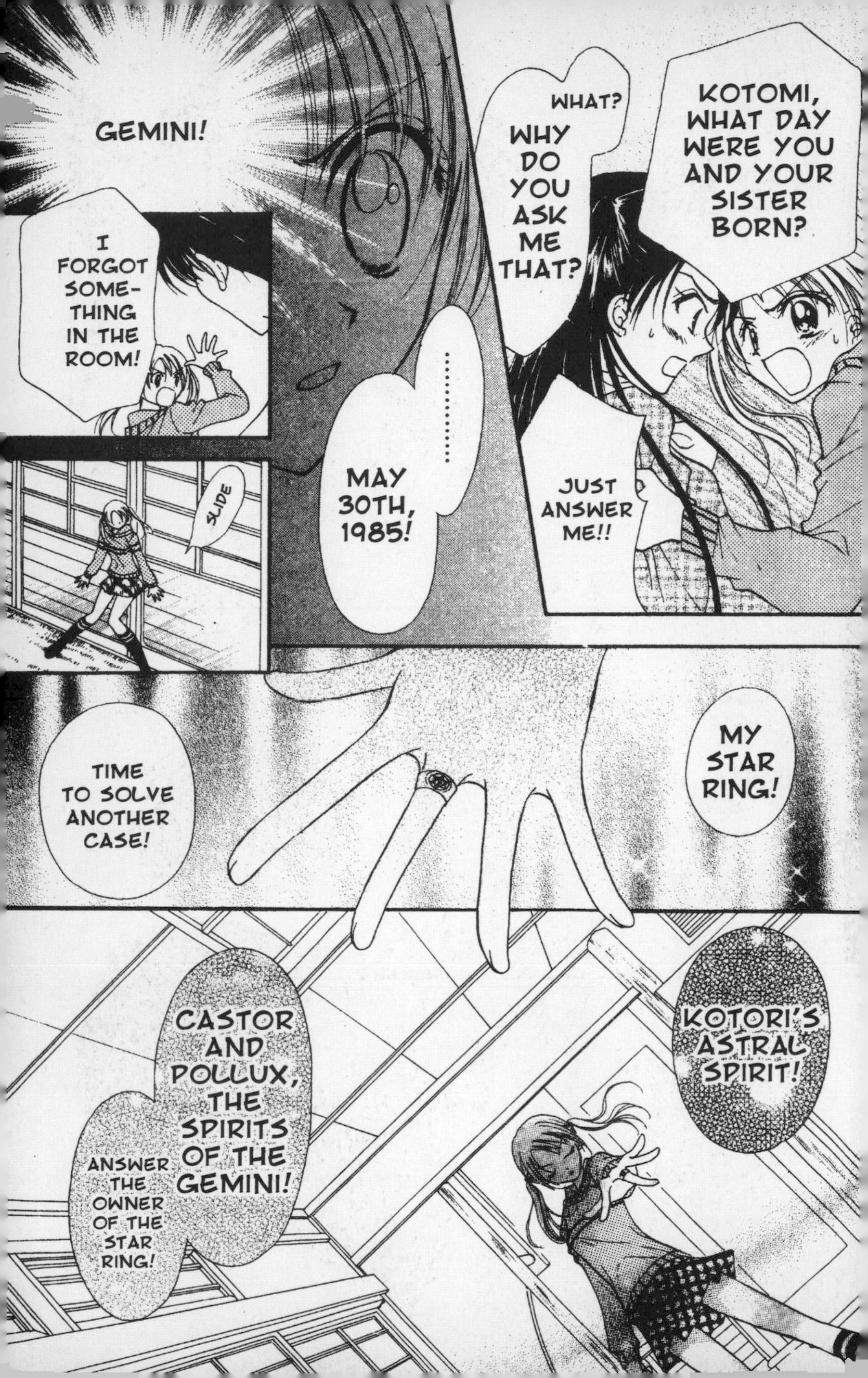
KOTOMI, WHAT DAY WERE YOU AND YOUR SISTER BORN?
WHAT?
WHY DO YOU ASK ME THAT?
JUST ANSWER ME!!
......
MAY 30TH, 1985!
GEMINI!
I FORGOT SOME-THING IN THE ROOM!
SLIDE
MY STAR RING!
TIME TO SOLVE ANOTHER CASE!
KOTORI'S ASTRAL SPIRIT!
CASTOR AND POLLUX, THE SPIRITS OF THE GEMINI!
ANSWER THE OWNER OF THE STAR RING!

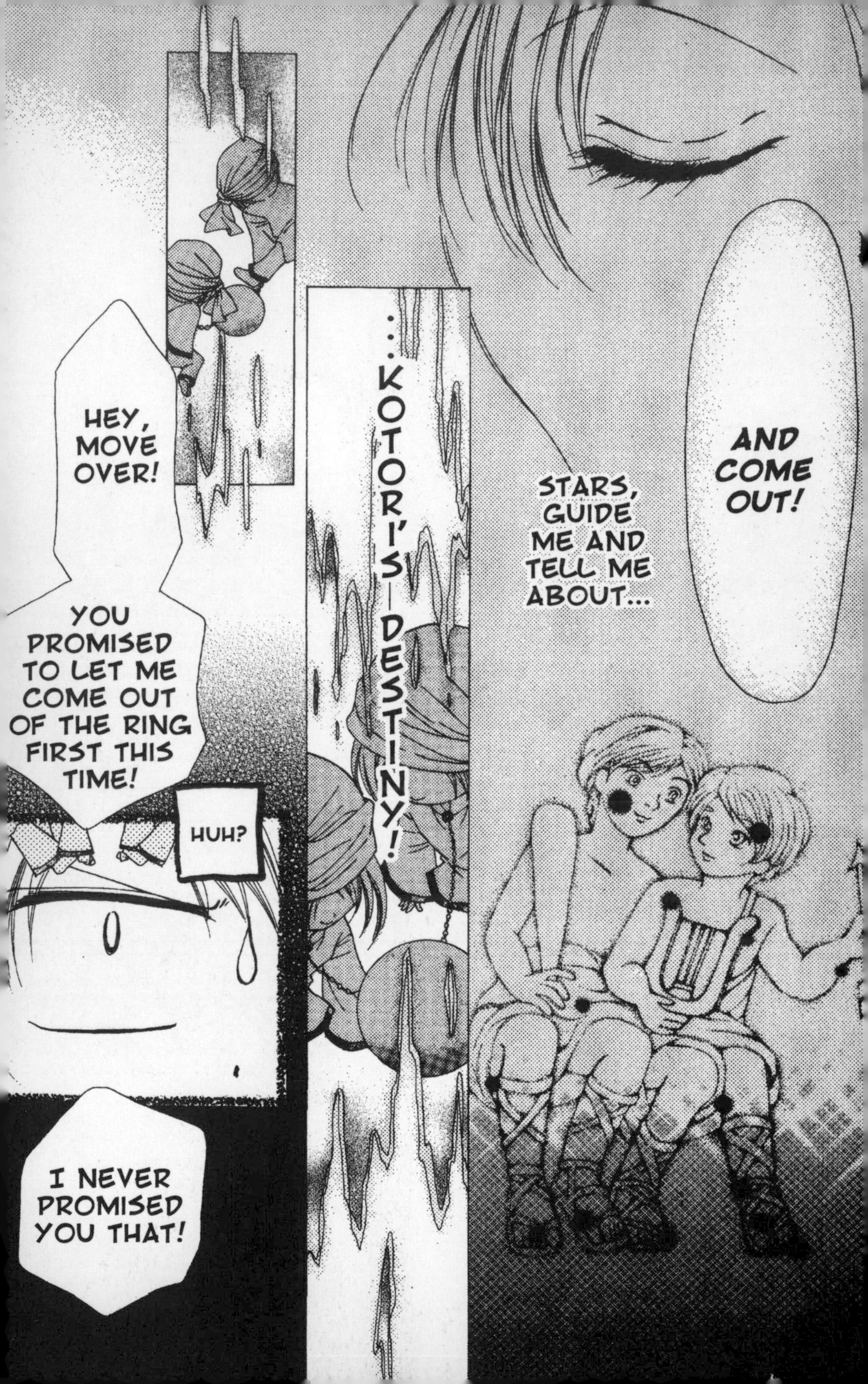
AND COME OUT!
STARS, GUIDE ME AND TELL ME ABOUT...
...KOTORI'S DESTINY!
HEY, MOVE OVER!
YOU PROMISED TO LET ME COME OUT OF THE RING FIRST THIS TIME!
HUH?
I NEVER PROMISED YOU THAT!

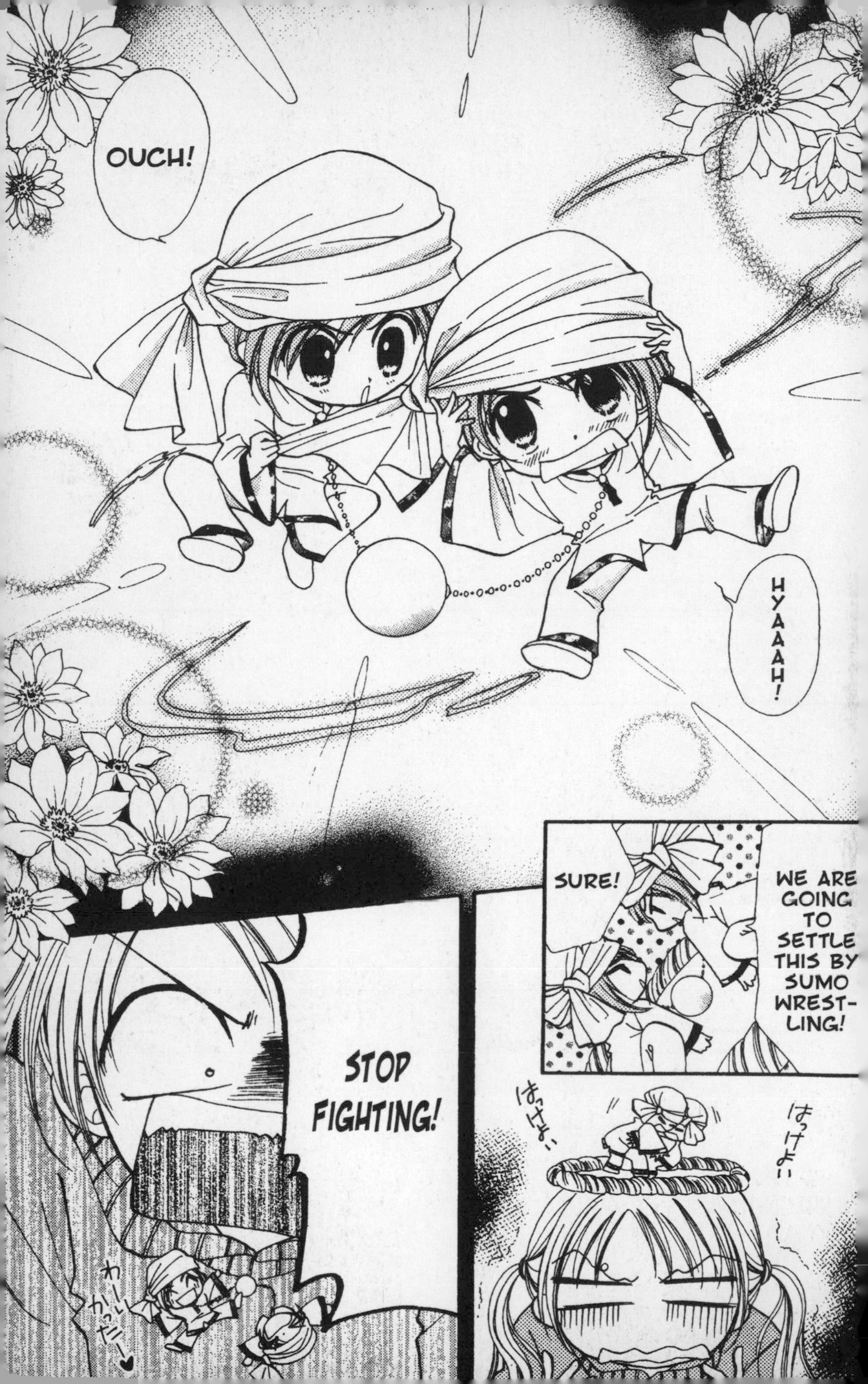

OUCH!
HYAAAH!
WE ARE GOING TO SETTLE THIS BY SUMO WRESTLING!
SURE!
はっけよい
はっけよい
STOP FIGHTING!
わーい かったー♥

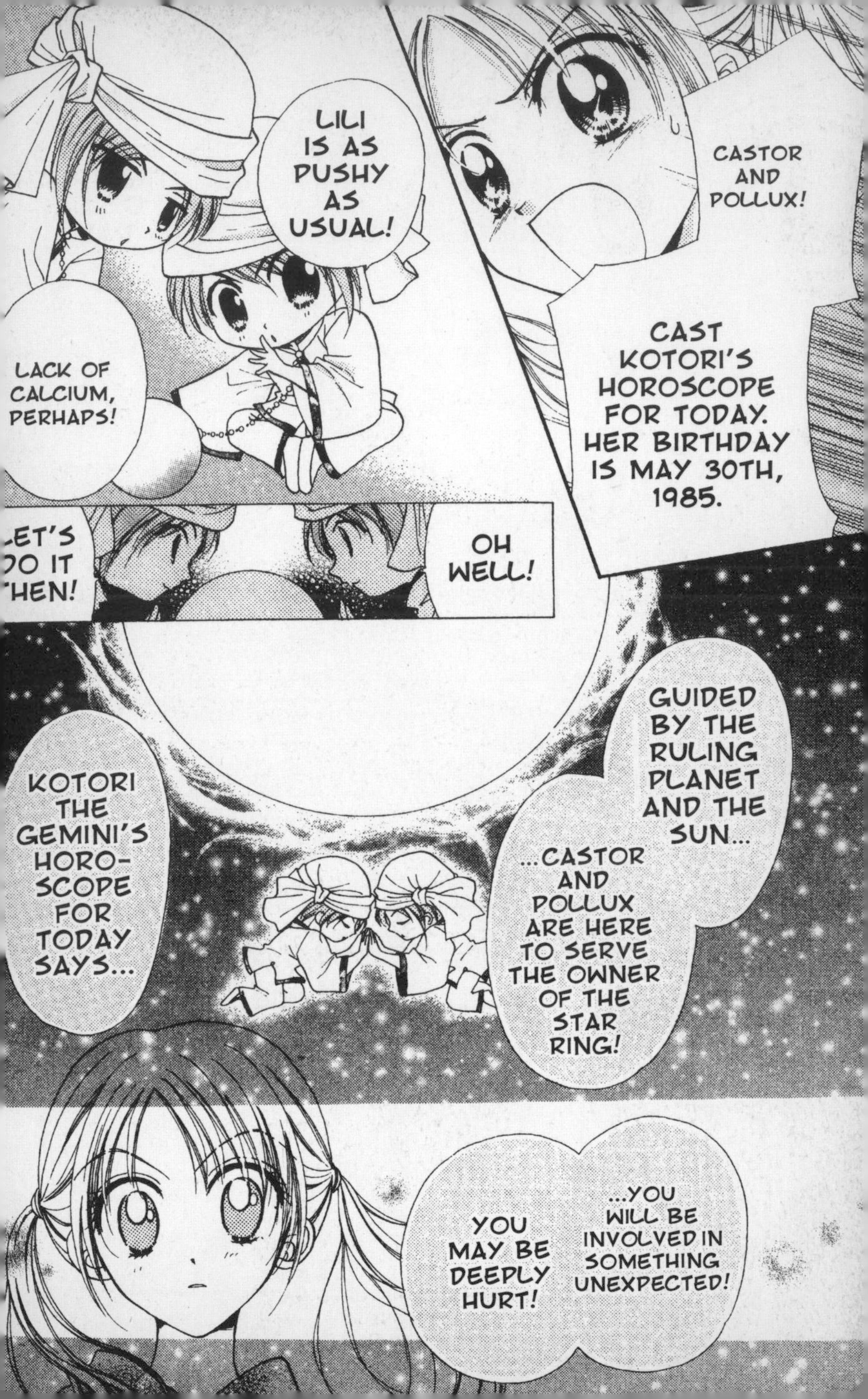
CASTOR AND POLLUX!
CAST KOTORI'S HOROSCOPE FOR TODAY. HER BIRTHDAY IS MAY 30TH, 1985.
LILI IS AS PUSHY AS USUAL!
LACK OF CALCIUM, PERHAPS!
OH WELL!
LET'S DO IT THEN!
GUIDED BY THE RULING PLANET AND THE SUN...
...CASTOR AND POLLUX ARE HERE TO SERVE THE OWNER OF THE STAR RING!
KOTORI THE GEMINI'S HORO-SCOPE FOR TODAY SAYS...
...YOU WILL BE INVOLVED IN SOMETHING UNEXPECTED!
YOU MAY BE DEEPLY HURT!

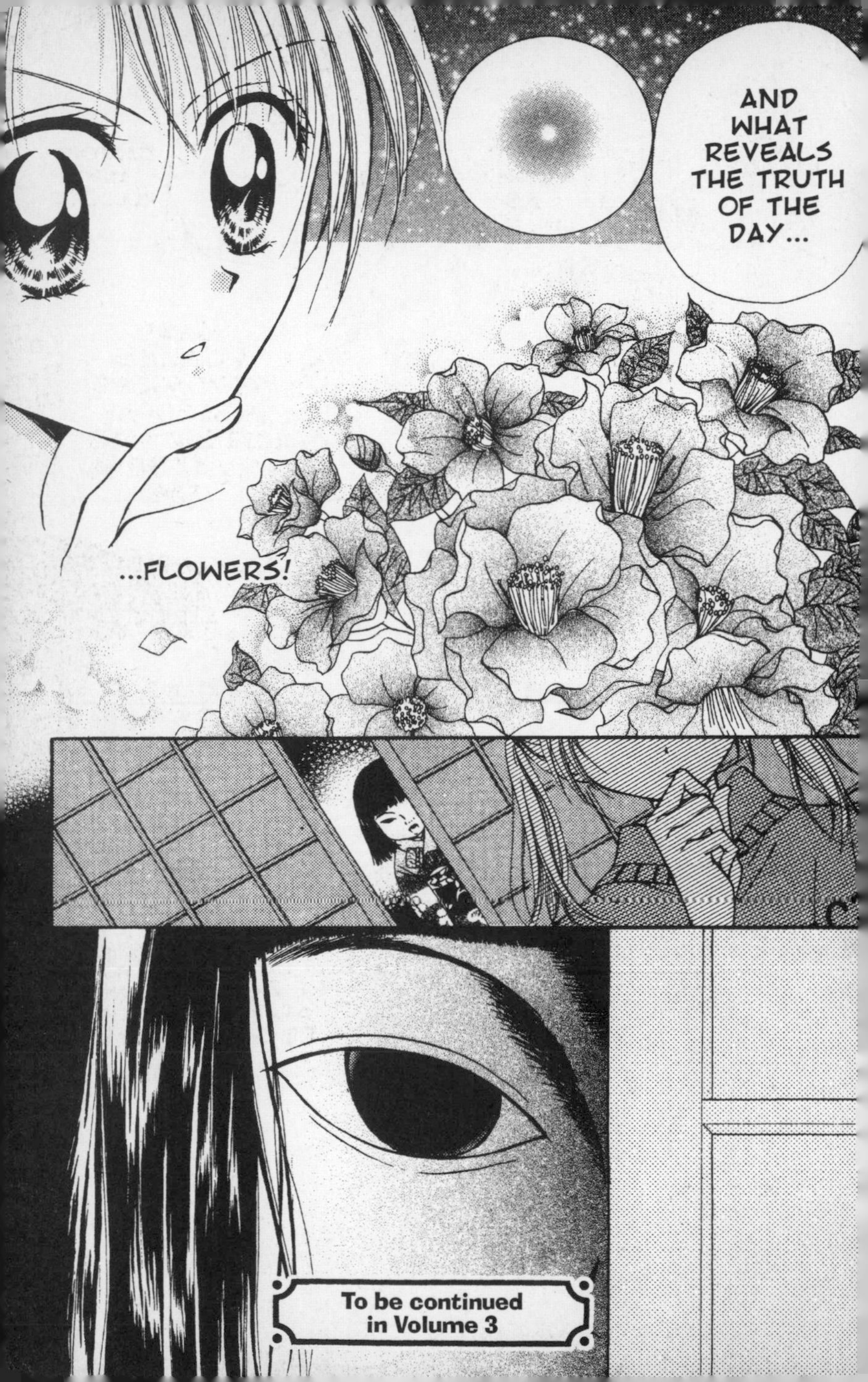
AND WHAT REVEALS THE TRUTH OF THE DAY...
...FLOWERS!
To be continued in Volume 3

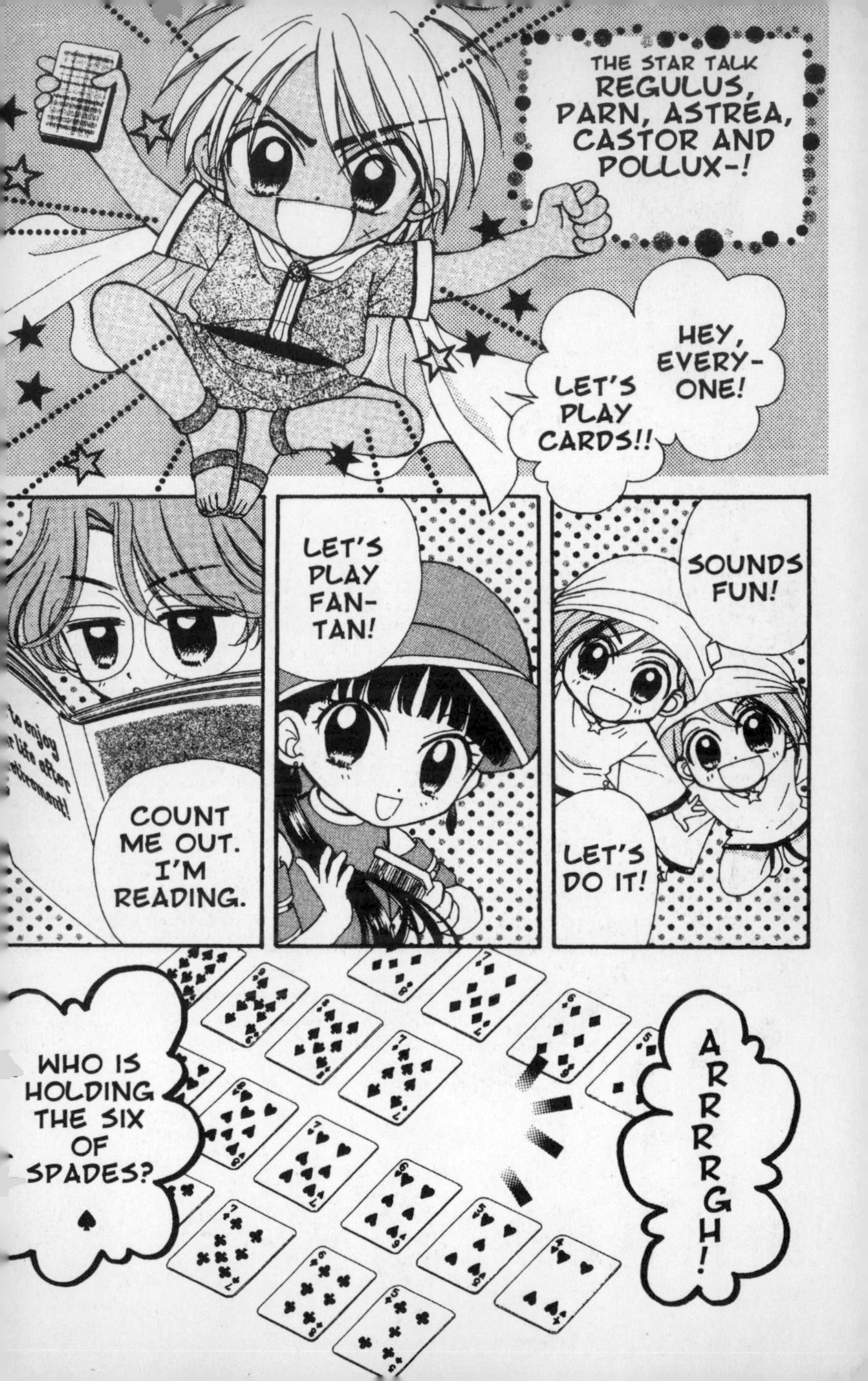
THE STAR TALK REGULUS, PARN, ASTREA, CASTOR AND POLLUX-!
HEY, EVERY-ONE!
LET'S PLAY CARDS!!
SOUNDS FUN!
LET'S DO IT!
LET'S PLAY FAN-TAN!
COUNT ME OUT. I'M READING.
ARRRRGH!
WHO IS HOLDING THE SIX OF SPADES?

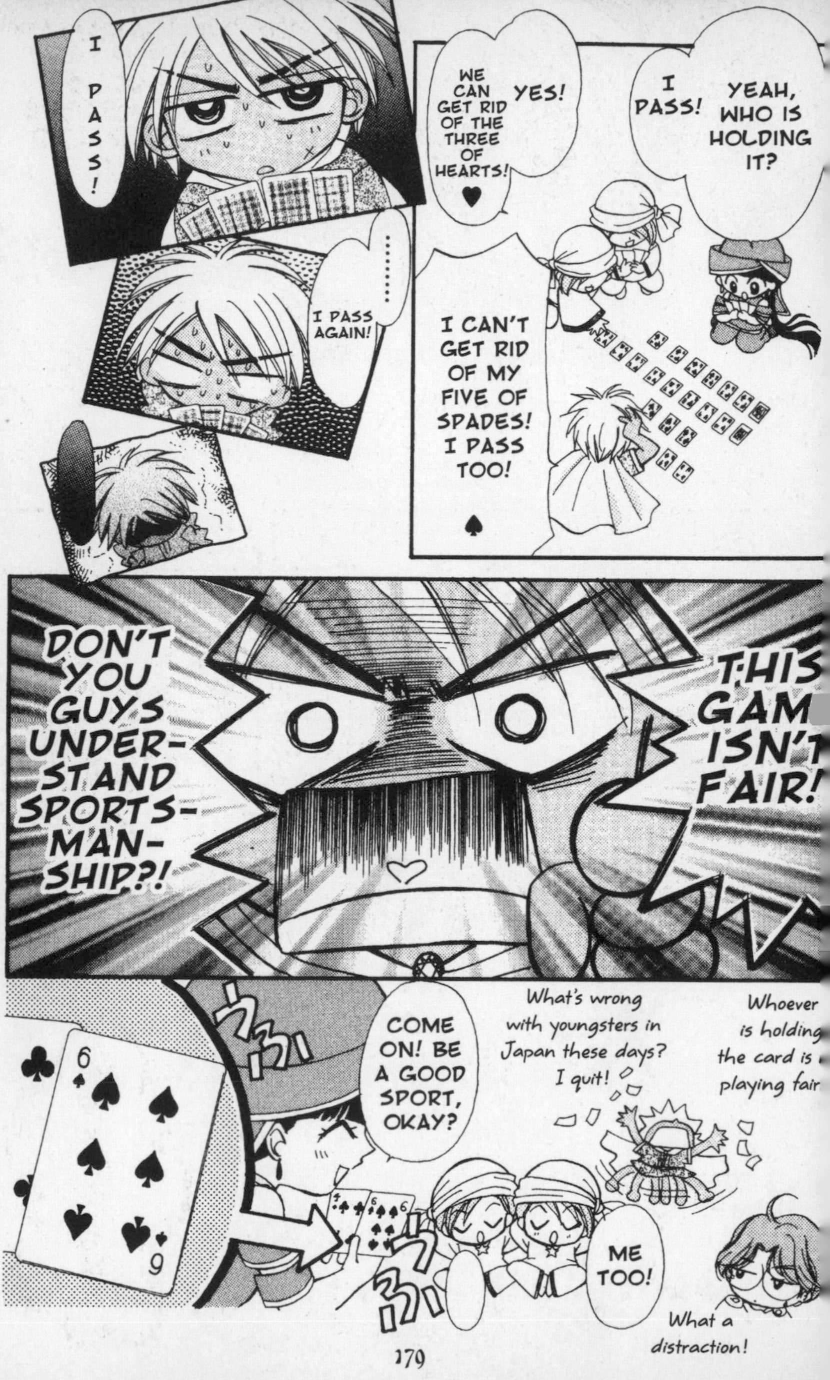
YEAH, WHO IS HOLDING IT?
I PASS!
YES!
WE CAN GET RID OF THE THREE OF HEARTS!
I CAN'T GET RID OF MY FIVE OF SPADES! I PASS TOO!
I PASS!
......
I PASS AGAIN!
THIS GAM ISN'T FAIR!
DON'T YOU GUYS UNDER-STAND SPORTS-MAN-SHIP?!
Whoever is holding the card is playing fair
What's wrong with youngsters in Japan these days? I quit!
COME ON! BE A GOOD SPORT, OKAY?
ME TOO!
What a distraction!

Coming Soon

Zodiac P.I.

Volume 3

Lili and her partner Hiromi are in Kyoto on their vacation. They stay at Hiromi's aunt's place, who runs an okiya and is a trainer of Geisha girls. Kotori, one of her trainees, shows them the way to the okiya. One day at the okiya, Gozo, a rude customer who favors Kotori, is found dead. Lili is determined to reveal the truth behind Gozo's death with a little help from the Star Ring. Will Lili figure it all out in time? Find out in Volume 3 of Zodiac P.I.!

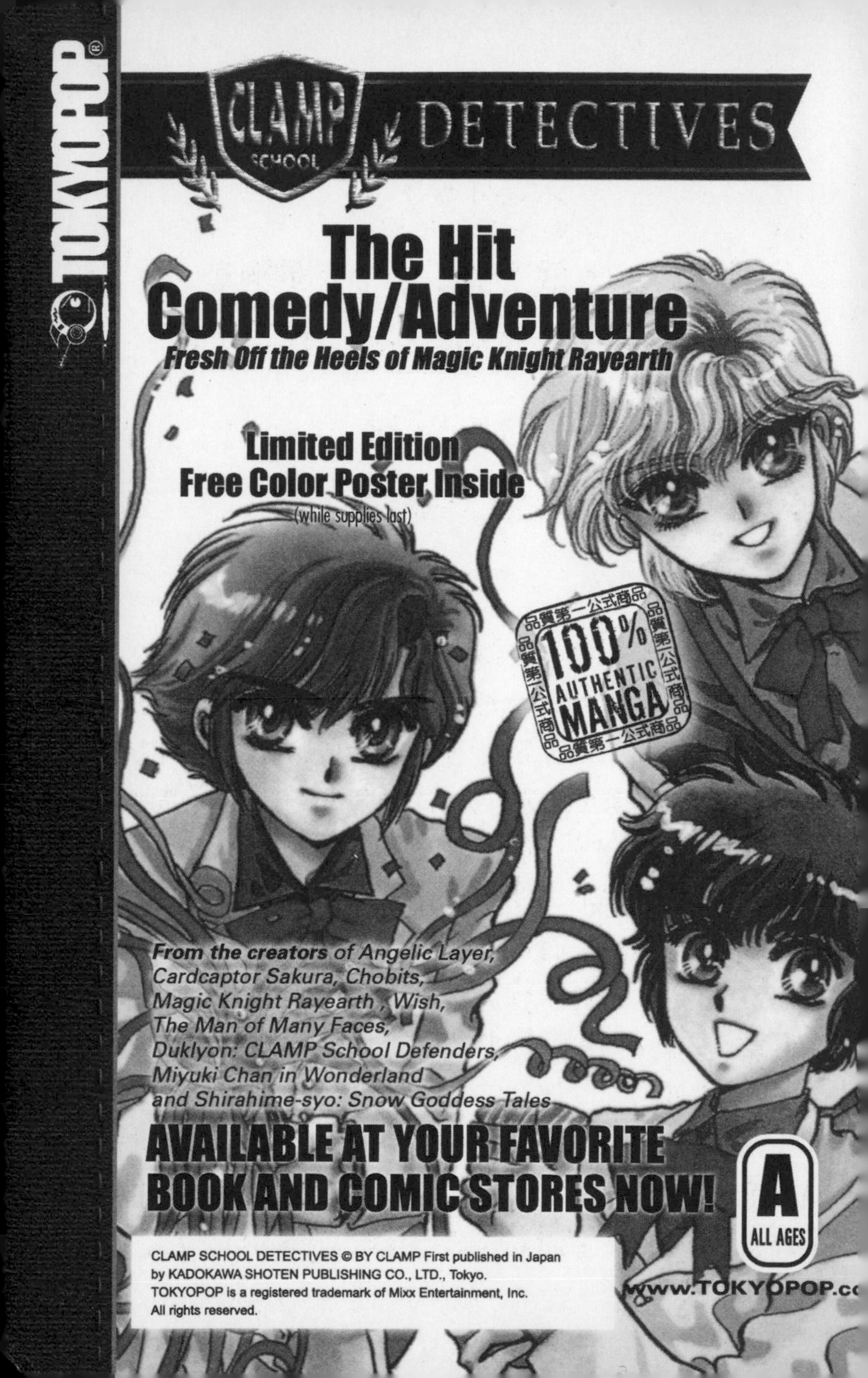
TOKYOPOP®
CLAMP SCHOOL DETECTIVES
The Hit Comedy/Adventure
Fresh Off the Heels of Magic Knight Rayearth
Limited Edition
Free Color Poster Inside
(while supplies last)
品質第一公式商品
100% AUTHENTIC MANGA
From the creators of Angelic Layer, Cardcaptor Sakura, Chobits, Magic Knight Rayearth , Wish, The Man of Many Faces, Duklyon: CLAMP School Defenders, Miyuki Chan in Wonderland and Shirahime-syo: Snow Goddess Tales
AVAILABLE AT YOUR FAVORITE BOOK AND COMIC STORES NOW!
A
ALL AGES
CLAMP SCHOOL DETECTIVES © BY CLAMP First published in Japan by KADOKAWA SHOTEN PUBLISHING CO., LTD., Tokyo. TOKYOPOP is a registered trademark of Mixx Entertainment, Inc. All rights reserved.
www.TOKYOPOP.co

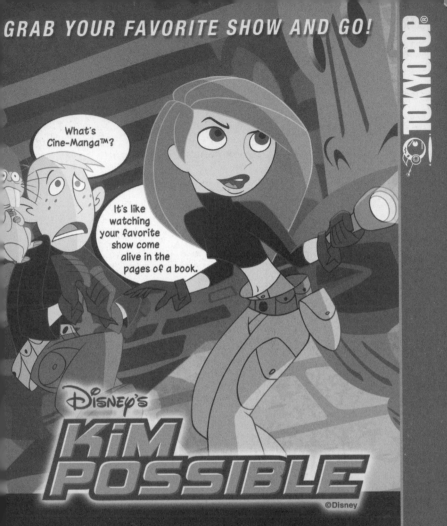

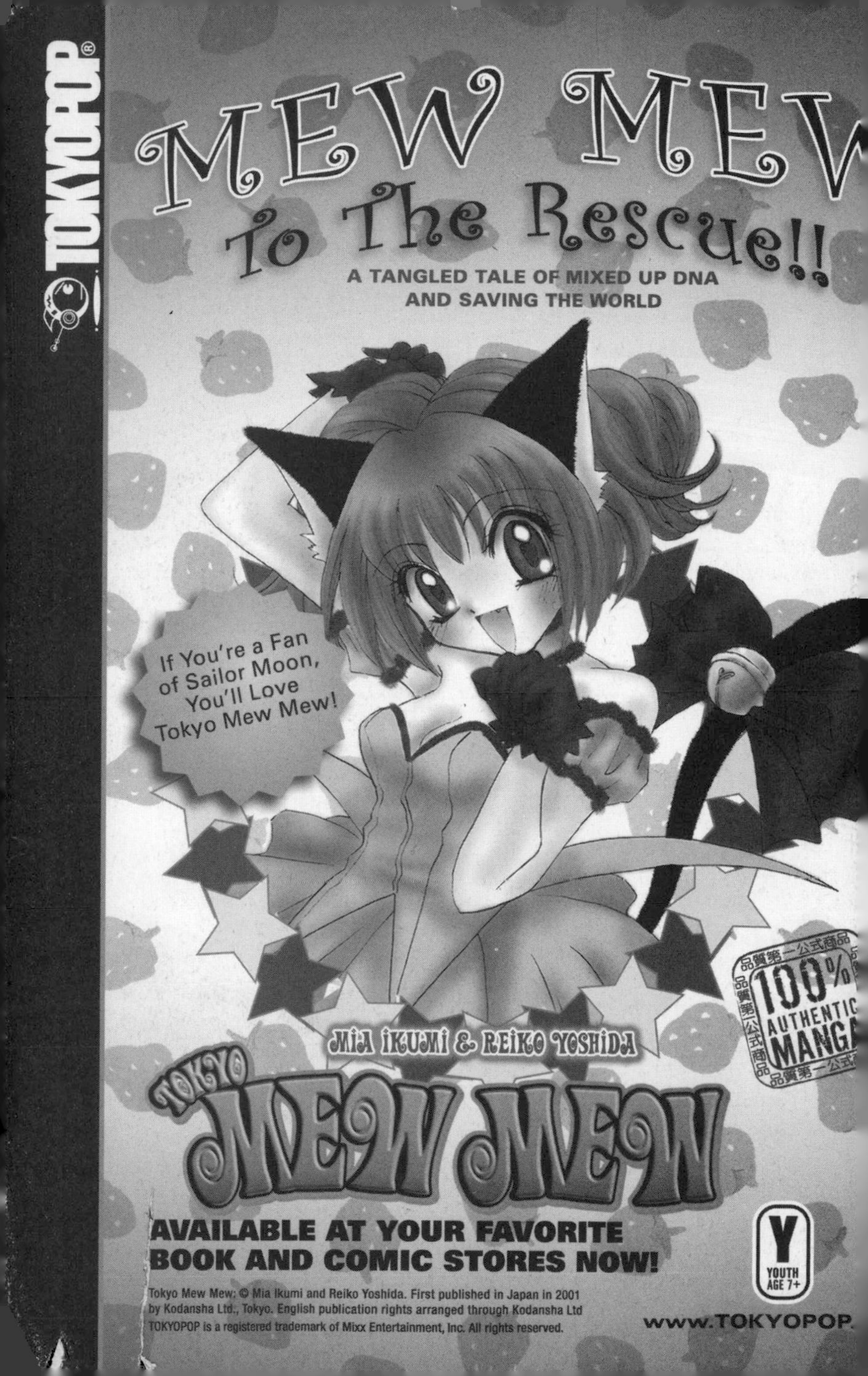
TOKYOPOP®
MEW MEW To The Rescue!!
A TANGLED TALE OF MIXED UP DNA AND SAVING THE WORLD
If You're a Fan of Sailor Moon, You'll Love Tokyo Mew Mew!
品質第一公式商品
100% AUTHENTIC MANGA
MIA IKUMI & REIKO YOSHIDA
TOKYO MEW MEW
AVAILABLE AT YOUR FAVORITE BOOK AND COMIC STORES NOW!
Y YOUTH AGE 7+
Tokyo Mew Mew: © Mia Ikumi and Reiko Yoshida. First published in Japan in 2001 by Kodansha Ltd., Tokyo. English publication rights arranged through Kodansha Ltd
TOKYOPOP is a registered trademark of Mixx Entertainment, Inc. All rights reserved.
www.TOKYOPOP.

STOP!

This is the back of the book.
You wouldn't want to spoil a great ending!

This book is printed "manga-style," in the authentic Japanese right-to-left format. Since none of the artwork has been flipped or altered, readers get to experience the story just as the creator intended. You've been asking for it, so TOKYOPOP® delivered: authentic, hot-off-the-press, and far more fun!

DIRECTIONS

If this is your first time reading manga-style, here's a quick guide to help you understand how it works.

It's easy... just start in the top right panel and follow the numbers. Have fun, and look for more 100% authentic manga from TOKYOPOP®!